THE NEW PHASE OF GLOBAL TERRORISM

The New Phase of Global Terrorism explores the nuances of the shift in the organization, strategy, and operation of terrorist groups into smaller and more robust terror groups in both the United States and international levels. To develop efficient counterterrorism measures, both domestically and globally, an understanding of the changing nature of terrorist group structure and strategy is essential. In this edited collection, authoritative scholars use relevant theories of sociology and psychology, as well as evidence from leading counterterrorism agencies such as the FBI, to support analysis, examples, and explanations of the landscape of terrorism around the world.

Part I discusses the evolution, theories, and psychology of terrorism. In this part, the authors outline the rationale of the book, capturing how terrorism has changed over the years. In Part II, the book explores the new phase of domestic terrorism, drawing on left-wing extremism, right-wing extremism, and jihadist attackers in the United States with a focus on their use of lone actor attacks and decentralized networks. Part III focuses on the new phase of international terrorism and discusses operational organization and strategies of international terror groups and their capabilities in the form of combat operations and small group operatives in Sub-Saharan Africa, the Middle East, and South-East Asia. Part IV covers terrorists' use of technology for propaganda, recruitment, training, and operations, with examples from the use of technology in recruiting and training by Al-Qaeda and Islamic State in Iraq and Syria (ISIS). Part V brings this information together and analyzes the criminal justice response, including building partnerships with counterterrorism agencies, intelligence sharing, and the use of courts to bring terrorist actors to justice.

Ideal as a text in terrorism, counterterrorism, and homeland security courses, this book is highly readable for criminal justice, psychology, and sociology students and professors, as well as policymakers and practitioners concerned with countering terrorism at home and abroad.

Binneh S. Minteh is an assistant professor of Criminal Justice at Salem State University. He is a former Gambian Armed Forces First Lieutenant. He attended the Turkish Land Forces Command School in Istanbul and the Turkish Gendarmerie Officers School in

Ankara. He was the Gambia National Gendarmerie training school commander, where he taught courses on National Security, Police and Society, Intelligence, Leadership, and Terrorism and Counterterrorism. He immigrated to the United States in 1997 as a refugee. Dr Binneh Minteh has published articles on terrorism and counterterrorism, social movements, police and society, organized crime, cybercrime, cyberspace, and cybersecurity. His research interests include social movements, peace and security studies, terrorism and counterterrorism, cybercrime, organized crime, and police and society.

James Bacigalupo is a doctoral student at the University of Massachusetts Lowell. His primary focus is on domestic political extremism. He is currently exploring the impact of partisanship on counterterrorism. James also applies his real-world experience from his full-time role as a correctional officer in Boston, MA, to the topic of institutional corrections, where he has gained insights into areas including inmate subcultures, misconduct, and rehabilitation.

Kevin Borgeson is an associate professor of Criminal Justice and former research fellow for the Center for Holocaust and Genocidal Studies at Salem State University. Dr Borgeson has published articles and op-eds on skinheads, cyberhate, profiling, serial crime, and right-wing domestic terrorism for the *Boston Globe*, *Boston Herald*, *Buffalo News*, *USA Today*, and the *London Daily Telegraph*. Dr Borgeson is the author and editor of ten books covering the topics of serial crime, skinheads, domestic terrorism in the United States, cyberhate, and criminal profiling. He has appeared on media outlets in Canada, Great Britain, Brazil, Russia, Ukraine, and India, as well as the United States, as an expert on hate crimes, hate groups, domestic terrorism, serial offenders, and child abductions. Over the past 25 years, Professor Borgeson has worked as a consultant to various law enforcement agencies conducting profiles and case linkage analysis, assisting in cold cases of serial murder, serial rape, and child abduction. Dr Borgeson has served as a consultant to many colleges and universities on issues dealing with hate on campus and is the main editor and researcher for the website Understanding Deviance, which provides op-eds, podcasts, and analysis of serial crime, both domestic and international.

Robin Maria Valeri is a professor of psychology at St. Bonaventure University. Valeri studies hate, extremism, and terrorism, with an emphasis on the role cyberspace plays in the spread of hate and terrorism, especially on the social influence tactics used by purveyors of hate and terrorism to convince potential acolytes to accept extremist beliefs and act on them.

THE NEW PHASE OF GLOBAL TERRORISM

Edited by Binneh S. Minteh, James Bacigalupo, Kevin Borgeson, and Robin Maria Valeri

Routledge
Taylor & Francis Group
NEW YORK AND LONDON

Designed cover image: Getty Images

First published 2025
by Routledge
605 Third Avenue, New York, NY 10158

and by Routledge
4 Park Square, Milton Park, Abingdon, Oxon, OX14 4RN

Routledge is an imprint of the Taylor & Francis Group, an informa business

ISBN: 9781032450766 (hbk)
ISBN: 9781032450735 (pbk)
ISBN: 9781003375265 (ebk)

DOI: 10.4324/9781003375265

Typeset in Sabon
by Deanta Global Publishing Services, Chennai, India

CONTENTS

CONTRIBUTORS

Ashlie Perry Banerjee is an associate professor of Criminal Justice and Security Studies at Endicott College, specializing in security studies and political psychology. Dr Perry Banerjee has published on the topics of terrorism, social movements, and identity politics. Perry Banerjee's research focuses on the intersectionality of identity and violent political action and has spent over a decade researching and writing in this area. She teaches classes that range from Race and Justice to Terrorism Studies. Outside of academia Dr Perry Banerjee is a member of Alpha Kappa Alpha Sorority, Inc., and the Midwest Political Science Association. Dr Perry Banerjee currently resides in the greater Boston area with her husband and son. She can be reached at aperry@endicott.edu.

Chris Mackowski is a writing professor in the Jandoli School of Communication at St. Bonaventure University in Allegany, NY, where he also serves as associate dean for undergraduate programs. He is the editor-in-chief and co-founder of Emerging Civil War, a digital platform of public historians, and he's the series editor of the award-winning Emerging Civil War Book Series. Chris has authored or co-authored more than two dozen books of his own and edited a half-dozen essay collections on the Civil War, and his articles have appeared in all the major Civil War magazines. In 2023, he was named a Copie Hill Civil War Fellow at the American Battlefield Trust.

Michael J. Mills is a criminal justice researcher with a professional background in policing and a research background in security studies. His research interests include pathways into extremism, social perceptions of extremist violence, and correctional policy responses to ideological extremism. This has led to previous studies looking at extremist organizational tactics and racially motivated vigilante violence, as well as an ongoing project looking into perceptions of racial violence. Outside of research, Josh lives in New Hampshire with his wife, Caitlin, where they spend their time hiking the White Mountains, wrangling literal cats, and trying to adjust to New England's winters after spending their first quarter century in Texas.

Nicholas Stone is an assistant researcher and collaborator with Dr Borgeson. He has written on and researched hate, extremism, hate crimes, terrorism, and criminal profiling.

INTRODUCTION

Binneh Minteh

The concept of terrorism and terrorist activity is not unique to the 21st or even the 20th century. From a historical perspective, the term terrorism dates to the French Revolution when it was first applied to the French Reign of Terror that occurred between September 5, 1793, and July 27, 1794. During those months, the government arrested and punished people they believed to be anti-revolutionary. Typically, punishment was in the form of death. Since that time, definitions of terrorism as well as the tactics of terrorists have changed. The current text examines the state of terrorism in the 21st century.

The New Phase of Global Terrorism explores the changes in the organization, strategy, and operation of terrorist groups into newer, smaller, and more robust terror groups operating in the form of small groups and lone wolve operatives at the domestic level, and both combat and small group operatives, including lone wolves, at the international level. Effectively containing terrorist organizations requires understanding their changing nature in structure, operations, and strategy to ensure development of efficient counter-terrorism measures at both the domestic and international stages.

These changes began after the defeat of Al-Qaeda in Afghanistan and the Middle East and its affiliate organization the Islamic State of Iraq and ash Sham (ISIS). Following the defeat of Al-Qaeda in Afghanistan, key leaders of the organization sought new safe havens in parts of the world sympathetic to their cause. Prominent among their new safe havens are North Africa—Libya, Tunisia, and Algeria; Sub-Saharan Africa—Mali, Mauretania, Burkina Faso, Niger, Ivory Coast, and Nigeria; and Eastern Africa—Somalia and Kenya. The Federal Bureau of Investigation (FBI), in collaboration with its global counter-terrorism partners, found groups in North Africa to be led by senior Al-Qaeda operatives who fled Afghanistan following defeat at the hands of coalition forces. The leaders of groups operating in Tunisia and Algeria are also believed to be linked to the ISIS. Similarly, terror groups operating in Mali, Niger, and Burkina Faso are believed to be splinter groups of either Al-Qaeda or ISIS. In Nigeria, the terror group Boko Haram has pledged allegiance to ISIS, and in Somalia, al-Shabab has also pledged allegiance to ISIS.

While the changing nature of terrorism and terrorist strategies has intermittently changed from its traditional operational premises, it is evident that 21st-century changes

DOI: 10.4324/9781003375265-1

in terrorist activities have brought to light a new phase of global terrorism defined by lone wolves and small group operatives unleashing brutal attacks on soft targets in populated areas such as shopping centers, movie theaters, schools, and hospitals.

The book is divided into five parts. Part I discusses the evolution, theories, and psychology of terrorism. In this part, the authors outline the rationale of the book, capturing how terrorism has changed over the years. In Part II, the book explores the new phase of domestic terrorism in the United States, examining left-wing extremism, right-wing extremism, and jihadist attackers in the United States and their linkages to international terror groups. The authors discuss operational strategies in the form of lone wolves, small group operatives, choice of targets, and weapons used during attacks. Part III draws on the new phase of international terrorism. In this section, the book discusses operational organization and strategies of international terror groups and their capabilities in the form of combat operations and small group operatives in Sub-Saharan Africa, the Middle East, and South-East Asia. Furthermore, the authors will discuss the rationale for choice of targets and weapons used during attacks. Part IV of the book covers terrorist use of technology for propaganda, recruitment, training, and operations. In this part, the authors draw examples from Al-Qaeda and ISIS's use of technology in recruiting and training American and British citizens to join militants at training camps in Syria and Iraq and in some cases, carrying out isolated domestic terror attacks. In Part V, the book discusses the criminal justice response in building partnerships with counter-terrorism agencies, intelligence sharing, building capacity, and the use of courts to bring to justice terrorist actors, both at home and abroad. Considering the focus of the book on the new phase of terrorism, the book uses relevant theories of sociology and psychology as well as evidence from leading counter-terrorism agencies such as the FBI to support the analysis, examples, and explanations presented throughout the book.

PART I

Evolution, Theories, and the Psychology of Terrorism

1

THE BLOOD OF PATRIOTS

A Brief Overview of Terrorism in America

Chris Mackowski

Introduction

The FBI (n.d.) defines domestic terrorism as "violent, criminal acts committed by individuals and/or groups to further ideological goals stemming from domestic influences, such as those of a political, religious, social, racial, or environmental nature." In this chapter, author Chris Mackowski presents a variety of events in American history and asks you to consider whether they are acts of terrorism. When does protest become terrorism? Is an armed uprising against colonialism or foreign occupation terrorism? When does terrorism become war? In Chapter 2, we will consider how terrorism is defined and examine how definitions of terrorism are influenced by politics.

The Blood of Patriots versus Terrorism

Little remains of the massive elm tree that once stood along the main road in and out of Boston. In August 1775, British soldiers and loyalists—hemmed in the city since spring by the new Continental Army—took out their frustrations on the elm, chopping the tree into splinters.

The tree dated back to 1646, but on August 14, 1765, it had taken on a new life. Angry residents of the Massachusetts Bay Colony staged a daylong protest around the tree against new taxes imposed by the British Parliament. The Stamp Act, which authorized the taxes, had so infuriated colonists that they hung in effigy the merchant appointed by King George III to collect the taxes, Andrew Oliver, or "A.O." as a tag pinned to the effigy identified him.

Some of the neighbours [sic] offered to take it down, but they were given to know, that would not be permitted," wrote colonial governor Francis Bernard, mortified. The sheriff and his deputies tried, too, "but could not do it without imminent danger of their lives" (Bernard, 1765, p.126).

By nightfall, the crowd itself removed the effigy and placed it in a coffin, which they paraded through downtown. At the time, Oliver was in the process of building a new shop

DOI: 10.4324/9781003375265-3

near the city wharves; the crowd stopped there and "pulled it to the ground in five minutes," Bernard reported. They used the timber for a bonfire, then used the bonfire to burn the effigy, which they beheaded. In an attempt to find Oliver himself, they ransacked his house—which Oliver had wisely already fled—but they accosted the sheriff and lieutenant governor with "a volley of stones." The next day, advised that "his house would be immediately destroyed and his life in continual danger," Oliver resigned his position (Bernard, 1765, pp. 127–128).

Nearly two weeks later, on the evening of August 26, another crowd of tax protestors stormed the homes of three colonial officials, including the mansion of Lieutenant Governor Thomas Hutchinson. "[T]hey came, with intoxicated rage," Hutchinson later wrote. He and his family fled, and the protestors occupied his home all night. They "destroyed, carried away, or cast into the street, everything that was in the house; demolished every part of it…" Hutchinson lamented. When a half dozen people were later arrested for their part in the incident, another angry crowd confronted the jailor and "compelled him, by threats, to deliver to them the keys of the prison, which they opened, and then set the prisoners at liberty…." (Hutchinson, 1828, pp. 165, 166, 168).

Within weeks, the activist group at the heart of the protests affixed a copper plaque to the elm, calling it the "Tree of Liberty." They, in turn, took their name—the Sons of Liberty—as an offshoot from the tree. The tree's prominent position at the corner of Orange and Essex streets on the city's south side made it an ideal rallying site. The Sons raised a flagpole next to the tree to signal gatherings where angry colonists could hear fiery orations by such leaders as Samuel Adams. One of the Sons' key organizers, silversmith Paul Revere, featured the tree in an engraving. By the following February, a newspaper described "the Tree" as "a great Ornament to the Square. And we doubt not but the TREE of LIBERTY will thrive and flourish, when all the Friends to the Stamp Act will decay and perish" (Boston Gazette, 1766, p. 3).

Over the next decade, the feud between Bostonians and the British Parliament escalated in fits and starts but moved ever toward open rebellion. Colonists saw Parliament as oppressive, blatantly disrespectful, and acting beyond its authority. The colonists believed only King George, not Parliament, had dominion over them and that Parliament had no authority to levy taxes. That Parliament had done so to help defray the cost of defending the colonies during the Seven Years' War—known in America as the French and Indian War—was moot.

During that time, the 120-year-old tree continued to serve as the focal point for protest and became a powerful symbol. Protestors hung other effigies, tacked up the names of people they disliked, and made examples of people they had tarred and feathered. One "seditious handbill" posted in 1767 exhorted "the Sons of Liberty to rise on that day and fight for their rights" (Preble, 1880, p. 195).

By the time the tree came down in August 1775, one Boston newspaper noted that the elm had already propagated widely: hundreds of liberty trees had cropped up in emulation all across the continent (Lane, 2021). "[T]he GRAND AMERICAN TREE OF LIBERTY, planted in the centre of the united colonies of North America, now flourishes with unrivalled [sic], increasing beauty," wrote another; "and bids fair in a short time to afford under its wide-spreading branches, a safe and happy retreat for all the sons of liberty, however numerous and dispersed" (Moore, 1775, pp. 131–132).

Little of the physical tree remained, however. The felled elm reportedly furnished 14 cords of wood for the troops and loyalists hemmed in the city (Preble, 1880, p. 195).

"Wood was in demand..." explains Kanisorn "Kid" Wongsrichanalai, director of research for the Massachusetts Historical Society.

> They were under siege. The Continental Army surrounded them. They ate anything they could. They chopped down anything they could to make fires. Everything was in demand. And this tree, of course, was a great symbol—for both the British as well as for the colonists—of rebellion.
>
> *(K. Wongsrichanalai, personnel communication, June 2022)*

Wongsrichanalai stands next to a glass exhibit case on the second floor of the Society's Boylston Street Headquarters, about a mile and a half west of where the Liberty Tree originally stood. Inside the case, three small fragments taken from the roots of the Liberty Tree lie in a tiny bundle, bound by a thin strip of rust-colored fabric. Souvenir hunters, recognizing the tree's symbolic value, managed to snag small pieces that didn't turn into firewood.

"It's a complicated story, for sure," Wongsrichanalai (personal communication, June 2022) says, pointing out that symbols mean different things to different people. To the Sons of Liberty, the Liberty Tree became a revered icon representing freedom from tyranny; to residents of Boston who remained loyal to the British government, the tree represented disloyalty and chaos. Edward Oliver, Chief Justice of Massachusetts's Supreme Court, scorned it as something "consecrated for an Idol for the Mob to worship" (Adair & Schultz, 1967, p. 54). Loyalists "armed with axes, &c," made a furious attack upon it," reported a Boston newspaper at the time. "After a long spell of groaning, swearing, and foaming with malice diabolical they cut down a tree because it bore the name of 'Liberty'" (Moore, 1775, p. 131). Wongsrichanalai's colleague, Jonathan Lane, described it as "perhaps their most gleeful moment" (Lane, 2021).

When the Continental Army gained control of the city in March 1776, pro-colonial Bostonians reclaimed the site of the old elm, defiantly rechristening it "the Liberty Stump." But as time went on, Boston's city leaders let the story of the stump fade into obscurity. "Symbols have a way of shifting meaning," Wongsrichanalai cautions. Liberty Trees were not just places that symbolized liberty, he says: "They became places that symbolized mob rule, as well" (K. Wongsrichanalai, personnel communication, June 2022).

Consider the coerced resignations of public officials in the summer of 1765. "The town was...under the awe of this mob," recalled Hutchinson; "many of the magistrates, with the field officers of the militia, standing by as spectators; and nobody daring to oppose, or contradict..." Similarly, when a mob forced the subsequent release of suspects, "there was no authority, which thought it advisable to make any inquiry after them." The Sons—whom Hutchinson referred to as "the liberty party"—claimed "the late violences proceeded from a few abandoned, desperate persons" rather than from some orchestrated effort. But Hutchinson never believed for a second that the protests were not ginned up, decrying the "influence the mob was under, and that they might be let loose, or kept up, just as their keepers thought fit" (Hutchinson, 1828, pp. 166, 168, 177–178).

Historian Alfred F. Young discusses at length the use of the Liberty Tree as a scene for "popular justice" and contends that even the Sons of Liberty recognized the site as a double-edged sword. "Leaders seemed constantly aware of the need to head off potentially explosive activity at the tree," he writes (Young, 2006, p. 337).

It's little wonder, says Wongsrichanalai, that "over time, the liberty trees and the liberty poles so popular during the American Revolution faded away because that's not the story you want to tell when you're trying to establish a new government" (K. Wongsrichanalai, personnel communication, June 2022).

This insight illustrates a fundamental tension built into America's history: the idea that one person's "freedom fighter" is another person's "terrorist." The Sons of Liberty saw themselves as "Patriots," while the British saw them as "traitors." The discontented protestors that rallied at the Liberty Tree called themselves "crowds," while the British called them "mobs." When armed warfare erupted in the spring of 1775 at Lexington and Concord, was it a "glorious cause" as George Washington believed, or was it, as Chief Justice Oliver later called it, "the late horrid rebellion"?

The winner in any situation often determines history's answer. That's what allows us today to think of something like the Boston Tea Party as a quaint story of American patriotism rather than as the unlawful, targeted destruction of nearly 92,000 pounds of tea worth £10,000 (more than $1.7 million in 2023 dollars). The British Parliament reacted to the incident by blockading Boston Harbor, which in turn raised concerns in other colonies that Parliament might just as easily do the same to them, thus inspiring them to gather for the First Continental Congress. Political and military events raced ever quicker toward revolution.

The concept of "terrorism," as we understand it today, did not exist in the 1770s, although the word made its first appearance shortly thereafter to describe the effects of "the Terror," a phase of the French Revolution in 1792–1793 most notoriously known for its frequent public executions. For our purposes today, the Patriot Act of 2001 provides a clear definition:

> "domestic terrorism" means activities that involve acts dangerous to human life that are a violation of the criminal laws of the United States or of any State; appear intended to intimate or coerce a civilian population; to influence the policy of a government by intimation or coercion; or to affect the conduct of a government by mass destruction, assassination, or kidnapping; and occur primarily within the territorial jurisdiction of the United States.
>
> *(United States Code, 2331[5])*

A simpler working definition from the *Oxford English Dictionary* might also suffice: "the unlawful use of violence and intimidation, especially against civilians, in the pursuit of political aims." In either context, events like the Boston Tea Party or those that spun from the rallies around the Liberty Tree take on a far more sinister tone—one that clashes with the more idealistic self-image Americans prefer to embrace.

This darker arc bears a striking resonance with some of the reasons people employ terrorism today: revolution; the establishment of national independence/separate state; reactionary desires against progressive trends; religious beliefs or acting on behalf of God; and single-issue motivations that run the gamut from a desire for labor reform to a stand against animal cruelty to opposition to abortion (Weinberg, 2008). Modern terrorists engage in terrorism:

(1) to cause fear and anxiety among the public;
(2) to shine a spotlight on their cause;

(3) to provoke authorities into responding to their threat in a manner that is consistent with the terrorist's message, thus confirming the terrorists' accusations against the authorities and winning the terrorist organization new recruits; and
(4) to raise the morale of both the terrorist group and the segment of the population whose cause they are championing (Weinberg, 2008).

But this arc also illustrates the challenges of navigating a substantial gray area: When does civil disobedience become terrorism? When does terrorism become a revolution? How do you differentiate between mob violence and terrorism?

"Extremism in defense of liberty is no vice," declared 1964 Republican presidential nominee Barry Goldwater, a sentiment shared, no doubt, by Samuel Adams and the Sons of Liberty as well as protestors who stormed the United States Capitol on January 6, 2021. Modern audiences might look at one group as patriots and the other as insurrectionists, but many of those who stormed the Capitol would have, through Goldwater's lens, put themselves in the same camp as Adams's.

As a nation born from revolution—so important to our national identity that we capitalize the event as "the Revolution"—the idea of government overthrow (which today we might refer to as terrorism, depending on your side of the controversy) is literally written into the Declaration of Independence (1776). In justifying the colonies' break from Great Britain, the Declaration states:

> Governments are instituted among Men, deriving their just powers from the consent of the governed,—That whenever any Form of Government becomes destructive of these ends, it is the Right of the People to alter or to abolish it, and to institute new Government.

While the Declaration has no legal standing within the framework of American governance, it does serve as a powerful spiritual lodestar. If "the governed" do not consent, the Declaration states they are entitled to do something about it. We have come to traditionally understand that concept to mean the exercise of power through the ballot box. However, more robust understandings have manifested themselves in several political movements over the course of American history, and some have gone so far as to interpret the phrase as tacit approval for the use of force.

The first political challenge came in 1798 with the Virginia and Kentucky Resolutions, written anonymously by Thomas Jefferson and James Madison in reaction to the Alien and Sedition Acts passed during John Adams's Administration. The Alien and Sedition Acts attempted to censor speech, particularly by foreign nationals, that agitated against the government. Jefferson and Madison, incensed because members of their party were being persecuted under the Acts, wrote the Resolutions to shift the balance of sovereignty from the federal to the state level. The Resolutions contended that a state could "explicitly and peremptorily declare" federal laws invalid if the state disagreed (Madison, 1798). No other states signed on, but the Resolutions have had a lasting impact nonetheless.

In December 1814, representatives from New England states, disaffected by President James Madison's war with Great Britain (the War of 1812), met in Hartford, Connecticut, to consider splitting away from the rest of the country. Only General Andrew Jackson's victory at the Battle of New Orleans and the war's conclusion put an end to the rumblings.

As president, Jackson butted heads in 1832 and 1833 with his vice president, South Carolinian Charles C. Calhoun, over a state's ability to veto—or "nullify"—federal tariffs. The extended drama, similar in spirit to the Kentucky and Virginia Resolutions, became known as the Nullification Crisis. In the spring and summer of 1864, in the midst of the Civil War, authorities uncovered a plot by Southern sympathizers to try and draw the Old Northwest Territory—Ohio, Indiana, and Illinois—out of the U.S. With an abundance of exclamation points, *The New York Times* reported on "the existence of an extensive secret organization contemplating a distinct and effective movement to cooperate with the armed rebels in the overthrow of the Government...looking to the establishment of a Northwestern Confederacy (!) and including as part of the programme the forcible ejection of Mr. LINCOLN from the executive office!" The effort never materialized, and historians disagree on how serious the threat really was, but *The Times*'s threat assessment characterized the effort as "certainly calculated to startle the loyal people of this country, and to excite grave apprehensions of a fresh peril" (New York Times, 1864, p. 5).

Of course, the Civil War represented the most serious of these threats, beginning as a firebrand political movement that built through the 1850s and finally erupted into a full-blown Secession Crisis in late 1860 and early 1861, when eleven Southern States tried to quit the country altogether. Politics turned to violence, and it took four years of civil war to quell the rebellion. The Supreme Court later ruled Secession was unconstitutional, basing its decision not on any textual analysis but by essentially conceding the outcome of trial by combat (Icenhaur-Ramirez, 2019; Nicoletti, 2017).

Separatists of a different sort waged a terror campaign between 1974 and 1983. The Fuerzas Armadas de Liberación Nacional ("Armed Forces of National Liberation")—known as "FALN" for short—supported the independence of Puerto Rico from its status as an American territory. Over nearly a decade, FALN claimed responsibility for more than 130 bombings in New York City; Washington, D.C.; and Chicago. Two decades before FALN appeared, four separatist gunmen opened fire in the U.S. House of Representatives on March 1, 1954, and four years before that, on November 1, 1950, two Puerto Rican separatists tried to assassinate President Harry S. Truman. Had Puerto Rico gained independence, the pro-separatist "terrorists" would instead be remembered as "liberators."

Separation and secession movements continue to crop up. Northern and southern California occasionally talk of separation, and Texas occasionally talks of reverting to an independent country (Texas Tribune Staff, 2022). In May 2021, five counties in western Oregon approved a nonbinding resolution to secede from the state and become part of Idaho (Johnson, 2021). In 2022, a Georgia Congresswoman called for a "national divorce" (Weaver, 2023). In 2019, facing his first impeachment, President Donald Trump forecast via Twitter the possibility of another civil war; in 2023, Trump supporters again raised the specter of civil war in response to Trump's multiple criminal indictments. "The seedy jabbering about civil war is unlikely to stop anytime soon," warned *Washington Post* columnist Francis Wilkinson (2023), who called the term "'civil war' ... a shorthand for the varied threats of violence that MAGA deploys in response to its political, legal, and cultural failures." (MAGA has become shorthand for the Trump-inspired "Make America Great Again" movement.)

However, those "varied threats of violence" spring from the same spiritual lodestone that inspired the aforementioned political movements. In 1786–87, discontented farmers in western Massachusetts, led by Revolutionary War veteran Daniel Shays, rose up against the state government in protest of tax collections and poor economic conditions. Protestors tried but failed to ransack the federal armory in Springfield before finally being dispersed by state and private militia. The event became known as Shays' Rebellion. In 1791–1793, farmers on the western frontier rose up in protest against a new federal "whiskey tax." President George Washington, as commander in chief of the United States Army, took to the field personally to quell what became known as the Whiskey Rebellion, which ended without violence. In both cases, and in the similar spirit of the Boston Tea Party, protestors believed the government had overstepped its bounds enough that resistance—in these cases, armed resistance—was justified.

At the time of Shays' Rebellion, Thomas Jefferson was living in Paris as the American minister to the French court. In a private letter to William Smith, John Adams's son-in-law, written on November 13, 1787, Jefferson discussed the rebellion in words that have since been gleefully cherry-picked by extremists looking for Revolutionary credibility to justify violence against the government:

> what country can preserve its liberties if their rulers are not warned from time to time that their people preserve the spirit of resistance? let them take arms. ... the tree of liberty must be refreshed from time to time with the blood of patriots & tyrants. it is it's natural manure.
>
> *(Jefferson, Nov. 1787)*

Jefferson's ideas were an outgrowth of a notion expressed in a January letter earlier that year to James Madison, in which he said, "I hold it that a little rebellion now and then is a good thing, and as necessary in the political world as storms in the physical" (Jefferson, Jan. 1787). It's worth noting that Jefferson never advocated these ideas publicly, and he softened his views later in life after he saw the full scope of the French Revolution's bloodletting. It is also worth noting that none of the other Founders, individually or as a group, adopted this radical idea. Jefferson's cachet as an iconic Founder has given the words weight in radical fringes they never had in Jefferson's own time. Timothy McVeigh, when he blew up the Alfred P. Murrah Federal Building in Oklahoma City, wore a t-shirt with Jefferson's words emblazoned on the back, along with a sketch of a liberty tree. On the front: an image of Abraham Lincoln captioned with the phrase John Wilkes Booth shouted after shooting the president: *sic semper tyrannis*, "Thus always to tyrants."

McVeigh tried to imbue his attack with additional Revolutionary symbolism by staging it on April 19, 1995. Two hundred and twenty years earlier, British forces and Massachusetts militia clashed on Lexington Green and later at Concord's Old North Bridge, where colonists fired "the shot heard 'round the world.'" "To McVeigh, this bombing was in the spirit of the patriots of the American Revolution, the stand of a modern radical patriot against an oppressive government," wrote journalists Lou Michel and Dan Herbeck in their book *American Terrorist: Timothy McVeigh and the Oklahoma City Bombing* (2001, p. 226). In a February 1992 letter to his local newspaper, for instance, McVeigh made such an allusion as he railed against the government's failure to do anything about the state of the country. "We have no proverbial tea to dump ..." he wrote. "Is a Civil War Imminent? Do we have to shed blood to reform the current system? I hope it doesn't come to that. But it might" (McVeigh, 1992).

April 19 also marked the two-year anniversary of the Federal assault against the Branch Davidian compound in Waco, Texas. In February 1993, the Bureau of Alcohol, Tobacco, and Firearms tried to execute a search warrant related to a purported stockpile of illegal weapons at the Davidians' compound. The Davidians responded with a shootout that triggered a 51-day siege and resulted in the deaths of 82 Davidians and four federal agents. McVeigh showed up during the siege to show support for the Davidians. "The government is continually growing bigger and more powerful, and the people need to prepare to defend themselves against government control," McVeigh told student journalist Michelle Rauch from Southern Methodist University (Michel & Herbeck, 2001, pp. 122–124).

The fiery end to the siege in Waco—and a federal siege at Ruby Ridge, Idaho, in August 1992—served as inflection points. "McVeigh felt as though he had no alternative but to go on the attack," Michel and Herbeck concluded (2001, p. 14). Michael Fortier, later convicted as an accomplice, testified that McVeigh had decided "to blow up a building to cause a general uprising in America hopefully that would knock some people off the fence and urge them into taking action against the federal government" (Toobin, 2023, p. 121). On that fateful April morning in 1995, McVeigh parked a rental truck packed with a homemade, 7,000-pound fertilizer bomb outside the Alfred P. Murrah Federal Building and detonated it at 9:02 a.m., killing 168 people, including 19 children, and injuring 680 more. "It was a genuinely evil act of terrorism—traitorous, cruel, savage," Michel and Herbeck wrote. "[T]he worst act of homegrown terrorism in American history" (2001, pp. 10, 11).

The Oklahoma City bombing "had a lasting and sinister legacy," contends Jeffrey Toobin in his 2023 book *Homegrown: Timothy McVeigh and the Rise of Right-Wing Extremism*. "McVeigh's values, views, and tactics have endured and even flourished in the decades since his death" (pp. 10, 12). A direct line can be drawn from Waco, Texas, through Oklahoma City, Oklahoma, to the United States Capitol on January 6, 2021, surrounded by Proud Boys and Oath Keepers and other right-wing militia. In fact, the Proud Boys' plan to storm government buildings that day was called "1776 Returns." Prior to the demonstration, alt-right conspiracy radio talk show host Alex Jones rallied his listeners to "declare 1776 against the New World Order" and, claiming to be "under attack," urged them to "get on war-footing" (Toobin, 2023, p. 1).

Efforts to control the political and eventual historical narrative of January 6 began immediately, with horrified witnesses describing the event as "disrespectful and damaging, not only to that building but to our democracy" while sympathetic parties downplayed the same scene as a "normal tourist visit" (Itkowitz, 2021; McGraw, 2023;). In floor speeches delivered hours after the event, Senator Mitt Romney (R-UT) condemned the Capitol breach as "an unprecedented attack on our democracy," while Senate Minority Leader Mitch McConnell (R-KY) decried, "American citizens attacked their own government. They used terrorism to try to stop a specific piece of democratic business they did not like." McConnell later labeled the episode "a violent insurrection for the purpose of trying to prevent the peaceful transfer of power after a legitimately certified election." The House of Representatives eventually impeached President Donald Trump—for a second time—on charges of "incitement of insurrection." Trump, for his part, countered by describing January 6 as "a very beautiful time with extremely loving and friendly people" (Relman & Haltiwanger, 2021). The Republican National Committee cast the January 6 crowd as "ordinary citizens engaged in legitimate political discourse" (Kapur, 2022).

Such a rhetorical tug-of-war was no different from the one waged in Boston and Great Britain in the 1760s and 1770s. Who gets to tell the story, and what story do they get to tell?

As the protest of January 6 turned violent, participants considered themselves "patriots," not "insurrectionists," and many waved American flags to demonstrate their patriotism. Others wrapped themselves in Trump flags, and—in a scene that later became infamous—one man strutted through the building with a Confederate flag propped over his shoulder. Another flag of note was the Gadsden Flag, little known today by its actual name but widely recognized for its yellow background, coiled rattlesnake, and the motto "Don't Tread on Me." The flag warns that, if disturbed, the venomous snake will defend itself with a dangerous bite. Michael Fortier, convicted as one of Timothy McVeigh's accomplices in the Oklahoma City bombing, flew a Gadsden Flag in front of his Arizona home.

The flag was designed in 1775 by Christopher Gadsden, a South Carolina merchant and slave dealer. Gadsden, who was virulently pro-independence, served as a member of the first two Continental Congresses and was a signer of the Declaration. Known as "the Sam Adams of South Carolina," Gadsden is credited as the first voice, in 1766, to publicly advocate for colonial independence. As the story goes, he made his call beneath Charleston's liberty tree, a large oak that stood along Alexander Street just north of the intersection with what is today Calhoun Street. "[T]en years later," proclaims a bronze plaque that now marks the spot, "the Declaration of Independence was first heard [there] and applauded by South Carolinians."

"All men are created equal," the Declaration said—read aloud within earshot of Gadsden's Wharf, where as many as forty percent of enslaved Africans were imported to the colonies. Gadsden's Wharf was only two-tenths of a mile up Calhoun Street from the intersection with Alexander Street. Two-tenths of a mile in the opposite direction, down Calhoun, stands Mother Emanuel African Methodist Episcopal Church, site of a 2015 racially motivated mass shooting.

Mass shootings have become an unfortunate aspect of modern American life. Movie theaters, concert venues, nightclubs, parades, synagogues, and workplaces have all become scenes of seemingly random violence. A spate of post office shootings beginning in 1986 through 2011 even contributed the phrase "going postal" to the American lexicon (Vick, 1993). School shootings, in particular, have been especially heartbreaking. Perhaps the most notorious was the April 20, 1999, attack at Columbine High School in suburban Denver, Colorado, which led to the deaths of ten students, one teacher, and the two shooters, who were seniors at the school. Two dozen people were also injured. The damage could have been far worse, too, except the homemade bombs deployed by the shooters malfunctioned (Cullen, 2009). Between the incident at Columbine and the end of 2023, more than 356,000 students experienced gun violence at school in 386 incidents, according to a database maintained by *The Washington Post* (n.d.).

While such acts of violence do strike terror, they don't fit within our working definition of terrorism because they aren't typically carried out for political or other coercive reasons. Thus, acts of terrorism are distinct from "acts of terror."

In the case of mass shootings, according to research by the Columbia University Department of Psychiatry, they are often perpetrated by aggrieved individuals seeking revenge; by people—most often middle-aged men—"responding to a severe and acute stressor"; or by young men experiencing "a combination of nihilism, emptiness, anger, and a desire for notoriety…." Nearly half are associated with a desire for "suicide by cop." Mental illness, often cited as a "fundamental cause" of shootings, actually accounts "for a very small proportion…." (Girgis, 2022; Brucato et al., 2021, pp. 1–9).

The misrepresentation of mental illness as a cause of gun violence springs from conservative political motivations, often forwarded as a counterpoint to the calls for greater gun control that inevitably spring up after a mass shooting. The topic of gun control, as it happens, serves as one of the primary triggers for right-wing extremists, which gives mass shootings political context even if any particular shooting might not explicitly stem from a political motivation. Oklahoma City bomber Timothy McVeigh, for instance, considered the passage of the 1993 "Brady Bill" requiring background checks for some firearms purchases, followed by the 1994 assault weapons ban, as his "last straw," finally putting into motion his truck-bomb plan inspired by the far-right novel *The Turner Diaries*, a book that considers gun control the ultimate form of government tyranny (Toobin, 2023, p. 97). Journalist Jeffrey Toobin, writing about January 6, 2021, observed: "When the Capitol rioters spoke of the Constitution, it was almost always of only one provision—the Second Amendment. They regarded the right to 'bear arms' as a license for citizens to fight back against the government" (Toobin, 2023, p. 2).

The debate over guns reminds us that the frame used for discussing an issue makes a huge difference. As another example, long-running disputes over women's reproductive health have often been characterized as "pro-choice" or "pro-life." However, when the Supreme Court legalized abortion in its 1973 Roe v. Wade decision, opposition to abortion became increasingly heated—so much so that, according to the National Library of Medicine, "From 1977 to 1988, an epidemic of antiabortion violence took place in the United States, involving 110 cases of arson, firebombing, or bombing. The epidemic peaked in 1984, when there were 29 attacks" (Grimes et al., 1991, pp. 1263–1268). Violence against abortion providers continued even after the Supreme Court overturned Roe v. Wade in 2022 (Department of Justice, n.d.). What does it mean to be "pro-life" when pro-life activists assassinate doctors and firebomb clinics? Does the more recent use of the term "pro-birth" clarify, or does it vilify in a different way? And how do we differentiate between violent acts that hope to inspire an extrajudicial outcome from violent acts that stem from individual grievance—where is the line of "terrorism"?

Motives for terrorism can also be intertwined, as the case of Theodore "Ted" Kaczynski illustrates. Known as the Unibomber, Kaczynski detested modernity itself. "The Industrial Revolution and its consequences have been a disaster for the human race," he wrote in classic reactionary style, yet he refused to be labeled as such. While reserving his greatest venom for the "leftism" of liberal society—which he characterized as "the craziness of our world"—Kaczynski aimed at conservatives, too, lambasting them as "fools who whine about the decay of traditional values, yet … enthusiastically support technological progress and economic growth" (Kaczynski, 1995, p. 1). Conservatives, he said, "are just taking the average man for a sucker, exploiting his resentment of Big Government to promote the power of Big Business" (Kaczynski, 1995, pp. 31–32).

Intertwined with his reactionaryism was a call for "a revolution against the industrial system." It was "not to be a POLITICAL revolution," he said: "Its object will be to overthrow not government but the economic and technological basis of the present society" (1995, p. 1). While he said the revolution might or might not use violence, he obviously had no scruples about his own use of terrorist techniques to achieve his ends.

In 1978, Kaczynski detonated a primitive homemade bomb at Northwestern University in Chicago. "Over the next 17 years, he mailed or hand-delivered a series of increasingly sophisticated bombs that killed three Americans and injured nearly two dozen more," recounts the FBI's official website. "Along the way, he sowed fear and panic, even threatening to blow up airliners in flight" (FBI, n.d.). The FBI's designation as "University and Airline Bomber"—UNABOM for short—led to his Unabomber nickname.

An anti-technologist, Kaczynski lived off the grid in a remote Montana cabin, which enabled him to evade capture for so long. The case finally broke in 1995 when Kaczynski sent a 35,000-word "manifesto" to major media outlets, promising not to murder anyone else if someone published it verbatim. To much controversy, U.S. Attorney General Janet Reno encouraged its publication, hoping it might generate leads in the case. It appeared on September 19, 1995, in *The Washington Post*. Reno's hope paid off: Kaczynski's own brother recognized the writing style and turned him in. Convicted in 1998, Kaczynski died in prison by suicide in June 2023.

Just as the Unibomber's style of revolution was deeply reactionary, so too was Timothy McVeigh's. "There was a paradox in McVeigh's patriotism," points out Toobin, "just as there is among his ideological successors. They profess to love their country, but detest nearly everything about the contemporary United States" (2023, p. 6).

That characterization might likewise describe the South in the years immediately following the Civil War. In the wake of the Confederacy's surrender, white residents had to take a loyalty oath to the United States and its laws. When the Thirteenth, Fourteenth, and Fifteenth Amendments to the Constitution abolished slavery, conveyed citizenship to newly freed enslaved people, and granted the right to vote to Black men, it upended the old social order of the South. White Southerners forced to "profess" their love for their country detested nearly everything around them.

"We had to shoot negroes to get relief from the galling tyranny to which we had been subjected," former South Carolina Governor Ben Tillman matter-of-factly explained in a 1909 speech (Tillman, 1909). Tillman had once belonged to an extralegal group of "leading white men" who had made it their business to ride around in the dead of night, lynching, beating, burning, intimidating, and murdering their way back into power—not just in Tillman's South Carolina but all across the South. Seeking "relief from tyranny" meant such groups as the White League, the Red Shirts, and, perhaps most notoriously, the Ku Klux Klan inflicted a brutal tyranny of their own; "kukluxing" even entered the lexicon as a verb. "The terror began almost as soon as the Civil War ended in 1865," noted historian Stephen Budiansky; "it lasted until 1876, when the last of the governments of the Southern states freely elected through universal manhood suffrage was toppled in a well-orchestrated campaign of violence, fraud, and intimidation...." (2008, p. 1).

During this postwar period, known as Reconstruction, the United States government failed to secure the peace it had won in the Civil War. Despite early successes for African Americans at the ballot box, the promise of a racially equitable society died on the vine as Southern whites, bitter over the loss of their "peculiar institution"—their euphemism for slavery—engaged in systematic, clandestine campaigns of terror to restore the old social order. Federal troops occupied the South in an attempt to enforce the rights granted by the new amendments, but in practical terms, they could do little to protect African Americans from white-hooded midnight posses.

In 1884, the U.S. Supreme Court acknowledged that such individual violence put the government itself "at the mercy of ... those who respect no right but brute force." *Ex parte Yarbrough* was a kukluxing case prompted by voter intimidation in north Georgia. In his original ruling, District Court Judge Henry K. McCay framed the issue:

> Of what avail is the form of a republic, the machinery and parade of ballots and elections, if the voter may not cast his vote without fear? What is the right of suffrage worth if it is to be exercised under fear that, unless it be exercised so as to suit the notions of the mob, the vote[r] will be waked up at night by a lawless band and be shamefully and cruelly beaten[?] The acts of which [the defendants] have been found guilty are not therefore mere acts of violence; they are attacks upon the very vitals of the republic and if permitted to continue would make the right to vote a sham and a snare.
>
> *(*Atlanta Weekly Constitution, *1883)*

In upholding McCay's ruling, the Supreme Court said the government

> must have the power to protect the elections on which its existence depends from violence and corruption. If it has not this power, it is left helpless before two great and natural and historical enemies of all republics, open violence and insidious corruption.
>
> *(*Ex parte Yarbrough, *1884)*

By 1884, such a recognition constituted a legal distinction with limited practical applicability. Reconstruction was more than half a decade dead. In 1871, President Ulysses S. Grant signed the "Ku Klux Klan Act" into law to help protect the political and civil rights of formerly enslaved people, but by 1877, the lure of westward expansion had drawn American attention beyond the Mississippi, undercutting public support for Reconstruction. President Rutherford B. Hayes withdrew troops from the South, and white supremacists re-imposed their rule with restrictive Black Codes, "Jim Crow" laws, and violence.

The worst case of racial violence during Reconstruction happened in Louisiana, in Grant County (named after the president), on Easter Sunday in April 1873. Following a contested election, white supremacists violently overthrew a bi-racial local government and massacred between 60 and 150 members of a Black militia who were trying to defend the county courthouse. Perpetrators called the incident the "Colfax Riot" in an attempt to disingenuously shift blame to the victims, although the event has since been more accurately reframed as the "Colfax Massacre." Ultimately, no one was punished for the crimes, which suggested a kind of "permission" for whites to carry out similar extra-legal action—a tragic precedent that became a pattern (Varon, 2023).

In 1874, the White League of New Orleans—a white militia made up primarily of former Confederate veterans—rallied around a statue of Henry Clay (serving the function of a liberty tree) and, in a pitched battle, temporarily overthrew the duly elected bi-racial city government (Budiansky, 2008; Varon, 2023). In 1898, in Wilmington, North Carolina, a white supremacist-led coup overthrew the duly elected bi-racial Reconstruction government and killed as many as 300 Black residents (Zucchino, 2020). In 1921, a white mob destroyed 35 city blocks of the thriving Greenwood neighborhood of Tulsa, Oklahoma. As many as 300 Black residents died in the nightmare, which was later labeled a "race riot" so insurance companies would not have to pay benefits to Black residents and business owners (Tulsa Historical Society).

White supremacists also liberally used lynchings to enforce the social order. "Indeed, some public spectacle lynchings were attended by the entire white community and conducted as celebratory acts of racial control and domination," wrote the Equal Justice Initiative (EJI) in a comprehensive 2017 report. Nearly 4,100 lynchings took place between 1877 and 1950. "Lynchings were violent and public acts of torture that traumatized Black people throughout the country, and were largely tolerated by state and federal officials," wrote the EJI (2017). "These lynchings were terrorism."

When the Civil Rights Movement began to challenge the status quo beginning in the 1950s, African Americans again faced coordinated, clandestine campaigns of lynching, murder, arson, and assault. Federal intervention met opposition from community-led "massive resistance." Riots broke out. White-hooded Ku Klux Klansmen burned crosses in yards. In Birmingham, Alabama, the 16th Street Baptist Church was bombed, killing four young girls. Individual reactionaries targeted Civil Rights leaders for assassination: Medgar Evers in June 1963; Rev. Martin Luther King Jr. in April 1968; and Malcom X in February 1965.

By the late 1960s and into the early 1970s, the Civil Rights Movement lost momentum and splintered, with some factions becoming as militant as the groups who had opposed them. Racial progress has continued to advance since then, in fits and starts, but resistance has likewise remained. For instance, lynching only became a federal crime in 2022, and then only after 200 failed attempts to pass such a measure (McDaniel & Moore, 2022).

Reconstruction was one of the most tragic yet least understood chapters of American history. Its connections to the Civil Rights Movement and the parallel violence of that era are direct and causal. We can also draw the thread forward to racially motivated acts of terror often classified today as hate crimes, such as Dylann Roof's 2015 murders in Mother Emmanuel AME Church in Charleston, South Carolina, and Peyton Gendron's mass shooting of ten Black people in a supermarket in Buffalo, New York. Analysis of Gendron's online manifesto demonstrated that some 80 percent of it was lifted directly (i.e., plagiarized) from hate sites (Peterka-Benton & Benton, 2023).

One more race-centered example bears examination, this one from October 1859. Radical abolitionist John Brown—who had already established a reputation for political violence after killing five pro-slavery settlers in Pottawatomie, Kansas—led a band of twenty-one followers to capture the federal arsenal at Harpers Ferry, Virginia (now West Virginia). After securing the firearms he needed, Brown planned to sweep across Virginia and spark an uprising of enslaved people. The captured arms would allow them to self-emancipate by force. Brown's plan unraveled quickly, and Brown and most of his men found themselves barricaded in a firehouse on the grounds of the arsenal. The United States Army sent one of its most promising officers, Col. Robert E. Lee—later of Confederate fame—at the head of a contingent of Marines to quell the insurrection.

After his capture, Brown was quickly tried for treason and hanged, but he went to the gallows with the grim prediction "that the crimes of this guilty land will never be purged away, but with Blood." Brown proved sadly prophetic: the incendiary nature of the entire episode did much to bring on the Secession Crisis just over a year later (Gilot & Pawlak, 2023). For that, poet Herman Melville called Brown "the meteor of the war," but depending on a person's sympathies, Brown was either a fanatic or a martyr, and his cause was either criminal or noble (Melville, 1866). He was an "insane old man" to one Chicago newspaper and "man of rare common sense and directness of speech, as of action; a transcendentalist above all, a man of ideas and principles" to Henry David Thoreau (Chicago Press and Tribune, 1859; Thoreau, 1859).

Modern Americans continue to struggle with Brown's story. "Who was this lunatic, this mad man, this abolitionist hero, this saint, this martyr to freedom?" asked legal history scholar Paul Finkelman, writing for the National Archives and Records Administration. "Was he America's first terrorist?" After a wonderfully nuanced examination of the context of Brown's story, Finkelman argued no, suggesting Brown's actions "do not comport with what we know about modern terrorists." However, Finkelman made his ultimate conclusion based on the erroneous assertion that "There are no complete or certain definitions of terrorism." Writing in 2011, he was apparently unaware of the government's official definition offered in the Patriot Act of 2001 (Finkelman, 2011).

In the end, Finkelman concluded his examination with an ambivalent remark from Massachusetts Governor John A. Andrew, quoted widely in the John Brown literature: "[W]hether the enterprise of John Brown and his associates in Virginia was wise or foolish, right or wrong, I only know that, whether the enterprise itself was the one or the other, John Brown himself is right" (Finkelman, 2011; Villard, 1943, p. 557).

But it is a similar sense of "right" that has allowed terrorists to carry out their actions and confirm their beliefs that the end justifies their means. It allowed one of the Boston Marathon bombers of 2013 to justify "killing innocent people" because "The U.S. Government is killing our innocent civilians" in Afghanistan and Iraq (Levenson, 2015). It allowed Timothy McVeigh to point out his "kill ratio" of children to adults in Oklahoma City was lower than the federal government's was at Waco, where the government "set the rules for engagement" (Toobin, 2023, p. 226). It allowed John Brown to "vainly" flatter himself "that without very much blood shed" his effort to end slavery might be done (Gilot & Pawlak, 2023).

The small brick building where Brown and his men made their final stand—now called "John Brown's Fort"—served as the federal armory's firehouse and guard station. The building has hopscotched across the grounds of Harpers Ferry to four different locations in the last 160-plus years, disassembled each time, brick by brick, and moved. In 1891, it even went to the World Exposition in Chicago. Today, it sits in the lower part of the historic town, about 150 feet from its original location, not far from the confluence of the Shenandoah and Potomac Rivers, a location Thomas Jefferson once described as "one of the most stupendous scenes in Nature" (Jefferson, 1832, p. 17).

One can sit in the old firehouse, sharing space with an antique fire engine similar to the one once stored there. High glass windows provide plenty of light. Benches provide an opportunity for reflection. Hindsight allows us to know all that was to come as a result of Brown's raid: Civil War, emancipation, assassination, Reconstruction, racial strife, Civil Rights.

What was Brown thinking as he and his men were holed up in that small brick building? What was going through his mind as the Marines began smashing down the door? Knowing what we know now, would he have been as convinced of his righteousness? Would he have thought it would have all been worth it?

The windows from the sixth floor of the Texas Book Depository in downtown Dallas offer an excellent view of Dealey Plaza. At the southeast corner of the building, South

Houston Street intersects with Elm Street, forming a sharp "V" that doubles back on itself. On November 22, 1963, President John F. Kennedy's motorcade had to slow to a crawl to make the turn, making him an ideal target. Lee Harvey Oswald, hidden behind a wall of boxes he'd stacked up, waited in ambush.

A visitor can't stand in Oswald's exact spot because a reproduction of his rifle occupies it. However, a visitor can stand in the window immediately next to it. The view is nearly identical. Easily visible are the two X's painted on the pavement below, each marking Kennedy's location when struck by Oswald's rifle fire.

Police apprehended Oswald later on the same day he assassinated Kennedy. Jack Ruby, in turn, assassinated Oswald on November 24 as police escorted Oswald to the Dallas jail. Oswald's motive for the killing was never established. Did he have political, revolutionary, or religious motives? Was he, by our working definition, a terrorist?

Other assassinations, easier to classify, can provide context. John Wilkes Booth's assassination of President Abraham Lincoln in April 1865 was in retaliation for the South's defeat in the Civil War. Anarchist Leon Czolgosz's assassination of President William McKinley in September 1901 followed in the footsteps of a number of other assassinations-by-anarchists in Europe over the previous decade and a half. We could add to that the assassination of Sen, Robert F. Kennedy, younger brother to President Kennedy, who was assassinated in June 1968 while running for president—shot by a Palestinian for his support of Israel. All could be understood as acts of terrorism based on our working definition of the term.

President James Garfield's assassination in the summer of 1881 stands as an outlier. Garfield was shot in the back by Charles Guiteau, a dissolute office seeker whom Garfield had turned down—clearly a personal act of vengeance rather than an ideological or theological act. Presidents Theodore Roosevelt and Ronald Reagan both survived attempts on their lives by mentally unstable assailants.

But it's a display in the Sixth Floor Museum in the Texas Book Depository that perhaps offers us our best context (Mackowski, 2019). The self-guided museum tour tells the story of Kennedy's visit to Dallas, his murder there, and the aftermath of his death. One display near the end situates the Kennedy assassination within the context of "Acts of Violence against America." Other examples on the panel include the Japanese attack on Pearl Harbor that triggered American involvement in World War II, the Oklahoma City bombing, and the four terrorist attacks of 9/11. To that list, we should add the 1993 attack on the World Trade Center.

We could also look overseas and add the October 1983 attack on the U.S. Marines barracks in Beirut, Lebanon, which killed 241 service members, and the October 2000 attack on the U.S.S. *Cole* in Aden, Yemen, which killed 17 sailors and injured 40 others. We could also add the 444-day crisis at the American embassy in Iran in 1979–1980. Except Pearl Harbor, which qualifies as an act of war, all of these incidents involved the work of terrorists—although the terrorists themselves might have considered their actions acts of war against America.

Situated on that thread of history, JFK's assassination clearly stands out as an act of violence against America itself, as do the murders of McKinley, Lincoln, and even Garfield. Importantly, though, assassination in America has not served as an effective change strategy. Despite attempts at political disruption, American democracy has muscled onward.

Kennedy's death, in particular, has spawned a cottage industry of conspiracy theories and speculation. One can't stand on the sidewalk in Dealey Plaza without wondering about a mysterious second shooter on the grassy knoll. Standing in Ford's Theater, on the other hand, one can almost assume John Wilkes Booth's perspective—and proximity—and hear his cry of "Sic semper tyrannis!" echo across the empty stage. One can't help but be haunted by the possibilities of what might have happened had Lincoln not been shot. Even Garfield, hardly in office long enough to leave much of a mark, raises tantalizing questions in his absence. "It's an intriguing question, for Garfield was the smartest, the most devious, and the most political of all [the] Civil War presidents..." writes biographer James M. Perry. "[H]e was aggressive, ambitious, and knowledgeable. He had *possibilities*" (Perry, 2003, p. 294).

Conclusion

We can only wonder how these and other acts of terrorism have changed the arc of our national history. But they *can* prompt us to ask more constructive questions, too. For instance, how does America respond when terrorized? What things do our fear, our terror, make us do?

Consider:

- Fear of foreign agents stirring up trouble for the new nation led John Adams to sign into law the controversial Alien and Sedition Acts, which sought, in part, to curtail dissent by limiting free speech.
- Nat Turner's slave rebellion in Southampton Country Virginia, in August 1831—a four-day revolt that led to the deaths of as many as 65 white Virginians and the executions of as many as 175 Black people in retaliation—triggered draconian measures against enslaved people intended to dissuade any further uprisings.
- At the beginning of the Civil War, Lincoln suspended the writ of habeas corpus in Maryland out of fear that malcontents would trigger rebellion in the still-loyal border state—a suspension he would repeat at other times and in other situations during the war.
- After the bombing of Pearl Harbor, the Franklin D. Roosevelt administration feared the work of spies and saboteurs and thus relocated thousands of innocent Japanese-Americans into internment camps.
- The attacks of 9/11 led to the passage of the Patriot Act, which curtailed individual freedoms in the name of national security and created a new cabinet-level department: the Department of Homeland Security, including an instant new federal agency, the Transportation Security Administration (TSA).

Other reactions have been subtler, even if literally set in stone. "Taking greater precautions at guarding public buildings with metal detectors and armed officers, concrete barriers disguised as oversized flower pots, and a smattering of surveillance cameras, society chalked up [Timothy] McVeigh as a lesson learned," wrote Michel and Herbeck (2001, p. 13). One need only travel by air today—arriving at least two hours early to ensure enough time to get through the TSA screening process with your shoes off and your personal items stacked neatly in plastic bins—to wonder whether the 9/11 terrorists actually won in the long term.

As early as 1755, Benjamin Franklin questioned trade-offs like these. "Those who would give up essential Liberty, to purchase a little temporary Safety, deserve neither Liberty nor

Safety," he wrote (Franklin, 1755). Often taken out of context, Franklin's comment spoke to the right of a colonially elected legislature, as the voice of the people, to determine its own affairs—something he considered an "essential Liberty" that derived from and belonged to the people. In the post-9/11 era, his comment has been used by the political left and right alike to decry the curtailment of individual freedoms by the government in the name of national security (Siegel & Anderson, 2015).

We continue to grapple with terrorism's effects in ways even more subtle, perhaps even insidious. The 24/7 news cycle, even as it has shown us the impacts of terrorism, has desensitized us to its visceral nature. Portions of society more readily believe and accept racial and ethnic stereotypes. Partisan tribalism inspires right-leaning politicians to downplay the potential danger of far-right violence despite ample evidence from state and federal law enforcement agencies, and some of them bandy about terms like "civil war" as though the first one didn't cost as many as 750,000 lives and ruin millions more.

Thomas Jefferson, for his part, lived long enough to see what happened when the blood of patriots watered the tree of liberty. He had supported the notion in 1787, but by 1816, after the stunning bloodshed of the French Revolution and the European wars waged by the subsequent rise of Napoleon Bonaparte, he expressed serious second thoughts. "Your prophecies [about the French Revolution] ... proved truer than mine," he admitted to his longtime friend and political rival, John Adams, who had condemned the French Revolution with dire warnings, yet still "fell short" in his predictions. "[F]or instead of a million," Jefferson conceded, "the destruction of 8 or 10 millions of human beings has probably been the effect of these convulsions. I did not ... believe they would have lasted so long, nor have cost so much blood" (Jefferson, 1816).

It's a 205-mile drive from Dealey Plaza in Dallas, north up Interstate 35 to Oklahoma City. One passes over the border between the two states at the Red River, then onward through the rolling green hills of the Chickasaw Nation. The Oklahoma City National Memorial and Museum sit in the heart of downtown between Harvey and Robinson, although some might say it sits, still, at the heart of Oklahoma. A long reflecting pool, like a smooth plane of obsidian, spans the plaza between two black walls. One says 9:01, the other 9:03. In the moment between them, stretched out forever, everything changed. McVeigh's bomb went off.

One hundred and sixty-eight vacant chairs—explicitly reminiscent of H. S. Washburn's Civil War-era poem of that name—sit on a hillside where the Murrah Federal Building once stood. "The Field of Empty Chairs," as it's called, is arranged in nine rows, one row for each floor of the building, one chair for every victim; nineteen small chairs represent the children from the building's daycare killed in the blast.

On the north side of the reflecting pool, one of the bombing's most extraordinary survivors still stands vigil, an American elm now known as the "Survivor Tree." Planted sometime around 1920—a dozen or so years after Oklahoma achieved statehood—the elm stood as a downtown fixture through decades of building demolitions and parking lot construction, even as other trees came down. It stood only yards away from the Murrah Building and absorbed the full impact of the blast, which stripped away many of the elm's leaves and branches. Yet the tree lived. Today, visitors can purchase seedlings from the tree. The Memorial Museum calls it "an iconic symbol of hope" (Oklahoma City National Memorial Museum, n.d.).

When President Bill Clinton visited Oklahoma City on Sunday, April 23, for a prayer service at the Oklahoma City Fairgrounds, he shared a suggestion given to him by a young girl who had recently visited the White House. "She said, 'We should all plant a tree in memory of the children,'" Clinton replied

> So this morning before we got on the plane to come here, at the White House, we planted that tree in honor of the children of Oklahoma. It was a dogwood with its wonderful spring flower and its deep, enduring roots. It embodies the lesson of the Psalms—that the life of a good person is like a tree whose leaf does not wither.
>
> *(Clinton, 1995)*

This dogwood, this elm—these, too, are the trees of liberty.

References

Adair, D., & Schutz, J. A. (Eds.). (1967). *Peter oliver's "origin and progress of the American rebellion": A tory view.* Stanford University Press.

The Atlanta Weekly Constitution. (1883, December 25). pg. 6.

Bernard, F. (1868). Extract of a letter to the lords of trade, dated August 15, 1765. In *The parliamentary debate: Official reports* (Vol. 16). H. M. Stationary Office.

The Boston Gazette, and Country Journal (1766, February). *569*(24).

Brucato, G., Appelbaum, P. S., Hesson, H., Shea, E. A., Dishy, G., Lee, K., Pia, T., Syed, F., Villalobos, A., Wall, M. M., Lieberman, J. A., & Girgis, R. R. (2021). Psychotic symptoms in mass shootings v. mass murders not involving firearms: findings from the Columbia mass murder database. *Psychological Medicine,* 1–9. https://doi.org/ 10.1017/S0033291721000076

Budiansky, S. (2008). *The bloody shirt: Terror after appomattox.* Viking.

Chicago Press and Tribune. (1859, October 20). *Where the responsibility belongs.*

Clinton, W. J. (1995, April 23). *Oklahoma bombing memorial prayer service* [Address]. https://www.americanrhetoric.com/speeches/wjcoklahomabombingspeech.htm

Cullen, D. (2009). *Columbine.* Hachette.

Declaration of Independence. (1776, July 4). https://www.archives.gov/founding-docs/declaration-transcript

Department of Justice. (n.d.). *Recent cases on violence against reproductive health care providers.* https://www.justice.gov/crt/recent-cases-violence-against-reproductive-health-care-providers

Equal Justice Initiative. (2017). *Lynching in America: Confronting the legacy of racial terror* (3rd ed.). https://lynchinginamerica.eji.org/report/

Ex parte Yarbrough, 110 U.S. 651 (1884)

Federal Bureau of Investigation. (n.d.). *The unibomber.* https://www.fbi.gov/history/famous-cases/unabomber

Federal Bureau of Investigation. (n.d.). *Terrorism.* https://www.fbi.gov/investigate/terrorism

Finkelman, P. (2001). A look back at John Brown. *Prologue, 43*(1). https://www.archives.gov/publications/prologue/2011/spring/brown.html

Franklin, B. (1756). *Pennsylvania assembly: Reply to the governor, 11 November 1755* [letter]. Printed in Votes and Proceedings of the House of Representatives, 1755–1756. Founders Online, National Archives. https://founders.archives.gov/documents/Franklin/01-06-02-0107

Gilot, J., & Pawlak, K. (2023). *John Brown's raid: Harpers ferry and the coming of the civil war, October 16–18, 1859.* Savas Beatie.

Girgis, R. (2022, July 6). Is there a link between mental health and mass shootings? *Columbia Psychiatry News.* https://www.columbiapsychiatry.org/news/mass-shootings-and-mental-illness

Grimes, D. A., Forrest, J. D., Kirkman, A. L., & Radford, B. (1991). An epidemic of antiabortion violence in the United States. *American Journal of Obstetrics and Gynecology, 165*(5) (Pt 1), 1263–1268. doi:10.1016/0002-9378(91)90346-s. https://pubmed.ncbi.nlm.nih.gov/1957842/

Hutchinson, T. (1828). *The history of the province of massachusetts bay.* W. Clowes.

Icenhaur-Ramirez, R. (2019). *Treason on trial: The United States v. Jefferson Davis.* Louisiana State University Press.

Itkowitz, C. (2021, May 12). 'Normal tourist visit': Republicans recast deadly Jan. 6 attack by pro-Trump mob. *The Washington Post.* https://www.washingtonpost.com/politics/trump-riot-capitol-republicans/2021/05/12/dcc03342-b351-11eb-a980-a60af976ed44_story.html
Jefferson, T. (1787, January 30). *From Thomas Jefferson to James Madison, 30 January 1787* [letter]. Founders Online, National Archives. https://founders.archives.gov/documents/Jefferson/01-11-02-0095
Jefferson, T. (1787, November 13). *From Thomas Jefferson to William Stephens Smith, 13 November 1787.* Founders Online, National Archives. https://founders.archives.gov/documents/Jefferson/01-12-02-0348
Jefferson, T. (1816, January 11). *To John Adams from Thomas Jefferson, 11 January 1816* [letter]. Founders Online, National Archives. https://founders.archives.gov/documents/Adams/99-02-02--6568.
Jefferson, T. (1832) *Notes on the state of Virginia.* Lilly and Wait.
Johnson, K. (2021, May 21). Their own private Idaho: Five Oregon counties back a plan to secede. *New York Times.* https://www.nytimes.com/2021/05/21/us/oregon-idaho-secession.html
Kaczynski, T. (1995). *Industrial society and its future.* http://editions-hache.com/essais/pdf/kaczynski2.pdf
Kapur, S. (2022, February 8). McConnell calls Jan. 6 a "Violent insurrection," breaking with the RNC. *NBC News.* https://www.nbcnews.com/politics/congress/mcconnell-calls-jan-6-violent-insurrection-breaking-rnc-rcna15404
Lane, J. (2021, June 24). *Jonathan Lane on pieces of the roots of the liberty tree* [Video]. Massachusetts Historical Society. YouTube. https://youtu.be/cAkjGiA0nNk?si=xuGbwU1RNWIraqYM
Levenson, E. (2015, March 10). Here's the note Dzhokhar Tsarnaev wrote inside the boat where he was captured. *Boston Globe, 10.* https://www.boston.com/news/local-news/2015/03/10/heres-the-note-dzhokhar-tsarnaev-wrote-inside-the-boat-where-he-was-captured/
Mackowski, C. (2019, September 11). Acts of violence against America. *Emerging Civil War.* https://emergingcivilwar.com/2019/09/11/acts-of-violence-against-america/
Madison, J. (1798, December 21). Virginia resolutions. *Founders Online.* https://founders.archives.gov/documents/Madison/01-17-02-0128
McDaniel, E., & Moore, E. (2022, March 29). Lynching is now A federal hate crime after a century of blocked efforts. *National Public Radio.* https://www.npr.org/2022/03/29/1086720579/lynching-is-now-a-federal-hate-crime-after-a-century-of-blocked-efforts
McGraw, T. (2023, September 5). Interview with author. McGraw worked in the Congressional mailroom in the capitol and was present in the building during the attack.
McVeigh, T. (1992, February 11). Letter to the editor. *Union Sun & Journal.*
Melville, H. (1866). The portent. In *Battle pieces and aspects of war.* Harper & Brothers.
Michel, L., & Herbeck, D. (2001). *American terrorist: Timothy McVeigh and the Oklahoma City Bombing.* Harper.
Moore, F. (1859). *Diary of the American revolution, from newspapers and original documents* (Vol. 1). Charles Scribner. [reprinting article from 1 September 1775 *New England Chronicle.*]
New York Times. (1864, July 31). The alleged conspiracy; The plot to form a northwestern confederacy: Full details of the scheme. Names of the traitors implicated. An averred conspiracy. *New York Times.*
Nicoletti, C. (2017). *Secession on trial: The treason prosecution of Jefferson Davis.* Cambridge University Press.
Oklahoma City National Memorial Museum. (n.d.). *The survivor tree.* http://memorialmuseum.com/experience/the-survivor-tree/
Perry, J. M. (2003). *Touched with fire: Five presidents and the civil war battles that made them.* Public Affairs.
Peterka-Benton, D. & Benton, B. (2023, Summer). Online radicalization case study of a mass shooting: The Payton Gendron anifesto. *Journal for Deradicalization, 35,* 7.
Preble, G. H. (1880). *History of the flag of the United States of America: And of the naval and yacht-club signals, seals, and arms, and principal national songs of the United States, with a chronicle of the symbols, standards, banners, and flags of ancient and modern nations.* A. Williams and Company.
Relman, E. & Haltiwanger, J. (2021, November 15). Trump called January 6 'a very beautiful time with extremely loving and friendly people' in a March 2021 interview for a new book. *Business*

Insider. https://www.businessinsider.com/trump-called-january-6-capitol-very-beautiful-time-book-2021-11
Siegel, R., & Anderson, R. (2015, March 2). Ben Franklin's famous 'liberty, safety' quote lost its context in 21st century. *All Things Considered.* https://www.npr.org/2015/03/02/390245038/ben-franklins-famous-liberty-safety-quote-lost-its-context-in-21st-century
Texas Tribune Staff. (2022, June 20). No, Texas can't legally secede from the U.S., despite popular myth *Texas Tribune.* https://www.texastribune.org/2021/01/29/texas-secession/
Thoreau, H. D. (1859, October 30). *A Plea for John Brown.* Speech presented in Concord, MA.
Tillman, B. R (1909). *The struggles of 1876: How South Carolina was delivered from carpet-bag and negro rule* [speech]. Benjamin Ryan Tillman Papers, Clemson University.
Toobin, J. (2023). *Homegrown: Timothy McVeigh and the rise of right-wing extremism.* Simon and Schuster.
United States Code, Ch. 113B: "Terrorism," Sec. 2331. https://uscode.house.gov/view.xhtml?path=/prelim@title18/part1/chapter113B&edition=prelim
Varon, E. (2023). *Longstreet: The confederate general who defied the South.* Simon & Schuster.
Vick, K. (1993, December 17). Violence at work tied to loss of esteem. *Tampa Bay (FL) Times. Note:* This is the first-known usage of the term "going postal" in print. https://www.tampabay.com/archive/1993/12/17/violence-at-work-tied-to-loss-of-esteem/
Villard, O. G. (1943). *John Brown, 1800–1859: A biography fifty years later.* Alfred A. Knopf.
Washington Post. (n.d.). *School shootings database.* https://www.washingtonpost.com/education/interactive/school-shootings-database/
Weaver, A. (2023, February). Greene stirs up political storm with 'national divorce' comments *The Hill.* https://thehill.com/homenews/house/3870038-greene-stirs-up-political-storm-with-national-divorce-comments/
Weinberg, L. (2008). *Global terrorism.* Oneworld Publications.
Wilkinson, F. (2023, September 3). The only US 'civil war' will be a war on democracy. *Washington Post.* https://www.washingtonpost.com/business/2023/09/03/the-only-us-civil-war-will-be-a-war-on-democracy/51c6e488-4a54-11ee-bfca-04e0ac43f9e4_story.html
Young, A. F. (2006). Liberty tree: Made in American, lost in America. In *Liberty tree: Ordinary people and the American revolution.* New York University Press.
Zucchino, D. (2020). *Wilmington's Lie: The murderous coup of 1898 and the rise of White supremacy.* Atlantic Monthly Press.

2

DEFINITIONS AND THEORIES OF TERRORISM

Robin Valeri and Binneh Minteh

Introduction

Anyone searching for a definition of terrorism will quickly come to realize that there is no one universally agreed upon definition of terrorism either by governmental organizations or by academics.

Governmental organizations tend to take one of three strategies with regard to terrorism. Agencies either provide a description/definition of terrorism or terrorist behaviors, provide a list of actions they consider to be terrorism, or offer some combination of the two. For those governmental organizations that choose to define or describe terrorism, there are two main commonalities among the definitions. The definitions or descriptions of terrorism include (1) either the occurrence of or the threat of a criminal act (2) that is perpetrated either to spread fear among a population or to coerce a government or another authority to act in a specific way.

To begin, we will examine definitions provided by two global governmental organizations. Next, definitions from several regional inter-governmental organizations will be presented. The regional organizations selected from Africa, Asia, the Americas, the Middle East, and Europe were chosen because these are the ones most relevant to this text. Then, definitions of terrorism from agencies in the United States will be examined. Finally, we will examine definitions offered by academics.

Global Organizations

The two largest global organizations are the United Nations and the Organization of Islamic Cooperation (OIC).

The United Nations is currently made up of 193 Member States. At the United Nations, because Member States have failed to agree on an official definition of terrorism, when references to terrorism are made, they are typically accompanied by descriptions of terrorism. The purpose of these descriptions is to help States know when and how to act in

DOI: 10.4324/9781003375265-4

accordance with a given resolution. For example, *U.N. Resolution 49/60 Measures to Eliminate International Terrorism*, states

> Criminal acts intended or calculated to provoke a state of terror in the general public, a group of persons or particular persons for political purposes are in any circumstance unjustifiable, whatever the considerations of a political, philosophical, ideological, racial, ethnic, religious or any other nature that may be invoked to justify them.
>
> *(U.N. Resolution 49/60, 1995)*

While in *Resolution 1566 (2004) International Cooperation in the Fight Against Terrorism*, the description offered is a bit more expansive regarding the targets, actions, and goals of terrorism, stating that

> Criminal acts, including against civilians, committed with the intent to cause death or serious bodily injury, or taking of hostages, with the purpose to provoke a state of terror in the general public or in a group of persons or particular persons, intimidate a population or compel a government or an international organization to do or to abstain from doing any act, which constitute offences within the scope of and as defined in the international conventions and protocols relating to terrorism, are under no circumstances justifiable by considerations of a political, philosophical, ideological, racial, ethnic, religious or other similar nature, and calls upon all States to prevent such acts and, if not prevented, to ensure that such acts are punished by penalties consistent with their grave nature.
>
> *(U. N. Resolution 1566, 2004)*

The OIC is composed of 57 states, including the State of Palestine. The member countries of the OIC are spread across four continents: Europe, Asia, Africa, and South America. Unlike the United Nations, the OIC has been able to agree upon a definition of terrorism as well as a definition of terrorism crime. According to the 1999 *Convention of the Organization of the Islamic Conference on Combating International Terrorism*

> "Terrorism" means any act of violence or threat thereof notwithstanding its motives or intentions perpetrated to carry out an individual or collective criminal plan with the aim of terrorizing people or threatening to harm them or imperiling their lives, honour, freedoms, security or rights or exposing the environment or any facility or public or private property to hazards or occupying or seizing them, or endangering a national resource, or international facilities, or threatening the stability, territorial integrity, political unity or sovereignty of independent States.
>
> *(OIC, 1999)*

> "Terrorist Crime" means any crime executed, started or participated in to realize a terrorist objective in any of the Contracting States or against its nationals, assets or interests or foreign facilities and nationals residing in its territory punishable by its internal law.
>
> *(OIC, 1999)*

As part of this Convention the Organization of Islamic Cooperation further stipulates that criminal activities listed in a number of other conventions, provided that those

> conventions have been ratified by a state, are also considered terrorist crimes. Examples of the criminal activities identified in these Conventions include the unlawful seizure of aircrafts, hostage taking, terrorist bombing, and explosive making.

One significant difference between the OIC's definition of terrorism and that of the United Nations and many other governmental organizations is that armed national liberation efforts or self-determination struggles are not considered acts of terrorism. Article 2.a of the *Convention of the Organization of the Islamic Conference on Combating International Terrorism* states

> Peoples' struggle including armed struggle against foreign occupation, aggression, colonialism, and hegemony, aimed at liberation and self-determination in accordance with the principles of international law shall not be considered a terrorist crime.
>
> *(OIC, 1999)*

The Organization of African Unity (OAU, 1999), in its *OAU Convention on the Prevention and Combatting of Terrorism* and the League of Arab States's (LAS, 1998) *Arab Convention for the Suppression of Terrorism* include similar statements indicating that armed national liberation efforts or self-determination struggles are not considered acts of terrorism.

Given this national liberation exception to terrorism, one can see why some might view Hamas's October 7, 2023, attacks on Israel as an armed struggle for liberation against occupation, while others might view these actions as terrorism. Certainly, the causal attributions surrounding the ongoing war in Gaza highlight the politics of defining terrorism and the truth behind the oft-quoted truism that "One person's terrorist is another person's freedom fighter."

Region of Africa

As will be discussed in later chapters of this text, in recent years the continent of Africa has faced threats from several terrorist groups including Al-Shabab, Boko Haram, Jama'a Nusrat ul-Islam, and affiliates of the Islamic State. The regional organization addressing terrorism in Africa is the African Union (AU), which is composed of 55 Member States. Its predecessor was the OAU. The Organization of African Unity, in its 1999 *OAU Convention on the Prevention and Combatting of Terrorism* provided a very clear and detailed definition of terrorism. The Convention clearly states

> "Terrorist act" means: (a) any act which is a violation of the criminal laws of a State Party and which may endanger the life, physical integrity or freedom of, or cause serious injury or death to, any person, any number or group of persons or causes or may cause damage to public or private property, natural resources, environmental or cultural heritage and is calculate or intended to: (i) intimidate, put in fear, force, coerce or induce any government, body, institution, the general public or any segment thereof, to do or abstain from doing any act, or to adopt or abandon a particular standpoints, or to act according to certain principles; or (ii) disrupt any public service, the delivery of any essential service to the public or to create a public emergency; or (iii) create general

> insurrection in a State. (b) any promotion, sponsoring, contribution to, command, aid, incitement, encouragement, attempt, threat, conspiracy, organizing, or procurement of any person, with the intent to commit any act referred to in paragraph (a) (i) to (iii).
>
> *(OAU, 1999)*

Note that this definition of terrorism, unlike that of the descriptions offered by the United Nations or the OIC, includes the promotion or sponsoring of terrorism as criminal acts. The European Council, as will be discussed shortly, provides specific definitions of these.

According to the OAU Convention, and as was previously mentioned, armed national liberation efforts or self-determination struggles are not considered acts of terrorism. Article 3.1 of the *Convention on the Prevention and Combatting of Terrorism* states

> Notwithstanding the provisions of Article 1, the struggle waged by people in accordance with international law for their liberation or self-determination, including armed struggle against colonialism, occupation, aggression and domination by foreign forces shall not be considered terrorist acts.
>
> *(OAU, 1999)*

One of the mandates of the *Convention on the Prevention and Combatting of Terrorism,* which was adopted in 1999 and became effective in December 2002, is that each Member State must criminalize the terrorist acts as defined in the Convention under their own national laws.

Since the 1999 Convention, the AU, through its Plan of Action (2002), has sought to strengthen the commitment of Member States to the 1999 Convention, and recognized that "Severe conditions of poverty and deprivation...of the African population provide a fertile breeding ground for terrorist extremism" (I.6), noting the linkages between terrorism and "drug trafficking, illicit proliferation and trafficking of small arms and light weapons, corruption and money laundering..." (II.10.d.), and established the African Center for the Study and Research on Terrorism (III.H.).

Region of Europe

The European Union (EU) is currently composed of 27 countries. Similar to the AU, which required that Member States criminalize terrorist acts, the European Union, in Title II Article 3 of Directive (EU) 2017/541, provides a comprehensive list of serious offenses that EU countries must classify as terrorist offenses in their national laws when they are committed or there is a threat to commit them for one of three terrorist aims. The terrorist aims are

> (a) seriously intimidating a population; (b) unduly compelling a government or an international organisation to perform or abstain from performing any act; (c) seriously destabilising or destroying the fundamental political, constitutional, economic or social structures of a country or an international organisation.
>
> *((EU) 2017/541)*

The serious offenses listed include attacking, kidnapping, or killing an individual; destruction of a government or public facility, a transport system, or an infrastructure facility;

seizure of public or goods transport; manufacture, possession, acquisition, transport, supply, or use of explosives or weapons; release of dangerous substances, causing fires, floods, explosions, or the effect of which is to endanger human life; interfering with or disrupting the supply of water, power, or any other fundamental natural resource to endanger human life; illegal computer/technology or data system interference, or threatening to commit any of these acts (EU 2017/541).

The EU is a separate organization from the Council of Europe (COE). The Council of Europe, whose mission is "to promote democracy, human rights and the rule of law across Europe and beyond" (COE, n.d.), is currently composed of 46 states. In May 2005, the COE adopted the *Council of Europe Convention on the Prevention of Terrorism (CETS No. 196)*. According to this treaty, which became effective in June 2007, terrorist acts are described as having

> the purpose by their nature or context to seriously intimidate a population or unduly compel a government or an international organisation to perform or abstain from performing any act or seriously destabilise or destroy the fundamental political, constitutional, economic or social structures of a country or an international organisation.
>
> *(CETS No. 196)*

An important objective of this convention is the prevention of terrorism. Prevention efforts include making it a criminal offense to engage in activities that would lead to the commission of terrorist acts. These activities include publicly provoking terrorism, recruitment efforts, and terrorist training. According to this convention, public provocation is defined as

> the distribution, or otherwise making available, of a message to the public, with the intent to incite the commission of a terrorist offence, where such conduct, whether or not directly advocating terrorist offences, causes a danger that one or more such offences may be committed.
>
> *(CETS No. 196)*

While recruitment is described as efforts to

> solicit another person to commit or participate in the commission of a terrorist offence, or to join an association or group, for the purpose of contributing to the commission of one or more terrorist offences by the association or the group.
>
> *(CETS No. 196)*

And finally, training is defined as

> Provide[ing] instruction in the making or use of explosives, firearms or other weapons or noxious or hazardous substances, or in other specific methods or techniques, for the purpose of carrying out or contributing to the commission of a terrorist offence, knowing that the skills provided are intended to be used for this purpose.
>
> *(CETS No. 196)*

Please note that later in this text, in the chapters on cyberterrorism, the role of the internet and social media in the recruitment, training, and provocation of terrorism will be discussed. In October 2015, effective July 1, 2017, the European Council adopted the *Additional Protocol to the Council of Europe Convention on the Prevention of Terrorism (CETS No. 217)*. In this treaty, criminal acts related to terrorism were extended to include joining or associating with a group for the purpose of terrorism, receiving training in terrorism, and traveling abroad, funding the travel abroad, or organizing travel abroad to engage in terrorism (CETS No. 217).

Region of Asia

In the region of Asia, the intergovernmental organizations are the South Asian Association for Regional Cooperation (SAARC), the Association of South East Asian Nations (ASEAN), and the Shanghai Cooperation Organization (SCO).

The South Asia Association for Regional Cooperation is comprised of eight Member States: Afghanistan, Bangladesh, Bhutan, India, Maldives, Nepal, Pakistan, and Sri Lanka. At the second SAARC summit, which took place in Bangalore, November 16–17, 1986, these countries committed to the Bangalore Declaration in which

> They unequivocally condemned all acts, methods and practices of terrorism as criminal and deplored their impact on life and property, social economic development, political stability, regional and international peace and co-operation.
>
> *(SAARC, 1986)*

In November 1987, the SAARC adopted the *SAARC Regional Convention on the Suppression of Terrorism*. In this Convention, the SAARC, rather than creating a definition of terrorism, relied upon the definitions of terrorism provided in previous conventions. Specifically, the criminal act of terrorism was regarded as any offenses defined in (1) The Convention for the Suppression of Unlawful Seizure of Aircraft, (2) The Convention for the Suppression of Unlawful Acts Against the Safety of Civil Aviation, or (3) The Convention on the Prevention and Punishment of Crimes against Internationally Protected Persons, including Diplomats, as well as (4) any offense within the scope of any convention to which SAARC Member States concerned are parties (SAARC, 1987). It further defined terrorism as "murder, manslaughter, assault...offences related to firearms...when used as a means to perpetrate indiscriminate violence involving death or serious bodily injury to persons or serious damage to property or an attempt or conspiracy to commit [any of the previously listed offences]" (SAARC, 1987). In January 2004, SAARC adopted an *Additional Protocol to the SAARC Regional Convention on the Suppression of Terrorism* the purpose of which was

> to strengthen the SAARC Regional Convention on Suppression of Terrorism, particularly by criminalizing the provision, collection or acquisition of funds for the purpose of committing terrorist acts and taking further measures to prevent and suppress financing of such acts.
>
> *(SAARC, 2004)*

Members of the ASEAN are the states of Indonesia, Malaysia, Philippines, Singapore, Thailand, Brunei Darussalam, Viet Nam, Lao PDR, Myanmar, and Cambodia. In the

ASEAN Convention on Counter Terrorism, adopted in January 2007 and effective in May 2011, rather than creating their own definition of terrorism, ASEAN defined the criminal act of terrorism as any offenses defined in a number of treaties. These treaties include, but are not limited to, the International Convention for the Suppression of Terrorist Bombings, the International Convention for the Suppression of the Financing of Terrorism, and the International Convention for the Suppression of Acts of Nuclear Terrorism (ASEAN, 2007). They also include treaties against the hijacking of aircraft, seizing nuclear facilities, hostage taking, and the like (ASEAN, 2007). In September 2017, ASEAN adopted the Manila Declaration to Counter the Rise of Radicalization and Violent Extremism. This declaration included a commitment to "Counter radicalisation and violent extremism... through means such as the prevention of radicalisation, financing, recruitment, and mobilization of individuals into terrorist groups" (ASEAN, 2017) as well as a commitment to counter terrorism, not only through force or punitive measures, but also by rehabilitating radicalized or extremist individuals so that they can be reintegrated into society and avoid relapsing into militant or terrorist activities (ASEAN, 2017).

The Shanghai Cooperation Organization, which was founded in 2001, is currently comprised of nine Member States: China, India, Iran, Kazakhstan, Kyrgyzstan, Russia, Pakistan, Tajikistan, and Uzbekistan. In June 2001, the SCO, then composed of only six countries—China, Kazakhstan, Kyrgyzstan, Russia, Tajikistan, and Uzbekistan—adopted the *Shanghai Convention on Combating Terrorism, Separatism, and Extremism*. Similar to SAARC and ASEAN, the offense of terrorism was defined in terms of previous treaties. However, the SCO, in the *Shanghai Convention* also added its own definition of terrorism as well as definitions for separatism and extremism. According to the *Shanghai Convention*

1) "terrorism" means:
    a. any act recognized as an offense in one of the treaties listed in the Annex to this Convention... and as defined in this Treaty;
    b. other acts intended to cause death or serious bodily injury to a civilian, or any other person not taking an active part in the hostilities in a situation of armed conflict or to cause major damage to any material facility, as well as to organize, plan, aid, and abet such acts, when the purpose of such acts, by its nature or context, is to intimidate a population, violate public security, or to compel public authorities or an international organization to do or to abstain from doing any act, and prosecuted in accordance with the national laws of the Parties; (SCO, 2001)

In the *Shanghai Convention*, Separatism and Extremism are defined as

2) "separatism" means any act intended to violate territorial integrity of a state, including by annexation of any part of its territory or to disintegrate a state, committed in a violent manner, as well as planning and preparing, and abetting such acts, and subject to criminal prosecution in accordance with the national laws of the Parties;
3) "extremism" is an act aimed at seizing or keeping power through the use of violence or changing violently the constitutional regime of a state, as well as a violent encroachment upon public security, including organization, for the above purposes, of illegal armed formations and participation in them, criminally prosecuted in conformity with the national laws of the Parties. (SCO, 2001)

In June 2009, the SCO recognized the "necessity of increasing efforts against terrorism and re-affirming that all measures in preventing and combating terrorism should be undertaken" (SCO, 2009) and adopted the *Convention Against Terrorism of the Shanghai Cooperation Organization*. In this convention the terms terrorism, terrorist act, and terrorist organization were defined.

Terrorism was defined as

> an ideology of violence and a practice of influencing decision-making by the authorities or international organizations through the commission of or the threat of committing violent and (or) other criminal acts connected with intimidating a population and aimed at causing damage to the person, to society, and to the state.
>
> *(SCO, 2009)*

A terrorist act was defined as

> an act connected with intimidating a population and creating a danger to human life and health that is intended to cause significant property damage, an ecological disaster, or other serious consequences in order to achieve political, religious, ideological, or other ends by influencing decision-making by the authorities or international organizations, or the threat of committing such acts.
>
> *(SCO, 2009)*

And a terrorist organization was defined as

> a) a criminal group, unlawful armed unit, gang, or criminal society created to commit offenses and (or) that commits offenses covered by the present Convention; b) a juridical person in whose name, at whose direction, or in whose interests one of the offenses covered by the present Convention is planned, organized, prepared for, or committed.
>
> *(SCO, 2009)*

Region of the Middle East and Gulf

The League of Arab States was established in 1945 and is currently composed of 22 states, including the State of Palestine, which are situated primarily in North Africa and the Middle East. In 1998, the League of Arab States adopted the *Arab Convention for the Suppression of Terrorism*. In this Convention, terrorism is defined as

> Any act or threat of violence, whatever its motives or purposes, that occurs in the advancement of an individual or collective criminal agenda and seeking to sow panic among people, causing fear by harming them, or placing their lives, liberty or security in danger, or seeking to cause damage to the environment or to public or private installations or property or to occupying or seizing them, or seeking to jeopardize a national resources.
>
> *(LAS, 1998)*

Terrorist offenses are defined in terms of offenses specified in other conventions adopted by Member States. These conventions are similar to those listed by the SAARC and previously discussed. As was previously mentioned, this convention makes clear that armed national liberation efforts or self-determination struggles are not considered acts of terrorism.

Region of the Americas

Finally, the inter-governmental agency in the Americas is the Organization of American States (OAS), which is composed of all 35 states of the Americas. In documents of the OAS, rather than providing an explicit definition of terrorism, these documents offer descriptions of terrorism or reference offenses described in other conventions. For example, in 1971, the OAS drafted thirteen articles for the prevention and punishment of terrorism, referred to as the *Convention to Prevent and Punish the Acts of Terrorism Taking the Form of Crimes against Persons and Related Extortion that are of International Significance.* Article 1 of this Convention states, "terrorism, especially kidnapping, murder, and other assaults against the life or physical integrity of those persons to whom the state has the duty according to international law to give special protection, as well as extortion in connection with those crimes" (OAS, 1971) should be prevented and punished by the contracting states. In the 1996 *Declaration of Lima*, terrorism is referred to as

> ...a serious form of organized and systematic violence, which is intended to generate chaos and fear among the population, results in death and destruction and is a reprehensible criminal activity.
>
> *(OAS, 1996)*

In 1999, the OAS, in accordance with the Resolution on *Hemispheric Cooperation to Prevent, Combat, and Eliminate Terrorism (AG/RES. 1650 (XXIX-O/99) (OAS, 1999)*, created the Inter-American Committee against Terrorism (CICTE). While the purpose of this committee is to prevent, combat, and eliminate terrorism through the cooperation of the Member States, neither the *Resolution on Hemispheric Cooperation* nor the statement regarding the nature, powers, and functions of CICTE (OAS, 1999) define or describe terrorism. However, this committee did play a key role in developing the 2002 Inter-American Convention Against Terrorism (AG/RES. 1840 (XXXII-O/02) (OAS, 2002) that was adopted after the September 11, 2001, terrorist attacks carried out by Al-Qaeda against the United States. This Convention does not define terrorism. In this Convention, efforts to prevent, punish, and eliminate terrorism center on enforcing a number of previously agreed upon conventions such as those involving hijacking aircrafts, attacks on civil aviation, terrorist bombings, and the like.

United States of America

In the United States, terrorism crimes and penalties are defined in 18 U.S. Code Chapter 113B, commonly referred to as the Patriot Act. The precise definitions of international and domestic terrorism are stated in 18 U.S.C. 2331.

According to 18 U.S.C. 2331, International Terrorism refers to activities that

> (A) involve violent acts or acts dangerous to human life that are a violation of the criminal laws of the United States or of any State, or that would be a criminal violation

> if committed within the jurisdiction of the United States or of any State; (B) appear to be intended (i) to intimidate or coerce a civilian population; (ii) to influence the policy of a government by intimidation or coercion; or (iii) to affect the conduct of a government by mass destruction, assassination, or kidnapping; and (C) occur primarily outside the territorial jurisdiction of the United States, or transcend national boundaries in terms of the means by which they are accomplished, the persons they appear intended to intimidate or coerce, or the locale in which their perpetrators operate or seek asylum.
>
> *(18 USC Ch. 113B: TERRORISM, Sec. 2331)*

Domestic terrorism refers to activities that

> (A) involve acts dangerous to human life that are a violation of the criminal laws of the United States or of any State; (B) appear to be intended (i) to intimidate or coerce a civilian population; (ii) to influence the policy of a government by intimidation or coercion; or (iii) to affect the conduct of a government by mass destruction, assassination, or kidnapping; and (C) occur primarily within the territorial jurisdiction of the United States.
>
> *(18 USC Ch. 113B: TERRORISM, Sec. 2331)*

While readers might assume that, within the United States, the above definitions are the only definitions of international and domestic terrorism, this assumption would be incorrect. The Federal Bureau of Investigation (F.B.I., n.d.) offers these definitions:

> International terrorism: Violent, criminal acts committed by individuals and/or groups who are inspired by, or associated with, designated foreign terrorist organizations or nations.
>
> *(state-sponsored)*

> Domestic terrorism: Violent, criminal acts committed by individuals and/or groups to further ideological goals stemming from domestic influences, such as those of a political, religious, social, racial, or environmental nature.

The definitions provided in the Patriot Act and by the F.B.I are similar in that they define terrorism as criminal acts. However, the Patriot Act focuses more on the desired outcome of those criminal acts, coercing, or intimidating either a civilian group or government. In contrast, the F.B.I's definition of domestic terrorism emphasizes the motivations of the perpetrator(s), specifically to further their ideological goals, while their definition of international terrorism emphasizes neither outcome nor motivation but instead focuses on an association with a terrorist group or organization.

As previously stated, there are two commonalities among the governmental descriptions and definitions of terrorism. These commonalities are (1) the engagement in or the threat to engage in criminal acts that will endanger human life whether by attacking people, physical structures, or virtual environments; (2) perpetrated either to spread fear among the population or a segment of it or to coerce a government or other authority to act in a specific way.

Academic Definitions of Terrorism

While the above definitions of terrorism are from governments or governmental agencies, academics also offer a variety of definitions of terrorism as well as myriad discussions about the difficulties in defining the concept of terrorism (Rapoport, 2017; Schmid, 2004, 2011, 2023; Weinberg, 2005; Weinberg & Davis, 1989; Weinberg et al., 2004). Schmid has made three attempts to create an academic consensus definition of terrorism, one in 1984, another in 1988, and a third in 2011. Each of these definitions can be found in the Appendix of Schmid's (2023) *Defining Terrorism*. The abbreviated version of Schmid's 2011 Academic Consensus version states:

1. Terrorism refers, on the one hand, to a doctrine about the presumed effectiveness of a special form or tactic of fear-generating, coercive political violence, and, on the other hand, to a conspiratorial practice of calculated, demonstrative, direct violent action without legal or moral restraints, targeting mainly civilians and non-combatants, performed for its propagandistic and psychological effects on various audiences and conflict parties;
2. Terrorism as a tactic is employed in three main contexts: (i) illegal state repression; (ii) propagandistic agitation by non-state actors in times of peace or outside zones of conflict; and (iii) as an illicit tactic of irregular warfare employed by state- and non-state actors.

At the National Consortium for the Study of Terrorism and Response to Terrorism (START), for the first Global Terrorism Database (GTD1) terrorism was defined as "the threatened or actual use of illegal force and violence by a non-state actor to attain a political, economic, religious, or social goal through fear, coercion, or intimidation" (START, n.d.) However, recognizing that there are differing definitions of terrorism, for the second Global Terrorism Database (GTD2), an incident was determined to be terrorism and included in the database as terrorism if it met the following criteria.

Each incident included in the GTD2 had to be an intentional act of violence or threat of violence by a non-state actor. In addition, two of the following three criteria also had to be met for inclusion in GTD2:

1. The violent act was aimed at attaining a political, economic, religious, or social goal;
2. The violent act included evidence of an intention to coerce, intimidate, or convey some other message to a larger audience (or audiences) other than the immediate victims; and
3. The violent act was outside the precepts of International Humanitarian Law. (START, n.d.)

Why is a universally agreed upon definition of terrorism important? For governments there are at least four reasons. First, without an agreed upon definition of terrorism, the term can be co-opted and misused by politicians or other leaders and applied to non-terrorist activities in order to curb or delegitimize those activities while legitimizing their own actions.

Second, it is difficult to establish legal sanctions for terrorism when the concept of terrorism is not clearly defined. Criminal acts need to be clearly defined as do the penalties for engaging in them. And this needs to be done prior to the commission of the criminalized act. For a state to bring charges of terrorism against someone the state needs to define terrorism and the penalties for it. For an international body to bring charges against someone the international body needs to define terrorism and the penalties for it. Third, differences in definitions between states and their regional organizations can result in conflict of law challenges regarding which law should prevail, that of the state or of the regional treaty. Fourth, in order for states to work together to stop terrorism they must agree on what constitutes terrorism.

Obviously, for academics to study terrorism it is helpful for them to have a clear definition as to what constitutes terrorism. Without such a definition, academics are forced to create their own definitions which may not align with those created by other researchers or with governmental definitions. Working from a shared definition facilitates comparison of results as well as their application. That being said, it is obvious from the plethora of articles and books on terrorism that the lack of a consensus definition has not hindered scholars in their research.

Theories of Terrorism

While a universally agreed upon definition would be beneficial to combatting terrorism understanding why terrorism occurs would benefit both efforts to prevent terrorism and efforts to counter it.

Implicit in the study of terrorism and counterterrorism are the concepts of radicalism and extremism, and various theoretical explanations that help in understanding terrorism and its violent machinations. While the literature on these common concepts provides explanations for the forms of terrorism, the theories provide an understanding of the causes or motivations for terrorism in our modern world.

Religious Theories of Terrorism

Traditionally, the term fundamentalism was used by American Protestants who sough a return to the fundamentals as a response to liberal Protestants who were seen as distorting their faith. In this sense, the term would not be easily applicable to other faiths such as Islam, Judaism and other faiths. However, in recent years a much broader definition was presented to be applicable to all other religions. For Dadosky (2004), the traits presented in contemporary fundamentalist conceptualization includes religious idealism, emphasizing communal and personal identity; a depiction of revealed truth as unified, undifferentiated and adherence to religious identity; a rejection of multivalent interpretations of sacred texts, which they fear may shape their behavior and identity; a mythologization of enemies; the establishment of boundaries for protection of identity and preservation of purity; and an intensive missionary fervor (Dadosky, 2004). Arguably fundamentalism or extremism is a simple reflection of identity crisis, and as Appleby and Marty(1993) noted, such a crisis is "one of identity experienced by a group of people who fear extinction as a people or absorption into an overarching syncretistic culture to such a degree that their distinctiveness is undermined in the rush to homogeneity" (Appleby and Marty, 1993).

Dadosky (2004) opined that fundamentalism and extremism falls on different paths of the ideological discourse, since extremist positions on fundamental religious values may not be shared by some fundamentalist, since they go against the authentic spirit on which the religion is founded. An extremist position on the fundamental value of love simply denotes "intolerance and hatred, which is more of an ideology than faithful adherence of religious values. Such are not authentic proponents of their faith, be it Christianity, Islam or Judaism" (Dadosky, 2004).

Political Theories of Terrorism

While religious theories provide an insight of modern terrorist activities in many aspects, it hasn't exhaustively captured ideological motivations of terrorism. Political theories of terrorism provide such explanations as driven by the quest for state power. The central assumption is that terrorist organizations use social movements in the form of collective action to bring about change. In this context, social movements may be violent or non-violent or may exhibit both actions in promoting their agenda for change. Operationally, (Tilly, 2004) defines social movements as "a type of group action that involves an ongoing effort to create social change by people with a common ideology."

Criminology Theories of Terrorism

The criminology theories of terrorism seek to explain the actions of terrorist operatives as the function of their criminal behaviors. These theories attempt to answer the key question why people choose to become terrorist and engage in violent terrorist activities. The theories include rational choice and sociological theories, routine activities theories and learning theories.

Rational Choice Theory: The central assumption of rational choice is that individuals have free will to engage in criminal behavior. Gaines and Miller (2022) belief that criminal activity is an expression of a rational decision-making process. The decision to commit a crime is a choice and only the fear of punishment can deter the choice to commit crime. In the context of terrorism, the rational choice theorist would argue that terrorism is the outcome of a rational decision by terrorist operative, since the individuals involve understand that their actions violate the law and harms society but choose to pursue their action. Prominent among the terrorist actions that validates the rational choice theory includes the September 11, 2001, attacks of the World Trade Center, the July 7, 2005, London Subway attacks, the April 15, 2013, Boston Marathon Bombing, the London Subway attacks and November 13, 2015, Paris attacks. Arguably the attackers involved in all these terrorist events calculatedly made the choice to carry out their deadly attacks for the purpose of unleashing death and destruction at such a magnitude.

Sociological Theories: These theories explore the development and functioning of groups of people who live together within a society (Gaines & Miller, 2022). These theories explore the function of social structure as it relates to crime. Gaines and Miller (2022) observed social disorganization, strain and cultural deviance as the three theories related to crime and social structures.

1. **Social Disorganization Theory:** This theory explores the failure of social institutions, breakdown of traditional institutions, chronic unemployment, state failure, high levels

of school dropouts, and the lack of amenities as it relates to crime. This theory is very much evident of terrorist groups operating in Sub-Saharan Africa and Southeast Asia, where terror groups recruit vulnerable unemployed youths to become active operatives. Under such abysmal social situations, terrorist organizations present themselves to be filling vacuums that governments are supposed to fill in providing human security. In Sub-Saharan Africa, terror groups such as Al-Qaeda, Boko Haram and Al -Shabab have recruited vulnerable young men and women from communities affected by failed social institutions and chronic unemployment. Similarly, in Southeast Asia, Al-Qaeda affiliate groups continue to tap into such vulnerable communities to recruit young men and women.

2. **Strain Theory:** This theory assumes that crime is the result of frustration felt by individuals who cannot reach their goals through legitimate means (Gaines & Miller, 2022). The theory looks at conditions in which individuals feel disconnected from society because of the breakdown of social norms. According to Gaines and Miller (2022) many people do not have access to the education and training necessary to reach their financial goals; this can lead to frustration and anger. In this context, communities that feel underserved and underrepresented can foster criminal activity (Gaines & Miller, 2022). In the past two decades alone, all major terrorist groups have taken advantage such vulnerable individuals across underserved and underrepresented communities by providing their economic and educational needs and recruiting them to serve as operatives.
3. **Cultural Deviance Theory:** The central assumption of this theory is that "members of certain subcultures reject the values of the dominant culture by exhibiting deviant behavior patterns" (Gaines & Miller 2022). Terrorist organizations look at liberal democracy and its political, economic and social systems as western ideology that is undermining their values and culture. Terrorist organizations such as Al-Qaeda, the Islamic State, Boko Haram and Al-Shabab have used anti-western slogans as a threat to their values and ways of life. In Nigeria, the name of the terror group Boko Haram means Western Education is forbidden. Boko Haram operations largely targeted symbols of western values such as schools, government institutions and transportation hubs. In the past decade, Al-Qaeda and its affiliate groups operating in Sub-Saharan Africa have targeted hotels and tourist destination centers as symbols of western culture in Mali, Niger, Burkina Faso and Ivory Coast.

Psychological Theories of Terrorism

Within the field of psychology, theories that are specific to terrorism, explaining why someone would become a terrorist or engage in terrorist activities are lacking. Rather, theories related to aggression, identity, and group dynamics are often used to explain these behaviors (See Valeri, 2018, 2023; Valeri & Kellogg, 2023 for a more detailed discussion of why people hate and engage in hate motivated aggression).

Although this section explores psychological theories of terrorism, to highlight the centrality of these psychological theories in explaining terrorism we are beginning with a sociological perspective on terrorism. Black (2004) describes terrorism as an intercollective (between groups), socially distant (against a different race, ethnicity, religion, etc.), upward directed (against a social superior) form of collective violence.

Let us first explore the concept of collective violence. Within the term collective violence there are two components, the collective, meaning a group, and violence, meaning aggressive behavior. According to Brown (2006, p. 4) “a group exists when two or more people define themselves as members of it and when its existence is recognized by at least one other [person outside of the group].” Brown’s definition, because it does not require that group members meet or have any direct interaction, is especially apropos in this era, when individuals who commit acts of terrorism, such as the perpetrator of the 2019 Mosque shootings in New Zealand, become radicalized online and engage in lone-wolf terrorism.

Groups have identities. Taylor and Louis (2005, p. 172) state that, “the collective identity of a terrorist organization describes the group’s beliefs, values, attitudes, and goals.” As Taylor and Louis (2005) explain, an individual’s personal identity is based on their collective identities and the collective identity that is most central to the individual’s personal identity is their cultural identity. Taylor and Louis (2005, p. 174) state “[t]hat a cultural identity provides its members with a shared history and a set of broadly based and valued goals, along with detailed informal normative information about how to pursue the valued goals as determined by the collective identity.” Therefore, the cultural identity of the group impacts the group as a whole as well as each individual member. While many cultural identities can help their members develop healthy collective and personal identities, some cultural identities, such as those offered by terrorist groups, will foster collective and personal identities centered around animosity toward an outgroup. The appeal of the terrorist group’s culture is that if offers an idealized history of the ingroup, one in which everyone is hardworking, honest, and happy. But whose ingroup was wrongly and/or unfairly brought-down by an external foe. The terrorist culture offers a promise of a return to the good-old days simply by destroying the external foe. This return to grandeur and idealized narrative is especially appealing to anyone who is disadvantaged, seeking validation that they are not to blame for their predicament, and searching for a clear path out of their woeful existence (Taylor & Louis, 2005; Valeri & Kellogg, 2023).

Groups deliberate and decide on actions. These actions are determined by the group’s goals. Examples of terrorist groups engaging in coordinated, collective terrorism include the October 7, 2023 attacks on Israel by Hamas; the November 13, 2015 attacks in Paris, France by members of the Islamic State; the November 26–29, 2008 attacks in Mumbai, India by Lashkar-e-Taiba, a militant Islamist organization from Pakistan; and the September 11, 2001 attacks on the United States by Al-Qaeda. In addition to collective actions individual members may also choose to engage in terrorist behaviors on their own. An individual member may choose to engage in terrorism to demonstrate their commitment to the group and the group’s beliefs, to gain the esteem of the group, to act in a manner consistent with both their own beliefs and those of the group, or to act in accordance with the group’s own instructions. For example, the Animal Liberation Front, Earth Liberation Front, and the Islamic State all encourage members to act on their own or act in small cells.

Whether it is the group’s decision to engage in terrorism or that of an individual member, the decision to engage in this extreme action may be influenced by group polarization. Research on group polarization reveals that after deliberation groups tend to make decisions that are more extreme than, but in the same direction of, the average of each individual member’s initial position. The consequence of group polarization is that the group’s position, as well as those of its individual members, tend to become more extreme.

As Black noted, terrorism occurs between socially distant groups, when the less powerful one decides to attack the more powerful group. Social identity theory, realistic group conflict, and relative deprivation can help us understand the animosity between the two groups and why the less powerful group might resort to violence. Research on social identity reveals that all that is needed for ingroup favoritism to develop is the presence of two groups. The mere act of dividing people into two groups, even based on some arbitrary criteria, results in group members liking their ingroup more and giving preferential treatment to their ingroup. According to realistic group conflict, groups will fight over scarce resources, whether it is land, water, oil, employment opportunities, etc. Psychologists debate whether it is the fighting, in and of itself, that leads to the development of negative attitudes toward the outgroup or whether negative attitudes are purposefully fostered to justify the fighting and taking of resources. Regardless of the cause, the result is that there are negative attitudes toward the outgroup. In contrast, relative deprivation does not require competition for scarce resources. According to relative deprivation, negative attitudes develop toward an outgroup when the outgroup is perceived as doing better than it should in comparison to one's own group. The perceived relative deprivation could be economic, political, or social. These three theories all point in the same direction, ingroup favoritism between two groups develops easily, and competition, whether it is for scarce resources or relative position and power, exacerbates those negative feelings and can lead to aggression.

The reformulated frustration-aggression hypothesis (Berkowitz, 1989, 1993) states that any negative event that leads to unpleasant feelings can result in emotional aggression. Negative feelings can be generated when one's goals are thwarted, from poverty, pain, or any number of other scenarios. Certainly, if a group feels like it is being disadvantaged in competition for scarce resources or is being relatively deprived, negative feelings may well result. While the frustration-aggression hypothesis focuses on the behavior of individuals, it is easy to see how the leader of a terrorist group can play on the frustration of members to foster terrorist behaviors. Sternberg (2003) in the Duplex Theory of Hate discusses how a leader can indoctrinate followers to devalue an outgroup so they come to be viewed as evil, less than human, and deserving of death. The leader accomplishes this through carefully crafted propaganda in which the outgroup is portrayed as a threat that needs to be feared and whose members are disgusting, repellent, subhuman, and worthy of contempt. Once these elements are in place the leader can use fiery speeches to purposefully incite a mob to violence, as was the case with Kristallnacht, or, through careful planning, engineer atrocities like the Holocaust or the genocide that occurred in Rwanda. Terrorist leaders can and have used these same tactics to incite their groups and its members to engage in terrorist actions.

Conclusion

This chapter attempted to define the concept of terrorism through a global and various regional lens. While there is no global consensus on the definition of terrorism, there is the consensus that acts of terrorism are criminal and states are obligated to codify terrorism into national laws for swift prosecutions based on national laws. The chapter further provided an in-depth explanation of the likely factors that leads to terrorism and terrorist behavior. The general conclusions that can be drawn from the chapter validate the notion that acts of terrorism are the function of human behavior shaped by the environment under which the human being functions. Using some of the most current incidents of terrorism and activities of terrorist groups, the chapter explored various political, sociological and psychological theories to understand the behavior of terrorist organizations and their respective operatives.

References

18 USC Ch. 113B: TERRORISM, Sec. 2331. https://uscode.house.gov/view.xhtml?path=/prelim@title18/part1/chapter113B&edition=prelim

African Union (2002, September 11–14). *Plan of action of the African union high-level intergovernmental meeting on the prevention and combating of terrorism in Africa.* Mtg/HLIG/Conv.Terror/Plan.(I). https://www.peaceau.org/uploads/au-anti-terrorism-plan-of-action.pdf

Appleby and Marty (1993). Fundamentalism and Society: Reclaiming The Sciences, The Family and Education. The University of Chicago Press.

Association of South East Asian Nations. (2007, January 13). *ASEAN convention on counter terrorism.* https://asean.org/wp-content/uploads/2021/01/ACCT.pdf

Association of South East Asian Nations. (2017, September 20). *Manila declaration to counter the rise of radicalization and violent extremism.* https://asean.org/wp-content/uploads/2021/01/Manila-Declaration-to-Combat-RRVE-Adopted-by-the-11th-AMMTC.pdf

Berkowitz, L. (1989). Frustration-aggression hypothesis: Examination and reformulation. *Psychological Bulletin, 106*, 59–73.

Berkowitz, L. (1993). *Aggression.* McGraw-Hill.

Black, D. (2004). The geometry of terrorism. *Sociological Theory, 22*(1), 14–25.

Brown, R. (2006). *Group processes.* Blackwell Publishing.

Council of Europe. (n.d.). *The council of Europe at a glance.* https://www.coe.int/en/web/portal/the-council-of-europe-at-a-glance

Council of Europe. (2005, May 16). *Council of Europe convention on the prevention of terrorism* (CETS No. 196). https://rm.coe.int/16808c3f55

Council of Europe (2015, October 22). *Additional protocol to the council of Europe convention on the prevention of terrorism* (CETS No. 217). https://rm.coe.int/168047c5ea

Dadosky (2004). *The Structure of Religious Knowing.* Sunny Press. https://doi.org/10.1515/9780791485187

European Union. (2017 March 15). *Directive (EU) 2017/541 of the European parliament and of the council of 15 March 2017 on combating terrorism and replacing council framework decision 2002/475/JHA and amending council decision 2005/671/JHA.* https://eur-lex.europa.eu/legal-content/EN/TXT/?uri=celex%3A32017L0541

F.B.I. (n.d.). *Terrorism definitions.* Federal Bureau of Investigation. https://www.fbi.gov/investigate/terrorism

Gaines, Larry K., & Roger L. Miller. (2022). *Criminal Justice in Action* (The Core) (11th ed.). Boston, MA: Cengage

League of Arab States. (1998, April). *The arab convention for the suppression of terrorism.* https://www.refworld.org/pdfid/3de5e4984.pdf

Organization of African Unity. (1999, July 1). *OAU convention on the prevention and combatting of terrorism.* https://au.int/sites/default/files/treaties/37289-treaty-0020_-_oau_convention_on_the_prevention_and_combating_of_terrorism_e.pdf

Organization of American States. (1971). *Convention to prevent and punish the acts of terrorism taking the form of crimes against persons and related extortion that are of international significance.* https://www.oas.org/juridico/english/Treaties/a-49.html

Organization of American States. (1996, April 23–26). *Declaration of lima to prevent, combat, and eliminate terrorism.* https://www.summit-americas.org/Terrorism/Lima-Declaration.htm

Organization of American States. (1999). *Resolution on hemispheric cooperation to prevent, combat, and eliminate terrorism (AG/RES. 1650 (XXIX-O/99).* https://www.oas.org/juridico/english/ga-res99/eres1650.htm

Organization of American States. (2002, June 3). *The inter-American convention against terrorism (AG/RES. 1840 (XXXII-O/02).* https://www.oas.org/xxxiiga/english/docs_en/docs_items/agres1840_02.htm
Organization of the Islamic Conference. (1999, July 1). *Convention of the organization of the islamic conference on combatting international terrorism.* https://www.refworld.org/docid/3de5e6646.html
Rapoport, D. C. (2017, September). Terrorism as a global wave phenomenon: Overview. *Oxford Research Encyclopedia of Politics.* doi: 10.1093/acrefore/9780190228637.013.299. https://www.researchgate.net/publication/320818342_Oxford_Research_Encyclopedia_Terrorism_Overviewpdf
Schmid, A. P. (2004). Frameworks for conceptualising terrorism. *Terrorism and Political Violence, 16*(2), 197–221.
Schmid, A. P. (2011). The definition of terrorism. In Schmid, A. P. (Ed.), *The Routledge handbook of terrorism research* (Routledge Handbooks) (pp. 39–98). Abingdon: Routledge.
Schmid, A. P. (2023, March). *Defining terrorism.* International Center for Counter-Terrorism. https://www.icct.nl/sites/default/files/2023-03/Schmidt%20-%20Defining%20Terrorism_1.pdf
Shanghai Cooperation Organization. (2001, June 15). *Shanghai convention on combatting terrorism, separatism, and extremism.* https://www.refworld.org/pdfid/49f5d9f92.pdf
Shanghai Cooperation Organization. (2009, June 16). *Convention on counter-terrorism of the Shanghai cooperation organization.* https://www.fidh.org/en/issues/terrorism-surveillance-and-human-rights/The-Convention-Against-Terrorism
South Asia Association for Regional Cooperation. (1986. Novmember 16–17). *Bangalore declaration.* https://www.saarc-sec.org/index.php/resources/summit-declarations/15-second-saarc-summit-bangalore-1986/file
South Asia Association for Regional Cooperation. (1987, November 2–4). *Regional convention on the suppression of terrorism.* https://treaties.un.org/doc/db/terrorism/conv18-english.pdf
South Asia Association for Regional Cooperation. (2004, January 2–6). *Additional protocol to the regional convention on the suppression of terrorism.* https://www.refworld.org/pdfid/49f6b7ad2.pdf
START. (n.d.). *Data collection methodology: Global terrorism database.* National Consortium for the Study of Terrorism and Response to Terrorism. Department of Homeland Security Emeritus Center of Excellence led by the University of Maryland. https://www.start.umd.edu/gtd/using-gtd/
Sternberg, R. J. (2003). A duplex theory of hate: Development and application to terrorism, massacres, and genocide. *Review of General Psychology, 7*, 299–328.
Taylor, D. M., & Louis, W. (2005). Terrorism and the quest for identity. In F. M. Moghaddam & A. J. Marsella (Eds.), *Understanding terrorism* (pp. 169–186). American Psychological Association.
Tilly, C. (2004). *Social Movements, 1768–2004*, Paradigm Publishers, Boulder, London.
United Nations Resolution 49/60. (1995, February 17). Measures to eliminate international terrorism. *U.N. General Assembly.* https://documents-dds-ny.un.org/doc/UNDOC/GEN/N95/768/19/PDF/N9576819.pdf?OpenElement
United Nations Resolution 1566. (2004, October 8). *Security council resolution 1566 (2004)* [on international cooperation in the fight against terrorism]. U.N. Security Council. file:///C:/Users/rvaleri/Downloads/S_RES_1566(2004)-EN.pdf
Valeri, R. M. (2018). Why do we hate? In R. M. Valeri & K. Borgeson (Eds.), *Hate crimes: Victims, motivations and typologies* (pp. 3–32). Carolina Academic Press.
Valeri, R. M. (2023). Why we hate. In R. M. Valeri & K. Borgeson (Eds.), *Hate crimes: Victims, motivations and typologies* (2nd ed.). Carolina Academic Press.
Valeri, R. M., & Kellogg, B. (2023). Crossing the divide: From virtual hate to actual harm. In R. M. Valeri & K. Borgeson (Eds.), *Hate crimes: Victims, motivations and typologies* (2nd ed.). Carolina Academic Press.
Weinberg, L. B. (2005). *Global terrorism.* Oneworld Publications.
Weinberg, L. B., & Davis, P. B. (1989). *Political terrorism.* McGraw-Hill Inc.
Weinberg, L. B., Pedahzur, A., & Hirsch-Hoefler, S. (2004). The challenges of conceptualizing terrorism. *Terrorism and Political Violence, 16*(4), pp. 777–794.

PART II

The New Phase of Domestic Terrorism

3

FROM VIRTUE TO VIOLENCE

Examining Contemporary Far-Left Extremism in the U.S.

James Bacigalupo

Introduction

On September 16, 1920, Mario Buda, a member of the Galleanists—a decentralized network of revolutionary anarchists—is suspected to have carried out what was, at the time, the deadliest terrorist attack until the Oklahoma City bombing 75 years later (Simon, 2022). At approximately noon, a bomb hidden in a horse-drawn wagon detonated on the busy corner of Wall Street in Lower Manhattan, across from the J.P. Morgan & Co headquarters, killing more than thirty people and seriously injuring well over 100 more. Nearly a century later, William van Spronsen, an early member of the militant antifascist group, Puget Sound John Brown Gun Club, launched an attack on an Immigration and Customs Enforcement (ICE) detention center in Tacoma, Washington (Allam & Urquhart, 2020). He hurled Molotov cocktails at the building and vehicles, attempting to ignite a large propane tank in the process. The 69-year-old lifelong far-left activist, who was also armed with a rifle, was fatally shot by responding officers, making his death the sole casualty of the attack. These two events demonstrate the evolution of far-left extremism. Although the scale of violence in attacks may not match that of the early or mid-20th century, its contemporary manifestations continue to pose a threat.

According to terrorism scholar David Rapoport (2004), modern terrorism has unfolded in four waves: the anarchist wave, the anti-colonial wave, the New Left wave, and the religious wave. Despite being a prominent influence in the first three waves, left-wing ideology has not received attention commensurate with the politically motivated violence it has inspired. This chapter will address the lack of discussion surrounding the left-wing worldview and its relationship with political violence, while offering potential explanations for its underrepresentation. It will then seek to fill the gap on this issue by examining the repertoire of tactics employed by far-left adherents, including an analysis of recent "direct actions" identified through digital propaganda found in the far-left online landscape. The chapter will conclude with a discussion of the most recent mobilizing left-wing cause: Palestinian advocacy and anti-Zionism amid the Israel-Hamas war.

DOI: 10.4324/9781003375265-6

The Moral Veil of the Far-Left

One of the key distinctions between far-left and far-right extremists lies in the perceived moral standing of their respective belief systems. Describing the ideological motivations of the far-left, Jenkins (2022) notes that historically, they have focused on specific issues such as "protection of organized labor, women's liberation, equal rights for all races and sexual orientations, opposition to nuclear weapons or the Vietnam War, environmental protection, anti-capitalism, opposition to police shootings, and anti-fascism" (p. 27). In contrast, right-wing extremism, as described by Jenkins, encompasses a collection of overlapping causes including "white nationalism, anti-Semitism, anti-Muslim sentiment, fears of replacement by imported minorities, opposition to immigration, anti-feminism, antigay sentiment, anti-abortion sentiment, opposition to restrictions of private gun ownership, and fervent opposition to the federal government" (p. 27). The moral asymmetry of these belief systems has significant ramifications for the attention they receive, resulting in a disproportionate focus on far-right extremism, which is perceived as a more prominent threat.

Ideological Sympathy

While far-right ideologies, such as neo-Nazism, are universally identified as extreme, this is not necessarily the case for far-left ideologies, particularly in the eyes of scholars who may be sympathetic to these views themselves. To focus on a particular category of political extremism is to associate a belief system with violence. Individuals sympathetic to a particular ideology may be reluctant to draw a throughline between its ideas and violence. This is especially true in the current context of political polarization, where researchers may fear their work will be used to draw negative attention to a political cause that they support.

The professoriate is widely regarded as one of the most left-leaning occupations in the U.S. This is especially true in the social sciences, where terrorism is likely to be studied. Gross and Simmons (2007) found that among professors in the social sciences, 62% identified as either an activist, a radical, or a Marxist, while only 4% identified as conservative. Moreover, several former members of notorious left-wing domestic terrorist organizations eventually transitioned into roles as professors or other positions in higher education (Moynihan, 2017). According to Moynihan, "there is a rather ignoble tradition within academia of welcoming those with fringe views and violent backgrounds, provided their politics were 'misguided' in the appropriate direction." This potential obstacle to objectivity is often overlooked or ignored, yet it can significantly undermine the credibility and influence of scholarly work, particularly among those outside the academic community.

Further threatening the validity of scholarship is the fact that terrorism lacks an agreed-upon definition, and is not commonly adjudicated under terrorism laws (Smith, 1994), particularly in the case of domestic terrorism (Jensen & Akers, 2024). As a result, official crime data sources, such as the Uniform Crime Report (UCR) or the National Incident-Based Reporting System (NIBRS), cannot be used to measure the prevalence of terrorism as they can for other types of crime. Databases that do track terrorism, such as the Global Terrorism Database (GTD) and the Center for Strategic and International Studies (CSIS), rely on open-source material to determine if a case meets their inclusion criteria, which often vary between databases. In assessing the accuracy and potential bias in two terrorism datasets, CSIS and New America Foundation (NAF), Allison (2021) found that through the coding process, the level of violence perpetrated by left-wing, Black nationalists, and anti-white extremists was obscured, leading to the impression of partisan influence. This illustrates how bias can find its way into quantitative data, potentially threatening the validity of some research findings.

Violent vs Nonviolent

Following violent protests, a debate often arises regarding the labeling of property destruction as "violence." Most recently, this debate took place during the 2020 protests following the fatal encounter between George Floyd and the Minneapolis, Minnesota police. For example, Nikole Hannah-Jones of the New York Times argued:

> Violence is when an agent of the state kneels on a man's neck until all of the life is leached out of his body. Destroying property, which can be replaced, is not violence. To use the same language to describe those two things is not moral.
>
> *(CBS News [@CBSNews], 2020)*

Similarly, Nathan Robinson of Current Affairs noted:

> One reason it's important to maintain a clear concept of what violence is and isn't, is because true violence is such a deeply terrible human experience. Actual violence leaves people with brain damage, nightmares, disability, and trauma. The destruction of human bodies is a moral horror that simply cannot exist in the same category as the breaking of objects.
>
> *(Robinson, 2020)*

In contrast, Rich Lowry of the *National Review* took a different position:

> The idea that, say, burning down a building isn't violence fails to pass the Merriam-Webster test. The dictionary defines violence as "the use of physical force so as to injure, abuse, damage, or destroy." And the blasé attitude about the destruction of property doesn't pass the common-sense test. Property is not an abstraction. It gives people shelter, and a sense of protection and stability. People pour themselves into their property, using their earnings to pay for it, improving it, becoming identified with it. If the property is a business, it often represents years of blood, sweat, tears and dreams.
>
> *(Lowry, 2020)*

These responses demonstrate partisan attitudes towards political violence, with Hannah-Jones and Robinson representing the left-wing perspective, and Lowry the more conservative position. The protests were in the service of a left-wing cause, which undoubtedly has influence on how it was reacted to, however, there is also a deep-rooted philosophical difference in how those on the political left and right value private property rights as well as law and order. This demonstrates how political ideology can shape how these activities are perceived, not just solely determined by the political affiliation of the groups involved, but based on how their behavior violates their version of norms, reflective of their ideology.

Irrespective of the debate surrounding the appropriateness of using the word "violence" to describe property damage, there is certainly an important distinction between attacking people and attacking property. In the following sections, tactics involving the targeting of people will be described as "violent" while the actions targeting property will be considered "nonviolent."

Comparing the Violence

Before discussing the violent elements of the far-left, it is essential to assess the extent of their violence relative to other forms of extremism, particularly in light of ongoing debates and disagreements about national security threats and the allocation of counterterrorism resources. Defined by the intent to kill or injure, Jasko et al. (2022) found that adherents of the far-left had 68% lower odds of engaging in violent behavior compared to those of the far-right. This is the most justifiable explanation for the disproportionate attention on the far-right, as scholars may prioritize violent forms of extremism over less violent ones. Duran (2021) compared far-left and far-right fatal violence from 1990 to 2020 using the Extremist Crime Database (ECDB). He found that when excluding the Oklahoma City bombing, deaths from the far-right averaged 11.5 per year, while the far-left killed far fewer with an average of 2.5 deaths per year. When examining ideologically driven mass shootings from 1970–2019, Silva (2023) compared far-right, far-left, and jihadist-inspired attackers. The far-right was found to have the most incidents (45), as well as the most fatalities with 104. The far-left and the jihadists carried out a similar number of mass shootings, 16 and 15 respectively; however, jihadist-inspired attacks produced more than double the number of fatal casualties with 104, compared to 45 attributed to the far-left.

The Violent Left

Black Nationalists

Since 2019, the federal government (Federal Bureau of Investigation [FBI] & Department of Homeland Security [DHS]) has classified domestic extremism into five categories:

1. Racially or Ethnically Motivated Violent Extremism.
2. Anti-Government or Anti-Authority Violent Extremism.
3. Animal Rights or Environmental Violent Extremism.
4. Abortion-Related Violent Extremism.
5. All Other Domestic Terrorism Threats.

Racially or Ethnically Motivated Violent Extremism (RMVE) is made up of two distinct groups:

> One set of RMVE threat actors use their belief in the superiority of the white race to justify their use of violence to further their political, cultural, and religious goals. A separate and distinct set of RMVE threat actors use real or perceived racism or injustice

> in American society, their desire for a separate Black homeland, and/or violent interpretations of religious teachings to justify their use of violence to further their social or political goals.
>
> *(FBI & DHS, 2023, pp. 4–5)*

While white supremacists pose the greater threat in this category, the comparative studies of lethal violent extremism (Duran, 2021; Silva, 2022) reveal that among left-wing attackers, RMVEs motivated by Black nationalism and racial injustice are responsible for a disproportionate number of left-wing killings. Duran found that racial motivation was the most significant driver of fatal attacks for both the far-left and far-right from 1990 to 2020. In the examination of ideologically motivated mass shootings, Silva notes that there is "a specific type of far-left extremist that engages in a mass shooting: Black Nationalists" (p. 15).

The most prominent of these recent left-wing RMVE attacks have come in the wake of controversial police killings of Black civilians. On July 7, 2016, Micah Xavier Johnson ambushed Dallas police officers who were working at a protest that was organized in response to the police killings of Alton Sterling and Philando Castille. Johnson killed five officers and wounded nine others, making it the deadliest attack on law enforcement since 9/11 (Park, 2016). In conversations with law enforcement attempting to negotiate his surrender, Johnson claimed that he was angry about recent police shootings and that he wanted to kill white people, especially white officers (Cherelus & Seba, 2016). He was eventually killed with the use of a bomb-carrying robot after hours of negotiations had failed (Kenning, 2018). Only ten days later, another attack took place, where Gavin Eugene Long shot six officers, killing three, in Baton Rouge, Louisiana (Johnson, 2017).

Both attackers were motivated by police violence towards the Black community. In a note left by Long, he said that he "must bring the destruction that bad cops continue to inflict on my people" (The Advocate, 2017). These attackers both expressed interest in Malcolm X and the Nation of Islam, but Johnson showed more of an interest towards Black militant groups including the New Black Panther Party (NBPP), the Black Riders Liberation Party, and the African American Defense League, who called for violence against police on their Facebook page days before the attack (Lankford, 2023). It was later revealed that Long was a member of the Washitaw Nation, a Moorish Sovereign movement that believes African Americans are indigenous to the continent and are above all state and federal laws (Kansas City Star, 2016). He was likely also inspired by Johnson's attack as he celebrated the mass shooting on social media stating, "He was one of us!" (Lankford, 2023, p. 11).

Groups and ideologies that fall under the category of Black nationalism are not a monolith. According to Johnson (2017), "The Black Nationalist Movement represents a swath of anti-government, anti-police, racist, and radical religious ideologies." In the 1960s and 1970s, Black militant groups were more closely aligned with far-left political ideologies. For example, the Black Panther Party (BPP) was possibly the most prominent group to arise from the New Left era, alongside notorious leftist groups such as the Weather Underground and the Symbionese Liberation Army. The BPP was regarded as "the vanguard" by other revolutionary groups, demonstrating their influence on the movement (Falciola, 2016). Although Black nationalism was an aspect of their movement, the BPP was fundamentally left-wing. Similarly, the Black Liberation Army (BLA), a lethal offshoot of the BPP that operated through the 1970s, was heavily influenced by Carlos Marighella, the Brazilian

Marxist-Leninist militant. The BLA waged a war against police with guerilla tactics, killing at least 20 (Rosenau, 2013).

In describing the tactics of leftist groups in the 1970s, Falciola (2016) differentiates between traditional leftist groups, which he describes as "white leftists," and anti-colonial groups such as the BPP, the American Indian Movement (AIM), and the Puerto Rican Fuerzas Armadas de Liberación Nacional (FALN). He argues that white leftist groups shifted away from targeting individuals and instead focused on property damage, while groups like the BPP engaged in retaliatory violence against people. This distinction highlights the diverse tactics among leftist groups of that era, with anti-colonial groups motivated by racial and ethnic liberation opting for more violent actions, a trend that seems to exist contemporarily to some degree. Groups like FALN and AIM demonstrate that these tactics were shared by broader ethnic liberation movements, not just Black liberation.

Black nationalist groups and movements associated with violent extremism in recent years have diverged from traditional left-wing ideologies. For example, the NBPP, which was founded in 1989, has been described as a "Black racist hate group" by members of the original group (Southern Poverty Law Center [SPLC], n.d.). While they do share some causes with the original group, including opposition to police brutality, it is vehemently anti-white and anti-Semitic, advocating a separatist ideology. In 1993, former Ku Klux Klan grand dragon, Tom Metzger, spoke at a NBPP rally, because his white supremacist belief system aligned with their belief of racial separation (SPLC, n.d.).

Many members of the NBPP are current or former members of the Nation of Islam (NOI), which represents another faction of the Black Power movement that includes religious extremism. The NOI, which is estimated to have between 10,000 to 50,000 members, is not considered a mainstream Muslim religious group and teaches that Jews and the U.S. government conspire to control the Black population (Anti-Defamation League [ADL], 2021). Like other Black nationalists, the NOI is anti-police and has called for violence following police killings of Black suspects. The controversial leader Louis Farrakhan stated, "So if the federal government will not intercede in our affairs, then we must rise up and kill those who kill us; stalk them and kill them and let them feel the pain of death that we are feeling!" (Johnson, 2017). Other radical religious ideologies have also been linked to violence in recent years. The Black Hebrew Israelites have been described as "regrettably understudied" for their role in domestic terrorism (Program on extremism [PoE], 2022). The extremist fringe of this group believes that modern-day African Americans are the descendants of the Israelites in the Old Testament of the Bible and that white Europeans are the descendants of Satan, while white Jews are considered imposters.

Like other forms of extremism, the threat from left-wing RMVEs often comes from lone actors rather than organized groups. This trend holds true for Dallas sniper Micah Johnson, who was denied membership in multiple Black nationalist organizations after failing a background check that was conducted by one of the groups (Glawe & Bertness, 2017). Although Johnson was not granted membership in the Black Riders Liberation Party, the group's leader, Lakesia Washington, acknowledged him after the attack, posting on social media, "R.I.P. Micah...X...Johnson!!!...RBG 4 LIFE" (Glawe & Bertness, 2017). "RBG" represents the colors of the Pan-African flag: red, black, and green. It appears that Johnson may have been attempting to paint these letters in his own blood before dying.

Given the significant level of violence associated with militant Black nationalism compared to many other extremist movements, it is surprising that it has received so little attention from terrorism scholars. The various directions that this movement has gone are worthy of examination. While they are classified in many databases as left-wing, some movements, including the Black Hebrew Israelites, have very little in common with the left-wing ideology. In fact, they have an almost identical ideology to the Christian Identity movement, which is a white supremacist theology adhered to by notorious right-wing organizations such as the Aryan Nations (PoE, 2022).

There is increased sensitivity and scrutiny surrounding the coverage of these groups, reflecting the politicization of this area of research. When the FBI warned about the threat from "Black Identity Extremists," critics decried it as racist (Winter & Weinberger, 2017). When the FBI stopped using the term and put Black nationalists and white supremacists together in the same category (RMVE), it was criticized as creating a false equivalency of the threat that these movements pose (PoE, 2022). The SPLC, a nonprofit organization dedicated to combating hate and bigotry through legal action and by providing intelligence briefs on hate groups, updated its coverage of these extremists by removing the Black Separatist category. Groups in this category were moved to various other categories, such as "General Hate." In an article on their website, the SPLC describes its rationale by noting that they "reject federal law enforcement's false and misleading contention regarding threats from Black separatists" and that it can be "used to justify the over-policing and surveillance of communities of color" (Hodges, 2020).

Militant Antifascists (Antifa)

Militant antifascists, commonly known as "antifa," gained widespread public attention through their physical confrontations with far-right groups that were galvanized by the launch of Donald Trump's first presidential campaign. Although the group seemed to emerge from relative obscurity, militant anti-fascism has been present in the United States since the late 1970s, with organizations such as the John Brown Anti-Klan Committee (JBAKC), SHARP (Skinheads Against Racial Prejudice), RASH (Red and Anarchist Skinheads), and Anti-Racist Action (ARA) paving the way for the contemporary antifa movement (Copsey & Merrill, 2021). The most significant clash between antifascists and the far-right during this era was known as the "Greensboro Massacre." In 1979, in Greensboro, North Carolina, five anti-Klan protesters were shot and killed by the United Racist Front, an umbrella organization for the KKK and the American Nazi Party (Copsey & Merrill, 2021).

Unlike Black nationalists, antifa activists are committed far-left ideologues. The black and red flags on their logo represents two left-wing ideologies: anarchism and communism, respectively. Many of the members also cross-pollinate with other left-wing groups and movements (Vysotsky, 2021). Not all antifascist activity is violent; they also employ tactics such as intelligence gathering and public shaming through doxing. However, their notoriety is due to their militant tactics of disrupting far-right activities and confronting far-right activists (Vysotsky). They see this violence as necessary to prevent the growth and implementation of fascist ideas in society. The physical confrontations between the far-left and far-right have, in some instances, escalated into both fatal and near-fatal violence. A deadly attack occurred in August 2020 when self-described antifascist Michael

Reinoehl followed and fatally shot Aaron Danielson, a member of the right-wing group Patriot Prayer, in Portland, Oregon (Wilson et al., 2020). In another incident, Alexander Contompasis stabbed two members of the right-wing Proud Boys at a rally in Albany, New York, in January of 2021 (Gavin, 2022). It is not just far-right groups that have been targeted with violence by antifa. On the one-year anniversary of the deadly far-right Unite the Right rally, antifa reportedly attacked journalists and police with water bottles, eggs, and fireworks (Williams, 2018). During the 2020 George Floyd protests, law enforcement became a primary target for these activists, as they view police brutality as related to fascism (Logan & Sigon, 2021).

Antifa has certainly succeeded in disrupting speeches by some prominent far-right figures, including Richard Spencer and Milo Yiannopoulos with the use of violence; however, the overall success of antifa's strategy is less clear. It appears that their presence has galvanized the far-right by providing a common enemy. If antifa's presence had a significant deterrent effect, then far-right groups would be actively avoiding them. In reality, it appears the opposite is true. According to Vysotsky (2021), "These fascist events are deliberately organized in locations that will draw a vigorous and militant antifascist response, and event organizers often explicitly goad antifascists into confrontation by bragging about their strength and threatening antifa activists on social media" (p.84). The far-right has embraced the violence and has used it as a tool to mobilize. Vysotsky further explains, "Such rallies increasingly draw attendees from across the country who are energized by fascist leaders to clash with antifa activists and other perceived movement leaders" (p.84).

Some responses to antifa, including those from lawmakers, indicate that there is a lot of confusion as to what the movement is. For example, on May 32, 2020, tPresident Trump announced on social media that he was going to designate antifa as a terrorist organization (Smith, 2020). During a debate with President Trump, the then-Democratic nominee, Joe Biden, described antifa as "an idea, not an organization" (Bernstein, 2020). The opposing positions by Trump and Biden highlight how partisanship shapes perceptions of extremists. The truth lies somewhere in between. There is a decentralized antifascist network, "Torch," that is comprised of various antifascist groups, but there are also antifa groups that operate outside the network (Copsey & Merrill, 2020). Antifa is certainly not an organization in any typical sense, and they are ideologically opposed to hierarchy. They operate primarily in loosely organized affinity groups with approximately four to twenty members (Michael, 2023). Some scholars have advocated for them to be categorized as street gangs, considering they have a collective identity and engage in illegal activity (Pyrooz & Densley, 2018).

Protest Violence

The death of George Floyd at the hands of police officer Derek Chauvin on May 25, 2020, sparked some of the largest protests in U.S. history, which continued for months. The demonstrations were often associated with Black Lives Matter (BLM), an organization that was started seven years earlier by Alicia Garza, Patrisse Cullors, and Opal Tometi after community watch volunteer George Zimmerman, was acquitted for killing Trayvon Martin, a Black 17-year-old (Garza, 2014). BLM's founders identify as Marxists and have been associated with far-left thinkers (Gonzalez, 2021). They advocate for a range of ideologically driven goals, but the movement is often perceived primarily through its focus on addressing police violence against Black individuals. Since 2013, they have organized in response to controversial police killings of Black civilians. While the group has been able to generate large-scale demonstrations, some of which ended in violence, the protests that they were instrumental in organizing following George Floyd's killing were unprecedented, in both scale and intensity.

The Armed Conflict Location & Event Data Project (ACLED) (2021) reported that 94% of pro-BLM demonstrations were peaceful. However, the violence and property destruction that did occur was severe, underscoring the sheer scale and intensity of these protests. One of the most significant instances was the burning of the police precinct where the officers charged with Floyd's death had worked. After days of assaults on the building and those attempting to protect it, protesters managed to infiltrate and set multiple fires inside the building. Mayor Jacob Frey made the decision to evacuate the precinct, which was later destroyed by the fire (Gutierrez et al., 2020).

While there were certainly politically motivated attacks that occurred amid these protests, the bigger threat seemed to be the destabilizing effects that the demonstrations had on law enforcement. It can be argued that the number of demonstrations, peaceful or not, stretched the police beyond their capabilities, leaving them unable to maintain order, resulting in approximately 25 deaths perpetrated by opportunistic criminals who wreaked havoc in their absence (The Guardian, n.d.). One such example was the killing of retired St. Louis Police Captain, David Dorn, who was shot and killed by a rioter as he was trying to protect his friend's pawn shop from looters (Bernstein, 2022).

Another example that illustrates the link between violence and the 2020 BLM protests was the Capitol Hill Occupation Protest (CHOP), which took place in the Capitol Hill area of Seattle, Washington. Due to daily violent conflicts between police and protesters in this area, Seattle Mayor Jenny Durkan ordered the Seattle Police Department (SPD) to abandon its East Precinct in an attempt to deescalate the situation (Rosas, 2022). Activists took hold of the surrounding 6-block area, where they implemented their ideology of police abolition in a real-world setting. The individuals occupying this neighborhood were described by journalist Julio Rosas (2022) as "a loose coalition of Black Lives Matter activists, community members, and Antifa/black bloc agitators, all of whom were in the zone at different times and different days, and many of whom had differing ideas of how things should be organized" (p. 27). Interestingly, in the security vacuum that was created by the evacuation of the police, law and order was ushered in by activists using aggressive means—ironically, the same authoritarian methods that they were supposedly rebelling against.

In reporting on CHOP, Nelle Bowles (2020) describes a harrowing experience for the residents and business owners located within the confines of the zone. Many businesses didn't last as customers were unwilling to venture inside CHOP as it was populated by swaths of masked protesters openly carrying firearms. Others paid for private security. When residents and business owners did call 911, police notified them that they would not be responding to CHOP. Many businesses were threatened by activists, while other activists would offer security for a fee. One business owner responded to a break-in at his auto repair shop to find someone actively attempting to set the building on fire. The police never showed up, but armed activists did, falsely claiming that the store owner abducted the would-be arsonist. The confrontation was livestreamed on an anti-police website that labeled the business owner as a "snitch" and "cop caller" (Bowles, 2021).

After 24 days, the occupied zone was taken back by Seattle police after four shootings, two of which were fatal. While the shootings may not have been ideological, it is likely that the removal of police invited the uptick in violence. Piza and Connealy (2022) empirically examined the relationship between CHOP and the prevalence of crime. They found that crime inside the CHOP zone was 132.9% higher than the weighted control area, while the encompassing 2-block area was 77% higher. Overall, in the East Precinct service area, crime was higher than the control area by 27.8% over this period. These findings could potentially be an undercount considering the police were not responding to the CHOP zone, which reduced the proactive discovery of crime by officers. Additionally, individuals found to have notified law enforcement would likely face repercussions, which would have an impact on the willingness of reporting crime.

Nonviolent "Direct Action"

A distinguishing feature of the far-left is its use of a diverse range of tactics, most of which do not involve targeting people with violence; however, they can be highly disruptive. For example, in April 2024, pro-Palestinian activists blocked roadways to some of the country's busiest airports, resulting in massive traffic jams and numerous missed flights (NPR, 2024). In contrast, other tactics, such as shoplifting live seafood from a grocery store have a less significant impact. The spectrum of these ideologically driven acts, both legal and illegal, are often referred to as "direct action" (Borum & Tilly, 2005). According to Williams (2019), "Instead of asking other people to act on one's behalf, the philosophy of direct action encourages people themselves to act. Direct action can be contrasted against indirect or representative action, which requires going through an intermediary, official, or lobbyist" (p. 108). This section will focus on illegal direct actions, exploring their geographic, tactical, and ideological characteristics.

While violent tactics are often covered by the media and are included in terrorism datasets or intelligence reports, nonviolent tactics sometimes go unnoticed. This is because activities such as smashing windows may not be recognized as ideologically motivated or considered too minor to make the news. To address this gap, digital propaganda from an anarchist website, which chronicled direct actions from May 1, 2022, to March 19, 2023, was used to construct a dataset of over 140 incidents, including descriptive variables for each incident.

Methodology

Data

The data for this study came from digital propaganda derived from the website itsgoingdown.org. According to the "About" section of the website, it is described as follows: "In search of new forms of life, It's Going Down, is a digital community center and media platform featuring news, opinion, podcasts, and reporting on autonomous movements across so-called North America from an anarchist perspective" ("About," n.d.). One of the features of this site is *Night Owls*, which is described as "a seasonal chronicle documenting actions against power, claimed and unclaimed, from across the territory occupied by the United States." This propaganda describes the direct actions carried out by left-wing adherents, and links to a website (often a blog) where the perpetrators have posted a communiqué outlining their motivations and detailing their actions. In some cases, no communiqué is posted; instead, the propaganda links to an online news source that has reported on the incident.

This analysis uses cases from three separate editions of *Night Owls*. The first edition, titled *Seasonal Chronicles of Sabotage and Direct Action* summarizes activities beginning on May 1, 2022, to early June of the same year. The start date has ideological significance; May Day (May 1st) is an important date for leftists as it commemorates the struggles and gains made by workers. The next edition, titled *Summer of Sabotage* highlights direct actions from June to late September of 2022. The third edition, titled *Autumn Offensive* describes attacks from late September through the end of 2022. The final edition of *Night Owls* used in this analysis is titled *Winter's Embers*, and it includes direct actions from the start of 2023 up until March 19, 2023. In total, 141 incidents are included in this study.

Variables

The variables in this analysis include location, political cause, tactics, target, violence, and newsworthiness. The source of these actions, either a communiqué, news article, or both, contains information for recording these variables. For political cause, the primary or most apparent cause will be recorded unless it was made explicit that the act was done in support of multiple causes. To assess newsworthiness, Google will be used to search any reporting on the incident, using keywords, dates, and specifics from the communiqué to determine if any mainstream news agency has covered it. The location will be recorded based on the state where the incident occurred, and the presence of violence will be coded based on whether individuals were targeted with violence. In many instances, multiple tactics were employed; each will be recorded. All targets will be included as well, however, in only a few incidents there was more than one target.

Results

Location and Political Cause

Out of the 50 U.S. states, 27 recorded at least one direct action. The states with the highest number of recorded incidents are Georgia (26), Pennsylvania (15), Oregon (13), California (12), and Michigan (11). Georgia having the most activity is not surprising when considering the political causes of these actions. Table 3.1 indicates that over 50% of incidents were carried out in opposition to the development of a public safety training center in Atlanta, Georgia. "Cop City," what opponents have dubbed the project, has galvanized environmental extremists that continue to fight to keep the public safety complex from being constructed on land that was once home to Native Americans (Jarvie, 2023). It is not just on environmental grounds that has the far-left up in arms; some are motivated by what they see as the expansion of militarized police departments.

The second most common political cause was pro-choice, which includes some serious attacks, including the arson of "pro-life centers." These began following the leak of the draft majority opinion in Dobbs v. Jackson Women's Health Organization in early May 2022, which ultimately overruled Roe v. Wade and clarified that the Constitution does

TABLE 3.1 Political causes that motivated direct actions

Cause	*Count*	%
Cop city	71	50.35
Pro-choice	25	17.73
Environmental	11	7.80
Housing (gentrification, homelessness)	11	7.80
Anti-police	8	5.67
Animal liberation	5	3.55
Anti-prison	4	2.84
Anti-colonialism	3	2.13
Political prisoner solidarity	2	1.42
Other	5	3.55

Note: Percentages do not sum to 100% because some incidents may involve multiple causes.

not confer a right to abortion. Fifteen of these were identified as being perpetrated by Jane's Revenge. This group has garnered a significant amount of attention in the press for their involvement in pro-choice attacks on pro-life centers. These attacks often include graffitied phrases: "If abortions aren't safe, neither are you" and "Jane's Revenge." In an interview with Vice, Mark Pitcavage noted, "The people who've been inspired by this concept of Jane's Revenge that emerged could be doing it on their own, anywhere" (Sherman, 2022). Essentially, this is a completely autonomous and decentralized movement (for a more detailed account of these attacks, see Norris, 2022).

Tactics and Violence

As shown in Table 3.2, graffiti emerged as the most frequently used tactic, appearing in 45.4% of incidents. Often, it was used in conjunction with other tactics, such as breaking windows. In only ten instances, graffiti was the sole tactic used. It is logical for graffiti to be the most prevalent tactic, as it allows the perpetrators to communicate their political message. When extreme violence like a mass shooting occurs, the motive is sought by the media and law enforcement; however, this is not the case for most nonviolent property damage. Graffiti can ensure that the message is delivered. Although this analysis is focused on nonviolent tactics, 11 (7.8%) incidents did involve direct targeting of individuals, predominantly law enforcement. In one incident, Cop City activists targeted police vehicles and construction equipment with rocks, bricks, Molotov cocktails, and aimed fireworks at police, resulting in state-level domestic terrorism charges (Keenan & Fawcett, 2023).

This study reveals that in contrast to Black nationalists and antifascists discussed earlier in the chapter, leftists motivated by environmental issues (Cop City) and pro-choice activists prefer targeting property as opposed to people. These findings are consistent with other studies that have examined the tactics of environmental extremists (Leader & Probst, 2003; Carson et al., 2012; Loadenthal, 2017).

Targets

As depicted in Table 3.3, Cop City linked companies were the most targeted group with 46 incidents (32.62%). Companies such as Atlas Technical Consulting faced various forms of

TABLE 3.2 Tactics used in direct actions

Tactic	*Count*	%
Graffiti	64	45.4
Smash windows	58	41.1
Arson	34	24.1
Throw rocks	7	4.96
Building sabotage	7	4.96
Equipment vandalized	7	4.96
ATM sabotage	6	4.26
Vehicle sabotaged	5	3.55
Vehicle vandalized (non-arson)	5	3.55
Theft	4	2.84
Animal release	4	2.84
Building vandalized (non-arson)	4	2.84
Spike trees	3	2.13
Blockade	3	2.13
Shoot fireworks	3	2.13
Surveillance equipment vandalized	3	2.13
Prison misconduct	2	1.42
Other	6	4.26

Note: Percentages do not sum to 100% because each incident may involve multiple tactics.

TABLE 3.3 Targets of direct actions

Target	*Count*	%
"Cop City" linked companies	46	32.62
Pro-Life centers	20	14.18
Construction equipment/vehicles	20	14.18
Police vehicles	7	4.96
Police buildings	6	4.26
Homes	6	4.26
Police officers	4	2.84
Farms	4	2.84
Trucks	4	2.84
Churches	3	2.13
Civilians	3	2.13
Correctional institutions	3	2.13
Statues	3	2.13
Subways/railways	3	2.13
Surveillance equipment	3	2.13
Forests	2	1.42
Other	7	4.96

Note: Percentages do not sum to 100% because each incident may involve multiple targets.

attack, including assaults on their offices, vehicles, and even employees' homes. Targeting these affiliated companies enabled activists from across the country to participate in the opposition to Cop City. Prominent banks and other related companies were also targeted nationwide in solidarity with the movement. Pro-life centers and construction equipment/vehicles tied as the second most frequent targets. Most attacks on construction equipment were associated with Cop City, while attacks on pro-life centers were most intense during the first half of 2022. However, the focus on pro-life centers diminished relatively quickly, highlighting the evolving nature of these reactive tactics.

Newsworthiness

Of the sample, 53 (37.59%) incidents were reported by mainstream online news sources. In searching for these incidents, it was discovered that most of them were published in other far-left/anarchist websites. While opting for small-scale nonviolent tactics, there is certainly a trade-off on newsworthiness, however, incidents involving violence towards individuals were only slightly more likely (45.45%) to be reported in the news compared to the overall sample. This suggests that there is likely a threshold of violence required to attract more attention. It is important to note that the primary goal of these activists may not always be to impact the broader public. Many of these direct actions were sabotage tactics, sometimes referred to as "monkey-wrenching." Unlike terrorism, which seeks to spread a message, the aim of these actions is often to "stymie the efforts of authoritarian or unjust institutions" (Williams, 2019, p. 108).

Conclusion

In criminology, the concept known as "the dark figure of crime" refers to the amount of crime that remains unknown. To some extent, this study reveals that there is a dark figure of political crime, manifesting as a spectrum of criminal acts carried out by left-wing adherents in support of their political cause. Less than half of the direct actions in the sample were reported by mainstream online news sources. Due to terrorism scholars focusing on larger-scale examples of political violence, and many databases relying on news media, these acts fall through the cracks. Without insight into the far-left online ecosystem, where these attacks are actively covered, the broader public remains largely unaware of these ideologically motivated crimes.

Free Palestine: The Current Catalyst for Far-Left Mobilization

This chapter has demonstrated that political violence perpetrated by the left does not occur in isolation. Many Black nationalist attacks appear to be motivated by controversial police killings of Black civilians, while antifascists typically mobilize against far-right public organizing. Additionally, protest violence arises for a variety of causes, but often intensfies in the context of perceived lawlessness. Similarly, a vast majority of the nonviolent direct actions were also not merely ideological manifestations, but reactions to specific events, such as the overturning of Roe v. Wade and the planned creation of a public safety training center. The far-left's most recent impetus for mobilization has come in response to the October 7, 2023, terrorist attack in Israel, carried out by Hamas, the Palestinian Islamist militant organization that governs Gaza. This was the worst attack on Jews since the Holocaust, with approximately 1,200 brutally murdered and another 250 abducted by the group (Byman et al., 2023).

While one might assume that the left-wing attraction to this issue was in sympathy with the Israeli casualties and hostages, but this was not the case. In just days after the attack, BLM Chicago posted a now-deleted image of a person paragliding with a Palestinian flag attached to the parachute and "I stand with Palestine" written underneath (Propper, 2023). The post appears to be celebrating the attack, where Hamas used fan-powered paragliders to cross the border fence into Israeli territory (Byman et al., 2023). Other left-wing groups also expressed solidarity with the attacks. Various chapters of the Democratic Socialists of America (DSA) issued statements like, "It is not terrorism or anti-Semitism to fight against this injustice," while the Party for Socialism and Liberation (PSL) declared that "The actions of the resistance over the last day are a morally and legally legitimate response to occupation" (ADL, 2023).

To understand how far-left activists and jihadists find common cause, sometimes referred to as the "Red-Green Alliance," Karagiannis and McCauley (2013) used framing theory and the concept of the master frame. Essentially, a master frame can be described as a schema that is widely interpretive and resonates with a broader audience for the purpose of mobilizing. Two master frames, anti-globalization/anti-capitalism and anti-colonialism/anti-imperialism resonate with both Islamists and leftists. Of these, the anti-colonialism/anti-imperialism frame is more relevant in understanding the sympathy that the far-left has with the jihadist attackers. According to Karagiannis and McCauley, Islamists see American wars in the Middle East as attempts to take resources and land from the global Islamic community ("Ummah"), while leftists see it mainly in economic terms. Israel represents the keystone of the Red-Green alliance:

> What brings together Islamists and Leftists is deep hostility for what Israel represents. From the Islamist point of view, the Jewish State is an artificial entity and an obstacle to the restoration of the Caliphate. For Leftists, Israel must be fought as Washington's colonialist ally in the Middle East.
>
> *(p. 178)*

As the Israel-Hamas war has continued since the attack and the number of Palestinian casualties continue to rise, left-wing opposition to Israel and "Zionism"—the political movement supporting the establishment and maintenance of a Jewish State in Israel—has intensified. This pro-Palestinian sentiment has motivated large-scale demonstrations, protests, and extreme tactics, both violent and nonviolent. In many instances, this activity has manifested as overt anti-Semitism. According to the ADL (2024), U.S. anti-Semitic incidents spiked 360% in the aftermath of the attack on Israel. Jewish individuals, businesses, and religious institutions have been targeted. U.S. universities have become the epicenter of this activity, as large-scale demonstrations have been organized, including the occupation of buildings. At George Washington University, protesters projected a U.S. flag in flames on a school building with the phrase "Long live the student intifada," referencing a violent rebellion against Israel (Makoii, 2024). In response to these protests, a member of Hamas's political bureau stated that "Today's students are the leaders of the future" (Ruiz-Goiriena, 2024), while Iranian Supreme Leader Ayatollah Ali Khamenei, whose government funds Hamas and other militant groups in the region, praised the students as being "on the right side of history" (Mesa, 2024). Even Al-Qaeda has voiced appreciation of the student demonstrations (Truzman, 2024).

With notable exceptions, the contemporary far-left in the U.S. has generally avoided tactics that target individuals directly with violence, largely constrained by the desire to maintain a moral high ground compared to other extremist movements. However, this approach may be changing; the intense mobilization for Palestine in the wake of such a brutal terrorist attack against the Israeli population, and finding common cause with some of the deadliest terrorist organizations in existence, suggests a shift. This evolution in strategy could foreseeably lead to an increase in violent tactics in the future.

References

The Advocate. (2017, June 3). *Read suicide note left by Gavin Eugene Long, gunman in deadly Baton Rouge officer shooting in July 2016*. https://www.theadvocate.com/baton_rouge/news/baton_rouge_officer_shooting/read suicide-note-left-by-gavin-eugene-long-gunman-in-deadly-baton-rouge-officer shooting/article_9748d2c0-5daa-11e7-af6d-ab3966e08d70.html

Allam, H., & Urquhart, J. (2020, July 23). 'I am antifa': One activist's violent death became a symbol for the right and left. *National Public Radio*. https://www.npr.org/2020/07/23/893533916/i-am-antifa-one-activist-s-violent-death became-a-symbol-for-the-right-and-left

Allison, B. V. (2021). The devil's in the details—or is he? The ethics and politics of terrorism data. *Perspectives on Terrorism*, *15*(2), 125–141.

Anti-Defamation League (ADL). (2021, September 1). *Nation of Islam*. https://www.adl.org/resources/profile/nation-islam

Anti-Defamation League (ADL). (2023, October 12). *Fringe-left groups express support for Hamas's invasion and brutal attacks in Israel*. https://www.adl.org/resources/blog/fringe left-groups-express-support-hamass-invasion-and-brutal-attacks-israel

Anti-Defamation League (ADL). (2024, January 9). *U.S. antisemitic incidents skyrocketed 360% in aftermath of attack in Israel, according to latest ADL data*. https://www.adl.org/resources/press-release/us-antisemitic-incidents-skyrocketed-360 aftermath-attack-israel-according

The Armed Conflict Location & Event Data Project (ACLED). (2021, May). *A year of racial justice protests: Key trends in demonstrations supporting the BLM movement*. https://acleddata.com/2021/05/25/a-year-of-racial-justice-protests-key-trends-indemonstrations-supporting-the-blm-movement/

Bernstein, B. (2020, September 29). Biden says antifa is 'an idea, not an organization' during presidential debate. *National Review*. https://www.nationalreview.com/news/biden-says antifa-is-an-idea-not-an-organization-during-presidential-debate/

Bernstein, B. (2022, October 5). BLM rioter who murdered retired St. Louis Police Captain sentenced to life in prison without parole. *National Review*. https://www.nationalreview.com/news/rioter-who-murdered-retired-st-louis-police captain-sentenced-to-life-in-prison-without-parole/

Bowles, N. (2021, August 7). Abolish the police? Those who survived the chaos in Seattle aren't so sure. *New York Times*. https://www.nytimes.com/2020/08/07/us/defund-police-seattle protests.html

Borum, R., & Tilly, C. (2005). Anarchist direct actions: A challenge for law enforcement. *Studies in Conflict & Terrorism*, *28*, 201–223.

Byman, D., McCabe, R., Palmer, A., Doxsee, C., Holtz, M., & Duff, D. (2023, December 19). *Hamas's October 7 attack: Visualizing the data*. Center for Strategic & International Studies. https://www.csis.org/analysis/hamass-october-7-attack-visualizing-data

Carson, J. V., LaFree, G., & Dugan, L. (2012). Terrorist and non-terrorist criminal attacks by radical environmental and animal rights groups in the United States, 1970–2007. *Terrorism and Political Violence*, *24*(2), 295–231.

CBS News [@CBSNews]. (2020, June 2). *Violence is when an agent of the state kneels on a man's neck until all of the life is leached out of his body. Destroying property, which can be replaced, is not violence. To use the same language to describe those two things is not moral*

[Tweet]. X (formely Twitter). https://x.com/CBSNews/status/1267877443911778306?ref_src=twsrc%5Etfw%7Ctwca p%5Etweetembed%7Ctwterm%5E1267877443911778306%7Ctwgr%5E932716f9e62dccee85fc275cfa176e4698a7f35%7Ctwcon%5Es1_&ref_url=https%3A%2F%2Fwww.re clearpolitics.com%2Fvideo%2F2020%2F06%2F02%2Fnyts_nikole_hannah jones_destroying_property_which_can_be_replaced_is_not_violence.html

Cherelus, G., & Seba, E. (2016, July 9). Dallas shooting suspect's online posts reflect anger, frustration. *Reuters*. https://www.reuters.com/article/world/dallas-shooting-suspects online-posts-reflect-anger-frustration-idUSKCN0ZO2BI/

Copsey, N., & Merrill, S. (2020). Violence and restraint within antifa. *Perspectives on Terrorism*, *14*(6), 122–138.

Copsey, N., & Merrill, S. (2021, April). *Understanding 21st-century militant anti-fascism*. Centre for Research and Evidence on Security Threats (CREST).

Duran, D. (2021). Far-left versus far-right fatal violence: An empirical assessment of the prevalence of ideologically motivated homicides in the United States. *Criminology, Criminal Justice, Law & Society*, *22*(2), 33–49.

Falciola, L. (2016). A bloodless guerrilla warfare: Why U.S. white leftists renounced violence against people during the 1970s. *Terrorism and Political Violence*, 28(5), 928–949.

Federal Bureau of Investigation & Department of Homeland Security. (2023, June). *Strategic intelligence assessment and data on domestic terrorism*. https://www.dhs.gov/sites/default/files/2023-07/23_0724_opa_strategic-intelligence assessment-data-domestic-terrorism.pdf

Garza, A. (2014, October 7). A herstory of the #BlackLivesMatter movement by Alicia Garza. *The Feminist Wire*. https://collectiveliberation.org/wp content/uploads/2015/01/Garza_Herstory_of_the_BlackLivesMatter_Movement.pdf

Gavin, R. (2022, November 18). Man sentenced to 20 years for stabbing two members of the Proud Boys. *Times Union*. https://www.timesunion.com/news/article/Alexander Contompasis-to-be-sentenced-for-Jan-6-17589543.php

Glawe, J., & Bertness, S. (2017, April 13). Dallas cop-killer Micah Johnson was blacklisted by Black-power groups as 'unstable'. *The Daily Beast*. https://www.thedailybeast.com/dallas cop-killer-micah-johnson-was-blacklisted-by-black-power-groups-as-unstable

Gonzalez, M. (2021). *BLM: The making of a new Marxist revolution*. Encounter Books.

Gross, N., & Simmons, S. (2007, October). *The social and political views of American professors*. Working Paper presented at a Harvard University Symposium on Professors and Their Politics, Cambridge, MA.

The Guardian. (n.d.). *At least 25 Americans were killed during protests and political unrest in 2020*. https://www.theguardian.com/world/2020/oct/31/americans-killed-protests-political unrest-acled

Gutierrez, G., Li, D. K., & Romero, D. (2020, May 29). Minneapolis police precinct burns as George Floyd protests rage; CNN crew arrested. *NBC News*. https://www.nbcnews.com/news/us-news/protests-looting-erupt-again-minneapolis-area following-death-george-floyd-n1216881

Hodges, E. (2020, October 8). Equity through accuracy: Changes to our hate map. *SPLC*. https://www.splcenter.org/hatewatch/2020/10/08/equity-through-accuracy-changes-our hate-map

It's Going Down. (n.d.). *About*. https://itsgoingdown.org/about/

Jarvie, B. (2023, March 15). The latest epicenter for anti-police protests: 'Cop City' in Atlanta. *Los Angeles Times*. https://www.latimes.com/world-nation/story/2023-03-15/stop-cop-city-forest-camp-atlanta

Jasko, K., LaFree, G., Piazza, J., & Becker, M. H. (2022). A comparison of political violence by left-wing, right-wing, and Islamist extremists in the United States and the world. *Proceedings of the National Academy of Sciences*, *119*(30), e2122593119.

Jenkins, B. M. (2022, October). Feature commentary: Elements of a pragmatic strategy to counter domestic political violence. *CTC Sentinel*, *15*(10), 24–44.

Jensen, M. A., & Akers, E. (2024). Prosecuting terror in the homeland: An empirical assessment of sentencing disparities in United States federal terrorism cases. *Perspectives on Terrorism, 18*(1), 8–36.

Johnson, D. (2017, August 8). *Return of the violent Black nationalist*. Southern Poverty Law Center. https://www.splcenter.org/fighting-hate/intelligence-report/2017/return-violent blacknationalist

Kansas City Star. (2016, July 18). *Kansas City man identified as suspect in killings of three Baton Rouge police officers.* https://www.kansascity.com/news/local/article90183857.html
Karagiannis, E., & McCauley, C. (2013). The emerging red-green alliance: Where political Islam meets the radical left. *Terrorism and Political Violence*, *25*(2), 167–182.
Keenan, S., & Fawcett, E. (2023, March 5). Protesters damage property at site of planned police center in Atlanta. *New York Times.* https://www.nytimes.com/2023/03/05/us/atlanta-cop city -protests.html#:~:text=ATLANTA%20 %20Hundreds%20of%20activists%20breached,fireworks%20toward%20officers%20stati oned%20nearby.
Kenning, C. (2018, January 31). No charges for Dallas officers who killed sniper with robot bomb. *Reuters.* https://www.reuters.com/article/world/no-charges-for-dallas-officers who-killed-sniper-with-robot-bomb-idUSKBN1FL3HQ/
Lankford, A. (2023). A close examination of the 2016 Dallas and Baton Rouge police killers: Identifying potential risk factors and influences for copycat violence. *International Criminal Justice Review*, *33*(1), 5–22.
Leader, S. H., & Probst, P. (2003). The earth liberation front and environmental terrorism. *Terrorism and Political Violence*, *15*(4), 37–58.
Loadenthal, M. (2017). "Eco-terrorism": An incident-driven history of attack (1973–2010). *Journal for the Study of Radicalism*, *11*(2), 1–34.
Logan, M. K., & Ligon, G. S. (2021). Come one, come all: individual-level diversity among anti-fascists. *Dynamics of Asymmetric Conflict*, *14*(2), 209–224.
Lowry, R. (2020, June 3). Of course destruction of property is violence. *Politico.* https://www.politico.com/news/magazine/2020/06/03/of-course-destruction-of-property isviolence299759#:~:text=Harming%20a%20person%20is%20much,aren't%20acts%20 f%20 violnce.&text=Rich%20Lowry%20is%20editor%20of,contributing%20editor%20 ith%20 Politico%20Magazine.
Makoii, A. (2024, May 8). Pro-Palestinian protesters project 'student intifada' slogan onto university. *The Telegraph.* https://www.telegraph.co.uk/us/news/2024/05/08/police-pro palestine-camp-george-washington-university/
Mesa, J. (2024, May 30). Ayatollah tells American college students they're on 'right side of history.' *Newsweek.* https://www.newsweek.com/ayatollah-tells-american-college students-theyre-right-side-history-1906281
Michael, G. (2023). Antifa: Anatomy of a movement. In J. P. Zúquete (Ed.), *The Palgrave handbook of left-wing extremism* (Vol. 2, pp. 19–39). Palgrave Macmillan.
Moynihan, M. (2017, July 11). How 1960's radicals ended up teaching your kids. *The Daily Beast.* https://www.thedailybeast.com/how-1960s-radicals-ended-up-teaching-your-kids
Norris, J. (2022). "If abortions aren't safe, neither are you": A mixed-method study of Jane's Revenge and other post-Dobbs militancy. *Journal for Deradicalization*, *33*, 108–149.
NPR. (2024, April 16). *Pro-Palestinian demonstrators shut down airport highways and bridges in major cities.* https://www.npr.org/2024/04/16/1244990246/pro-palestinian demonstrators-shut-down-airport-highways-and-bridges
Park, M. (2016, July 11). Dallas shooting is deadliest for police officers since 9/11. *CNN.* https://www.cnn.com/2016/07/08/us/deadliest-attacks-on-police/index.html
Program on Extremism (PoE). (2022, September). Contemporary violent extremism and the Black Hebrew Israelite movement. *The George Washington University.* https://extremism.gwu.edu/sites/g/files/zaxdzs5746/files/ContemporaryViolentExtremis -BlackHebrewIsraeliteMovement090722.pdf on-police/index.html
Propper, D. (2023, October 11). BLM Chicago admits it 'isn't proud' of deleted post showing paragliding terrorist after outrage. *New York Post.* https://nypost.com/2023/10/11/blm-chicago admits-it-isnt-proud-of-deleted-post-of-hamas-paraglider/
Piza, E. L., & Connealy, N. T. (2022). The effect of the seattle police-free CHOP zone on crime: A microsynthetic control evaluation. *Criminology & Public Policy*, *21*(1), 35–58.
Pyrooz, D. C., & Densley, J. A. (2018). On public protest, violence, and street gangs. *Society*, *55*, 229–236.
Rapoport, D. C. (2004). The four waves of modern terrorism. In A. K. Cronin & J. M. Lodes (Eds.), *Attacking terrorism: Elements of a grand strategy* (pp. 46–73). Georgetown University Press.
Robinson, N. J. (2020, June). Why damaging property isn't the same as "violence". *Current Affairs.* https://www.currentaffairs.org/news/2020/06/why-property-destruction-isnt violence

Rosas, J. (2022). *Fiery (but mostly peaceful): The 2020 riots and the gaslighting of America*. DW Books.

Rosenau, W. (2013). "Our backs are against the wall": The Black Liberation Army and domestic terrorism in the 1970s America. *Studies in Conflict & Terrorism*, *36*(2), 176–192.

Ruiz-Goiriena, R. (2024, April 25). Hamas and Iran celebrate anti-Gaza war protests taking colleges by storm. https://www.usatoday.com/story/news/politics/2024/04/24/hamas-iran support-college-protests/73447123007/

Sherman, C. (2022, July 28). The right is freaking out over Jane's Revenge. But what is it? *Vice*. https://www.vice.com/en/article/y3ppmj/what-is-janes-revenge-abortion-rights

Silva, J. R. (2022). Ideologically motivated mass shootings: a crime script analysis of far-right, far-left, and jihadist-inspired attacks in the United States. *Journal of Policing, Intelligence and Counter Terrorism*, *18*(1), 1–23.

Simon, J. D. (2022). *America's forgotten terrorist: The rise and fall of the Galleanists*. Potomac Books.

Smith, A. (2020, May 31). Trump says he will designate antifa a terrorist organization as GOP points fingers at extremists. *NBC News*. https://www.nbcnews.com/politics/politics news/trump -says-he-will-designate-antifa-terrorist-organization-gop-points-n1220321

Smith, B. L. (1994). *Terrorism in America: Pipe bombs and pipe dreams*. State University of New York Press.

Southern Poverty Law Center (SPLC). (n.d.). *New black panther party*. https://www.splcenter.org/ fighting-hate/extremist-files/group/new-black-panther-party

Truzman, J. (2024, May 28). Al-Qaeda's general command lauds attacks against Jews commends anti-Israel protests on western campuses. *Long War Journal*. https://www.longwarjournal.org /archives/2024/05/al-qaedas-general-command-lauds attacks-against-jews-commends-anti-israel -protests-on-western-campuses.php

Vysotsky, A. (2021). *American Antifa: The tactics, culture, and practice of militant antifascism*. Routledge.

Williams, D. M. (2019). Tactics: Conceptions of social change, revolution, and anarchist organisation. In C. Levy & M. S. Adams (Eds.), The Palgrave handbook of anarchism (pp. 107–123). Palgrave Macmillan.

Williams, J. (2018, August 12). Antifa clashes with police and journalists in Charlottesville and DC. *Vox*. https://www.vox.com/identities/2018/8/12/17681986/antifa-leftist-violence clashes-protest s-charlottesville-dc-unite-the-right

Wilson, C., Freda, K., & Neuman, S. (2020, September 4). Suspect in fatal shooting of Portland right-wing protester killed by law enforcement. *NPR*. https://www.npr.org/2020/09/04/909515885/ protester-suspected-in-portland-shooting death-killed-by-law-enforcement

Winter, J., & Weinberger, S. (2017, October 6). The FBI's new U.S. terrorist threat:'Black identity extremists'. *Foreign Policy*. https://foreignpolicy.com/2017/10/06/the-fbi-has identified-a-ne w-domestic-terrorist-threat-and-its-black-identity-extremists/

4

TIMELINE OF TERROR

The Evolution of Right-Wing Terrorism in the U.S.

Nicholas Stone, James Bacigalupo, and Kevin Borgeson

Right-wing terrorism has persisted over time as a devastating reminder of the deep divisions in the U.S. While some elements have remained constant, the ideologies, tactics, movements, and organizations of the far-right have evolved over time. This chapter provides a detailed timeline tracing the evolution of right-wing terrorism, from the founding of the Ku Klux Klan in 1865 to its most recent manifestations. The far-right operates within a broader context of political and social factors. Therefore, the timeline also integrates key events that have shaped the far-right's development. The chapter will then examine the far-right's latest obsession of gender roles and the rise of incels. Relevant theories will be introduced to help explain this shift. Finally, the chapter will apply theories to the two primary methods of right-wing violent extremism: lone actor attacks and group-level protest violence. This analysis will include a detailed examination of the deadly attacks perpetrated by James Alex Fields Jr. and Robert Bowers.

Timeline

- The Ku Klux Klan was founded in 1865 in the aftermath of the Civil War by Confederate veterans in Pulaski, Tennessee. The Klan evolved into a loose network of terrorist cells that lynched and brutalized Black people and their white allies across the Reconstructionist South to intimidate Black people from voting and exercising their civil rights (Southern Poverty Law Center [SPLC], 2023; Tures, 2016).
- In 1871, President Ulysses S. Grant passed the KKK Act, which made the deprivation of certain civil rights a federal offense and allowed the president to send in federal troops to combat the Klan and similar white supremacist militias. Between the prosecutions of hundreds of Klansmen, and the emerging Jim Crow laws enshrining white supremacy, the first Klan would be dissolved (Scaturro, 1999).
- Amid growing antisemitism toward the large influx of Jewish immigrants from Europe, a Jewish factory director named Leo Frank is lynched in Georgia in 1915 after he is accused of the murder of 13-year-old Mary Phagan. The consensus among modern researchers is that Frank was innocent. The incident would lead to the founding of

DOI: 10.4324/9781003375265-7

both the Anti-Defamation League and the Second Ku Klux Klan (Augustyn, 2015; Feldberg, n.d.)

- After the revisionist pro-KKK blockbuster film Birth of a Nation sweeps the nation, the second Klan was founded in Stone Mountain, Georgia, in 1915. The second Klan became a multi-level marketing-style fraternal organization, attracting millions of members nationwide. The second Klan is characterized less by anti-Black sentiment and more by antisemitism, xenophobia, anti-Catholicism, anti-communism, and a growing fear of moral degradation that threatened traditional American life. The Klan flourished into the mid-20s, before scandals, infighting, and poor publicity led to its rapid decline (Fryer & Levitt, 2007; SPLC, 2023; TIME, 1965).
- Henry Ford's weekly newspaper, *The Dearborn Independent*, published numerous anti-Semitic conspiracies, most notably the Protocols of the Elders of Zion in 1920. Originating from the Russian Empire in 1903, the Protocols are a fabricated document that purports to be the secret plan of a Jewish cabal for international domination. The document would popularize anti-Semitic conspiracies of International Jewry attempting total global control. Lawsuits and boycotts would lead Ford to close the paper in 1927 (Feldstein, 2021).
- The 1910s and 1920s were marked by the pervasive and endemic lynching of Black people, with the most brutal culminating in race riots and massacres, most notably in Rosewood and Tulsa. Between 1883 and 1941, 4,467 people were lynched in the United States (Seguin & Rigby, 2019; Tulsa Historical Society & Museum, 2022; EJI, n.d.).
- Pro-Nazi organizations, like the German American Bund, Teutonia Society, and Christian Front, attempted to normalize Nazism in America. This culminated in a Nazi rally in Madison Square Garden in 1939, attended by over 20,000 people (Kramer, 2019; Lederhendler, 2017).
- Teenager Emmett Till was accused of wolf-whistling at a white woman and was brutally murdered by her husband and his half-brother in 1955. Photographs of Till's mutilated body shocked the nation and increased support for the civil rights movement (Brown, 2018).
- In response to the growing civil rights movement, the third KKK emerged to intimidate Black people and preserve segregation. The third Klan resembled the first as a mob of loosely connected terrorist cells and committed a litany of attacks, including the murders of three civil rights activists in Mississippi and the Baptist Street Church bombing in Birmingham, which resulted in the deaths of four children. These acts turned the public against the Klan and eventually culminated in the signing of the Civil Rights Act of 1964 (TIME, 1965; SPLC, 2023; McWhorter, 2013).
- Martin Luther King Jr. was assassinated in Memphis, Tennessee, on April 4, 1968. James Earl Ray was convicted of the crime, though a civil court later found that a conspiracy of local white business owners, the mafia, and the federal government was more likely. Regardless of the true perpetrator, the assassination was met with mixed reactions from the American public, as King had continued his activism to include opposition to the Vietnam War and support for socialist causes. The assassination would lead to riots and national unrest (Encyclopedia Brittanica, 2024a, 2024b; Stanford University, n.d.).
- The end of the Vietnam War led to the stabbed-in-the-back narrative, in which the far-right believed the war could have been won, but the government capitulated to

leftists to save face. Louis Beam and David Duke would use this narrative to sculpt the post-war far-right, in which neo-Nazi, KKK, and anti-government factions would converge. This movement would focus on militarism, anti-communism, leaderless resistance, anti-immigrant sentiments, and establishing ties to the mercenary movement (SPLC, 2024; Barrouquere, 2019; Berger, 2019).

- The Turner Diaries was published by William Luther Pierce in 1978. The novel depicts a dystopian future in which the world is run by a cabal of Jewish elites, and through a race war and nuclear holocaust, neo-Nazi rebels overthrow the government and exterminate all non-whites and Jews. The book would become a staple of the far-right and would continuously inspire acts of domestic terror (Romano, 2021).
- In 1979, members of the KKK and the American Nazi Party shot and killed five members of the Communist Workers Party (CWP) in Greensboro, North Carolina. The violence was preceded by inflammatory rhetoric on both sides and culminated in a shootout during an anti-racist march held by the CWP (Keating & Assael, 2019).
- Between 1983 and 1984, a neo-Nazi terrorist group called the Order launched an armed robbery campaign to finance a rebellion against the "Zionist Occupied Government" (ZOG). The group would steal $4.1 million and distribute it throughout the far-right. After the group murdered Jewish radio host Alan Berg, leader Bob Mathews died in a shootout with the FBI, and the remaining members were incarcerated (Martin, 2011; Egan, n.d.).
- The 1980s farm crisis led to the rise of the Posse Comitatus, a far-right anti-government group opposed to income tax, debt-based currency, and debt collection, deeming them to be tools of Jewish oppression against the working man. The popularity of the group would endear anti-tax activists to far-right ideology and create the broader sovereign citizen movement (SPLC, 1998; Balleck, 2014).
- White supremacists became some of the earliest adopters of the internet. In 1990, former KKK grand wizard Don Black started Stormfront as a message board for fellow white supremacists. By 1995, it became a website and would be followed by hundreds of hate sites across the internet (SPLC, n.d.-b; Swain & Nieli, 2010).
- The FBI and ATF blunders in the Ruby Ridge and Waco siege incidents inspired a national wave of backlash and a surge in militia and far-right recruitment (Niebuhr, 1995; Wilson, 2017).
- In 1995, Timothy McVeigh and accomplices used a fertilizer bomb to destroy the Alfred P. Murrah Federal Building in Oklahoma City. The blast killed between 168 and 169 people, including 19 children. The bombing was the deadliest terrorist attack in the U.S. before 9/11 and remains the deadliest domestic terrorist attack in United States history (Enyclopedia Brittanica, 2024d).
- The September 11, 2001, attacks created an immense wave of Islamophobic backlash in the U.S., leading to a large spike in hate crimes against Muslims. The attacks also split the far-right, with some being outraged by them and others like Aryan Nations leader August Kreis celebrating the killings and proposing collaboration with jihadists against their "common enemy" (Al Jazeera, 2022; Schuster, 2005).
- Throughout the early 2010s, French white supremacist writer Renaud Camus developed the Great Replacement Theory, a conspiracy theory that elites are betraying native Europeans by replacing them with Muslim populations from Africa. The popularity of this theory among the far-right would help bolster the more extreme white genocide

theory, in which an explicitly Jewish cabal is attempting to exterminate white people globally through the immigration of racial minorities. These theories have become tenets of the far-right and have frequently been cited by terrorists (ADL, 2022; Flanagan & Wilson, 2022; ISD, 2023).

- In 2014, Elliot Rodger murdered six people in Isla Vista, California. Rodger's manifesto spread across the internet, filled with rants against women for rejecting him and dystopian visions of a world where women are enslaved for procreation. Rodger would become an icon of the violent side of the incel movement (Yelimeli & Mineiro, 2015; Glasstetter, 2014; BBC, 2018a).
- Between 2014 and 2015, an online harassment campaign known as Gamergate emerged, targeting women working in the video game industry, and decrying feminism and political correctness. The movement would give a large rise to far-right troll culture on the internet, normalize misogyny in many online spaces, and inspire the subsequent alt-right movement (Dewey, 2014).
- In 2015, white supremacist Dylann Roof murdered nine people in a historic Black church in Charleston, South Carolina. Roof's online radicalization and frequent posing with the confederate flag led to a fierce debate over the display of confederate iconography and the rise of internet-made terrorists (Rogers, 2015).
- The election of Donald Trump in 2016 fueled the far-right, with a rise of hate crimes under his presidency, direct advocacy for fringe right positions, and appointment of extremist personalities to his cabinet, including Steve Bannon, Stephen Miller, and Sebastion Gorka (SPLC, n.d.-a; Galvan & Kunzelman, 2021; ADL, 2018; Banic & Smith, 2017).
- In 2017, a collection of far-right and white supremacist activists organized a rally against the removal of a Robert E. Lee statue in Charlottesville, Virginia. Dubbed Unite the Right, the rally descended into chaos when wide-scale fights between the hundreds of protesters and counter-protesters broke out, with one man, James Alex Fields, using his car to ram into protesters and kill a woman. The incident led to an intense political debate over the rise of the far-right, especially after President Trump blamed both sides for the violence (Merica, 2017; TIME, 2017).
- The mid to late 2010s hosted a dramatic rise in far-right terror attacks. Between 2014 and 2018, right-wing terror attacks rose 320%. Prominent among these are high-profile mass shootings targeting religious sites, minority community centers, and abortion clinics (Auger, 2020).
- The COVID-19 pandemic's Chinese origins fueled anti-Asian racism, with a large uptick in hate crimes targeting Asian Americans reported in 2020 and 2021. The pandemic also fueled wide-ranging anti-government conspiracies of a "plandemic" and a surge in anti-vaccine ideology (Ruiz et al., 2023; Dongen, 2021).
- The murder of George Floyd by police officers in Minneapolis triggered the George Floyd protests, characterized by an opposition to systemic racism and police violence. The protest became the largest of its kind in U.S. history and resulted in both peaceful protests and riots, with police often engaging in violent retaliation. The chaotic nature of the riots attracted some far-right and anti-government extremists to further the discord in the hopes of sparking a race war or the collapse of the federal government. Activities ranged from misinformation campaigns and participation in riots to violent terror attacks and murders of police officers. Notable groups who capitalized on the

unrest included the Boogaloo Bois, the Oath Keepers, the Three Percenters, and the Proud Boys (Taylor, 2020; Olson, 2020).

- The 2020 election loss of Donald Trump surged conspiracy theories of a stolen election, fueled by Trump himself. The increasing agitation of the far-right culminated in the January 6, Capitol attack, in which Trump supporters stormed the U.S. Capitol building to delay the certification of the election. The level of malice and premeditation of the rioters ranged, with the majority acting impulsively as the mob began surging into the Capitol building. Other more dedicated extremists had conspired over social media sites weeks in advance and came prepared with tactical gear, zip ties, and bombs, although none were detonated. Some of the rioters had planned to hold congress people hostage, and in some instances to execute them. This included Vice President Mike Pence, whom rioters blamed for allowing the certification to take place. The seditious conspiracy included the leadership of the Proud Boys and Oath Keepers, and members of various QAnon, white supremacist, neo-Nazi, and neo-Confederate groups. Donald Trump would receive criticism for his reluctance to speak against the riots, and would later embrace the rioters as patriots and would make their clemency a campaign promise. Trump would be impeached after the attack, though he avoided removal from office. He was later indicted in 2023 on federal election interference charges, which pertained in part to his involvement in the Capitol attack. Over 890 rioters were convicted of their role in the attempted insurrection. The riot resulted in the deaths of five people, including a police officer who suffered a stroke and a rioter who was shot trying to invade the Capitol building. The event still spurns controversy as to the scope of those involved in its planning and execution (Diaz, 2023; Duignan, 2024; Rabinowitz & Lybrand, 2024).
- In 2022, British-American influencer Andrew Tate rose in popularity. A prominent manosphere personality, Tate pushes deeply misogynistic ideology into the mainstream, popularizing a lifestyle dominated by the use of women as sexual objects. Tate is particularly resonate with teenage boys, resulting in an increasing fear that his rape apologia and far-right views are becoming prominent among young people. In December of 2022, Tate and his brother were arrested in Romania on charges of rape and sex trafficking, and are still awaiting trial (Hermant & Yussuf, 2024; Radford, 2024).
- On October 7, 2023, the Palestinian terror group Hamas launched a massive attack on Israel that led to over 1,000 deaths. Israel responded with an invasion of Gaza that has resulted in a war mired in controversy over Israel's methods and treatment towards the Palestinian people. The ongoing conflict has led to anti-Arab, Islamophobic, and anti-Semitic incidents surging globally (Encyclopedia Brittanica, 2024c; Atkinson & Swann, 2023).

Gender Roles and the Rise of Incels in the Contemporary Far-Right

One of the most notable trends of modern far-right terror is the incorporation of manosphere elements in its extremism. Strict gender roles and an expectation of female compliance and obedience have always been a hallmark of the radical right. The Nazi Party slogan *Kinder, Kuche, Kirche* (Children, Kitchen, Church) proscribed the functions of women in Aryan society, and the Ku Klux Klan would terrorize and publicly humiliate women whom they accused of immoral acts (Baldwin, 2011; BBC, 2023). The reactionary tendency to subjugate and control women as chattel and objects of conquest dates back millennia and far outdates the modern radical right sphere in the United States.

The modern extreme right has incorporated a new kind of misogyny into its ethos: manosphere ideology. The manosphere is a modern internet movement that spans a variety of sexist communities and forums and that is united in its rejection of contemporary feminism and promotion of vitriolic views of women, an ideology known as the "red pill." Becoming prominent in 2016, the manosphere houses a variety of misogynistic outlooks. Among these include the onslaught of Andrew Tate-style influencers and internet gurus who proscribe an obsession with wealth and sex, and the status of women as status objects. Also among them are MGTOW (men going their own way), which idealizes men's lives as being improved without the "the corruption of modern feminism," pick-up artists who teach men that women are like machines that can be easily manipulated for sex, and incel ideologies.

The incel movement (involuntary celibate) is primarily comprised of disillusioned young men who are either virgins or dissatisfied with their sex lives, and focus all their frustration and animus towards women, whom they blame as being "evil, selfish and materialistic." All of these ideologies are united in hatred towards modern feminism, which they charge as being a corrupting influence that has disrupted traditional gender roles and weakened Western society (Bates, 2021). The average incel or internet misogynist is typically young, insecure, anti-social, and more prone to blame others for their misfortune and unhappiness rather than embrace introspection and seek mental help. This combination of isolation and misanthropy makes them ideal targets for radicalization.

The extreme right, like other radical ideologies and cults, is highly predatory and manipulates that frustration to radicalize them. A case and example would be the Daily Stormer and its founder Andrew Anglin. The neo-Nazi website is littered with rhetoric decrying women as deceivers, with one article reading, "Women use their bodies like Jews use their Jew gold—as a manipulation tool to get what they want." Anglin isn't simply preaching to the choir with this message, he is intentionally trying to court misogynists, implying Nazism is an ideological parallel (ISD, 2022). Incels and others radicalized by the manosphere commonly espouse other reactionary terminally online viewpoints. Their outlook is often polluted with racism, homophobia, transphobia, anti-Semitism, and paranoia of conspiracies against them.

An example would be Nikolas Cruz, who carried out a mass school shooting on February 14, 2018, at the Stoneman Douglas High School in Parkland, Florida. His social media was littered with a hatred for women, particularly white women who had interracial relationships, as well as Jews, gay people, Mexicans, Muslims, and Black people among others (McLoughlin & Park, 2018; Murphy, 2018). Cruz also professed hero worship for other mass killers, including Elliot Rodger, likely the most infamous incel killer, who is often praised by other incels as the "Supreme Gentleman." Rodger also had an ideology that mixed hatred of women with other far-right beliefs, having a fixation with Nazis, hating Black people, and targeting and killing three Asian men in his attack, whom he felt were inferior (Glasstetter, 2014).

Cruz and Rodger are far from the only men whose misogyny led them down the alt-right pipeline into becoming killers. Between 2014 and 2020, law enforcement estimates 50 murders were committed by violent incels in the United States and Canada. (Hoffman,

2020). One of the most prominent reasons incels become violent is due to nihilism. A common platitude of the incel community is the Blackpill, a bleak mindset that if you are unattractive or unwealthy, no amount of growth or self-improvement will ever yield any success in finding a partner. This mindset is consistent with the incel perception of women as being shallow and pernicious and traps its victims in a spiral of stagnation and doom, in which their only sense of catharsis and control over their lives becomes deepening frustration and contemplation of violent fantasies. This nihilistic and aggrieved state of mind towards the world around them can push them toward other forms of radicalization (ADL, 2019).

The mindset that they are never at fault for their misery and that it is the fault of everyone else begins to spread to others. Jews, minorities, gay and trans people, Muslims, and the government can all become objects of their spite, invisible enemies in their world that surely must be working against them in clandestine ways. This absorption of other extremist tenets can also be attributed to emotional contagion. When they open themselves up to one extreme element on the internet, they are subjected to the influence of other extreme parties online, whom they may relate to and exchange ideas with. This can happen person to person or informed by a larger group in which ideologies are exchanged and combined, before many of the exposed leave with a hybridized ideology in which the possessor of one of these beliefs leaves with all of them (Green et al., 2023).

This can happen organically, in which the subject happens upon these gateways and communities, or intentionally seeks them out themselves. This can also be done through an active sense of recruiting. Former neo-Nazi Christian Picciolini expressed how he was radicalized after a neo-Nazi caught him smoking marijuana and exclaimed "That is exactly what the Jews and Communists want you to do" (p. 3), Picciolini was an unhappy and angry youth who was skeptical of the world around him, and that active act of recruitment sucked him into a subculture of violence and hate (Picciolini & Jett, 2017). With the increasing interconnectedness of the internet, the ability to be exposed through intention or happenstance has increased exponentially. This is helped by the nature of internet algorithms, if unchecked tend to recommend and advertise increasingly extreme materials in higher quantities after engaging with one. Studies have indicated that the alt-right pipeline has been a contributing factor to the rise in domestic terrorism, and many social media websites acknowledge its existence and vow measures to curb it (Ribeiro et al., 2020; Roose, 2019; Munn, 2019).

Another element that may push these killers to violence is the copycat effect (Coleman, 2014). It is frequently observed that mass murderers and spree killers tend to obsess over previous notorious murders, and on occasion cite them as inspirations. Unibomber Ted Kaczynski was cited as an inspiration by neo-Nazi spree killer Anders Breivik, who was in turn praised in the manifesto of Christchurch shooter Brenton Tarrant (Coaston, 2019; Follman & Andrews, 2015; van Gerven Oei, 2019) The likes of other notorious mass killers like the Columbine shooters, Elliot Rodger, and Dylann Roof are all common hallmarks in the manifestos or frequent search histories of domestic terrorists (BBC, 2018b; Follman & Andrews, 2015; ADL, 2022).

Most lone-wolf terrorists commit acts of terror out of a desperate attempt to reestablish control and power over a world they rationalize has victimized them. This sense of desire for power works in tandem with a desire for infamy, and so many killers look to other notorious killers and the media sensationalism surrounding their crimes as a point of inspiration to commit them themselves. Additionally, in doing so, the disgruntled individual who felt that they lacked any sense of belonging or status in the world feels that they have established themselves in a league of infamy with the likes of the other killers that they have worshiped as heroes.

The Pathway to Terror: Theories that Explain Right-Wing Extremism

Identification with the Aggressor

Sigmund Freud introduced the concept of identification in the 1800s as a psychological mechanism through which a person takes on aspects of another person's personality (Freud, 1990). Initially, this theory was conceived of as a process by which an infant internalizes the virtues of a parent or caregiver into one's life. Anna Freud extended this concept when she introduced identification with the aggressor in her work in the early 1900s. The theory was meant to help explain situations where individuals adopt the behaviors, attitudes, or values of those with dominance or power over them. (Ekins & Freeman, 1998).

Anne Freud's ego defense theory is complex, and she created several mechanisms the ego engages in to deal with such feelings as anxiety. The theoretical concept that is most applicable to understanding right-wing terrorists is the concept of cognitive dissonance, which is widely used among sociologists and psychologists. Although some theorists suggest it only happens in severe anxiety-induced scenarios, this psychological process happens in everyday situations as well. For instance, when someone is buying a new car and finally decides on the vehicle they will buy, the person downplays negative things about the car they bought and plays up the negative things about the car they did not buy. In situations like this, people feel discomfort when their views or actions challenge one another. Anxieties such as fear, dependency, or survival can affect a person's willingness to accept or adopt the approach or behaviors of those they view in positions of authority in their specific situation (Freud, 1979).

At times, the interpretation of Anna Freud's work on Identification with the Aggressor has not been applied appropriately. According to Anna Freud, she believed that an individual could identify with the aggressor or with the aggression (A. Freud, 1979). Individuals can connect not just the person but also with the aggression used to accomplish violent actions of domestic terrorism. When the person identifies with the aggression, it is seen as a means to an end.

Identification with the aggressor/aggression can become noticeable in situations of intense emotion. People may adopt values or beliefs in tense situations to deal with their current situation. According to Anna Freud, this defense mechanism shows how situations of control can shape an individual's psychological outlook and reactions to behavior. The implications of identification with the aggressor can extend very quickly to the field of right-wing domestic terrorism. On a macro level, some people may have feelings of relative deprivation and feel they have been mistreated. When these people identify with strong power figures, they may continue to vilify groups and envision acts of violence to possibly be martyrs of their individual or group beliefs (Borgeson & Valeri, 2018).

Emotional Contagion

Emotional contagion occurs when people copy emotions from those around them, often without conscious awareness (Hatfield et al., 1993). Although one might not think so, emotions can spread nationally and internationally, much like a pandemic virus like COVID-19 did in 2020. This concept, extensively studied in psychology and sociology, demonstrates the complexities of human emotions—especially when combined with a massive audience with a social network and an intense emotional range. They use avenues for the emotion to spread to those willing to receive the emotional message. When the message comes to the attention of terrorists, they, in turn, can accept the emotion and act on it like others have.

According to some modern theorists, emotional contagion can operate through face-to-face and social media platforms. The brain picks up conscious and unconscious emotional cues from those we associate with. Whether it is a smile, frown, or an inflection of one's voice, people can internalize and imitate those emotions. For example, we have all been in a social situation where someone begins to laugh. Others will join in, even if they do not fully understand what the group is laughing at.

A critical application of this theory to domestic terrorism is in the use of empathy (Hatfield et al., 1993). When we empathize with someone, we recognize their emotion(s) but also can internalize them to an extent and begin to experience similar feelings. Shared emotions can create a sense of belonging among those exposed. Because this psychological process is an emotion, it has direction. In other words, emotional contagion can be positive or negative, depending on the social context it is used in. Emotions, whether positive or negative, have the capacity to spread through a group and create feelings of fear, anxiety, and frustration. Experiences like those described above can lead social groups to conflict among those sharing the collective experience (Hatfield et al., 1993).

Emotional contagion is not limited to just face-to-face. Emotions have the capacity to transmit, through social media and face-to-face interactions, at unprecedented speed and can affect many. For right-wing terrorists, videos evoking instances that provoke outrage can trigger a torrent of displeasure and frustration across both in person and online communities, which in turn can increase the development of new terrorist movements or create moral panics where violence breaks out—as in the instance of the domestic terrorist act which happened at the Charlottesville Rally on August 11, 2017.

When anxiety spreads rapidly through communities, it can impact an individual's conduct and overall processing, as well as their interpretation of social cues. Politicians can develop more effective ways of managing public perceptions by trying to understand how these feelings are transferred in social situations, both in person and via social media networks.

Because this is psychological, and personalities vary, not everyone will engage in it—personality, social situations, and intellect can all influence the susceptibility of this emotional response to those exposed to it. Emotions can accelerate when not controlled by individuals, groups, or society.

Definition of the Situation

Social psychologists in symbolic interactionism created the theory definition of the situation. Social psychologist William I. Thomas invented the theory, extended later by the great social psychologist Erving Goffman. This theory states that "if somebody defines something as real, it becomes real in its consequences" (Manis & Meltzer, 1972).

The definition of the situation is when people act based on how they socially construct an event or an interaction rather than its actual meaning. These perceptions can be shaped by various social situations or how individuals see themselves (Berger & Luckmann, 1966).

The definition of the situation relies on what social psychologists refer to as the social construction of reality, especially in the meaning one gives to social situations (Manis & Meltzer, 1972). This process happens when an individual weighs something as necessary based on their interpretation of social cues, symbols, and shared meaning. These meanings guide their actions and dealings with others. This meaning is dynamic, quite fluid, and can change over time and social context. Individuals place importance on things they experience and socially construct meaning from these shared experiences, which theorists state is done through communication with others. The constant process of change and compromise contributes to how a person interprets and reinterprets their social experience.

Erving Goffman (1959) extended the theory by adding what he referred to as "dramaturgy." Goffman hypothesized that social interactions are the same as a performance on a stage by "actors," where they adopt roles and engage in what he called "impression management." Within the framework of the theory, individuals deliberately present themselves in ways they want to be perceived by those in the "audience" and accomplish this by drawing on "cultural scripts" within individual or group norms (Lemert & Branaman, 1997). This theory explains the normalcy of domestic terrorists, how they go undetected in society, and how their actions go undetected for a very long time. These people become the person who lived next door, and everyone thought "he was nice and kept to himself." Ideologies are not detected until they become exposed to other like-minded terrorists and the right situation arises.

Within psychological explanation lie the concepts of "front stage" and "backstage" (Goffman, 1959). According to Goffman, the front stage is where individuals conduct a performance of themselves that they believe an audience wants to see. This performance is engaged to elicit reactions from those in the "audience" (Goffman, 1959). In contrast, the backstage is where individuals cannot pretend and behave authentically, reflecting how they are.

The definition of the situation tells us a lot about the way right-wing terrorists make sense of their social surroundings. One highlight of the theory is the role of interpreting how we create social constructs of the world we see (Brown, 1985). By emphasizing the context of meaning in social contexts, this theory provides insights into how individuals deal with the complex social milieus they encounter daily and explains why a terrorist act does not take place until their situation is defined as accurate. They engage in violence to "correct" the views they believe exist in the larger social context. According to social psychologists of the symbolic interactionist school, this construction is done through everyday conversations and word choices with others. Individual meanings that are constructed are used when one interprets the social situations they become engaged in. Through a constantly changing back-and-forth discourse with the language they used. People begin to navigate meanings and shared understandings, which influence social behavior such as terrorism. This social construction to action model can happen via groups or in the larger social order, in which they begin to define their problem accurately.

The definition of the situation can be applied very quickly to how these violent individuals and groups construct reality (Valeri & Borgeson, 2018). By emphasizing interpretation, shared meaning, and the social context it is shared in, this theory provides insights into how a person deals with everyday life and, in turn, engages with like-minded terrorist ideologies represented in real life and on social media.

Case Studies in Far-Right Violence: Theoretical Insights into Lone Actor Attacks and Group-Level Protest Violence

The contemporary far-right employs two primary forms of violence: lone actor attacks and group-level protest violence. This analysis examines these distinct tactics through case studies that apply relevant theories of violent extremism. While each case is unique, the examples discussed illustrate broader patterns in far-right violence. Although instances of protest violence resulting in fatalities are relatively rare, the James Fields Jr. case is representative of the violent conflicts that have been escalating between the far-right and far-left in recent years.

James Alex Fields Jr. and the Charlottesville Tragedy

Predictably, the August 12, 2017, Unite the Right rally in Charlottesville, Virginia, ended in violence. Numerous right-wing demonstrations prior to this event, including several earlier that year in Berkeley, California, also resulted in violent clashes (Lenz, 2017). The rally, organized by white nationalist Jason Kessler, aimed to oppose the removal of a statue of Confederate General Robert E. Lee from a Charlottesville park. It was claimed that the rally intended to bring together various factions of the right-wing; however, promotions for the event advertised appearances of far-right figures, including Richard Spencer, who was the unofficial leader of the alt-right.

The night before the scheduled event, white nationalists led a torch march through the University of Virginia campus, chanting slogans such as "blood and soil" and "Jews will not replace us." This march ended in violent clashes, but it was only a preview of what was to come the following day. The next morning, hundreds of far-right demonstrators participated in the march equipped with shields and protective gear. Some, especially those affiliated with militia groups, were armed with rifles. Among the participants was James Alex Fields Jr., who can be seen wielding a shield bearing the logo of Vanguard America, the white supremacist group he was affiliated with before they rebranded to Patriot Front following the events of the day (ADL, 2024a).

The protective gear worn by demonstrators was logical given the likelihood of encountering a violent confrontation with counter-protesters, including militant anti-fascists (antifa). Seemingly coming out of nowhere, antifa has origins in the U.S. dating back to the mid-1980s. Following Donald Trump's 2016 presidential campaign, they grew in prominence by frequently clashing with far-right groups energized by Trump's rise (Michael, 2023). Although it is relatively uncommon for antifa to use firearms, approximately 20 members of the group Redneck Revolt were armed with rifles (Stockman, 2017). As anticipated, violence erupted, with footage showing participants using weapons such as pepper spray, batons, and flag poles to attack each other, sometimes severely. A state of emergency was declared by the governor at 11:06 am, and shortly after, at 11:30 am, an unlawful assembly was declared by officials.

At 1:40 pm, James Fields Jr. drove his Dodge Challenger down a narrow street in downtown Charlottesville, barreling into a group of counter-protesters. Multiple people were hit, including Heather Heyer, who was tragically killed. In court, his defense did not dispute that he was the driver, but claimed he was motivated by self-protection. In contrast, prosecutors alleged that months before the incident, he had posted pictures on social media of a group being struck by a car (BBC, 2018a). Ultimately, Fields Jr. pleaded guilty to 29 violations of the Mathew Shepard and James Byrd Jr. Hate Crimes Prevention Act and was sentenced to life in prison (Department of Justice [DOJ], 2019).

One way to explain the violence carried out by Fields Jr. is through the concept of cumulative extremism. Originally coined by Eatwell (2006), cumulative extremism describes how various forms of extremism, including far-right, jihadist, and anti-fascist movements, "feed off and magnify other forms" (p. 205). Littler and Feldman (2015) described the phenomenon as "the cyclical ratcheting up of violent activity between opposing communities," where violent acts by a sub-group of one community trigger retaliatory violence from another community. Carter (2020) notes that since its inception, variations of the concept have been developed including "tit-for-tat radicalization" and "reciprocal radicalization"; however, they are essentially the same phenomenon. While it has garnered the attention of both policy experts and academics alike for its application in Western European contexts, its application to political violence in the U.S. remains limited.

According to Vysotsky (2021), militant anti-fascists see violent tactics not only as acceptable but necessary to counter fascist political organizing. The presence of these groups at right-wing events greatly increases the likelihood of physical confrontation as they consider violent opposition imperative. Right-wing groups adapted to antifa's tactics by preparing for, and seemingly embracing the violence. Antifa has provided these groups with a common enemy. Instead of political demonstrations, many of these events more accurately resemble groups going into battle, with the expectation and even intention of physical confrontations. Fields Jr.'s attack with his car exemplifies a devastating escalation consistent with cumulative extremism. The trend of protest violence has continued since with fatal attacks from both sides. In 2021, over half of all domestic terrorist incidents occurred in the context of urban demonstrations (Doxsee et al., 2022).

Robert Bowers and the Tree of Life Massacre

The deadliest anti-Semitic attack in United States history occurred on October 27, 2018, at the Tree of Life Synagogue in Pittsburgh, Pennsylvania (Fattal, 2018). On that morning, three congregations—Tree of Life, Dor Hadash, and New Light—were gathered for Shabbat services when Robert Bowers entered the building, armed with a rifle and three handguns (DOJ, 2023). He opened fire, killing 11 and wounding six before responding police engaged him in a firefight and eventually took him into custody. After being found guilty on 63 counts, including hate crimes resulting in death and obstruction of free exercise of religion resulting in death, a jury unanimously recommended the death penalty for Bowers (DOJ, 2023).

One way to make sense of how someone can bring themselves to commit such a horrific act of violence on an innocent group of people is through social identity theory (SIT). SIT has been useful for analyzing intergroup dynamics in extremism (Berger, 2018). Key studies (Tajfel et al., 1971; Billig & Tajfel, 1973; Turner, 1978) were integral to the development of SIT, which was later formalized by Henri Tajfel and John Turner in their seminal works (Tajfel, 1978; Tajfel & Turner, 1979). Essentially, SIT argues that individuals categorize themselves and others as members of two competing groups: the in-group and out-group. Although individuals tend to favor their own group, these statuses are not necessarily a value judgment, and in a pluralistic society, many accept and celebrate differences between individuals. Berger defines extremist ideology as "a collection of texts that describe who is part of the in-group, who is part of the out-group, and how the in-group should interact with the out-group" (p. 26). Additionally, he defines violent extremism as "the belief that an in-group's success or survival can never be separated from the need for violent action against an out-group" (p. 46).

Bower's adherence to white supremacy and his view of Jews as enemies of the white race align with Berger's (2018) definition of violent extremism. He came to believe that the survival of his in-group, the white race, depended on violent action against the out-group, Jews. While white supremacists have targeted various non-white groups, Jews are often portrayed as the orchestrators of the plot to destroy the white race, known as "white genocide" (Borgeson & Bacigalupo, 2022). Evidence suggests that Bowers may have been influenced by Christian Identity (CI) (Wexler et al., 2024), a white supremacist theology that posits white Europeans are the true descendants of the biblical Israelites and that non-whites are lower species, with some adherents believing Jews are descended from Satan (Sharpe, 2000). Bowers posted a verse (John 8:44) commonly associated with CI adherents, as well as a screenshot of a CI Wikipedia entry. While it is unknown if Bowers was a CI believer, his final social media post demonstrates his extreme anti-Semitism, which appeared to have reached a fever pitch. His mention of HIAS refers to the Hebrew Immigrant Aid Society, which is a nonprofit that provides humanitarian aid to refugees: "HIAS likes to bring invaders in that kill our people. I can't sit by and watch my people get slaughtered. Screw your optics, I'm going in" (Amend, 2018).

Dr Richard Rogers, who evaluated Bowers, reported that Bowers truly believed that he was going to be honored with medals and a parade for his actions, viewing them as heroic (Souza & Levenson, 2023). Siddhartha Nadkami, a neurologist who also assessed Bowers, noted that he did not see Jews as human, but described them as "silhouette targets," demonstrating severe dehumanization. These perceptions are consistent with SIT's explanation of how individuals can devalue out-group members and justify violence against them. These delusional beliefs were likely magnified by his mental health issues. Bowers had been involuntarily committed multiple times since adolescence and suffered from schizophrenia. The relationship between Bowers' mental health issues and radicalization demonstrates how mental health conditions can interact with extreme ideologies, increasing the likelihood of violent behavior. This may have also been a factor with James Field Jr.'s case as well, considering he was also diagnosed at a young age with schizophrenia (Kang & Sewall, 2017). The conspiratorial nature of white supremacist narratives about out-groups, and the threat they pose, likely resonated with these attackers' existing paranoia, contributing to the tragic outcome.

Conclusion

This chapter has put the contemporary far-right in context within the historical timeline of right-wing terrorism. The most significant development in recent decades is the transformative impact of the internet. It has become the primary means for extremists to interact, organize, disseminate, and consume information. The rise of the incel movement, as discussed in this chapter, demonstrates how a right-wing subculture can develop online and lead to real-world violence. The group-level dynamics of the far-right are currently most notable in protest violence, while the deadliest attacks appear to be carried out by unaffiliated lone actors who are members of digital communities. The theories and case studies presented illustrate how these individuals can transition from online engagement to violent extremism. With extremists' social lives existing primarily online, it is crucial for counterterrorism efforts to focus on these digital spaces to effectively counter the threat posed by far-right adherents.

References

Al Jazeera. (2022, September 11). *Decades after 9/11, Muslims battle islamophobia in US*. https://www.aljazeera.com/news/2022/9/11/decades-after-9-11-muslims-battle islamophobia-in

Amend, A. (2018, October, 28). *Analyzing a terrorist's social media manifesto: The Pittsburgh synagogue shooter's posts on Gab*. Southern Poverty Law Center. https://www.splcenter.org/hatewatch/2018/10/28/analyzing-terrorists-social-media manifesto-pittsburgh-synagogue-shooters-posts-gab

Anti-Defamation League (ADL). (2018). *Steve Bannon: Five things to know*. Anti-Defamation League. https://www.adl.org/resources/backgrounder/steve-bannon-five-things know?gad_source=1&gclid=CjwKCAjw_Na1BhAlEiwAM dm7L6RTtuxwSV3M4meWKjHvwyVL6CuLBL3zSBMIz5ac5OQOAImCXllBoCHTIQAvD_BwE&gclsrc=aw.ds

Anti-Defamation League (ADL). (2019). *The extremist medicine cabinet: A guide to online "pills."* Anti-Defamation League. https://www.adl.org/resources/blog/extremist medicine-cabinet-guide-online-pills

Anti-Defamation League (ADL). (2022, May 14). *Buffalo shooter's manifesto promotes "great replacement" theory, antisemitism and previous mass shooters*. Anti-Defemation League. https://www.adl.org/resources/blog/buffalo-shooters-manifesto-promotes-great replacement-theory-antisemitism-and-previous-mass-shooters

Anti-Defamation League (ADL). (2024a, March 20). *Men going their own way (MGTOW): What you need to know*. https://www.adl.org/resources/blog/men-going-their-own-way mgtow-what-you-needknow

Anti-Defamation League (ADL). (2024b, July 7). *Backgrounder: Patriot front*. https://www.adl.org/resources/backgrounder/patriot-front

Atkinson, E. & Swann, S. (2023, December 29). Police record rise in religious hate crimes after Israel-gaza war. *BBC News*. https://www.bbc.com/news/uk-67836607

Auger, V. A. (2020). Right-wing terror: A fifth global wave? *Perspectives on Terrorism*, *14*(3). http://www.jstor.org/stable/10.2307/26918302?refreqid=fastly-default

Augustyn, A. (2015). *100 years since the death of Leo Frank*. Encyclopædia Britannica. https://www.britannica.com/story/100-years-since-the-death-of-leo-frank

Baldwin, R. B. (2011, February 9). Baldwin: Local Klan enforced their version of law here. *The Randolph Leader*. https://web.archive.org/web/20190326234155/http://www.therandolphleader.com/opini n/columns/article_d1c0b824-a217-57b5-ad03-509e0fe88125.html

Balleck, B. (2014). *Allegiance to liberty: The changing face of patriots, militias, and Political Violence in America*. Praeger, an imprint of ABC-CLIO, LLC.

Banic, V., & Smith, A. (2017, April 8). A Nazi-linked group was "proud" after Trump aide wore its medal. *NBC News*. https://www.nbcnews.com/news/world/sebastian-gorka-made nazi-linked-vitezi-rend-proud-wearing-its-n742851

Barrouquere, B. (2019, May 17). *White Shadow: David Duke's lasting influence on American white supremacy*. Southern Poverty Law Center. https://www.splcenter.org/hatewatch/2019/05/17/white-shadow-david-dukes-lasting influence-american-white-supremacy

Bates, L. (2021). *Men who hate women: The extremism nobody is talking about*. Simon & Schuster.

BBC. (2018a, April 25). Elliot Rodger: How misogynist killer became "incel hero." *BBC News*. https://www.bbc.com/news/world-us-canada-43892189

BBC. (2018b, November 29). *Charlottesville driver James Alex Fields Jr acted in anger, trial told. https://www.bbc.com/news/world-us-canada-46394995*

BBC. (2023, January 13). Nazi views on the role of the family - life for women and the family in nazi germany - CCEA - GCSE history revision - CCEA - BBC Bitesize. *BBC News*. https://www.bbc.co.uk/bitesize/guides/zxb8msg/revision/1

Berger, P., & Luckmann, T. (1966). *Social construction of reality*. First Anchor Books.

Berger, J. M. (2018). *Extremism*. MIT Press

Berger, J. M. (2019, August 7). The strategy of violent white supremacy is evolving. *The Atlantic*. https://www.theatlantic.com/ideas/archive/2019/08/the-new-strategy-of-violent white-supremacy/595648/

Billig, M., & Tajfel, H. (1973). Social categorization and similarity in intergroup behavior. *European Journal of Social Psychology*, *3*, 27–52.

Borgeson, K., & Bacigalupo, J. (2022). When cyberhate turns to violence. In J. Bacigalupo, K. Borgeson, & R. Valeri (Eds.), *Cyberhate: The far right in the digital age* (p. 119136). Lexington Press.

Brown, D. (2018). Emmett till's mother opened his casket and sparked the civil rights movement. *The Washington Post*. https://www.washingtonpost.com/news/retropolis/wp/2018/07/12/emmett-tills-mother opened-his-casket-and-sparked-the-civil-rights-movement/

Brown, R. (1985). *Social psychology*. Free Press.

Carter, A. J. (2020). *Cumulative extremism: A comparative historical analysis*. Routledge.

Coaston, J. (2019, March 15). The new zealand shooter's manifesto shows how white nationalist rhetoric spreads. *Vox*. https://www.vox.com/identities/2019/3/15/18267163/new zealand-shooting-christchurch-white-nationalism-racism-language

Coleman, L. (2014). *The copycat effect: How the media and popular culture trigger the mayhem in Tomorrow's headlines*. Pocket Books.

Department of Justice (DOJ). (2019, June 28). *Ohio man sentenced to life in prison for federal hate crimes related to August 2017 car attack at rally in Charlottesville, Virginia*. https://www.justice.gov/opa/pr/ohio-man-sentenced-life-prison-federal-hate-crimes related-august-2017-car-attack-rally

Department of Justice (DOJ). (2023, August 2). *Jury recommends sentence of death for Pennsylvania man convicted for tree of life synagogue shooting*. https://www.justice.gov/opa/pr/jury-recommends-sentence-death-pennsylvania-man convicted-tree-life-synagogue-shooting

Dewey, C. (2014). The only guide to Gamergate you will ever need to read - The Washington Post. *Washington Post*. https://www.washingtonpost.com/news/the intersect/wp/2014/10/14/the-only-guide-to-gamergate-you-will-ever-need-to-read/

Diaz, J. (2023, August 2). The charges facing Trump in the Jan. 6 investigation, explained. *NPR*. https://www.npr.org/2023/08/01/1191493880/trump-january-6-charges-indictment count s#:~:text=6%20case%3A%20The%20special%20counsel%20indictment%20expla ned%20%3A%20NPR&text=Donate,Trump%20Jan.,to%20obstruct%20an%20official 20proceeding.

Dongen, T. van. (2021, August 5). *Assessing the threat of covid 19-related extremism in the West*. ICCT. https://www.icct.nl/publication/assessing-threat-covid-19-related extremism-west

Doxsee, C., Jones, S. G., Thompson, J., Hwang, G., & Halstead, K. (2022). *Pushed to extremes: Domestic terrorism and polarization and protest*. Center for Strategic & International Studies. https://www.csis.org/analysis/pushed-extremes-domestic-terrorism-amid polarization-and-protest

Duignan, B. (2024, August 8). *January 6 U.S. capitol attack*. Encyclopædia Britannica. https://www.britannica.com/event/January-6-U-S-Capitol-attack#ref348114

Eatwell, R. (2006). Community cohesion and cumulative extremism in contemporary Britain. *The Political Quarterly*, *77*(2), 205–216.

Egan, N. (n.d.). *The order*. Encyclopædia Britannica. https://www.britannica.com/topic/The Order

EJI. (n.d.). *Jan. 5, 1923: White Mob destroys black community of Rosewood, Florida*. calendar.eji.org. https://calendar.eji.org/racial-injustice/jan/05

Ekins, R., & Freeman, R. (Eds.). (1998). Selected writings: Anna Freud. Penguin Books.

Encyclopædia Britannica, inc. (2024a, July 22). *Conspiracy theories*. Encyclopædia Britannica. https://www.britannica.com/event/assassination-of-Martin-Luther-King-Jr/Conspiracy theories

Encyclopædia Britannica, inc. (2024b, July 22). *The assassination*. Encyclopædia Britannica. https://www.britannica.com/event/assassination-of-Martin-Luther-King-Jr/The assassination#ref339200

Encyclopædia Britannica, inc. (2024c, July 29). *Arab-israeli wars*. Encyclopædia Britannica. https://www.britannica.com/event/Arab-Israeli-wars#ref377011

Encyclopædia Britannica, inc. (2024d, July 29). *Oklahoma City bombing*. Encyclopædia Britannica. https://www.britannica.com/event/Oklahoma-City-bombing

Fattal, I. (2018, October 28). A brief history of anti-semitic violence in America. *The Atlantic*. https://www.theatlantic.com/politics/archive/2018/10/brief-history-anti-semitic-violence america/574228/

Feldberg, M. (n.d.). *Leo Frank*. Jewish Virtual Library. https://www.jewishvirtuallibrary.org/leofrank

Feldstein, Z. (2021, April 28). Henry Ford and antisemitism: The notorious "Dearborn independent." *American Jewish Archives*. https://www.americanjewisharchives.org/snapshots/henry-ford-and-antisemitism-the notorious-dearborn-independent/

Flanagan, A., & Wilson, J. (2022, May 17). *The racist "great replacement" conspiracy theory explained*. Southern Poverty Law Center. https://www.splcenter.org/hatewatch/2022/05/17/racist-great-replacement-conspiracy theory-explained?gad_source=1&gclid=CjwKCAjw_Na1BhAlEiwAM dm7HtgZjahVn4ajx4BiTHFJYrtZKtIFOHpMBgmtIuoCJneyg5bpV3MBxoC1FIQAvD BwE

Follman, M., & Andrews, B. (2015, October 5). How columbine spawned dozens of copycats. *Mother Jones*. https://www.motherjones.com/politics/2015/10/columbine-effect-mass shootings-copycat-data/

Freud, A. (1979). *The ego and the mechanisms of defense*. International University Press.

Freud, S. (1990). *Inhibitions, symptoms and anxiety*. W.W. Norton.

Fryer, R., & Levitt, S. (2007). *Hatred and profits: Getting under the Hood of the Ku Klux Klan*. https://doi.org/10.3386/w13417

Galvan, A., & Kunzelman, M. (2021, May 1). Trump words linked to more hate crime? Some experts think so. *AP News*. https://apnews.com/article/az-state-wire-tx-state-wire-race and-ethnicity-el-paso-caribbean-7d0949974b1648a2bb592cab1f85aa16

Glasstetter, J. (2014, May 24). *Elliot Rodger, Isla Vista shooting suspect, posted racist messages on misogynistic website*. Southern Poverty Law Center. https://www.splcenter.org/hatewatch/2014/05/23/elliot-rodger-isla-vista-shooting suspect-posted-racist-messages-misogynistic-website

Goffman, E. (1959). *Presentation of self in everyday life*. Anchor Publications.

Green, R., Fowler, K., & Palombi, A. (2023). The black pill pipeline: A process-tracing analysis of the incel's continuum of violent radicalization. *Sexualities*, 136346072311695. https://doi.org/10.1177/13634607231169509

Hatfield, E., Cacioppo, J., & Rapson, R. (1993). *Emotional contagion*. Cambridge University Press.

Hermant, N., & Yussuf, A. (2024, April 2). Teachers are quitting due to Andrew Tate's ideology driving sexual harassment and misogyny in class. *ABC News*. https://www.abc.net.au/news/2024-04-02/andrew-tate-effect-in-australian classrooms/103657122

Hoffman, B. (2020, January 12). Incels: America's newest domestic terrorism threat. *Default*. https://www.lawfaremedia.org/article/incels-americas-newest-domestic-terrorism-threat

ISD. (2022). *The "manosphere."* https://www.isdglobal.org/explainers/the-manosphere explainer/

ISD. (2023). *White genocide*. https://www.isdglobal.org/explainers/white-genocide-conspiracy/

Kang, D., & Sewall, D. (2017, August 13). Crash suspect's ex-teacher says he idolized Hitler, Nazism. *Associated Press*. https://apnews.com/article/93d3cba12d134836ae243af285b27eaf

Keating, P., & Assael, S. (2019). *The massacre that spawned the alt-right - politico magazine*. https://www.politico.com/magazine/story/2019/11/03/greensboro-massacre-white nationalism-klan-229873/

Kramer, S. K. (2019, February 20). When Nazis took Manhattan. *NPR*. https://www.npr.org/sections/codeswitch/2019/02/20/695941323/when-nazis-took manhattan

Lederhendler, E. (2017). *American jewry: A new history*. Cambridge University Press.

Lemert, C., & Branaman, A. (Eds.), (1997). *The Goffman reader*. Wiley Blackwell.

Lenz, R. (2017, May 1). The battle for Berkeley: *In the name of freedom of speech, the radical right is circling the ivory tower to ensure a voice for the alt-right*. Southern Poverty Law Center. https://www.splcenter.org/hatewatch/2017/05/01/battle-berkeley-name-freedom speech-radical-right-circling-ivory-tower-ensure-voice-alt

Littler, M., & Feldman, M. (2015). *Annual monitoring, cumulative extremism, and policy implications*. Centre for Fascist, Anti-Fascist and Post-fascist Studies. https://www.tellmamauk.org/wp content/uploads/pdf/Tell%20MAMA%20Reporting%202014-2015.pdf

Manis, J. G., & Meltzer, B. (1972). *Symbolic interaction: A reader in social psychology*. Allyn and Bacon.

Martin, G. (2011). *The Sage encyclopedia of terrorism* (2nd ed.). SAGE Publication.

McLaughlin, E. C., & Park, M. (2018, February 16). Social media paints picture of Racist "professional school shooter." *CNN*. https://edition.cnn.com/2018/02/14/us/nikolas cruz-florida-shooting-suspect/index.html

McWhorter, D. (2013). *Carry me home: Birmingham, Alabama, the climactic battle of the civil rights revolution*. Simon & Schuster.
Merica, D. (2017, August 16). Trump: "both sides" to blame for Charlottesville | CNN politics. *CNN*. https://www.cnn.com/2017/08/15/politics/trump-charlottesville-delay/index.html
Michael, G. (2023). Antifa: Anatomy of a movement. In J. P. Zúquete (Ed.), *The Palgrave handbook of left-wing extremism* (Vol. 2, pp. 19–30). Palgrave Macmillan.
Munn, L. (2019). Alt-right pipeline: Individual journeys to extremism online. *First Monday*. https://doi.org/10.5210/fm.v24i6.10108
Murphy, P. P. (2018, February 18). Exclusive: Group chat messages show school shooter obsessed with race, violence and guns. *CNN*. https://www.cnn.com/2018/02/16/us/exclusive-school-shooter-instagram group/index.html
Niebuhr, G. (1995, April 26). Assault on Waco sect fuels extremists' rage. *The New York Times*. https://www.nytimes.com/1995/04/26/us/terror-in-oklahoma-religion-assault-on-waco sect-fuels-extremists-rage.html
Olson, E. (2020, June 27). Hawaiian shirts, guns and anticipation of war: Who are the "Boogaloo boys"? *ABC News*. https://www.abc.net.au/news/2020-06-28/antifa boogaloo-extremists-at-us-floyd-protests/12388260
Picciolini, C., & Jett, J. (2017). *White American Youth: My descent into America's most violent hate movement -- and how I got out*. Hachette Books.
Rabinowitz, H., & Lybrand, H. (2024, January 6). It may be a long time, if ever, before everyone involved in January 6 is punished. here's why | CNN politics. *CNN*. https://www.cnn.com/2024/01/06/politics/january-6-rioters-justice/index.html
Radford, A. (2024, March 12). Who is Andrew Tate? the self-proclaimed misogynist influencer. *BBC News*. https://www.bbc.com/news/uk-64125045
Ribeiro, M. H., Ottoni, R., West, R., Almeida, V. A., & Meira, W. (2020). *Auditing radicalization pathways on YouTube*. Proceedings of the 2020 Conference on Fairness, Accountability, and Transparency. https://doi.org/10.1145/3351095.3372879
Rogers, K. (2015, June 19). Charleston shooting reignites debate about Confederate Flag. *The New York Times*. https://www.nytimes.com/2015/06/20/us/charleston-shooting reignites-debate-about-confederate-flag.html
Romano, A. (2021, January 28). How a dystopian neo-nazi novel helped fuel decades of white supremacist terrorism. *Vox*. https://www.vox.com/22232779/the-turner-diaries-novel links-to-terrorism-william-luther-pierce
Roose, K. (2019, June 8). The making of a YouTube radical. *The New York Times*. https://www.nytimes.com/interactive/2019/06/08/technology/youtube-radical.html
Ruiz, N. G., Tian, Z., & Im, C. (2023, November 30). 4. Asian Americans and discrimination during the COVID-19 pandemic. *Pew Research Center*. https://www.pewresearch.org/2023/11/30/asian-americans-and-discrimination-during the-covid-19-pandemic/
Scaturro, F. J. (1999). *President grant reconsidered*. Madison Books: Distributed by National Book Network.
Schuster, H. (2005). *An unholy alliance*. CNN. https://www.cnn.com/2005/US/03/29/schuster.column/index.html
Seguin, C., & Rigby, D. (2019). National crimes: A new national data set of lynchings in the United States, 1883 to 1941. *Socius: Sociological Research for a Dynamic World*, *5*, 237802311984178. https://doi.org/10.1177/2378023119841780
Sharpe, T. T. (2000). The identity christian movement: Ideology of domestic terrorism. *Journal of Black Studies*. *30*(4), 604–623.
Southern Poverty Law Center (SPLC). (1998, January 1). *Hate group expert Daniel Levitas discusses posse comitatus, Christian identity movement and more*. https://www.splcenter.org/fighting-hate/intelligence-report/1998/hate-group-expert daniel-levitas-discusses-posse-comitatus-christian-identity-movement-and
Southern Poverty Law Center (SPLC). (2023). *Ku Klux Klan*. https://www.splcenter.org/fighting-hate/extremist-files/ideology/ku-klux-klan
Southern Poverty Law Center (SPLC). (2024). *Louis beam*. https://www.splcenter.org/fighting-hate/extremist-files/individual/louis-beam
Southern Poverty Law Center (SPLC). (n.d.-a). *Stephen Miller*. https://www.splcenter.org/fighting-hate/extremist-files/individual/stephen-miller

Southern Poverty Law Center (SPLC). (n.d.-b). *Stormfront.* https://www.splcenter.org/fighting hate/extremist-files/group/stormfront

Souza, S., & Levenson, E. (2023, June 23). Pittsburgh synagogue gunman was 'blatantly psychotic' and viewed himself as hero, psychologist testifies. *CNN.* https://www.cnn.com/2023/06/28/us/pittsburgh-synagogue-shooter-trial schizophrenia/index.html

Stanford University. (n.d.). *Assassination of Martin Luther King, Jr..* The Martin Luther King, Jr. Research and Education Institute. https://kinginstitute.stanford.edu/assassination-martin lutherkinjr#:~:text=At%206%3A05%20P.M.%20on,deaths%20nationwide%20and%20 xtensve%20property

Stockman, F. (2017, August 14). Who were the counterprotesters on Charlottesville? *The New York Times.* https://www.nytimes.com/2017/08/14/us/who-were-the counterprotesters -incharlottesville.html

Swain, C. M., & Nieli, R. (2010). *Contemporary Voices of white nationalism in America.* Cambridge University Press.

Tajfel, H. (Ed.). (1978). *Differentiation between social groups: Studies in the social psychology of intergroup relations.* Academic Press.

Tajfel, H., Billig, M., Bundy, R. P., & Flament, C. (1971). Social categorization and intergroup behaviour. *European Journal of Social Psychology, 1*, 149–178.

Tajfel, H., & Turner, J. C. (1979). An intergrative theory of intergroup conflict. In W. G. Austin & S. Worchel (Eds.), *The social psychology of intergroup relations* (pp. 33–47). Brooks/Cole.

Taylor, D. B. (2020, May 30). George Floyd protests: A timeline. *The New York Times.* https://www .nytimes.com/article/george-floyd-protests-timeline.html

TIME. (1965, April 9). The various shady lives of the ku klux klan. *Time.* Retrieved 2024, from https://web.archive.org/web/20100514210524/http://www.time.com/time/magazine/artic e/0 ,9171,898581-1,00.html.

TIME. (2017, August 15). *Charlottesville: "Unite the right" rally, state of emergency.* https://time .com/charlottesville-white-nationalist-rally-clashes/

Tulsa Historical Society & Museum. (2022, November 3). *1921 Tulsa Race Massacre.* https://www .tulsahistory.org/exhibit/1921-tulsa-race-massacre/

Tures, J. A. (2016, July 6). General Nathan Bedford forrest versus the ku klux klan. *HuffPost.* https://www.huffpost.com/entry/general-nathan-bedford-fo_b_7734444

Turner, J. C., & Brown, R. J. (1978). Social status, cognitive alternatives and intergroup relations. In H. Tajfel (Ed.), *Differentiation between social groups* (pp. 201–234). Academic Press.

Valeri, R, & Borgeson, K. (2018). *Terrorism in America.* Routledge Press.

van Gerven Oei, V. W. J. (2019, March 15). Anders Breivik: On copying the obscure. *Continent.* https://continentcontinent.cc/archives/issues/issue-1-3-2011/anders-breivik-on-copying the-obscure

Vysotsky, S. (2021). *American antifa: The tactics, culture, and practice of militant antifascism.* Routledge.

Wexler, S., Lewis, J., Mellea, J., & Tyler, M. B. (2024, August). *Christian identity reborn: The evolution and revitalization of an antisemitic ideology.* Program on wxtremism: The George Washington University. https://extremism.gwu.edu/sites/g/files/zaxdzs5746/files/2024-08/christian-identity reborn.pdf

Wilson, J. (2017, August 26). Ruby Ridge, 1992: The day the American militia movement was born. *The Guardian.* https://www.theguardian.com/us-news/2017/aug/26/ruby-ridge 1992-moder n-american-militia-charlottesville

Yelimeli, S., & Mineiro, M. (2015, February 20). *Sheriff releases report detailing events, investigation of 2014 I.V. mass murder: The daily nexus.* The Daily Nexus | The University of California, Santa Barbara's independent, student-run newspaper. https://web.archive.org/web/20210616043022/https://dailynexus.com/2015-02-20/sheriff releases-report-detailing-even ts-of-2014-i-v-mass-murder/

5

THE EVOLUTION OF DOMESTIC JIHADIST TERRORISM

Michael J. Mills

Introduction

In the late morning hours on August 12, 2022, a young man named Hadi Matar made his way into the Chautauqua Institution in Chautauqua, New York. Like others in attendance, Matar was present to see author Salman Rushdie. The event was centered around a discussion of the United States of America being a safe haven for exiled writers and artists. Rushdie himself had been living under the threat of violence since 1988 when a fatwa was issued by Ayatollah Khomeini calling for Rushdie's assassination after the publication of Rushdie's controversial novel, The Satanic Verses. While Rushdie himself had managed to evade various attempts on his life prior to 2022, translators, publishers, and others involved with Rushdie in Italy, Japan, and elsewhere had been targeted for their apparent complicity in blaspheming Islam (Hida & Ives, 2022). By 2022, however, over 30 years had passed since Khomeini's own death, and little had been made of the lingering fatwa in the intervening years. Rushdie himself had opted to live his life as freely as he could to avoid allowing the threat of violence to dictate his movements (Remnick, 2023). Years of inaction on the part of others and an appetite for irony apparently led Matar to take it upon himself to follow-through on the death warrant hanging over Rushdie's head. After entering the venue, Matar identified Rushdie on the stage, hurriedly approached, and before law enforcement could intervene stabbed the author multiple times. After the two were separated, Rushdie was rushed to the hospital and Matar detained until additional law enforcement personnel arrived to take him into custody (Root et al., 2022; Schuessler, 2022). This act not only further compounded the legacy of Rushdie and discussions around political persecution of artists, but also placed Matar within the ever-growing pantheon of individuals who adopt violence as a tactic to promote their religious interpretations.

Instances of Islamic extremist violence were not a particularly unique phenomenon in 1989 when Rushdie drew the ire of Ayatollah Khomeini, and have certainly not become less prevalent in the 35 years since. If anything, the specter of Islamic extremism post-2001 has only grown more omnipresent in the cultural consciousness. Since the late 1960s, instances of religiously motivated extremism have remained one of the foremost concerns within

DOI: 10.4324/9781003375265-8

discussions of terroristic violence broadly. While other forms of extremist violence might pose a more recurring threat (i.e. the rise of white supremacist violence in the 2010s), concerns around religiously motivated extremism and particularly "Jihadist" terrorism have drawn consistent attention. However, while the mainstream discourse revolving around Islamic extremism tends to fixate on the potential for dangers stemming from international sources, some of the most notable instances of Islamic extremism within the United States have boiled up from the domestic space. Actors like Matar, born in California and living in New Jersey at the time of Rushdie's stabbing, bring up questions about why an individual born and raised in the United States might opt to engage in violence in direct antagonism of their adopted home. Prior to Matar, the primary perpetrator of the 2015 San Bernardino shooting, Syed Rizwan Farook, and the perpetrator of the Pulse Nightclub shooting in 2016, Omar Mateen, were individuals born and raised within the United States with some prosocial pursuits prior to their engagement in Jihadist terrorism (Byman, 2017; Fitzpatrick, 2018; C. Lee et al., 2016; Alvarez & Pérez-Peña, 2016). Such instances of domestic extremism have naturally evolved with the rapid expansion of online-based globe-spanning subcultures. Cases like those involving Farook and Mateen, in particular, seem to hinge on the influencing (and potentially motivating) capacity of online sources in their movement into extremism as well as the decision to engage in overt action (Goffard, 2015; Nagourney et al., 2015; Peralta, 2015; Pilkington & Roberts, 2017; Segal, 2016). This indicates a need for a greater understanding of the potential factors leading to a movement by individuals toward extremist violence as well as the kind of mitigating factors that can influence movement toward or away from religious extremism (Burroni, 2018; Conway, 2017; Doxsee et al., 2024; Ghosh et al., 2017; Iannaccone & Berman, 2006; Jenkins, 2017; Lane, 2017; Liebman, 1983; Simons, 2016; Wibisono et al., 2019).

The current chapter is interested in the evolution and ongoing threat posed by Jihadist terrorism. Such a broad focus would prove impractical to shoehorn into a single chapter, however. In order to better capture the scope of "Jihadism" as a threat to domestic security in 2024 and beyond, a three-pronged focus is implemented here. To start, Islamic extremism and the concept of "Jihad" will be explored within the broader historical narrative. This will assist in homing in on the types of patterns in extremist engagement and action that can contextualize the threat of Jihadist terrorism broadly. Jihadist terrorism as a tactic did not spring forth onto the global stage fully formed. Decades of evolution, setbacks and successes, and ingenuity have coalesced into something of note within broader discussions of terrorism and religious extremism. Secondly, space will be afforded for certain theoretical constructs to be explored within this historical context. Looking to concepts like extreme overvalued beliefs and the quest for significance will help in our establishment of the potential motivators and drives toward religiously motivated violence. While exact theoretical explanations for the "why" of extremism are not something that can be grounded in irrevocable fact (particularly within the religious extremist tradition), observing the historical trajectory of Jihadist terrorism using these theoretical framings can assist in conceptualizing the broader problem of domestic Jihadist terrorism in 2024 and beyond. This segues into the final question about how we understand the threat posed by domestic Jihadist terrorism in the evolving decade. Might the past 20 years' worth of external-facing priorities potentially be missing the proverbial forest for the trees? This question seems especially prescient considering the ongoing geopolitical instability and evolving responses to religious extremism and radicalization on the domestic front.

Jihadism as a Tactic

Jihadist terrorism or Jihadism, as a concept, has evolved in the half-century it has been a more pointedly visible tactic in the Western world. Point of fact, "Jihadism" as a term has varied wildly in definition depending on who is doing the defining. The most common definitions fluctuate between a broad and inaccurate assertion that the term means "holy war," or a straightforward promotion of Islam through violence. A slightly more accurate translation of "Jihad" would be an act of struggling or striving toward a higher good, not necessarily through violence (Barlas, 2003; Brachman, 2008; Esposito, 2003; Khosrokhavar, 2015; Maher, 2016). Striving toward a higher good is a core tenet of most world religions in some capacity and, often in the case of Islam, a striving that can take on less militant forms. Such peaceful expressions of religious devotion rarely warrant attention in security studies spaces, however. It is instances where this striving crosses into emphasizing a need to defend Islam and the Islamic community from aggression (real or perceived) through violent retaliation that this struggle becomes cause for concern. This could be where a movement toward "extremism" begins to emerge. Berger's definition of extremism is predicated on the idea that an individual or group moving into extremism has to come to a belief that their success or survival cannot be separated from the overwhelming need for hostile action directed at the out-group (Berger, 2018). Put within the current chapter's context, when an adherent of Islam becomes convinced that the survival of their in-group (adherents of Islam) is threatened by violence from an out-group (non-adherents of Islam), engaging in a mass shooting at a San Bernardino County Department of Public Health Christmas party becomes the only viable option to achieve the desired "higher good" (Fitzpatrick, 2018; C. Lee et al., 2016).

Observing the broad context of Jihadist terrorism, many of the most notable cases seen in the domestic space also involve at least some element of "leakage." Prior to engaging in overt violence, an individual expresses an affinity or, at the very least, an appreciation for the need for some kind of action against the perceived out-group. Would-be extremist actors note, either in private correspondence or public proclamations through social media channels, that something needs to or should be done to offset the harm being done to the in-group (Cohen et al., 2014; Dudenhoefer et al., 2021; Ellis et al., 2016; Rose & Morrison, 2023). Much was made in the wake of the Pulse Nightclub shooting in 2016 when stories of odd or troubling behavior began to surface around Mateen in the event's aftermath. Whether these were grounded in Omar Mateen's lived reality or simply hyperbolized remembrances by former friends and colleagues in the wake of horrific violence is not entirely clear. However, the fact that Mateen expressed frustration at ongoing violence perpetrated against his perceived in-group and, eventually, acted on an apparent drive toward violent reprisal is well established (Alvarez & Pérez-Peña, 2016; Byman, 2017; Greenwald et al., 2019; Pilkington & Roberts, 2017). Following in the previously defined parameters of "extremism," this would seem to indicate the movement from perceived victim of violence to active participant in retaliatory violence could apply at the very least in certain cases of self-styled Jihadist terrorism.

Our current understanding of Jihadist terrorism in 2024 and beyond is best contextualized within the broader history of Islamic extremism. While a discussion could be had regarding the philosophical grounding of "Jihad" within the core tenets of the Islamic faith, an understanding of the tactic within a homeland security context is best begun several centuries after the religion's initial foundation. The social and political upheaval of the late 1960s across the globe led to a variety of lingering outcomes. Tendrils of right- and left-wing extremism can trace some of their earliest roots back to movements either born or reinvigorated in the tumult of the era. Islamic extremism in particular saw a significant evolution in the wake of 1967's Six-Day War when Palestinian militants began to view traditional military engagements as a less amenable tactic. A greater impact could be made if political grievances were brought out of traditional theaters of war and into more visible (civilian) settings (Hoffman, 2007; Moghadam, 2003; Oren, 2003). Palestinian terroristic violence targeting both the Israeli diaspora and those seen as tacitly supporting Israeli interests (most notably, Robert Kennedy in 1968 [Fischbach, 2022]) was a recurring concern throughout the 1970s and into the mid-1980s. This wave of anti-Israeli terrorism in the United States stemmed from a combination of independent actors with only ideological ties to broader extremist groups and more formal organizations like the Black September Organization (Abrahms, 2004; Cooley, 2015; Oakley, 1985; Silke & Filippidou, 2020; Singh, 2015). This, reflecting later evolutions in Jihadist extremism in the 1990s and early 2000s that followed similar trajectories. Some events involving actors independent of any organizational oversight and others more formal terroristic apparatuses with clearly articulated goals and stratagems.

The most notable Jihadist group from this period would be the militant organization spearheaded by Osama Bin Laden, Al-Qaeda. Adopting similar tactics to those of the Palestinian terrorists before them, Al-Qaeda was organized in the mid to late 1980s as a means of combating the ongoing Soviet occupation of Afghanistan. After the Soviet-Afghan war ended in 1989, the focus of Bin Laden and Al-Qaeda began to hone in on the United States (Blanchard, 2010; Burke, 2021). Prior to the attacks on September 11, 2001, the 1993 World Trade Center bombing would prove to be a precursor to the eventual attack that would bring the twin towers down eight years later. This attack also brought the issue of international Jihadist terrorism on a grand scale into stark relief after decades of left and right-wing domestic terrorism pulled the majority of the security focus in the United States. Other international incidents, like the simultaneous attacks on U.S. embassies in Nairobi, Kenya, and Dar es Salaam, Tanzania, in 1998, and the bombing of the USS Cole in 2000, compounded the reputation of Al-Qaeda and the concern that their influence could continue to reach into the domestic front (Gerges, 2011; Gunaratna, 2002). The primary focus of the domestic security apparatus during this period stemmed from concerns around infiltration through porous borders. Instances like what was seen in the failed "borderbomb" plot from Ahmed Ressam in 1999, the failed plot to detonate a bomb in the Port Authority Trans-Hudson tunnel from Assam Hammoud and others in 2006, or the failed Christmas day "underwear bomber" plot from Umar Farouk Abdulmutallab in 2009 (Flynn, 2000; Jenkins, 2017; Jenkins & Trella, 2012; Kilroy et al., 2013; Savage, 2012). A focus on the potential for attacks coming from international spaces via subversion and infiltration remained in spite of the fact that, with certain large-scale exceptions like the 1993 and 2001 attacks on the World Trade Center, most internationally based plots either failed to materialize on the domestic front or were stymied before they could come to fruition.

Some of these operational difficulties could be seen as the result of haphazard or poorly operationalized tactics. However, the heavy emphasis by the United States on rooting out terrorist organizations at their source post-9/11 led to difficulties for Al-Qaeda in effectively getting impactful operations out of the planning stages. As a result, operations in the tradition of the World Trade Center attacks in 1993 and 2001 and the dual embassy bombings in 1998 began to take less precedence over incidents of homegrown domestic Jihadist terrorism. Individuals sympathetic to the core tenets espoused by Al-Qaeda but without formal ties to the organizational apparatus others within the same tradition may have had previously. The culmination in this sea change reached its apparent zenith when, in 2009, multiple instances of domestic Jihadist extremism came to the fore. Plots to attack a synagogue in New York, an Army recruiting office in Little Rock, Arkansas, the Marine Corps training base in Quantico, Virginia, suicide bombings in New York City subways, and Nidal Hasan's attack at Fort Hood in Texas all involved domestic actors with only limited linkages to Al-Qaeda via formal training or online-specific communications (Dao, 2010; Gilmore, 2009; Jenkins, 2017; Poppe, 2018) . An ongoing precedent was thus set going into the 2010s as the latest evolution of Jihadist violence in the United States began to ferment in online channels (Hughes & Meleagrou-Hitchens, 2017; Liang, 2015; McNeal, 2006; Nance & Sampson, 2017; Neumann, 2013; Winter et al., 2020; Zeiger et al., 2015; Zeiger & Gyte, 2020).

Al-Qaeda was not entirely absent from these online channels, but a smaller organization tracing its roots to the earliest days of the Iraqi insurgency in 2004 would eventually supplant the older organization it had once operated in tandem with as the most prominent Jihadist group in the global zeitgeist. The Islamic State, otherwise known as the Islamic State of Iraq and the Levant (ISIL) or the Islamic State of Iraq and Syria (ISIS), debuted under a new name and new organizational modus operandi in 2014. The organization declared itself a caliphate, quickly moved to consolidate territory in Iraq and Syria, and began to undertake actions to establish itself in the global Jihadist ecosystem (Byman, 2015; Gerges, 2014; Harris, 2018; Hashim, 2014; Kirdar, 2011; Weiss & Hassan, 2016; Zelin, 2014). A byproduct of this shift from Al-Qaeda to ISIS as the epicenter of Jihadist terroristic tactics was a move away from the spectacular and large-scale operations preferred by the previous trendsetters, to the more rapid and less rigidly structured tactics popularized by the new generation. These tactics opened the door for even more potential acolytes of a militant brand of Jihadism to pick up the mantle without having to formally engage with leadership or training apparatuses. An individual like Omar Mateen with a sympathy for the work being done by ISIS need not formally engage with anyone in the group. The alternative path Mateen took into radicalization was through online-based extremist propaganda and discourse alongside interactions with other domestic actors going through similar radicalizing processes (Pilkington & Roberts, 2017; Segal, 2016). Conceptualizing and implementing a plan to engage in a mass shooting and swearing allegiance to ISIS during said attack was then enough to warrant posthumous inclusion in the organization's ranks.

As Jihadist tactics continued to shift with the cultural tides during this era, the rapid expansion and diversification of online-based networks and social platforms only compounded the difficulty in crafting an effective response. Cases like that of Ardit Ferizi, (pseudonym: Th3Dir3ctorY), a citizen of Kosovo were a sharp reminder of the dangerous capacity of individuals with a willingness and means to provide direct support to terrorist groups. In the summer of 2016, Ferizi utilized his technical acumen to gain access to a U.S.-based company out of Arizona, culling their database for personally identifiable information of military or government personnel. This information was compiled into a "hit list" of 1,300 persons who could potentially be targeted due to their symbolic value as proxies for the United States government. The hit list was disseminated by notable ISIL hacker Junaid Hussain, who worked closely with Ferizi in the implementation of the operation (Egloff, 2021; Hamid, 2018; Iqbal & Iqbal, 2017). While no known incidents of targeted violence came to fruition in the aftermath of the hit list's publication (and subsequent removal), this case became another in the ongoing discussions around the evolution of Islamic extremist tactics going into the new decade.

As technological limitations decreased leading to an explosion of potential for even the most technologically inhibited terrorist to engage in potential violence alongside the increasing ubiquity of the Internet in day-to-day life, more concerns began to arise regarding the potential "radicalizing" effect online spaces and discourse could wield. Extremist organizations and extreme ideas had been online well before the social media boom (see early adopters like Stormfront.org or the Internet Black Tigers [Denning, 2007; Donovan et al., 2019]), but as more of the world's daily life migrated into predominantly online spaces, Jihadist terrorist operations followed suit. Notable recruiters for ISIS operating on X (née Twitter) were a concern for both their notoriety within the space leading to wider potential influence, but also their capacity to spread propaganda and recruit effectively from a variety of international spaces (Egloff, 2021; Hamid, 2018; Iqbal & Iqbal, 2017).

In the same vein, the online patterns of behavior from Jihadist terrorists came under increasing scrutiny in the aftermath of attacks in an attempt to root out potential warning signs for future incidents. The difficulty in effectively establishing what qualifies as a warning sign, already a difficult delineation in a real-world space, is compounded exponentially by the nature of online communication. An expression of frustration over the marginalization of Muslims in the world does not seem like the kind of sentiment that warrants concern in a vacuum. However, when viewed in hindsight of an event like the 2015 San Bernardino shooting or the 2016 Pulse Nightclub attack, might such expressions take on a more sinister subtext? The efficacy of "recognizing" warning signs in hindsight of extreme violence is already fraught with complications and contradictions due to a variety of factors (Kydd & Walker, 2006; Lankford, 2018; Nowopolski et al., 2018; Phillips & Pohl, 2020; Springer, 2009). Compounding this complication is the devolution of context in many online spaces where a statement can be read divorced entirely from its initial expression. The continued rise of lone-wolf or unaffiliated domestic Jihadist actors post-2009 led to much discourse on the need to recognize the channels and means of online radicalization (Conway, 2017; Neumann, 2013; Correa & Sureka, 2013; Whittaker, 2022). However, not for lack of trying, no firmly established response has proven to be entirely effective at delineating between those who warrant homeland security concern and those who are simply engaging in poor online etiquette.

As the 2020s carry on and online-based Jihadist operations appear poised to remain a concern for the foreseeable future, further evolutions of tactical approaches can be observed. While certain individuals within the online Jihadist space rely on tried and true propagandizing methodologies, others have been noted to adopt the more abstract language of memes to spread their word (Asyari et al., 2023; Farag, 2017; Kala, 2022). A formal definition of meme would be a cultural element or behavioral system that is passed between individuals via imitation or other non-genetic means (Blackmore, 1998; Castaño Díaz, 2013). A less-formal definition would be pictures, phrases, hand gestures, or almost any other visual, audio, or sensory expression that can carry an in-joke or specific meaning to the group it originates from. The malleability of memes as a form of expression makes it nigh impossible to establish a clear-cut "definition" or all-encompassing description of their nature. While the majority of such expressions tend to be innocuous at best, their utility as potential tools for propaganda or recruitment into extremist movements is an oft-repeated concern within the broader security studies literature (Bogerts & Fielitz, 2019; Fisher, 2021; Kingdon, 2021; B. Lee, 2020; Zannettou et al., 2018). Whether such tactics alone have actually led to overt engagement with the planning and operationalization of Jihadist violence against a domestic target still remains to be seen.

In the ongoing struggle to define Jihadism and how it functions within the domestic space, it is paramount to recognize these past and present evolutions. The previous three decades have seen significant shifts in how Jihadism is exercised and the type of individuals undertaking it as a tactic. The one fixture that remains static throughout the decades of change is the recurring goal of each generation of Jihadist terrorists: the promotion and preservation of (their interpretation of) Islam. Religious extremism is not a novel phenomenon in 2024, but reckoning with this evolving threat and how it has come together to reach its current form in the mid-2020s is an important step in understanding our responses to it.

Theories of Extremism

A question all of this naturally dredges up is what kind of factors might be influencing these individuals' movements toward extreme religious violence? Certainly, basic misinterpretation could play a role, but simply writing off extremist actors as "theologically misguided" does not satisfactorily address the underlying logic of such religious expressions. Individuals like Hadi Matar, Syed Rizwan Farook, and Omar Mateen expressed an interpretation of Islam counter to a majority of their fellows, but the factors that led to this contrary interpretation and subsequent violence are the primary concern.

Returning to Berger's previously established definition in this context, there may have been a fear that these individuals' religious expressions were being threatened by an external force and a violent defense of those religious expressions became necessary. Without making speculative inferences about the motivations of now-deceased persons, what might have led to this particular understanding? The phenomenon of an extreme overvalued belief (EOB) is defined as an overwhelming fixation on an idea or belief that dominates the mind of an individual or in-group that is not shared by broader society (Jones & Watson, 1997; Logan, 2014; Overholser, 2018; Rahman, 2018; Rahman et al., 2019; Veale, 2002). This, in theory, could be at least a partial explanation for the motivating factors behind the actions of men like Matar, Mateen, and Farook. All three were convinced of the absolute necessity of violent action to protect the in-group, amplified that belief through engagement with peers of similar ideological bent, and reached a point where the necessity to retaliate against those in the out-group became unavoidable.

A follow-up question to the exploration of extreme overvalued beliefs would be how such belief systems are perpetuated and escalate to the point of being extreme and overvalued in the first place. Some of this could tie back to differential association as would-be extremist actors simply ingratiate themselves within in-groups who overvalue a particular belief to the point of extremity. Or, for proponents of Burgess and Akers' explanation, a process of operant conditioning leads an individual to buy into the tenets of an extreme overvalued belief, which then morphs into a collective over-selling of the importance of that belief (Burgess & Akers, 1966). Qualifying an individual's movement toward radical violence as a simple process of overvaluing a belief and then being conditioned by others within an in-group of fellow over-believers does not necessarily provide the most robust of explanations for movement toward violent extremism, however. Adhering to bad ideas and enjoying the company of others with similar bad ideas is a fairly standard human behavior, all things considered. Jihadist violence, particularly within the domestic space, requires a movement of greater specificity.

Kruglanski's theory of the quest for significance could provide at least an initial framing by which to rationalize such movements. If an individual feels that they have lost some measure of individual significance due to personal or professional failings, social stigmatization, or removal from a preferred in-group (real or perceived), this then might lead to a movement (or quest) toward significance attainment. An engagement with a means quest could manifest initially as a strict devotion to a religious ideal, affiliation with other zealous ideologues, and an eventual justification of the need for more overt action. Looking again at the cases of Farook and Mateen, their individual movements toward Jihadist violence both appeared to take on a more extreme bent over the course of months and years prior to their full submersion in terroristic tactics. Both appeared to be engaging with ideological peers with similar extreme beliefs as well as justifications for the necessity of violence as a tactic prior to their eventual move toward planning and executing their own terrorist actions. Their respective means quests appeared to coincide with a lowering of inhibitions toward violence as a tactic well before either overtly engaged with violence (Dugas & Kruglanski, 2014; Jasko et al., 2017; Kruglanski et al., 2009, 2013, 2015; Kruglanski & Orehek, 2011; Lyons-Padilla et al., 2015; Webber et al., 2017; Webber & Kruglanski, 2018).

If individual significance is not the primary motivating factor, might more grandiose aspirations be relevant? Individual significance could be a secondary concern for some who alternatively find their purpose through the significance gleaned from placement in a broader ideological movement (Jasko et al., 2019; Kruglanski & Orehek, 2011; Kruglanski et al., 2014; Orehek & Vazeou-Nieuwenhuis, 2014; Webber et al., 2017). Farook displayed clear sympathies for ISIL and the broader Jihadist movement, and Mateen overtly acknowledged his ideological support for ISIS and desire to draw attention to their cause (Byman, 2017; Fitzpatrick, 2018; C. Lee et al., 2016; Alvarez & Pérez-Peña, 2016). This indicates, at the very least, an unconscious acknowledgment of their respective placement within the larger pantheon of ideological peers fighting for a similar cause. This "fight" was not a singular act of violence by an individual, but an ongoing war fought by a wide-reaching Jihadist movement. Others within the movement could then pick up where one fallen soldier fell and carry the proverbial baton further. This then provides retroactive weight (or significance) to the actions undertaken by individuals like Farook and Mateen, even if they do not live to see it. This could play into both the gravitas of these actors' self-perceptions (calling back to extreme overvalued beliefs), as well as the additional significance one can attain by placing themselves within such an ideological movement.

Going further with the potential of significance quest theory, it is also worth dissecting the theoretical model proposed by Moghaddam: the staircase to terrorism. According to Moghaddam's theory, an individual's pathway toward violence can be viewed as an escalating sequence of steps (or a staircase). While most individuals will never leave the "ground floor" (those who do not engage with extremist or radical ideations), others make their way up a series of steps toward an acceptance of and a need to engage in extremist violence. This process begins when an individual perceives unfair treatment (or a loss of significance) and instigates a search for a means to counteract this unfairness (*step 1*). Farook and Mateen, alongside others previously mentioned, all expressed some measure of discontent with the treatment of Muslims in the world. The persecution of Muslims is, in itself, not "radicalizing" any more than any other acknowledgment of religious persecution. However, as was seen in the cases of Farook and Mateen, when a means of overcoming the persecution cannot be found, a process of displacing aggression can occur where blame is shifted onto a perceived aggressor (*step 2*). The aggressor in this case was the country Farook and Mateen were born into. Once an aggressor is identified, a process of moral justification begins to occur where whatever actions are taken against this aggressor are ultimately justifiable (*step 3*). If the violence being perpetrated against the in-group is of such a degree that violence in response is necessary, this might eventually lead to a belief that terroristic violence is not only appropriate but necessary (*step 4*). This segues quickly into the final step of Moghaddam's model where an individual circumvents prior psychological inhibitors and engages in violent action against the perceived aggressor or an appropriate proxy (*step 5*) (Moghaddam, 2005; Moghaddam et al., 2013). The proxies in the cases of Farook and Mateen being a San Bernardino County Department of Public Health Christmas party and the Pulse Nightclub, respectively.

Attempting to understand the factors that lead to religious violence both globally and in the domestic space has proven slippery for as long as there has been religious violence (i.e. Since the beginning of recorded history). However, conceptualizing these actors and their movements toward Jihadist terrorism is a necessary part of the ongoing discussions around domestic Jihadist terrorism as simply observing the history of a tactic in a vacuum does not fully capture the scope of such tactics. If we are to understand the threat Jihadist terrorism poses to domestic security going forward, it behooves us to understand its evolution as well as potential explanations for the movements of the individuals leading that evolution.

Jihadist Extremism Moving Forward

If the pattern of Jihadist terrorism over the last 30 years in the domestic space has been one of evolution, it stands to reason that further shifts should be expected. What might those shifts look like? Will the continued proliferation of Jihadist terrorist operations online lead to others like Farook and Mateen sprinting up the staircase toward extreme violence? There is certainly a precedent for online-fueled radicalization pathways leading to real-world violence based on the influx of actors from the extreme right who trace their path toward terroristic violence directly to online spaces (Caiani & Parenti, 2013, 2016; Castle, 2012; Conway, 2017; Futrell, Simi & Gottschalk, 2006). Could a return to decades-old fears of international infiltration see a resurgence in the wake of the ongoing crisis at the Southern border? Just because Ressam, Hammoud, and Abdulmutallab were unsuccessful in their attempts to cross into the United States and detonate a bomb does not mean more technologically savvy Jihadist terrorists cannot overcome the obstacles that flummoxed their predecessors. Or, perhaps more realistically, will we see a continued ebb and flow to what kind of extremist movements demand the most focus in a given era? With twenty years of fixation, domestic Jihadist terrorists may naturally cede ground to a resurgence in other less-religiously inclined extremist movements for a time.

Considering the nigh-omnipresence of online channels of connection, communication, coordination, and collaboration in 2024, it seems highly unlikely that domestic Jihadist terrorism will not continue to have at least some online presence going forward. Ardit Ferizi's collaborator, Junaid Hussain, is not likely to be involved as he ceased playing a role in Jihadist action post-2015, but others with similar technological capacities and extremist sympathies pose a particular threat as more critical infrastructure and individual's personally identifiable information migrates online. Perhaps more simply, the capacity of social media algorithms to supercharge extremist content into the view of sympathetic watchers might help maintain the ranks (official or otherwise) of Jihadist-oriented groups or organizations (Ledwich & Zaitsev, 2019; Schmitt et al., 2018; Whittaker et al., 2021).

Discussions of bad actors carrying tools of violence across unguarded borders is another recurring point of contention within the broader political discourse that is likely to only grow louder as the 2020s approach middle-age (Cinoglu & Altun, 2013; Fratianni & Kang, 2017; Hataley, 2007; Shelley, 2006). While these concerns are not without some merit, they are frequently couched in hyperbolic language or simply fail to account for the realities of domestically based Jihadist terrorism. A group like ISIS does not necessarily need to expend the resources to train, equip, and transport a bomber into the United States if they can prompt a charismatic operative to open an account on X (née Twitter) and recruit an individual sympathetic to their cause already present within the United States to engage in their own training, equipping, and transportation in service of the same end goal. This does not invalidate the need for effective border security, but hyper-fixation on one potential channel where Jihadist terrorism might stem from fails to account for the reality of the threat seen over the last twenty years.

Hadi Matar was not born at the time The Satanic Verses was published and Salman Rushdie became a target of Ayatollah Khomeini's fatwa. In the intervening years, Rushdie would go into hiding for a period, Khomeini would pass away, groups like Al-Qaeda would consolidate influence, and Jihadist terrorist actors would look for in-roads to attack those they felt threatened their in-group. Much of the furor around The Satanic Verses' publication had quieted in the wake of other controversies and concerns by the late 1990s when Matar was born in California. Over the course of the next two decades, Rushdie would become less hidden as the fatwa faded into the past and the face of terrorism on the domestic front shifted. However, even after events like the 2001 World Trade Center attack, the 2009 Fort Hood, 2015 San Bernardino, and 2016 Pulse Nightclub shootings, the fatwa persisted. A shift in focus from the Jihadist terrorism of the mid-2000s to white supremacist and extreme right terrorism led to further distance between the concerns of 1989 and this new era. However, for reasons that are still not entirely clear, Matar, an individual with no apparent prior connection to Rushdie, chose to target the author for his offenses against the perpetrator's in-group. This case serves as a grim reminder that even if the flow of extremism has shifted elsewhere in recent years, the continued reality of Jihadist terrorism is not likely to quietly slip into the annals of history.

References

Abrahms, M. (2004). Are terrorists really rational? The Palestinian example. *Orbis (Philadelphia)*, *48*(3), 533–549.

Alvarez, L., & Pérez-Peña, R. (2016, June 12). Orlando Gunman attacks gay nightclub, leaving 50 dead. *The New York Times.* https://www.nytimes.com/2016/06/13/us/orlando- nightclub -shooting.html
Asyari, A., Jumarim, J., & Kadri, K. (2023). The battle between moderate and fundamentalist Islamic groups in covid-19 memes on social media. *Jurnal Penelitian Keislaman, 19*(2), 142–158.
Barlas, A. (2003). Jihad, holy war, and terrorism: The politics of conflation and denial. *American Journal of Islam and Society, 20*(1), 46–62.
Berger, J. M. (2018). *Extremism.* Mit Press.
Blackmore, S. (1998). Imitation and the definition of a meme. *Journal of Memetics-Evolutionary Models of Information Transmission, 2*(11), 159–170.
Blanchard, C. M. (2010). Al Qaeda: Statements and evolving ideology. *Al-Qaeda: An Organization To Be Reckoned With*, 11–28. Diane publishing.
Bogerts, L. & Fielitz, M. (2019). "Do You Want Meme War?" Understanding the Visual Memes of the German Far Right. In M. Fielitz & N. Thurston (Ed.), *Post-Digital Cultures of the Far Right: Online Actions and Offline Consequences in Europe and the US* (pp. 137–154). Bielefeld: transcript Verlag.
Brachman, J. M. (2008). *Global jihadism: Theory and practice.* Routledge.
Burgess, R. L., & Akers, R. L. (1966). A differential association-reinforcement theory of criminal behavior. *Social Problems, 14*, 128.
Burke, P. (2021). Al-Qaeda. In P. Burke & S. Miller (Eds.), Global jihadist terrorism (pp. 10–35). Edward Elgar Publishing.
Burroni, M. R. (2018). *The homegrown Jihadi terrorist: The threat of ISIS-inspired radicalization in the United States* (Doctoral dissertation). Naval Postgraduate School, Monterey, CA.
Byman, D. (2015). Terrorism in Africa: The imminent threat to the United States. *Prepared Testimony before the Subcommittee on Counterterrorism and Intelligence of the House Committee on Homeland Security, 29.* (pp. 1–18).
Byman, D. (2017). How to hunt a lone wolf: Countering terrorists who act on their own. *Foreign Affairs, 96*, 96–105.
Caiani, M., & Parenti, L. (2013). Extreme right organizations and online politics: A comparative analysis of five western democracies. In P. G. Nixon, R. Rawal, & D. Mercea (Eds.), *Politics and the internet in comparative context* (pp. 135–153). Routledge.
Caiani, M., & Parenti, L. (2016). *European and American extreme right groups and the internet.* Routledge. https://doi.org/10.4324/9781315580845
Castaño Díaz, C. M. (2013). Defining and characterizing the concept of Internet Meme. *Ces Psicología, 6*(2), 82–104.
Castle, T. (2012). Morrigan rising: Exploring female-targeted propaganda on hate group websites. *European Journal of Cultural Studies, 15*(6), 679–694. https://doi.org/10.1177/1367549412450636
Cinoglu, H., & Altun, N. (2013). Terrorism, international migration and border control. *European Scientific Journal, 9*(20), 100–114.
Cohen, K., Johansson, F., Kaati, L., & Mork, J. C. (2014). Detecting linguistic markers for radical violence in social media. *Terrorism and Political Violence, 26*(1), 246–256.
Conway, M. (2017). Determining the role of the internet in violent extremism and terrorism: Six suggestions for progressing research. *Studies in Conflict & Terrorism, 40*(1), 77–98. https://doi.org/10.1080/1057610X.2016.1157408
Cooley, J. K. (2015). *Green March, Black September (RLE Israel and Palestine): The story of the palestinian arabs.* Routledge.
Correa, D., & Sureka, A. (2013). Solutions to detect and analyze online radicalization: A survey. *arXiv preprint arXiv:1301.4916.*
Dao, J. (2010, February 17). A Muslim son, a murder trial, and many questions. *The New York Times.* https://www.nytimes.com/2010/02/17/us/17convert.html
Denning, D. E. (2007). A view of cyberterrorism five years later. In K. Himma (Ed.), Internet security: Hacking, counterhacking, and society (pp. 123–140). Jones and Bartlett Publishers.
Donovan, J., Lewis, B., & Friedberg, B. (2019). Parallel ports: Sociotechnical change from the alt-right to alt-tech. In M. Fielitz & N. Thurston (Eds.), Post-digital cultures of the far right: Online actions and offline consequences in Europe and the US (pp. 49–65). transcript Verlag.

Doxsee, C., Palmer, A., & McCabe, R. (2024, February 8). *The global terrorism threat assessment 2024*. Center for Strategic and International Studies. https://csis-website- prod.s3.amazonaws.com/s3fs-public/2024-02/240208_Doxsee_Global_Terrorism.pdf?VersionId=yNcjxwHMs48w8NFB0EMnpbA2OToZaPs7

Dudenhoefer, A. L., Niesse, C., Görgen, T., Tampe, L., Megler, M., Gröpler, C., & Bondü, R. (2021). Leaking in terrorist attacks: A review. *Aggression and Violent Behavior*, *58*, 101582.

Dugas, M., & Kruglanski, A. W. (2014). The quest for significance model of radicalization: Implications for the management of terrorist detainees: Significance quest and the management of terrorists. *Behavioral Sciences & the Law*, *32*(3), 423–439. https://doi.org/10.1002/bsl.2122

Egloff, F. J. (2021). Intentions and cyberterrorism. In P. Cornish (Ed.), The Oxford handbook of cyber security (pp. 187–200). Oxford University Press.

Ellis, C., Pantucci, R., de Roy van Zuijdewijn, J., Bakker, E., Smith, M., Gomis, B., & Palombi, S. (2016). Analysing the processes of lone-actor terrorism: research findings. *Perspectives on Terrorism*, 10(2), 33–41.

Esposito, J. L. (2003). *Unholy war: Terror in the name of Islam*. Oxford University Press.

Farag, D. (2017). From Tweeter to terrorist: Combatting online propaganda when Jihad goes viral. *American Criminal Law Review*, *54*, 843.

Fischbach, M. R. (2022). Sirhan Sirhan and the assassination of Robert F. Kennedy: Palestinian rage and the depoliticization of a tragedy. *The Middle East Journal*, *76*(2), 245–264.

Fisher, M. (2021, April 30). From memes to race war: How extremists use popular culture to lure recruits. *Washington Post*. https://www.washingtonpost.com/nation/2021/04/30/extremists-recruiting-culture-community/

Fitzpatrick, T. M. (2018). Global radicalization and the San Bernardino Attack. Evolving extremist US domestic threat. *International Relations and Diplomacy*, *6*(9), 500–506.

Flynn, S. E. (2000). Beyond border control. *Foreign Affairs*, *79*(6), 57–68. https://doi.org/10.2307/20049967

Fratianni, M., & Kang, H. (2017). Borders and international terrorism. In J. J. Kirton (Ed.), New perspectives on global governance (pp. 119–135). Routledge.

Futrell, R., & Simi, P. (2004). Free spaces, collective identity, and the persistence of US White power activism. *Social Problems*, *51*(1), 16–42.

Futrell, R., Simi, P., & Gottschalk, S. (2006). Understanding music in movements: The white power music scene. *The Sociological Quarterly*, 47(2), 275-304.

Gerges, F. A. (2011). *The rise and fall of Al-Qaeda*. Oxford University Press.

Gerges, F. A. (2014). ISIS and the third wave of Jihadism. *Current History*, *113*(767), 339–343.

Ghosh, R., Chan, W. A., Manuel, A., & Dilimulati, M. (2017). Can education counter violent religious extremism?. *Canadian Foreign Policy Journal*, *23*(2), 117–133.

Gilmore, G. J. (2009, September 25). FBI, navy foiled alleged terror plot on quantico. *US Department of Defense News*.

Goffard, C. (2015, December 5). They met online, built a life in San Bernardino — and silently planned a massacre. *Los Angeles Times*. https://graphics.latimes.com/san-bernardino- syed-farook-tashfeen-malik/

Greenwald, G., Hussain, M., & Greenwald, G. (2019, May 28). As the trial of omar mateen's wife begins, new evidence undermines beliefs about the pulse massacre, including motive. *The Intercept*. https://theintercept.com/2018/03/05/as-the-trial-of-omar-mateens-wife-begins-new-evidence-undermines-beliefs-about-the-pulse-massacre-including-motive/

Gunaratna, R. (2002). *Inside Al Qaeda: global network of terror*. Columbia University Press.

Hamid, N. (2018). The British hacker who became the Islamic state's chief terror cybercoach: A profile of Junaid Hussain. *CTC Sentinel*, *11*(4), 30–37.

Harris, L. G., & US Army Command and General Staff College Fort Leavenworth United States. (2018). ISIS vs. Al Qaeda: An ideological comparison. *School of Advanced Military Studies*. (Tech report).

Hashim, A. S. (2014). The Islamic state: From al-Qaeda affiliate to caliphate. *Middle East Policy*, *21*(4), 69–83.

Hataley, T. (2007). Catastrophic terrorism at the border: The case of the Canada-United States border. *Homeland Security Affairs*, *1*, 1–27.

Hida, H., & Ives, M. (2022, August 14). Salman Rushdie attack recalls murder of his Japanese translator. *The New York Times*. https://www.nytimes.com/2022/08/13/world/asia/ rushdie-attack-japanese-translator.html

Hoffman, B. (2007). Terrorism in history. *Journal of Conflict Studies*, *27*(2), 8–28.
Hughes, S., & Meleagrou-Hitchens, A. (2017). The threat to the United States from the Islamic State's virtual entrepreneurs. *CTC Sentinel*, *10*(3), 1–8.
Iannaccone, L. R., & Berman, E. (2006). Religious extremism: The good, the bad, and the deadly. *Public Choice*, *128*, 109–129.
Iqbal, Z., & Iqbal, K. (2017). Cyber terrorism: A case study of islamic state. *Journal of Social Sciences and Humanities*, *56*(2), 67–79.
Jasko, K., LaFree, G., & Kruglanski, A. (2017). Quest for significance and violent extremism: The case of domestic radicalization: Quest for significance and violent extremism. *Political Psychology*, *38*(5), 815–831. https://doi.org/10.1111/pops.12376
Jasko, K., Webber, D., Kruglanski, A., Gelfand, M., Taufiqurrohman, M., Hettiarachchi, M., & Gunaratna, R. (2019). Social context moderates the effects of quest for significance on violent extremism. *Journal of Personality and Social Psychology*, *118*. https://doi.org/10.1037/pspi0000198
Jenkins, B. M. (2017). *The origins of America's Jihadists* (p. 99). Rand Coporation.
Jenkins, B. M., & Trella, J. (2012). *Carnage interrupted: An analysis of fifteen terrorist plots against public surface transportation.* (No. CA-MTI-12-2979). Mineta Transportation Institute.
Jones, E., & Watson, J. P. (1997). Delusion, the overvalued idea and religious beliefs: A comparative analysis of their characteristics. *The British Journal of Psychiatry*, *170*, 6.
Kala, G. (2022). *Internet memes as instruments of subversion in the context of Islam and Muslims* (Doctoral dissertation). University of Westminster.
Khosrokhavar, F. (2015). *Inside jihadism: Understanding jihadi movements worldwide*. Routledge.
Kingdon, A. (2021). The meme is the method: Examining the power of the image within extremist propaganda. In A. Lavorgna & T. J. Holt (Eds.), Researching cybercrimes (pp. 301–322). Palgrave Macmillan.
Kirdar, M. J. (2011, June). *Al Qaeda in Iraq. Case study, 1.* Center for Strategic and International Studies. https://csis-website-prod.s3.amazonaws.com/s3fs-public/legacy_files/files/ publication/110614_Kirdar_AlQaedaIraq_Web.pdf
Kilroy, R. J., Sumano, A. R., & Hataley, T. S. (2013). *North American regional security: A trilateral framework?.* Lynne Rienner Publishers.
Kruglanski, A. W., Bélanger, J. J., Gelfand, M., Gunaratna, R., Hettiarachchi, M., Reinares, F., Orehek, E., Sasota, J., & Sharvit, K. (2013). Terrorism—A (self) love story: Redirecting the significance quest can end violence. *American Psychologist*, *68*(7), 559–575. https://doi.org/10.1037/a0032615
Kruglanski, A. W., Chen, X., Dechesne, M., Fishman, S., & Orehek, E. (2009). Fully committed: Suicide bombers' motivation and the quest for personal significance: Significance quest and suicide terrorism. *Political Psychology*, *30*(3), 331–357. https://doi.org/10.1111/j.1467-9221.2009.00698.x
Kruglanski, A. W., Gelfand, M. J., Bélanger, J. J., Hetiarachchi, M., & Gunaratna, R. (2015). Significance quest theory as the driver of radicalization towards terrorism. In J. Jerard & S. M. Nasir (Eds.), Resilience and resolve: Communities against terrorism (pp. 17–30).
Kruglanski, A. W., Gelfand, M. J., Bélanger, J. J., Sheveland, A., Hetiarachchi, M., & Gunaratna, R. (2014). The psychology of radicalization and deradicalization: How significance quest impacts violent extremism: Processes of radicalization and deradicalization. *Political Psychology*, *35*, 69–93. https://doi.org/10.1111/pops.12163
Kruglanski, A. W., & Orehek, E. (2011). The role of the quest for personal significance in motivating terrorism. In J. P. Forgas, A. W. Kruglanski, & K. D. Williams (Eds.), The psychology of social conflict and aggression (pp. 153–166). Psychology Press.
Kydd, A. H., & Walter, B. F. (2006). The strategies of terrorism. *International Security*, *31*(1), 49–80. http://www.jstor.org/stable/4137539
Lane, J. E. (2017). Can we predict religious extremism?. *Religion, Brain & Behavior*, 7(4), 299–304.
Lankford, A. (2018). Identifying potential mass shooters and suicide terrorists with warning signs of suicide, perceived victimization, and desires for attention or fame. *Journal of Personality Assessment*, *100*(5), 471–482.
Ledwich, M., & Zaitsev, A. (2019). Algorithmic extremism: Examining YouTube's rabbit hole of radicalization. *arXiv preprint arXiv:1912.11211*.

Lee, B. (2020). 'Neo-nazis have stolen our memes': Making sense of extreme memes. In M. Littler & B. Lee (Eds.), Digital extremisms: Readings in violence, radicalisation and extremism in the online space (pp. 91–108). Springer International Publishing.
Lee, C., Walters, E., Borger, R., Clem, K., Fenati, G., Kiemeney, M., Seng, S., Yuen, H., Neeki, M., & Smith, D. (2016). The San Bernardino, California, terror attack: Two emergency departments' response. *Western Journal of Emergency Medicine*, *17*(1), 1.
Liang, C. S. (2015). Cyber Jihad: Understanding and countering Islamic State propaganda. *GSCP Policy Paper*, *2*(4), 6.
Liebman, C. S. (1983). Extremism as a religious norm. *Journal for the Scientific Study of Religion*, *22*(1), 75–86.
Logan, M. H. (2014). Lone wolf killers: A perspective on overvalued ideas. *Violence and Gender*, *1*(4), 159–160. https://doi.org/10.1089/vio.2014.0036
Lyons-Padilla, S., Gelfand, M. J., Mirahmadi, H., Farooq, M., & van Egmond, M. (2015). Belonging nowhere: Marginalization & radicalization risk among Muslim immigrants. *Behavioral Science & Policy*, *1*(2), 1–12. https://doi.org/10.1353/bsp.2015.0019
Maher, S. (2016). *Salafi-Jihadism: The history of an idea*. Oxford University Press.
McNeal, G. S. (2006). Cyber embargo: Countering the internet jihad. *Case Western Reserve Journal of International Law*, *39*, 789.
Moghadam, A. (2003). Palestinian suicide terrorism in the second intifada: Motivations and organizational aspects. *Studies in Conflict and Terrorism*, *26*(2), 65–92.
Moghaddam, F. M. (2005). The staircase to terrorism: A psychological exploration. *American Psychologist*, *60*(2), 161–169. https://doi.org/10.1037/0003-066X.60.2.161
Moghaddam, F. M., Warren, Z., & Love, K. (2013). Religion and the staircase to terrorism. In R. F. Paloutzian & C. L. Park (Eds.), Handbook of the psychology of religion and spirituality (pp. 632–648). The Guilford Press.
Nagourney, A., Lovett, I., Turkewitz, J., & Mueller, B. (2015, December 8). Couple kept tight lid on plans for San Bernardino shooting. *The New York Times*. https://www.nytimes.com/ 2015/12/04/us/san-bernardino-shooting-syed-rizwan-farook.html
Nance, M., & Sampson, C. (2017). *Hacking ISIS: How to destroy the cyber jihad*. Simon and Schuster.
Neumann, P. R. (2013). Options and strategies for countering online radicalization in the United States. *Studies in Conflict & Terrorism*, *36*(6), 431–459.
Nowopolski, M., BaNasik, M., & Gierowski, J. K. (2018). Warning behaviours and risk factors preceding acts of individual terrorism. *Problems of Forensic Sciences*, *116*, 323–338.
Oakley, R. B., & United States Department of State, Office of Public Communication, Editorial Division. (1985). Terrorism: Overview and developments. U.S. Department of State, Bureau of Public Affairs, Office of Public Communication, Editorial Division.
Orehek, E., & Vazeou-Nieuwenhuis, A. (2014). Understanding the terrorist threat: Policy implications of a motivational account of terrorism. *Policy Insights from the Behavioral and Brain Sciences*, *1*(1), 248–255. https://doi.org/10.1177/2372732214549747
Oren, M. B. (2003). *Six days of war: June 1967 and the making of the modern Middle East*. Presidio Press.
Overholser, J. C. (2018). From puddles to potholes: The role of overvalued beliefs in emotional problems. *Journal of Contemporary Psychotherapy*, *48*(1), 41–50. https://doi.org/10.1007/s10879-017-9364-9
Peralta, E. (2015, December 9). San Bernardino attackers were radicalized before meeting, FBI director says. *NPR*. https://www.npr.org/sections/thetwo-way/2015/12/09/459074323/ san-bernardino-attackers-were-radicalized-before-meeting-fbi-director-says
Phillips, P. J., & Pohl, G. (2020). How terrorism red flags become weak signals through the processes of judgement and evaluation. *Journal of Police and Criminal Psychology*, *35*, 377–388.
Pilkington, E., & Roberts, D. (2017, November 28). FBI and Obama confirm Omar Mateen was radicalized on the internet. *The Guardian*. https://www.theguardian.com/us-news/ 2016/jun/13/pulse-nightclub-attack-shooter-radicalized-internet-orlando
Poppe, K. (2018). *Nidal Hasan: A case study in lone-actor terrorism*. George Washington University.
Rahman, T. (2018). Extreme overvalued beliefs: How violent extremist beliefs become "normalized." *Behavioral Sciences*, *8*(1), 10.

Rahman, T., Meloy, J. R., & Bauer, R. (2019). Extreme overvalued belief and the legacy of carl wernicke. *The Journal of the American Academy of Psychiatry and the Law*, *47*(2), 8.

Remnick, D. (2023, February 6). The defiance of Salman Rushdie. *The New Yorker*. https://www.newyorker.com/magazine/2023/02/13/salman-rushdie-recovery-victory-city

Root, J., Gelles, D., Harris, E. A., & Jacobs, J. (2022, August 13). Salman Rushdie is attacked onstage in Western New York. *The New York Times*. https://www.nytimes.com/2022/ 08/12/nyregion/salman-rushdie-attacked.html

Rose, M. M., & Morrison, J. (2023). An exploratory analysis of leakage warning behavior in lone-actor terrorists. *Behavioral Sciences of Terrorism and Political Aggression*, *15*(2), 179–214.

Savage, C. (2012, February 11). Nigerian's bomb plot detailed in court filings. *The New York Times*. https://www.nytimes.com/2012/02/11/us/underwear-bomb-plot-detailed-in-court-filings.html

Schmitt, J. B., Rieger, D., Rutkowski, O., & Ernst, J. (2018). Counter-messages as prevention or promotion of extremism?! The potential role of YouTube: Recommendation algorithms. *Journal of Communication*, *68*(4), 780–808.

Schuessler, J. (2022, August 16). The stabbing of Salman Rushdie renews free speech debates. *The New York Times*. https://www.nytimes.com/2022/08/15/arts/salman-rushdie-free- speech.html

Segal, O. (2016, June 15). The Orlando shooter's many paths to violence. *Anti-Defamation League*. https://www.adl.org/resources/blog/orlando-shooters-many-paths-violence

Shelley, L. (2006). Border issues: Transnational crime and terrorism. In M. Caparini & O. Marenin (Eds.), Borders and security governance: Managing borders in a globalised world (pp. 255–269). LIT Verlag Münster.

Silke, A., & Filippidou, A. (2020). What drives terrorist innovation? Lessons from Black September and Munich 1972. *Security Journal*, *33*, 210–227.

Simons, G. (2016). Islamic extremism and the war for hearts and minds. *Global Affairs*, *2*(1), 91–99.

Singh, S. (2015). Black September: A turning point in the Palestinian national movement. *International Journal of Applied Social Science*, *2*(5/6), 135–145.

Springer, N. R. (2009). *Patterns of radicalization indentifying the markers and warning signs of domestic lone wolf terrorists in our midst* (Doctoral dissertation). Naval Postgraduate School, Monterey, CA.

Veale, D. (2002). Over-valued ideas: A conceptual analysis. *Behaviour Research and Therapy*, *40*(4), 383–400. https://doi.org/10.1016/S0005-7967(01)00016-X

Webber, D., Klein, K., Kruglanski, A., Brizi, A., & Merari, A. (2017). Divergent paths to martyrdom and significance among suicide attackers. *Terrorism and Political Violence*, *29*(5), 852–874. https://doi.org/10.1080/09546553.2015.1075979

Webber, D., & Kruglanski, A. W. (2018). The social psychological makings of a terrorist. *Current Opinion in Psychology*, *19*, 131–134. https://doi.org/10.1016/j.copsyc.2017.03.024

Weiss, M., & Hassan, H. (2016). *ISIS: Inside the* army *of* terror (updated ed.). Simon and Schuster.

Whittaker, J. (2022). Rethinking online radicalization. *Perspectives on Terrorism*, *16*(4), 27–40.

Whittaker, J., Looney, S., Reed, A., & Votta, F. (2021). Recommender systems and the amplification of extremist content. Internet Policy Review, 10(2).

Wibisono, S., Louis, W. R., & Jetten, J. (2019). A multidimensional analysis of religious extremism. *Frontiers in Psychology*, *10*, 2560.

Winter, C., Neumann, P., Meleagrou-Hitchens, A., Ranstorp, M., Vidino, L., & Fürst, J. (2020). Online extremism: research trends in internet activism, radicalization, and counter-strategies. *International Journal of Conflict and Violence (IJCV)*, *14*, 1–20.

Zannettou, S., Caulfield, T., Blackburn, J., De Cristofaro, E., Sirivianos, M., Stringhini, G., & Suarez-Tangil, G. (2018, October). On the origins of memes by means of fringe web communities. In Proceedings of the Internet Measurement Conference 2018 (pp. 188–202). Association for Computing Machinery.

Zeiger, S., Aly, A., Neumann, P. R., El Said, H., Zeuthen, M., Romaniuk, P., Omelicheva, M. Y., Ellis, J. O., Schmid, A. P., Lucas, K., & Samuel, T. K. (2015). *Countering violent extremism: Developing an evidence-base for policy and practice*. Curtin University, Perth, Western Australia.

Zeiger, S., & Gyte, J. (2020). *Prevention of radicalization on social media and the internet*. International Centre for Counter-Terrorism (ICCT).

Zelin, A. Y. (2014). The war between ISIS and al-Qaeda for supremacy of the global jihadist movement. *The Washington Institute for Near East Policy*, *20*(1), 1–11.

PART III

The New Phase of International Terrorism

6

TERROR GROUPS IN SUB-SAHARAN AFRICA

Binneh Minteh and Ashlie Perry Banerjee

Background of Terror Groups in Sub-Saharan Africa

Since the emergence of Boko Haram as a formidable local terrorist group in the West African state of Nigeria, its operational dynamism has brought to light one of the most daunting challenges for regional and global security professionals. The effectiveness of its operations and capabilities to operate and hit targets in a country duped as one of Africa's security powerhouses remains to be a security challenge for counterterrorism operations. Amid a wanton trail of bombings, kidnappings, and assassinations, several variations around the group's ideology, strategies, techniques, and linkages emerged over the years. While many scholars are of the view that Boko Haram and its affiliate organizations have only local agendas, many others opine it has deeply rooted ties to mainstream terrorist organizations on the global stage.

With the emergence of Sub-Saharan Africa as the new front for operatives defeated in Afghanistan, Iraq, and Syria the power and influence of these groups are evident from their operations in Mali, Nigeria, Niger, Libya, Ivory Coast, Burkina Faso, and Benin. Al-Qaeda in the Maghreb (AQIM) is operating in splinter groups, linking it to groups battling international forces in Northern Mali, Niger, Burkina Faso, Ivory Coast, and Benin. And Al-Shabab continues to pose one of the most complex security dilemmas for the East African peninsula.

Many of the terrorist groups in this chapter are rooted in the concept of the "global jihad." As discussed in other chapters, many of these groups claim that their interpretation of jihad is linked to Islam's more classical roots. Generally, there are four recognized Sunni jurisprudence or schools of thought: Maliki (jurist Malik Ibn Anas jurist), Hafani (jurist Muhammed al-Sahybani), Shafi'i (jurist al-Shafi'i), and Hanbali (jurist Ibn Qudama) schools (Toutounji, 2017). However, Islamic jihadists in Sub-Saharan Africa subscribe more to the modern ideologies of "jihad," specifically those ideologies rooted in defensive jihad, like that of Sayyid Qutb and Mohammed ibn Abdul Wahhab.

Mohammed ibn Abdul Wahhab led the 18th-century purification movement and favored a militant application of Islam. This form of Islam, this Wahhabism, took root in the then

DOI: 10.4324/9781003375265-10

"Arabia" which advocated for a puritanical sect of Islam. Sayyid Qutb had written bodies of work around the idea of armed struggle against the Egyptian regime. His works are at the root of many Sunni jihadist groups, ranging from Al-Qaeda to Hamas. Many of the groups discussed in this chapter have ideologies rooted in the teachings of these two Islamic scholars and their interpretation of jihad.

Al-Shabab—East Africa

Al-Shabab or "The Youth" is an Al-Qaeda-linked Wahhabi—jihadist militant group and U.S.-designated Foreign Terrorist Organization (FTO) that emerged in Somalia in 2006 after the collapse of the Union of Islamic Courts in Somalia. The group was a breakaway military wing of the Islamic Courts Union (ICU) with origins rooted in support for global jihadism and strict interpretation of Sharia Law.

The group is a powerful force capable of mobilizing Somalis and feeding the population with nationalist sentiments and grievances. It has an estimated membership of over 7,000 fighters, including 300 of its most ideologically radicalized members holding positions of importance (Abdulkadir, 2012). Al-Shabab recruits young men through its financial security network, sometimes through force and through propaganda methods. The group's recruiting process is quite appealing to young Muslims beyond Somali borders. It is estimated that "at least 20 young American men have been enlisted by Al-Shabab with one of the recruits, Shirwa Ahmed, becoming one of its first suicide bombers in October 2008" (Abdulkadir, 2012).

The aim of the group is the creation of a Fundamentalist Islamic State in Somalia with significant influence in the region. By 2007, Al-Shabab had gained control of southern Somalia and parts of Puntland and Somaliland, and as it gained power, it began building a formidable army with recruits from the United States, Canada, and East Africa (Abdulkadir, 2012). The operation of the group is mainly centered within Somalia. However, recent activities and capabilities show the group operating in neighboring countries, including coordinated attacks in the Ugandan capital, Kampala, in 2010, and a deadly raid on the Westgate shopping mall in Nairobi, Kenya, in 2013.

The spiritual leader of the group is Sheikh Hassan Dahir Aweys, who fought against Ethiopia as a colonel in the Siad Barre regime in the 1970s. In 2006, Aweys handed operational command of Al-Shabab to a young Somali jihadi, Aden Hashi Ayro, who was killed in a U.S. missile strike in May 2008. Ayro had links to an Islamic movement called Al Ittihad Al Islamiya (AIAI) that disbanded in 1997 and then later joined the ICU. His time in the organization gained Ayro and others, the opportunity to loosely create Al Shabaab as a military-like wing of the ICU (Stanford, 2019).

Ayro's death in 2008 began a violent retaliation by Al Shabaab, focusing many of its attacks on foreign presences in Somalia, like United Nations workers/peacekeepers and United States troops. Following the death of Ayro, Ahmed Abdi Godane, known as Abu Zubayr, one of Al-Shabab's founders, served as the group's top commander. He was designated a global terrorist by the United States in November 2008.

In July of 2010, the group launched its first attack outside of Somalia's borders when a suicide bomber attacked a restaurant in Uganda during the final FIFA World Cup match, killing 74 people. As the group lost more territory in Somalia, it amplified its attacks against unarmed civilians and security personnel. In 2011, the group engaged in a four-day siege at Kenya's Westgate mall. The attack garnered international attention but left 68 people killed. Another attack that gained international attention included the 2015 Garissa University College attack that also took place in Kenya. The group went through the college, attacking non-Muslims and other civilians. If the Al-Shabaab militants encountered someone and they could not cite the Koran, the person was killed. The Garissa University College attack left more than 147 students, faculty, and staff dead (Stanford, 2019).

In September 2014, the U.S. Department of Defense confirmed that Ahmed Godane, the then-leader of Al-Shabaab, was killed as a result of a U.S. military targeted airstrike in Somalia. The death of Godane is thought to be the reason behind the group's fragmentation, with sub-groups forming within the organization. Attacks by the group continued in 2016 and 2017, with attacks occurring in crowded, high-visibility places, and against civilians and military personnel. The African Union Mission to Somalia (AMISOM) base in Kenya was attacked by the group in January of 2016, leading to over 100 soldiers' deaths. This was one of the deadliest attacks in AMISOM's history (Stanford, 2019). In 2017 the group carried out Somalia's equivalent of 9/11, when two truck bombs were detonated in downtown Mogadishu. The number of innocent civilians killed in the attack is estimated to be over 500.

The U.S. involvement in combating Al-Shabaab increased in 2018 when the Trump Administration carried out 47 drone strikes. The Trump Administration also changed the rules of engagement for the group, allowing preemptive airstrikes. An estimated 300 Al Shabaab militants were killed due to the policy shift. The current leader of Al Shabaab is Ahmad Umar. Umar was deathly ill in late 2017, which brought about a power struggle within the group (Stanford, 2019). Hussein Ali Fiidow was a possible successor and attempted a coup in 2018, but Umar has maintained overall leadership of the group. Fiidow is a financial administrator for the group and continues to remain active in the group. In late 2022, the U.S. Department of State's Rewards for Justice Program announced a $10 million reward for information that would lead to the capture or arrest of Umar.

Tactics of the group include bombings, suicide attacks, attacks against civilians (private and/or Christian), and generally against symbolic governmental targets (Stanford, 2019). The goal of the organization is to overturn the Somalian government and install strict Sharia Law. The group bans music, videos, bras for women, shaving for men, Western media outlets, etc. While the group's mission calls for control of Somalia, it has expanded its attacks to Kenya and Uganda. The group has a relationship with Al-Qaeda.

Boko Haram—West Africa

The origin date of the formation of Boko Haram is 2002, but the group was not formally known as Boko Haram but as a youth group (Al-Jazeera, 2010). At its inception, Boko Haram was more of a highly opinionated group but had mixed messaging and the mission of the group was still unclear at that time. The group's origins are rooted in an Islamic youth group studying the Koran in Maiduguri. The city and its political leaders were declared corrupt by the group and its leader, Mohammad Yusef (Al-Jazeera, 2010). The group relocated to the city of Kanama near Chad. They were known locally as the "Nigerian Taliban" (Walker, 2012), and the Yusufiyyah sect, with many of the youth group being sons of wealthy Nigerian families (Onuoha, 2010).

The group is an Islamic sect that believes politics in Northern Nigeria has been seized by a group of corrupt false Muslims. The group then declared the political leaders of the city corrupt and later relocated to Kanama on what is embarked as a hijira (a withdrawal along the lines of the Prophet Muhammad's withdrawal from Mecca to Medina) (Walker, 2014). At Kanama, it set up a separatist community run on hardline Islamic principles. The group's leader at the time Mohammed Ali espoused anti state ideology and called on other Muslims to join the group he group's leader at the time, Mohammed Ali espoused anti state ideology and called on other Muslims to join the group and return under true Islamic law, with the aim of making a more perfect society away from the corrupt establishment (Walker, 2014).

The organization attracted community support and membership by providing community aid (i.e., free food, shelter, etc.). The sect, organization, is alleged to have received outside funding (Onuoha, 2010). In 2007, Sheik Ja'afar Mahmoud Adam was assassinated during prayer; he had publicly objected to the radical ideology of the group (Walker, 2014). Later that same year, group leaders Mohammad Yusef and Mohammad Damagun were arrested and tried on charges related to terrorism. Damagun was arrested on three counts: being a member of the "Nigerian Taliban," as it was dubbed; receiving a total of $300,000 from Al-Qaeda to train and recruit Nigerians as terrorists; and participating in acts of terrorism. Yusef was accused of five counts, one of which included receiving money from Pakistani operatives belonging to Al-Qaeda (Onuoha, 2010).

The group progressively became more violent, and in 2009 the group engaged in terroristic acts after the controversial, and shrouded, death of Mohammed Yusuf while in Nigerian police custody) (Aduku 2021). They attacked police stations and Yusef released videos sermons about the state and police (Walker, 2012). The Baurchi government responded with a crackdown that resulted in the incarceration of more than 700 group members. For three days, members of the group killed police, Muslim, and Christian civilians indiscriminately (Walker, 2012).

The 3-day reign prompted the government to detain and kill anyone suspected of being a member of Boko Haram. Yusef was one of the members who was captured and executed without a trial (Walker, 2012). Many members fled the region during the 2009–2010 period, with some leaving the country. By mid-2010, Boko Haram returned to the Nigerian forefront. With members having potentially received training while in hiding, the organization returned with a new vigor. The group's return included a campaign of assassinations and attacking police checkpoints. On Christmas Eve in 2010, the group detonated more than half a dozen bombs near churches and markets. Several people were killed in the attacks. A few days later, on New Year's Eve, a bomb was detonated in a popular market area, killing 10 people (Walker, 2012).

From its formation, Boko Haram has transitioned from a group of insurgents using poisoned arrows to coordinated car bombing. Between 2010 and 2015 the violence and intensity of the attacks by the group continued to increase. In 2011, the Subcommittee on Counterterrorism and Intelligence Committee on Homeland Security found Boko Haram to be a threat to U.S. interest and homeland security. The committee also found the organizations evolution to be like that of Al-Qaeda in the Arabian Peninsula (AQAP) and the Tehrik-i-Taliban Pakistan (TTP) (Homeland Security, 2011).

The group sparked international interest in 2015 when they abducted 276 schoolgirls in Chibok, Borno State. The abduction and attack became known as the Chibok girls kidnapping. The news of the kidnapping made its way to the White House and drew international attention to Boko Haram. The group's message, mission, and lethality of attacks highlighted Nigeria's security threat. The kidnapping of the Chibok girls solidified Boko Haram's proclivity to use kidnapping of women, as well as bombings, raids, and looting. The group has kidnapped hundreds of women, with an estimated 700 in their custody in 2019 alone, in what the Islamic State would later tout as "the revival of slavery" (Pearson & Zenn, 2021). Shekau, and in turn Boko Haram, considers anyone not a part of the jihad an "infidel" and subject to abduction and enslavement. The group uses women and children as suicide bombers due to this ideology.

Strategically, in 2015, the group moved into Chad and committed its first known attack in the country when a suicide bomber bombed a market area, killing 15 people (National Counterterrorism Center, 2021). The group continued with attacks, that included two female suicide bombers killing at least 60 displaced people in Borno State in 2016. Then, in 2017, in the Diffa Region of Niger, the group abducted 33 women and 6 children, making it the first major abduction by Boko Haram in that country (Pearson & Zenn, 2021).

In 2017, the Nigerian Air Force confused a camp for displaced people with the group's hideout and killed over 100 innocent civilians (Aduku, 2021). Deadly confrontations between the Nigerian government and Boko Haram continued to escalate between 2017 and 2020, with confrontations that led to hundreds of civilian casualties. In December 2020, the group attacked several villages, including those in neighboring Niger, where over 1,000 homes were destroyed, civilians were killed or attacked, and the group looted supplies.

Islamic State West Africa Province

The death of Mohammed Yusef in 2009 created a competition for ruling power with Boko Haram. Many of his top followers, like Khalid Al-Barnawi, Mammah Nur, Abubakar Shekau, and others, rose to the top for succession after Yusef (Aduku, 2021). Abubakar Shekau, Yusef's deputy leader, eventually became the group's leader around 2009 and helped organize the direction of the group. During the same year of the Chibok Girls kidnapping (2015), Boko Haram pledged allegiance to a rapidly growing terrorist organization emerging from Syria/Iraq, named the Islamic State (ISIS). Dissent and splintering in the group that remained from concern about lost territories in 2015, tactical concerns and the still present resentment of Shekau's succession after Mohammed Yusef's death became much deeper. Within the organization the group splintered into two separate organizations, the Islamic State West Africa Province (ISWAP) and Boko Haram (Aduku, 2021). Shekau maintained leadership of Boko Haram and Musab Al-Barnawi became the appointed leader of ISWAP in 2016 (Aduku, 2021).

Using similar tactics but still operating distinctly separate from Boko Haram, ISWAP also actively engages in attacking Nigeria. An ideological distinction that ISWAP makes is that it claims to not attack Muslims who do not aid/abet the Nigerian government (Pearson & Zenn, 2021). This is one of the ideological differences that caused many in Boko Haram to splinter into ISWAP. The group claims that it will not attack or abduct "civilians" but only "apostates." ISWAP has openly criticized Shekau for sanctioning the abduction of Muslim "civilian" women.

One of the most influential strategies that this group obtains is allowing civilians the freedom to maintain their livelihood activities and then tax them for their livelihood. The group focuses on winning the hearts and minds of the community as it focuses on the poorest sections of Cameroon. These areas have lacked public services and assistance by the government and ISWAP helps these communities by providing assistance in building schools, roads, hospitals, etc., making these areas more receptive to their advances (Salkida, 2019). The group makes the distinction from Boko Haram by promising to treat civilians better than previous groups, and the public responds well to the taxations that the group puts forth as they find themselves living in much better conditions (Pike, 2021). It is known that ISWAP disciplines members within its own group if someone displays unacceptable behavior towards community members.

Another strategy ISWAP uses is propaganda. They often inflate their true success rate to threaten others. When raiding the Multinational Joint Task Force (MNJTF) bases, they claimed to have taken the lives of many while the MNJTF claims it did not, in fact take any (United Nations, 2020). The group also attempts to claim they have obtained large amounts of weaponry from rival bases when, in some cases, none were taken (Salkida, 2019). This installs panic in the minds of any opposing group or individual, thus gaining followers persuaded by fear. As the group is in an ongoing rivalry with Boko Haram, the group tries to isolate itself from the ideology and messaging of Boko Haram by placing value on Muslim civilian life and condemning abduction/slavery of Muslim women and children.

In 2017, ISWAP launched a failed attack on the Nigerian military and U.S. Special Forces. In 2018, the group kidnapped 110 schoolgirls from Yobe state. Originally thought to be another Boko Haram attack, ISWAP claimed responsibility for the attack (BBC, 2018).

Islamic State in West African Province was responsible for over 45 attacks throughout 2022. Their main targets were Christian worshipers (approximately 100 deaths) as well as the invasion of military bases and schools (12). Their most well-known attack in 2022 occurred on June 5, in which four gunmen stormed a church, killing 40 civilians.

In 2021, splinter divisions of Boko Haram (including ISWAP) abducted at least 211 children, with at least 88 being killed, and over 53 girls were subjected to sexual violence. In December of 2022, the group attempted to assassinate Nigeria's president, Muhammadu Buhari, when a vehicle explosive device (VEBID) went off. The attack killed four but was unsuccessful in assassinating Buhari (SITE Intelligence Group, 2023). Since military operations launched in 2009 (while still part of Boko Haram), ISWAP has carried out over 1,480 attacks throughout Nigeria. These attacks resulted in the deaths of approximately 15,111 victims and left over 3.2 million Nigerians displaced as a result.

Islamic State in West African Province is currently led by Ba-Lawan since its previous leader's execution in 2020. Today, it has approximately 3,500–5,000 fighters and between 800,000 and over 3 million civilians live under their rule as of 2022 (Australian National Security, 2023). In an attempt to gain young militants, the group has established a "Khilafah Cadet School" for 8–16 year old boys where they receive militant training.

Ansar al-Dine—Mali

A Salafist group, Ansar al-Dine, was a United States-designated Foreign Terrorist Organization operating in Mali and Tunisia in close cooperation with AQIM. It is also known as Defenders of Faith, Ansar Eddine, Salafist Warriors of Religion, AAD, etc. Some accounts credit this group as a splinter group of AQIM, while others accredit it as a separate group that received support from AQIM since its infancy (National Counterterrorism Center, 2022).

The group's ideology was rooted in a Sunni doctrine of Islamic Sharia Law. The mission of the group was to create an Islamic State in Mali. Primary targets include civilians, Malian/governmental forces, peacekeepers, and foreign troops (National Counterterrorism Center, 2022). Ansar Dine did not seek independence for Northern Mali but rather a country unified under Islam, a mission supported by AQIM.

The organization originally formed as a Tuareg rebel group in late 2011 under the leadership of Iyad Ag Ghali (National Counterterrorism Center, 2022). It received support from AQIM in its fight against Malian and French forces, most notably in the capture of the Malian towns of Agulhok, Tessalit, Kidal, Gao, and Timbuktu, between January and April 2012 (U.S. Department of State, 2013). When the moderate town of Timbuktu was seized, Ansar al-Dine and AQIM imposed strict Sharia Law. Those in their territories that were not compliant with the Sharia Law enforced were executed, tortured, or harassed (National Counterterrorism Center, 2022). In March 2012, the group attacked the Northern Malian town of Aguelhok and executed 82 Malian soldiers and kidnapped 30 more (U.S. Department of State, 2013).

A coup of the Malian government in 2012 allowed the group to seize control before the French intervention in January 2013. Ansar al-Dine was forced to retreat and regroup until their re-emergence in 2016 with a series of attacks that killed 21 civilians and wounded another 35 (National Counterterrorism Center, 2022). After the unrest, a mentee of Ghali (Amadou Kouffa) formed the Macina Liberation Front (FLM) as an affiliate of Ansar al-Dine. The goal of FLM was to coordinate its operations in central and southern Mali with Ansar al-Dine (Stanford University, 2022).

In 2017, the group merged with Al Mourabitoun, the local jihad group Macina Liberation Front, and AQIM's Sahara branch to form Jama'at Nusrat al-Islam wal-Muslimin (JNIM). Iyad Ag Ghali, leader of Ansar al-Dine, became the leader of the newly formed JNIM in March of 2017 (National Counterterrorism Center, 2022). Al-Qaeda in the Maghreb and Al-Qaeda (AQ) Central approved the merger and accepted the new group (Stanford University, 2022).

Al Mourabitoun

Al Mourabitoun, also known as "The Sentinels" formed in 2013 after the merger of two terrorist groups. Al Mourabitoun is a self-proclaimed jihadist group operating in West Africa. The group founders were Mokhtar Belmokhtar and Adnan Abu Waleed al-Sahrawi. Its operations were mainly carried out in Mali, and by 2015 the group pledged allegiance to Al-Qaeda. In December of 2015, the group merged with Al-Qaeda in the Islamic Maghreb (National Counterterrorism Center, 2022). The merger was marked with a joint attack on a hotel in the Malian capital of Bamako. Since then, the group has led AQIM operations in Mali.

In 2012, Belmokhtar created al-Mulathamum Battalion (The Masked Men), a splinter group from AQIM (Al-Qaeda in the Islamic Maghreb) (National Counterterrorism Center, 2022). The group accused France of various atrocities and carried out attacks in Algeria. In

2011, the Movement for Unity and Jihad in West Africa (MUJAO) splintered from AQIM after disputes within the group about leadership (Stanford University, 2022).

MUJAO group members kidnapped three European aid workers from a refugee camp in Algeria in 2011 (Stanford University, 2022). The group carried out attacks from 2011 to 2013 with groups like AQIM, Ansar al-Dine, and National Movement for the Liberation of Azawad (MNLA). Under the leadership of al-Sahrawi, MUJAO merged with al-Mulathamum Battalion in 2013. MUJAO and al-Mulathamum Battalion (AMB) carried out joint suicide bombings in 2013 in Niger that killed at least 20 people (National Counterterrorism Center, 2022).

In January of 2013, AMB gained international attention with a southeastern Algeria attack. In August of 2013, the two AQIM affiliated groups, the Movement for Unity and Jihad in West Africa (MUJAO) and AMB, merged to form Al-Mourabitoum. Tension within the group increased in 2015 when Adnan Abu Walid al Sahrawi, then leading spokesperson, claimed allegiance of Al—Mourbitoun to IS. Sahrawi left the group and joined the IS-affiliated Islamic State in the Greater Sahara (ISGS) (Stanford University, 2022). Under new leadership, the group became AQIM affiliated in August 2015 and has continued ties with AQIM.

In 2017, the group expanded the partnership to include marginalized Libyan groups (United Nations, 2017). This allowed the group to expand its operations beyond Mali. The expansion into Libya allowed for another merger, that between Al Mourabitoun, Ansar al-Dine, and the Macina Liberation Front. The merger of the three groups led to the formation of JNIM (Thomas, 2017).

Jama'a Nusrat ul-Islam

Jama'at Nusrat al-Islam wal-Muslimin (JNIM) is a Salafi-Jihadist organization that formed in March 2017 after the merging of four different terrorist organizations: Al-Qaeda in the Maghreb-Sahara Branch, Al Mourabitoun, Ansar al-Dine, and te Macina Liberation Front (Stanford University, 2022). The formation of JNIM was a consolidation of AQ affiliates in the area, as a better way to manage resources, better occupy territory, and create unity among groups with the same ideology and affiliation. The group's mission is to build a Salafi-Islamist state in West Africa and to rid the region of Western influences.

A Tuareg rebellion in 2012 forced the varying AQ affiliates to work together to address the threat. They additionally worked together to thwart French, Malian, and UN forces that intervened on the ground during the rebellion (Chivvis & Liepman, 2013). The collaboration eventually led to the formation of JNIM in 2017.

Like the Islamic State in the Greater Sahara (ISGS), JNIM has suffered losses due to repeated conflicts with France's counterterrorism forces associated with Operation Barkhane (Stanford University, 2022). A series of February 2018 attacks by the French forces resulted in the deaths of 20 JNIM fighters and six of its leaders. In June of 2018, the group responded to counterterrorism tactics but claiming responsibility for a suicide bombing of the Malian headquarters of the G5 Sahel. The attack killed two soldiers and one civilian.

Additional challenges the group faces are ethnic clashes with other groups in the Sahel, Mali in particular. Many members of JNIM are ethnically Fula and have engaged in conflicts supporting other Fulanis (Stanford University, 2022).

Iyad ag Ghali, the group's emir and leader since its formation, has stated that JNIM's strategy is to train "soldiers"/militants to fight any enemies, increase the groups presence across West Africa, win "hearts and minds" or locals by providing resources, education, etc., and by signing local agreements (National Counterterrorism Center, 2022). Jama'at Nusrat al-Islam wal-Muslimin has many higher-up leaders, as it is the result of the coalescing of four groups. Iyad Ag Ghali, founder of Ansar Dine and JNIM, is the emir and top leader of JNIM (Stanford University, 2022). However, other members of leadership include Hasan al-Ansari (a co-founder of Al Mourabitoun and founder of JNIM), Abu Abdul Rahman al Sanhaji (deputy leader of Al Mourabitoun), Yahya Abu Hammam (head of AQIM operations-Sahel and emir of AQIM in Timbuktu), and Amadou Kouffa (a former emir of the MLF and a Fulani imam).

Islamic State in the Greater Sahara

The Islamic State in the Greater Sahara (ISGS) is an Islamic State affiliated organization that formed in May of 2015. The group is mainly composed of former Al Mourabitoun members that splintered from Al Mourabitoun after Adnan Abu Walid al Sahrawi swore allegiance to the Islamic State (IS) and Abu Bakr al-Baghdadi in 2015 (Stanford University, 2022). Sahrawi's ideology contrasted with fellow Al Mourabitoun member Mokhtar Belmokhtar. Belmokhtar was the founder of AQIM and wanted Al Mourabitoun to remain loyal to Al-Qaeda. In 2015, Sahrawi created Islamic State in the Greater Sahara (ISGS) in order to pledge full allegiance to IS. Belmokhtar took over leadership of Al Mourabitoun and the group reaffirmed its allegiance to Al-Qaeda (Stanford University, 2018). Clashes between members of Al Mourabitoun and ISGS began, and assassination attempts were made by Al Mourabitoun members against Sahrawi during this time.

In 2016, IS recognized ISGS as an affiliate in West Africa, but it is not clear what type of support the Islamic State offers ISGS. There is a notable lag from Sahrawi's audio tape pledging allegiance to the Islamic State and IS recognizing it as an affiliate.

The Islamic State in the Greater Sahara operates in Mali, Niger, and Burkina Faso. It recruits members by fostering disenfranchisement of ethnic minority youths. The group has carried out several attacks, with its most conspicuous attack occurring in October of 2017. More than 100 fighters attacked a U.S.-Nigerian patrol in Niger, killing both an interpreter and U.S. and Nigerian soldiers. ISGS has struggled to gain traction, as Al-Qaeda still has a strong presence in the region (Max Security Report, 2024). In 2018, the group began to experience strong counterterrorism efforts by France, Operation Barkhane, and Malian forces (Kishi & Nsaibia, 2018). Also in 2018, ISGS announced a possible collaboration with the AQ-affiliated group Jama'at Nusrat ul-Islam (JNIM). The last known attack by the group was the kidnapping and execution of a local town leader, Hamada Ag Mohamed. Mohamed was a former member of Groupe d'Autodéfense Tuareg Imghad et Alliés (GATIA), a Tuareg pro-government Malian militia group, and a member of the High Council for Azawad Unity (HCUA) (Attacks claimed by the Islamic State, 7).

Islamic State Central Africa Province

Islamic State Central Africa Province (ISCAP) is also an Islamic State affiliated organization. Locally known as the Allied Democratic Forces (ADF), the group began in 1995 as a rebellion group in the Democratic Republic of the Congo (DRC) (Weiss, Farrell, Candland

& Poole, 2023). The ADF has gradually become a regional terrorist threat, ISCAP, as it now carries out acts beyond the DRC to include Uganda and terrorist attempts were made in Rwanda.

Many of ADF's members were a part of the Ugandan Muslim Freedom Fighters movement, with a very Uganda-centric agenda. The group was relatively peaceful in the Congo between 2007 and 2010 until the Congolese military began a crackdown on the group in 2010. The group began targeting local civilians in response. In 2014, ADF clashed with the Uganda peoples' defense force and fled Uganda to avoid defeat by the group. The ADF responded with a series of brutal civilian attacks that led to a local and international backlash (Weiss et al., 2023).

The ADF began affiliations with the Islamic State between 2014 and 2016 but received no funding from the IS (Weiss et al., 2023). Jamil Mukulu, leader of the ADF until his arrest in 2015, was a prominent figure in the group's financing network. Mukulu's arrest proved to be a pivotal moment in the group's history, as their funding drastically decreased until a critical point in 2017. The ADF had ideologies that aligned with IS and the group was looking for a partnership, especially one that would benefit them financially. Mukulu objected to the potential IS affiliation, but the group's next successor, Musa Baluku, made the connection.

Under Baluku, the group transitioned from a clandestine group to a group more vocal about their goals and objectives. In 2016, the group took on the name Madinat Tauheed wau Muwahideen (MTM). In 2017, one of its leaders, Ahmed Muhamood, released a video calling for an "Islamic State in the Congo" (Weiss et al., 2023). As the group slowly morphed into ISCAP, it officially began to receive funding from IS starting in 2016.

By 2019 the group officially became ISCAP and propelled itself to a regional group by utilizing suicide and urban bombings (Weiss et al., 2023). On April 18, 2019, IS made its relationship with ISCAP public when it claimed its first attack in the DRC, when ISCAP attacked and killed Congolese soldiers (Stocker 2019). The use of IS' network and money is directly linked to the 2021 bombings in Uganda, the DRC, and Rwanda. The IS connection has also allowed the group to rebuild its forces into the more recognized group that ISCAP is today.

Islamic State Central Africa Providence's evolution has followed a trajectory similar to that of IS, its main benefactor. Money for the group came from (1) IS when it had control of large territories in Iraq and Syria and (2) local funds distributed among IS-affiliated groups in the area. Regional IS groups set up financial networks to "raise" and pool resources. The money is transported through routes in the area. This approach utilizes a financial system that utilizes both a global and local components. Other IS affiliates, like the Islamic State's West Africa Province (splinter of Boko Haram), have benefited from the financing network that the IS brand affords (Weiss et al., 2023).

Islamic State Central Africa Providence carries out a bombing campaign, in the name of the Islamic Caliphate, that now spans across Central and East Africa (Weiss et al., 2023). Self-funding comes in the form of extortion and taxing civilians. These heavy taxes are called zakat, an Islamic concept, suggesting that it is almsgiving to the jihadist group. The tactics the group engages in includes kidnapping and using charitable causes as fundraisers.

Conclusion

A growing sense of secular invasion, government corruption, and misrule has laid the foundation for violent clashes between civilians and governments. Like in other regions of the world, Sub-Saharan Africa is not exempt from the spread of extremism. Many of the terrorist groups reviewed in this chapter are Islamic extremists and are rooted in the concept of the "global jihad." Wahhabism is a brand of Islamic extremism that many of the groups discussed subscribe to.

Things like the lack of resources, disenfranchisement, being on the periphery of the political process, tribal/communal differences, etc., are all exacerbated by religious affiliations and weak governments. Groups like Al-Qaeda and ISIS exploit weak governments and local grievances to mobilize civilians into their organizations.

Al-Qaeda has two official branches in Africa: AQIM/Al-Qaeda in the Maghreb (North Africa region down to Mali), founded in the early 2000s, and al Shabaab (Somalia and East Africa) that was founded in 2006. Jihadist groups that are part of the Al-Qaeda network or have a form of alliance with Al-Qaeda in Africa includes: Ansar al Din (Mali, founded in 2011), Ansar al Sharia Libya (founded in 2011), Ansar al Sharia Tunisia (founded in 2011), Ansaru (Nigeria, founded in 2012), Al Mourabitoun (North Africa and Mali, founded in 2013), and Uqba bin Nafi Brigade (Tunisia, founded in 2012). Corruption, coupled with local grievances and weak borders has allowed Al-Qaeda to spread its ideology, resources, and fighters throughout the region.

Other groups, like IS, have also expanded to Africa, especially in Sub-Saharan Africa. Without its territory, or Caliphate, IS further expanded and depended, on its affiliates. This is particularly true of Africa. The 2024 Annual Threat Assessment (ATA) noted a shift of the "Sunni global jihad to Africa." Currently, the group uses its affiliates in Africa, the Middle East, and Asia to exert its presence globally. IS affiliates in Africa include Islamic State in Libya, ISWAP, Islamic State in the Sahel Province, Islamic State in the Democratic Republic of Congo, Islamic State in Mozambique, ISCAP, Islamic State in the Greater Sahara (ISGS), and Islamic State in Somalia.

Groups like ISWAP, ISCAP, and Islamic State in the Greater Sahara (ISGS) are groups in Sub-Saharan Africa that have adopted the ideology and tactics of the Islamic State. ISIS is a known splinter group of Al-Qaeda and adopted the Wahhabi interpretation of jihad from its predecessor. Abubakar Shekau, of Boko Haram, claimed that the hostage taking and kidnapping tactics were allowed in the religious texts (Hussein, 2015). This proclamation paralleled ISIS's leader Abu bakr al-Baghdadi's similar claim for his group. Boko Haram raised the ISIS flag in allegiance, but internal clashes over the brute use of force, especially against Muslims, led to the splintering of Boko Haram. Islamic State in West African Province formed in 2015 after a group of members broke away from Boko Haram to pledge allegiance to the Islamic State and the brutal tactics of the group.

With the similarities in strategies, techniques, and operations to mainstream global terror groups, it is evident that Boko Haram is linked to Al-Qaeda on deeply rooted ideological bases of protecting the soul of Islam. Although its ideology of extremism is rooted in Nigeria, with the intention of implementing Sharia Law, the organization has gained international attention. The group has transitioned from utilizing poisoned arrows to adopting Al-Qaeda's tactics of kidnapping, coordinated car bombing, and assassinations.

A challenge for many, if not all, governments dealing with extremist groups in the region is the continued sense of grievance that many civilians face. From corruption to lack of resources, many civilians are left feeling disenfranchised from their governments. The aim of many groups, either Islamic jihadist or separatist, is to create a state where their identity group holds a position of power or has a political voice.

References

Abdulkadir, S. (2012, February). *Al Shabab's impact on peace in Somalia and the Horn of Africa.* Backgrounder.

Aduku, O. (2021). *Legal classification of conflict in Nigeria (Boko Haram case study).* SSRN. https://ssrn.com/abstract=3861496

Al-Jazeera. (2010, December 28). Muslim group claims Nigeria blasts | News. *Al Jazeera.* https://www.aljazeera.com/news/2010/12/28/muslim-group-claims-nigeria-blasts

Austrailian National Security. (2023, July 3). *Islamic state West Africa province.* Australian National Security. https://www.nationalsecurity.gov.au/what-australia-is-doing/terrorist-organisations/listed-terrorist-organisations/islamic-state-west-africa-province

BBC News. (2018, March 28). Islamic state and the kidnap of Nigerian schoolgirls from Dapchi. *BBC.* https://www.bbc.com/news/world-africa-43570488

Chivvis, C., & Liepman, A. (2013). *North Africa's menace: AQIM's evolution and the U.S.* Policy Response. https://www.rand.org/pubs/research_reports/RR415.html

Counter Extremism Project. (n.d.). *Al-Mourabitoun.* Counter Extremism Project. https://www.counterextremism.com/threat/al-mourabitoun/report

Hussein, W. (2015, March). The Islamic state in Africa. *Al- Monitor: The Pulse of the Middle East.* http://www.al-monitor.com

Kishi, R., & Nsaibia, H. (2018, March 3). In light of the recent attacks in Ouagadougou. *ACLED.* https://acleddata.com/2018/03/03/in-light-of-the-recent-attacks-in-ouagadougou/

Max Security. (2024). *West Africa analysis: Islamic State recognizes ISGS as West African affiliate following increased attacks in recent months, despite 17 month silence - | MAX Security.* Max Security. https://www.max-security.com/reports/west-africa-analysis-islamic-state-recognizes-isgs-as-west-african-affiliate-following-increased-attacks/

National Counterterrorism Center. (n.d.). *Counter terrorism guide: Boko Haram.* National Counterterrorism Center | Groups. https://www.dni.gov/nctc/groups/boko_haram.html

National Counterterrorism Center. (2022). *Counterterrorism guide: Ansar Al Dine (Mali).* National Counterterrorism Center | FTOs. https://www.dni.gov/nctc/ftos/ansar_al_dine_fto.html

National Counterterrorism Center. (2022, October). National counterterrorism center | FTOs. *Jama'a Nusrat.* https://www.dni.gov/nctc/ftos/jnim_fto.html

Onuoha, F. (2010). The Islamist challenge: Nigeria's Boko Haram crisis explained. *African Security Review, 19*(2), 54–67.

Pearson, E., & Zenn, J. (2021). *Boko Haram, the Islamic state, and the surge in female abductions in Southeastern Niger.* International Centre for Counter- Terrorism. https://www.icct.nl/sites/default/files/2022-12/Pearson-And-Zenn-research-paper.pdf

Pike, J. (2021, June 24). Islamic State West Africa Province (ISWAP). *GlobalSecurity.* Retrieved October 16, 2023, from https://www.globalsecurity.org/military/world/para/iswap.htm

Salkida, A. (2019, May 16). Facing the challenge of the Islamic State in West Africa province. *Crisis Group.* https://www.crisisgroup.org/africa/west-africa/nigeria/273-facing-challenge-islamic-state-west-africa-province

SITE Intelligence Group. (2023, January 2). *ISWAP claims car bombing outside palace of Okene ruler, in Nigeria's Kogi State.* SITE Intelligence Group. https://ent.siteintelgroup.com/

Stanford University. (n.d.). *MMP: Al Mourabitoun | FSI.* Center for International Security and Cooperation. https://cisac.fsi.stanford.edu/mappingmilitants/profiles/al-mourabitoun

Stanford University. (n.d.). *MMP: MUJAO | FSI.* Center for International Security and Cooperation. https://cisac.fsi.stanford.edu/mappingmilitants/profiles/mujao

Stanford University. (2018, July). *The Islamic State in the Greater Sahara.* Mapping Militant Organizations. https://cisac.fsi.stanford.edu/mappingmilitants/profiles/islamic-state-greater-sahara

Stanford University. (2019). *Al Shabaab.* Mapping Militant Organizations. https://cisac.fsi.stanford.edu/mappingmilitants/profiles/al-shabaab

Stanford University. (2022). *MMP: Ansar Dine | FSI.* Center for International Security and Cooperation. https://cisac.fsi.stanford.edu/mappingmilitants/profiles/ansar-dine

Stanford University. (2022). *MMP: Jamaat Nusrat al-Islam wal Muslimeen.* Center for International Security and Cooperation. https://cisac.fsi.stanford.edu/mappingmilitants/profiles/jamaat-nusrat-al-islam-wal-muslimeen

Stocker, J. (2019, April 18). ISIS claims first attack in DR Congo, saying it killed soldiers near Uganda border. *The Defense Post.* Retrieved October 15, 2023, from https://www.thedefensepost.com/2019/04/18/isis-killed-dr-congo-soldiers-kamango-uganda/

Subcommittee on Counterterrorism and Intelligence Committee on Homeland Security. (2011). *Boko Haram: Emerging threat to the U.S. Homeland.* Subcommittee on Counterterrorism and Intelligence Committee on Homeland Security.

Thomas, J. (2017). Analysis: Al Qaeda groups reorganize in West Afric. *Long War Journal.* https://www.longwarjournal.org/archives/2017/03/analysis-al-qaeda-groups-reorganize-in-west-africa.php

Toutounji, Y. (2017). *The double-edged Sword: Globalization and international Islamic terrorism.* American University in Cairo, Master's Thesis. AUC Knowledge Fountain. https://www.google.com/url?sa=t&source=web&rct=j&opi=89978449&url=https://fount.aucegypt.edu/cgi/viewcontent.cgi%3Farticle%3D1696%26context%3Detds

United Nations. (2020, February 22). *Islamic State West Africa Province (ISWAP) | United Nations security council.* United Nations Security Council. https://www.un.org/securitycouncil/content/islamic-state-west-africa-province-iswap-0

United Nations Security Council Counter Terrorism Committee. (2017, June 22). *Challenges in countering terrorism in Libya.* United Nations. https://www.un.org/sc/ctc/wp-content/uploads/2017/06/Concept-Note-Joint-open-briefing-on-Libya-22-Jun- 17.pdf

U.S. Department of State. (2013, March 21). *Terrorist designations of Ansar al-Dine.* Media Note. https://2009–2017.state.gov/r/pa/prs/ps/2013/03/206493.htm

Walker, A. (2012). What is Boko Haram? Special report. *United States Institute For Peace*, *17*, 1–13.

Walker, A. (2014, May 14). Why Nigeria has not defeated Boko Haram. *BBC.* Retrieved October 15, 2023, from https://www.bbc.com/news/world-africa-27396702

Weiss, C., O'Farrell, R., Candland, T., & Poole, L. (2023, June). *Fatal transaction: The funding behind the Islamic State's Central Africa province.* George E Washington Program on Extremism.

7

TERROR GROUPS IN THE MIDDLE EAST AND NORTH AFRICA

Islamic State of Iraq and ash-Sham, Armed Islamic Group, Aden-Abyan Islamic Army

Ashlie Perry Banerjee

Background of Terror Groups in the Middle East and North Africa

Three unique characteristics of an "Islamic movement" are identified: the "Umma," Dawa, and jihad (Azani, 2009). The Umma aspect of an Islamic movement is aimed at uniting all Muslims worldwide and the restoration of Islam as a leading factor in the world. Jihad and Dawa are the means by which the Umma is achieved. Dawa is rooted in nonviolence; it suggests that the means to fix Muslim society is through community education, indoctrination, and community unity. Jihad attempts to accomplish the aforementioned goals, but violence is a plausible tactic one. (Azani, 2009). It is noted that while jihad allows the use of violent measures, this does not signify that violent physical means are the only option. Islamic extremists embraced writings that encouraged physical violence and interpreted it as such. The Iranian Revolution is cited as one of the first instances of the Islamic Revolution, with an impact felt throughout the rest of the Arab world (Azani, 2009).

The era of the "Islamic Resurgence" began in the beginning of the 1970s. It revived Islamic movements and several religious leaders were at the helm of the movement (Harik, 2005). A growing sense of secular invasion, government corruption and misrule, and poverty grew. This was especially true for the Shiite population, who viewed themselves as the populous majority (Harik, 2005). The Shiite community experienced a surge in population due to high birth rates in the 1970s; the influx of births caused an aim to revise the power pendulum (Haddad, 2006).

North Africa has its own unique way of dealing with the growing impact of Islam on politics, producing domestic and foreign policy changes. Political violence in Tunisia, Libya, Algeria, and Morocco occurred in North Africa prior to the "Arab Spring." Extremists who claimed ties with Al-Qaeda in 2003 and 2006 called to light the growing influence of "political Islam" (Jofee', 2010). North Africa uses the political crisis and its security issues in a way that has altered its working relationship with the United States and Europe. Europe and the U.S. are more involved in the area protecting their security interests in the region (i.e., Trans-Saharan Counterterrorism Initiative). The North African model allowed the region to address external threats by focusing on foreign policy; however, this

DOI: 10.4324/9781003375265-11

did not address its own internal shortcomings such as corruption, economic disparity, etc (Jofee', 2010).

Islamic Extremism

Many of the terrorist groups in this chapter, and the next on terrorist groups in Southeast Asia, are rooted in the concept of the "global jihad." While many of these groups, like Al-Qaeda or ISIS in the Middle East and Abu Sayyaf in the Philippines, claim that their interpretation of jihad is linked to Islam's more classical roots, the path to a global jihad is neither clear nor direct path. Generally, there are four recognized Sunni jurisprudence, or schools of thought: Maliki (jurist Malik Ibn Anas jurist), Hafani (jurist Muhammed al-Sahybani), Shafi'i (jurist al-Shafi'i), and Hanbali (jurist Ibn Qudama) schools (Toutounji, 2017). Another, the Zahiri school (jurist Ibn Hazm), is frequently characterized as a fifth jurisprudence but it should be noted that it is generally outlined as four schools of Sunni thought.

These classical jurists, and their schools of thought, have shaped the foundations of Islam and have been cited by many extremist groups as the explanation for the use of force, especially against non-Muslims. However, many scholars agree that many classical jurists mentioned above understood jihad as offensive and generally held a spiritual connotation. Such jihad was aimed at internal struggles and desires. The current interpretation of jihad used by terrorist groups is modern and rooted in the context of warfare. Classical jurists made the stipulation that before engaging in fighting/violence, one would need to invite non-Muslims to Islam, a guideline often skipped by many modern-day groups. Some classical jurists (i.e., Malik, al-Shaybani, and Ibn Qudama) went as far as condemning those who are not able to fight. This would include women, children, the elderly, and anyone without the interest in fighting (i.e., monks, peasants, etc.). On the other hand, al-Shafi'i and Ibn Hazm did not hold such a stipulation and viewed all adult males as legitimate targets for attack (Badawi, 2014). The classical jurists did all agree that the accidental killing of women and children were a consequence of war (Toutounji, 2017).

Defensive jihad, used by modern terrorist groups, interprets Islam from their current sociopolitical viewpoint. This is supported by the articulated goals of the global jihad: ending Western hegemonies via violent/defensive jihad and establishing an Islamic State. The idea of a caliphate or Islamic State is based on the Westphalian premise of a "state"/ central government, a concept that was not around during the time of the classical jurists (Toutounji, 2017). Instead, the global jihad is largely influenced by the writings of modern writers such as Taqi al-Din Ibn Tamiyya, Mohammed Ibn Abdul Wahhab, Mawlana Mawdudi (Maududi), Sayyid Qutb, and Muhammad al-Farag. Most of these writers are discussed in greater detail in the chapter on South East Asia.

Taqi al-Din Ibn Taymiyya (1269–1328) lived during, and reacted to, the turbulent times of his age. The Mongols used brute force against captives, and the Christian Crusades attempted to forcibly install Christianity to the Muslim "non-believers." Also an Islamic scholar, Ibn Taymiyya attempted to find a solution within Islam. He called for jihad (struggle or effort) as the sixth pillar of Islam (White, 2020). Ibn Taymiyya laid the foundation for using Islam as a solution to political issues, like defending oneself from foreign invaders. Thus begins the path of using a sociopolitical viewpoint to interpret Islam.

Muhammad Ibn Abdul Wahhab (1703–1792) was greatly influenced by Taymiyyah. Wahhab started a purification movement in then Arabia, during the late 18th century. His aim was to remove some of the religious practices added after the death of the prophet Mohammad (PBUH). This more puritanical strand of Islam spread throughout Arabia to India and other parts of Asia. Now known as "Wahhabism," this is a strict interpretation of Islam (White, 2020). Ibn Abdul Wahhab felt that Muslims should return to the state envisioned by Mohammad (PBUH) and his initial followers.

It is important to note that Mawdudi/Maududi (1903–1979) formed Jamaat-e-Islami in British India in 1941 (Alam, 2024). He viewed British and French colonialism as one of the main hindrances of Muslim rule in the Middle East and South Asia (Toutounji, 2017). He concluded that jihad was a way to liberate Muslims from oppression and to bring about an Islamic State, where Muslims could rule once more. The writings of Mawdudi greatly influenced a young Egyptian by the name of Sayyid Qutb. While a member of the Muslim Brotherhood, Qutb would write a body of work embraced by terrorist organizations worldwide.

Muslim Brotherhood

The Muslim Brotherhood, and the ideological works that came from members of the group, provided an ideological basis for other prominent Islamist groups (Pew Research Center, 2010). The Muslim Brotherhood was founded in 1928 by a 22-year-old school teacher, Hassan al-Banna. Originally started as a social welfare and religious club, the group quickly became political and is now known as one of the oldest, largest, and powerful Islamic organization. al-Banna witnessed the influence of colonialism not only on Muslim life but also on Egyptians during the British occupation of Egypt (1882–1952) (Laub, 2019). al-Banna, like Mawdudi and other modernists, believed that the state of affairs for Muslims was weak because they were far removed from the original, more puritanical practices of Islam, and sought to restore Sharia/Islamic Law. The Muslim Brotherhood promoted the importance of civil society in Egypt and campaigned for an Islamic party that would expand beyond Egypt's border (Harik, 2005). The Brotherhood joined forces with a group of nationalist military leaders, the Free Officers, in its early days. In 1952, a coup d'etat led to the ousting of King Farouk and pitted the military against the Brotherhood (Laub, 2019). The Brotherhood did not agree with the plan for Egypt by the military government, which included a secular government, no social welfare programs planned, and the possibility of defeat by Israel. In 1954, a suspected member of the Brotherhood attempted to assassinate Gamal Nasser, a member of the Free Officers. Nasser began to view the group, and its opposition to a secular nationalist government, as a political threat (Pew Research Center, 2010). The new government and Nasser aimed to limit the influence of the Brotherhood.

The group was banned from involvement in elections and the government. The conflict between the group also resulted in many Brotherhood members being arrested at the behest of Nasser. One of those arrested was the newly returned to Egypt Sayyid Qutb. Qutb wrote bodies of work around the idea of armed struggle against the Egyptian regime. His works are at the root of many Sunni jihadist groups, ranging from Al-Qaeda to Hamas. His most famous body of work was *Milestones*, published in 1965 and outlined the ideology of jihadist revolution. The book was the preemptive for his second arrest in 1966 and his subsequent hanging by the government (White, 2020). His death became a form of martyrdom, with many extremists citing modern governments as apostate and subject to indiscriminate violence (Laub, 2019). Qutb called for the destruction of all enemies. He is the dubbed "father" of modern-day jihadism (Toutounji, 2017).

The group renounced violence in 1970, while the Egyptian Islamic Jihad engaged in numerous acts of violence. The Egyptian Islamic Jihad (EIJ) was formed by Aiman Muhammed Rabi al-Zawahiri, who later became a leader in Al-Qaeda (Shehata, 2015). The Brotherhood also struggled with the fragmented groups of Salafism that ranged from peaceful to violent. One such group, the Salafi Call, sought to dominate the Egyptian Islamist scene and challenged the authority of the Muslim Brotherhood (Shehata, 2015). In addition to Salafism, the group embraced Wahhabism, originated by the writer Mohammed Ibn Abdul Wahhab, as well.

The Arab Spring protests of 2011 led to the ousting of former Egyptian President Hosni Mubarak. The Brotherhood's political wing, the Freedom and Justice Party, won seats in Egypt's lower house of parliament. Additionally, their presidential candidate, Mohammed Morsi, was elected President. However, the victory was short-lived as Morsi was ousted in a military revolt in July of 2013. With the turn of political events, many Brotherhood members were imprisoned, exiled, or went underground (Laub, 2019). The Egyptian court also issued death sentences to hundreds of the Muslim Brotherhood members from 2013–2014, and again in 2018. By 2020, Egypt was ranked as the world's third most frequent user of executions. The Human Rights Watch estimated that 51 women and men were executed in the first 6 months of 2021 (Amnesty International, 2021). Despite these setbacks, the Muslim Brotherhood remains a conduit for grievances, an organization that provides social welfare, and one that promotes the Islamic faith, culture, and practices.

Saudi Arabia, UAE, and Iran

Saudi Arabia's role in the region, especially in Yemen, is a complicated one. Eyewitnesses in Abyan, Aden, and Taiz reported seeing Saudi Arabia airdrop weapons and money to militants, even those that fight with Al-Qaeda (Arrabyee, 2016). Saudi Arabia has provided airdrops to Hamoud al-Mekhlafi, leader of an anti-Houthi group and tribal leader. al-Mekhlafi has ties to Al-Qaeda and fights alongside the group. Saudi leadership has supported many anti-Houthi groups, ranging from the Muslim Brotherhood to Salafi groups. This even means indirectly supporting Al-Qaeda affiliated groups, like Al-Qaeda in the Arabian Peninsula (AQAP), that are part of the anti-Houthi movement.

The UAE also supports anti-Houthi groups but is less all-inclusive in the types of groups it supports. The UAE is less tolerant of some branches of the Muslim Brotherhood and has listed groups like Islamic State, Jabhat al-Nusra, and most Houthi groups as terrorist organizations (Arrabyee, 2016). The UAE has publicly admonished some groups, like the Islah Party. The 2015 airdrop by Saudi Arabia to support anti-Houthi groups, and indirectly Al-Qaeda, Taiz prompted the UAE to pause sending armored tanks from Aden to Taiz. It was a form of protest as the UAE saw the anti-Houthi rebels as a faction of the Muslim Brotherhood that they did not support (Arrabyee, 2016).

Extremist Groups

Al-Qaeda

The word *qaeda*, in Arabic, means "foundation" or "base of operations." Other translations of the word mean "method" or "precept" (Burke, 2009). However, Islamic militants often associate the term with the latter translations of "method" or "precept." The formation of Al-Qaeda (al-Qaida) extends well before Osama bin Laden's 1989 decree to stop non-Islamic forces with the use of violence (PBS, n.d.). Al-Qaeda formed as a splinter group of Maktab al-Khadamat (MAK) in 1987, not in 1988 as previously thought (Farrall, 2017).

The Soviet Union's invasion of Afghanistan in December of 1979 sparked the beginning of the "Afghan Jihad." In effect, the invasion created the Arab-Afghanistan identity and solidified ideologies and conflicts that would reverberate around the world (Farrall, 2017). The United States, via the Central Intelligence Agency, began Operation Cyclone (1979–1989) in Afghanistan shortly after the Soviet invasion (Lumen Learning, n.d.). Osama bin Laden began financial contributions to the Afghan Jihad very soon after the start of the war. Later on, he and Abdullah Azzam, another prominent Arab-Afghan supporter, would organize within the country and later finance the Service Officer (Maktab al-Khadamat, or MAK).

Operation Cyclone was a covert mission aimed at funneling money, weaponry, recruits, and training to the mujahideen on the ground (Associated Press, 2021). The U.S. worked with Pakistan's dictator Mohammad Zia-ul Haq and the Pakistan Interservice Intelligence Agency (ISI) as tools to help bolster financial and physical support for the mujahideen. Zia-ul Haq encouraged Muslims within and outside of Afghanistan to join the fight against the Soviets. Operation Cyclone was, and is still, one of the most expensive CIA operations, costing more than $20 billion in U.S. funds (Lumen Learning, n.d.). The U.S. chose to support groups favored by Zia-ul Haq, with those groups being more militant and Islamic focused than their Afghan counterparts. In a move that would further set the tone for U.S. support in the conflict, the United States invited Afghanis from the various sectors of the mujahideen to the Oval Office. On January 2, 1983, President Ronald Reagan called the group freedom fighters (Ronald Reagan Presidential Library, n.d.).

On the night of Ramadan during their 1984 Hajj, several Afghan leaders, Arab-Afghans, and other Arabs met to discuss a potential organization. Dubbed the Pakita Project, the meeting was to determine the role and scope of the organization (Farrall, 2017). Although Operation Cyclone saw an influx of American money, there were still concerns of getting supplies to where they were needed and the ever-present concern of corruption at the higher levels. The collaboration between Afghan leaders and Arab-Afghans would include one faction contributing forces/fighters (Arab leaders) and the other securing financing (Arab-Afghans) (Farrall, 2017). During the Pakita talks, Azzam was selected to lead the initiative of securing and distributing funding. Abdul Aziz would then ensure that the mujahideen received the supplies needed.

However, the project did not produce the intended results, with many shortcomings on the Arab leadership side. The one-sided partnership led the Arab-Afghans, specifically Jalaluddin Haqqani, to commission a report of the supplies and needs of Afghan groups. Mustafa Hamid, who was also at the Jaji meeting, created a detailed report (Farrall, 2017).

He outlined the supplies needed, infrastructure weaknesses, and the need for external support to reduce the possibility of corruption. Hamid also suggested a media presence, building their own ammunition, and education and military training. The overall plan aimed at better recruitment tactics and strategic planning that would tempt possible investors with a new, separate organization. The envisioned organization would include independent oversight and a better handle on logistical problems of disseminating goods to Arabs fighting in the Afghan-Soviet war (Farrall, 2017).

The Arab-Afghans accepted the proposal of Hamid's report and decided to move forward with the plan, without the input of Afghan leaders, with a coalition of Arabs leading the group. As with the Pakita Project, Azzam would remain responsible and a prominent figure to assess the organization's progress. Osama bin Laden would become the new group's initial benefactor. At its founding in October of 1984, MAK had an Amir, Azzam, and 12 other members (Farrall, 2017). Figures like Osama bin Laden, also known as Abu Abdullah, were transient figures that simply provided financial support.

Maktab al-Khadamat was established with the explicit intent of directly receiving funding in an attempt to thwart corruption and rectify supply chain concerns. However, after Azzam assumed control, he decided to increase the scope of the organization. He wanted to establish an Islamic State and expel the Soviets from Afghanistan (Farrall, 2017). While bin Laden may have supported the Islamic State idea, he did not believe that it was MAK's mission to do so. Azzam's change, or evolution, in focus eventually led to bin Laden parting ways with the organization.

Osama bin Laden traveled to the Afghan-Soviet frontline in 1986. He participated in the battle in Jalalabad (Toutounji, 2017). bin Laden traveled unannounced in order to get a realistic view of conditions for mujahideen fighting against the Soviets. Instead of the visit fueling support for the status quo and continued support of MAK, bin Laden decided to withdraw funding from the organization (Farrall, 2017). Also around this time, the U.S. began supplying the mujahideen with missiles. The use of missiles overwhelmed the Soviets, and they began signaling negotiations for withdrawals (Associated Press, 2021). In 1987, bin Laden fought in the Battle of Jaji. This was a move that further bolstered his reputation and increased his popularity in the Afghan Jihad (Richardson, 2021). Additionally, it continued to increase his confidence in his own capabilities as a leader in the movement. Around this time, Ayman al-Zawahiri, an important figure later in the formation of Al-Qaeda and operational leader of EIJ in Egypt, arrived in Afghanistan and began working with bin Laden (Toutounji, 2017).

Maktab al-Khadamat became famous for the way it recruited, trained, and housed its volunteers, especially for its foreign recruits. As this, and later chapters discusses on volunteers came from an array of countries that ranged from Yemen to South East Asia (Farrall, 2017). Maktab al-Khadamat and Azzam's first training camp in Zhawar for recruits was criticized by both Mustafa Hamid and Osama bin Laden for lacking rigor. Hamid once claimed that Azzam had established a "mosque, not a training camp." In 1986, bin Laden began searching for a location for his own training camps. Abu Burham al-Suri stepped in and drastically changed the quality of training recruits received at camps, improving MAK's training techniques. Osama bin Laden continued to search for a location to train recruits, even though MAK's training sites were improved.

Maktab al-Khadamat continued to suffer internal administrative problems that led to a weakening of the organization. Azzam continued tarbiyyah, or overall cultural training of recruits (Farrall, 2017). Osama bin Laden, with the help of Saudi nationals, discreetly began construction of his own camp in October of 1986. In early 1987, later called al-Masada base started the operations of Al-Qaida/Al-Qaeda. Located in Jaji, this site later became a famous battleground in the Afghan Jihad, one in which bin Laden would personally fight. The al-Masaada base recruits trained but also built up the infrastructure of the camp. Abu Ubaydah al-Banshiri joined bin Laden, under his payroll, to train recruits in January of 1987, officially beginning "al-Qaeda" as an organization (Farrall, 2017).

Recruits at al-Masada were eager to join in combat with their fellow mujahedeen. Osama bin Laden allowed the recruits to engage in small-scale attacks on the Soviets in April and May of 1987, leading to a retaliatory act by the Soviets. The Battle of Jaji in May 1987, was one that found bin Laden and his recruits on the frontline of the Afghan-Soviet war. Azzam sent his recruits to assist and do a large amount of the fighting for Osama bin Laden. The Battle of Jaji was a victory for the Afghan Jihad and cemented both bin Laden and his group as a legitimate military group. It also boosted the reputation of MAK, as many fighters were from their Saad training camp. Between 1987 and early 1989, Al-Qaeda membership grew to almost 400, compared to the 40 or so recruits at its inception (Farrall, 2017).

Azzam and bin Laden agreed that disbanding the Arab fighters and recruits post-Battle of Jaji would not be a good plan. Instead, Azzam came up with a plan to create a "base" or "foundation" to create the Islamic caliphate he'd dreamed up (Toutounji, 2017). Azzam dubbed this "base" as Al-Qaeda, or *Qaidat Ansarallah*. Azzam allowed more of his trainees to train at bin Laden's training camp in Jaji (Farrall, 2017). Bin Laden began to heavily recruit mujahideen and Zawahiri organized the training camps. Zawahiri suggested an umbrella structure for the organization, with independent cells underneath it (White, 2020).

On February 15, 1989, the last of the overwhelmed Soviet forces began to withdraw. Several resistance groups, and the Pakistani Interservice Agency, formed a coalition called the Afghan Interim Government, in hopes of controlling the country after full Soviet withdrawal (Farrall, 2017). Dubbed the Jalalabad campaign, the opposing Arab-Afghans coalition attempted to overthrow the newly forming government. This opposing coalition included Azzam's MAK recruits, Osama bin Laden's Al-Qaeda, the EIJ (with whom Zawahiri had an affiliation), and the Egyptian Islamic Group (Farrall, 2017). The Azzam/bin Laden coalition was badly defeated and suffered heavy losses with both human lives and morale. The defeat triggered a domino effect; widespread anger and dissatisfaction with bin Laden's leadership, bin Laden leaving for Saudi Arabia to work for his family's business, and the subsequent decline in momentum for Al-Qaeda.

An impromptu leadership change occurred when Abdullah Azzam was killed in a car bomb assassination in November 1989. By default, both bin Laden and Zawahiri became the leaders of Al-Qaeda (White, 2020). When bin Laden was on his self-imposed exile in Saudi Arabia, he had become independently wealthy working with his family's construction business. He also made several connections with a larger Saudi network. During the leadership transition phase, the directive for Al-Qaeda at the time was to avoid fighting and not cause any further friction in the region (Toutounji, 2017). However, in 1990, Iraq invaded Kuwait. The U.S.'s Operation Desert Shield (1990) morphed into Operation Desert Storm in February 1991 (White, 2020). The transition included U.S. troops operating in both Iraq and Kuwait and adding Saudi Arabia to their sights. A Western coalition of the United States, the

British, and other allies positioned themselves in holy cities like Mecca and Medina. Osama bin Laden saw this as an overreach and means for retaliatory action, positioning the United States as a "far enemy" of Al-Qaeda (Toutounji, 2017). The Saudi government's decision to allow foreign troops to intervene on Islamic soil was a decision that bin Laden fundamentally disagreed with. By that point, Zawahiri had returned to Egypt with the hope of creating an Islamic State in Egypt with the EIJ. Zawahiri focused on a "near enemy," the Egyptian government that he viewed as a proxy for Western countries. Zawahiri called on Egyptians who were trained in Afghanistan during the Afghan-Soviet war to join the EIJ (White, 2020).

In 1992, Osama bin Laden, now based in Sudan, employed and trained mujahideen there with the intent of striking back at the United States (Toutounji, 2017). He also began buying properties, creating multinational corporations, false charities, and other clandestine activities (White, 2020). His activities expanded into the Balkans, Philippines, Kashmir, and even Chechnya. He condemned the royal family for allowing U.S. troops in Saudi, for allowing the highly contested Oslo Accords between Palestinians and Israel, and not thwarting the Soviet presence in South Asia.

The group began an active agenda to attack its "Near" enemies in 1992. He had rekindled his alliance with Ayman al-Zawahiri. Zawahiri inspired bin Laden to broaden his scope from the Saudi royal family to a wider jihad. The two began transforming Al-Qaeda into an international organization, with numerous cells in various Muslim countries (Toutounji, 2017). From 1992–1995 the group engaged in several plans: Yemen hotel bombing aimed at U.S. troops (1992), the World Trade Center attack (1993), foiled NYC infrastructure attacks (1993), Black Hawk helicopter shot down in Mogadishu (1993), Bangkok truck hijacking to bomb the Israeli embassy (1994), and a bin Laden planned attack where EIJ members attacked Mubarak's motorcade (1995) (Counter Extremism Project, n.d.).

With pressure from the U.S., the Sudanese government expelled Al-Qaeda from its borders in 1996 (Toutounji, 2017). Bin Laden returned to Afghanistan and declared war on the United States. Afghanistan would remain Al-Qaeda's base of operations from 1996 to 2001. Bin Laden issued his first *fatwa* in 1996. It asserts that jihad was the only solution to the "Judeo-American" alliance that plagued many Muslim countries. Bin Laden established an alliance with the Taliban, under Mullah Omar's leadership. The Taliban benefited by gaining control of the country and funding, while bin Laden was able to operate training camps.

In 1997, Zawahiri joined bin Laden in Afghanistan, where Al-Qaeda issued two *fatwas*, and a document named *The World Islamic Front against Jews and Crusaders*. The aforementioned document united Islamic groups like EIJ, the Followers of the Prophet Movement (Harakat al-Ansar), the Bangladeshi Jihad Movement (Harakat al-Jihad), al-Jihad, and the Egyptian GI. The fatwas called for the killing of any American in any part of the world (White, 2020). In 1998, Al-Qaeda launched simultaneous suicide bombings at both U.S. embassies in Tanzania and Kenya, killing 258 people and wounding over 5,000 (Toutounji, 2017). The USS Cole attack in 2000, in collaboration with the newly formed Yemeni group Ayden Islamic Army, resulted in the death of 17 U.S. servicemen. Al-Qaeda's chief of naval operations was arrested for his involvement in the low-budget, but high-collateral attack (Counter Extremism Project, n.d.).

On September 11, 2001, Al-Qaeda solidified its global jihad movement when 19 of its operatives used 4 hijacked commercial planes as weapons of mass destruction (Toutounji,

2017). Two planes flew into the World Trade Center towers, while another crashed into the Pentagon. A fourth plane, possibly heading for the U.S. Capitol Building, crashed in a rural field in Pennsylvania (Counter Extremism Project, n.d.). The targeted locations were symbolic of the United States' "economic, material, and political power" (Migaux, 2007). More than 3,000 civilians were killed, with several 1,000 more injured. The attacks on 9/11 were significant beyond the scale and scope of the attacks, but it also signified Al-Qaeda's shift from a "near" enemy to that of a "far" enemy, as noted in the World Islamic Front document. It also allowed the group to give a view of the organization from within, with Al-Qaeda releasing testimonies and declarations via videotapes. The use of airplanes as weapons created a new, unknown type of scenario that would shift the focus on modern terrorism. Within six weeks of the September 11 attacks, the United States invaded Afghanistan in the hope of finding terrorist safe havens (Toutounji, 2017). From that point on, the organization of Al-Qaeda changed from a structured one to that of a loose, and franchised, one.

Both Osama bin Laden and Ayman al-Zawahiri became the faces of religious violence. Although Al-Qaeda asserted its theology and rationale for the use of violence, many Muslims rejected the claims of the group and disagreed with their interpretations of jihad and the role of Islam. With the U.S. invasion of Afghanistan, Al-Qaeda and its leaders operated out of Pakistan. The organization began to "franchise" terrorism. Zawahiri became core leadership of the group and used his alliances to branch the organization out within Pakistan and Southeast Asia (White, 2020). Within Pakistan, he was able to work in tribal areas, the Pakistani version of the Taliban and the Haqqani Network (whose founder was a mentor of Osama bin Laden). Outside of the region, he made an alliance with Lashkar-e-Taiba. Al-Qaeda continued attacks, either solo or with affiliates, showing its commitment to religious violence.

Attacks by the group include the 2002 bombing of a synagogue in Tunisia that killed 19 and injured 22, just one of many attacks that year (Counter Extremism Project, n.d.). The U.S. announced that its mission was "accomplished" in Afghanistan in 2003, but this did not slow down the attacks by the group. In 2004, the group detonated bombs on four rush hour trains in Madrid, killing 191 civilians and wounding more than 1,800 others. In 2007, the group aided Al-Qaeda in Iraq (AQI) in coordinated suicide bombings of five diesel trucks in Yazidi Kurdish villages in Iraq. Considered the worst terrorist attack in the post-Saddam Hussein era, the attack left over 300 people dead and wounded hundreds more (Counter Extremism Project, n.d.). There were several attacks in 2008, including the January suicide bombings that killed Belgium tourists, the grenade attack on the U.S. embassy in Sana'a, and the attacks on British and Italian embassies. There was also the bombing of a Japanese oil tanker in April of 2008.

Al-Qaeda has two official branches in Africa: Al-Qaeda in the Lands of the Islamic Maghreb (AQIM)/Al-Qaeda in the Maghreb (North Africa region down to Mali), founded in the early 2000s, and al-Shabaab (Somalia and East Africa) that was founded in 2006. Jihadist groups that are part of the Al-Qaeda network, or have a form of alliance with Al-Qaeda, include Ajnad Misr (Egypt and founded in 2013), Ansar al Din (Mali and founded in 2011), Ansar al Sharia Libya (founded in 2011), Ansar al Sharia Tunisia (founded in 2011), Ansar al Sharia Yemen (founded in 2011), Ansaru (Nigeria and founded in 2012), Al-Mourabitoun (North Africa and Mali, founded in 2013), Uqba bin Nafi Brigade (Tunisia and founded in 2012) and Al Muhajiroun (based in Saudi Arabia, operated in the

U.K. and founded in 1996). Al-Qaeda in Iraq, founded in 2004, was the first Al-Qaeda affiliate. In 2006, AQI renamed itself the Islamic State in Iraq. This group would go on to have its own turbulent and explosive trajectory (Congressional Research Service, 2024). As the franchise and affiliates grew, so did the scope of the attacks Al-Qaeda were involved in.

For example, Ansar al-Sharia in Libya attacked the U.S. consulate in Benghazi, which led to the death of U.S. Ambassador Chris Stevens and three other Americans (Counter Extremism Project, n.d.). Also in 2012, AQIM attacked a natural gas plant. Failed negotiations with Algerian forces led to the death of 37 hostages. Al-Qaeda in the Arabian Peninsula claimed responsibility for the 2015 Charlie Hebdo attacks. A month later, the group seized a large military base in Yemen, while Al-Qaeda fighters attacked a prison in Yemen and released six Al-Qaeda militants (Counter Extremism Project, n.d.). The group has remained active, either itself or through affiliates, to the present day. The last attack claimed by al-Qaeda, or an affiliate, was the August 2023 attack by Ansar al-Tawhid and the Turkistan Islamic Party in Syria.

Leadership for Al-Qaeda remained stable for many years with Osama bin Laden as the primary founder/financial backer of the organization and Abdullah Azzam as the architect of ideology for the group. Ayman al-Zawahiri stepped into a leadership role after the death of Azzam and became the chief leader of the group after Osama bin Laden's death in 2010. (Toutounji, 2017). Zawahiri led the group until his death in July of 2022 by a U.S. drone attack (Congressional Research Service, 2024). Saif (Sayf) al-Adl is the current de facto, leader of the group as he was the most senior person in the group at the time of Zawahiri's death.

Initial funding for Al-Qaeda came primarily from Osama bin Laden. Since then, the organization has become involved in extortion, donations via charities, private funds, state sponsorship, and illicit activities (drug trafficking, bank robbing, hostage-taking, unregistered money remittances, etc.) (Counter Extremism Project, n.d.). Prior to 9/11, it is estimated that Al-Qaeda maintained a $30 million annual budget, with donations being a large portion of the funding. By 2009, the group experienced a negative cash flow and even resorted to charging recruits for their weapons. Post bin Laden's death in 2011, the group expanded its funding sources to illicit crimes, like drug trafficking.

The group finds less regulated financial systems and exploits the ability to transfer funds. In September 2021, Turkey-based Al-Qaeda affiliates were caught moving funds and sending money to militants in Syria (Department of Treasury, 2022). They also use charities as a means to acquire funds. Groups like the Islamic Relief Agency (ISRA), based in Sudan, funneled nearly $5 million to Al-Qaeda's predecessor, MAK in 1997 (Counter Extremism Project, n.d.). This is a tactic that Al-Qaeda would continue. Other sources of funding for the group include private donors, like the "Golden Chain" which included some 20 Saudi financial donors, some related to bin Laden.

The U.S.'s response to Al-Qaeda over the years included earlier efforts to find weapons of mass destruction (WMD) and dismantling Al-Qaeda after the 9/11 attacks. While the power and control that Al-Qaeda has ebbed and waned over the years, the group remains active. Its adaptability in finding financial revenues, affiliates in varying countries, and loose networks with a few key leaders has proven to work in its favor. Since its creation in the 1980s, Al-Qaeda has been able to play the long game. Groups like ISIS rose very quickly in 2013 and was once a main competitor of Al-Qaeda. However, the United States continues to view Al-Qaeda as a more dangerous organization (Counter Extremism

Project, n.d.). Affiliates for the group range from Africa to Southeast Asia. The U.S.'s withdrawal from Afghanistan in August 2021 and the takeover of the country by the Taliban, many question if Al-Qaeda will use this opportunity to establish a base there.

Al-Qaeda in the Lands of the Islamic Maghreb

Al-Qaeda in the Lands of the Islamic Maghreb (Al-Qaeda in the Maghreb) operates in the Sahel (Mali, Mauritania, Chad, and Niger areas) with cells in Nigeria, Libya, and Tunisia (Masters & Laub, 2015). Like other groups under the Al-Qaeda franchise, AQIM has identified a "far enemy" and a localized one. Unlike Al-Qaeda, AQIM views France and Spain as its "far enemy," not the United States (Stanford University, n.d.). The group's origin traces back to the Islamist movement the Armed Islamic Group (GIA) during the Algerian Civil War in the 1990s (Masters & Laub, 2015). In 1998 Hassan Hattab and other GIA members formed the Salafist Group for Preaching and Combat (GSPC) when some of the violent tactics of GIA lost civilian support (Central Intelligence Agency, n.d.).

The group then entered a state of chaos in the early 2000s due to the counterterrorism tactics of Algeria. Under the leadership of Mokhtar Belmokhtar, AQIM took 32 Europeans hostage in Northern Mali. This 2003 attack led to a total of $6 million in ransom money for the group (Stanford University, n.d.). The group then merged with al-Qaeda to form AQIM in September of 2006 (Central Intelligence Agency, n.d.). In June of 2009, the group claimed responsibility for the murder of James Leggett, a U.S. citizen, in Mauritian on a missionary visit (National Counterterrorism Center, n.d.). This drew a lot of attention from the international community. A multinational counterterrorism raid in 2010 on AQIM camps disrupted the group and its membership (National Counterterrorism Center, n.d.).

As a result of a mixture of the Arab Spring, instability in the greater Middle East region, and internal differences, many fighters left the region and went to fight in larger conflicts. A group of Mauritanians left AQIM in 2011 and formed the Movement for Unity and Jihad in West Africa (MUJWA). The group coordinated the 2012 attacks in Mali with Ansar al-Dine and MUJAO against the Mali government. The attack included controlling the northern region of the country and imposing a severely strict brand of Sharia law (Masters & Laub, 2015).

In 2013, al-Mulathamun and MUJWA merged to form al-Mourabitoun. By late 2015, al-Mourabitoun was reintegrated back into AQIM. In 2017, the Mali branch of AQIM, along with al-Mourabitoun, joined Jama'at Nasr al-Islam wal-Muslimin (JNIM), a Mali-based Al-Qaeda coalition (Central Intelligence Agency, n.d.).

Group leadership includes Abdelmalek Droukdel (aka Abu Musab Abdul Wadud), who assumed a leadership role in June of 2004 and continues in that role. Droukdel succeeded Sahraoui as leader of the GSPC. Droukdel expanded GSPC operations and is credited with allying the GSPC with Al-Qaeda (AQ) when it formally became AQIM (Stanford University, n.d.). The group mainly views France and, in the periphery, Spain as targets. AQIM has an estimated 1000 base members in Algeria (Central Intelligence Agency, n.d.). At its height, it's estimated that AQIM had over 30,000 members (National Counterterrorism Center, n.d.). The group has worked with Boko Haram, al-Shabaab, and AQAP.

Tactics for the group include guerilla-style raids (keeping with the group's origins), kidnapping, assassinations, and suicide bombings. A large portion of funding comes from kidnapping for ransom, arms smuggling, trafficking cigarettes, and vehicles (Masters & Laub,

2015). The group is also known to engage in the illicit human and drug trade. It was once labeled "One of the wealthiest terrorist organizations in the world" (Stanford University, n.d.). While AQIM operates mainly in Algeria, it publicly expresses support for Islamist extremism in Afghanistan, Pakistan, Iraq, Yemen, Somalia, Chechnya, and Palestine.

Armed Islamic Group

The Groupe Islamique Arme' (GIA), or the Armed Islamic Group, is a Salafi-jihadist group that formed in Algeria in October of 1992 (Stanford University, n.d.). Dubbed as one of the most successful jihadi groups, the GIA came very close to overthrowing a regime (Thurston, 2017). The group was created by veterans, former mujahideen, of the Soviet-Afghanistan War that took place from 1979 to 1989 in Afghanistan (Council on Foreign Relations, 2009). The Algerian government banned the Islamic Salvation Front (FIS) in December of 1991, precipitating the creation of GIA (United Nations Security Council, 2018).

Based in Algeria, the group's founders were activists and radicals that started with the aim to create an Islamic State by overthrowing the Algerian government and establishing Sharia law. Heavily recruiting "Afghan Algerians," the group used Salafi-Jihadi to explain its use of violence (Thurston, 2017). The Groupe Islamique Arme' became a well-known extremist group due to its indiscriminate attacks on civilians, high-profile attacks, and its violent campaign (United Nations Security Council, 2018). The group disbanded in 2004 after many of its leaders were either arrested or killed due to counterterrorism policies.

The origins of GIA trace back to the 1988 riots when desperate and impoverished Algerians took to the streets to express discontent with the Algerian government. In response, the government allowed for new political parties to form (Thurston, 2017). One such group was an Islamist party, Front islamique de salut (Islamic Salvation Front, FIS). A diverse group, FIS united both Muslim Brotherhood-style/Qutbist-style Islamists with the Salafis. This moderate but mainstream Muslim party had some internal discourse about the use of force, jihadism, etc., but was able to maintain group cohesion (Thurston, 2017). In 1991 FIS won the first round of parliamentary elections and had garnered the support of many.

A precipitating event for the formation of GIA was Algeria's military government cancelling the country's election in 1992. The FSI was poised to win the election before the cancellation (Council on Foreign Relations, 2009) Frustration in the country was funneled into many outlets, ranging from activism to extremism. The Islamic Salvation Army (ISA), a militant group linked to FSI, was an immediate backlash. The ISA operated until its 1997 ceasefire and subsequent 2,000 disbanding. The ISA and the Armed Islamic Group (GIA) both operated with the goal of toppling the Algerian government (Thurston, 2017). As the country began a civil war, several militant groups began to appear.

The GIA had three groups of followers: Algerian Afghans who'd returned to the country, followers of the Mustafa Bouyali movement, and homegrown Salafi-Jihadists. This collection of followers allowed the GIA to establish a more purist ideology than the FSI. The GIA quickly emerged as a violent and brutal group, adopting Salafi-Jihadism and embracing violence. In 1993, the group was able to distinguish itself from other groups by indiscriminately targeting civilians (United Nations Security Council, 2018). Journalists and intellectuals were beheaded or killed during the civil war. Both military and anyone thought to be a sympathizer of the regime were targeted (Council on Foreign Relations, 2009).

The group evoked *takfir*, an extremist concept of excommunication, to justify attacking a Muslim they considered a military regime sympathizer. During the mid-1990s, the group produced a widely known newsletter, Al-Ansar, in London. Al-Ansar was a weekly publication that often published hate speech against Jews and Christians (Council on Foreign Relations, 2009). In 1995, Abu Qatada al-Filastini, a global jihadist and supporter of GIA, issued a *fatwa* on "the legality of killing children and women to ward off the danger of the rape of women and the killing of brothers" (Thurston, 2017). al-Filastini published fatwas like this in Al-Ansar. However, in 1995, the group murdered two former FIS leaders. Initially, Al-Ansar reported their deaths as attacks by the state and that the men were martyrs. It came to light that GIA was responsible for the men's deaths. Al-Ansar then published a statement admitting to their deaths (Thurston, 2017). There was public backlash from civilians and London-based jihadists, like al-Filastini, resulting in the slow decline of the newsletter. Many Al-Qaeda leaders, like prominent leader Omar Mahmoud Uthman, served as editors of the newsletter. Mostafa Kamel Mostafa Ibrahim became editor-in-chief of the newsletter in 1997. In 1998, he served as the unofficial spokesperson for the group during the "Ramadan massacres" in Algeria (United Nations Security Council, 2018).

Tactics of the group include ambushing Algerian security forces, hijackings, bombings, and attacking civilians. In 1994, the group hijacked an Air France flight with the intention of crashing it over the city of Paris. In 1995, the group set off a series of bombs throughout France, killing 10 and wounding over 200 people when subways, outdoor markets, and a Jewish school were targeted (United Nations Security Council, 2018). GIA members involved in the attacks were eventually convicted in France in 1999. Between 1995 and the late 1990s, the group is thought to have murdered several hundreds of civilians when they would attack entire villages. During their most active period, the group operated in France, Belgium, Britain, and Italy (Council on Foreign Relations, 2009).

The group was known for targeting the Algerian government, military personnel, civilians, and foreigners alike. An estimated 100 foreigners were killed by the GIA in Algeria between 1992 and 2002 (United Nations Security Council, 2018). The group also engaged in target attacks against women, specifically liberated women. They murdered women who did not wear hijabs and women with professional careers (Council on Foreign Relations, 2009). If a woman refused mu'ta, temporary marriages that men used for "pleasure marriages," the woman was also attacked. Another targeted group of women were the wives, family members, and children of military personnel. This practice did garner disdain from both civilians and even within the group (Council on Foreign Relations, 2009).

In 1998, dissension in the group over the targeting of civilians led to a splinter group breaking away from GIA. One of its commanders, Hassan Hattab, left to create the Salafist Group for Call and Combat (GSPC), with many GIA members following him (United Nations Security Council, 2018). GSPC took most of GIA's networks and financial resources with it, leaving the group vulnerable (Council on Foreign Relations, 2009). The GSPC would later become Al-Qaeda in the Lands of the Islamic Maghreb (AQIM) (National Counterterrorism Center, n.d.). In 2004 the Algerian police forces engaged in a large-scale crackdown of all local terrorist groups. An estimated 400 GIA and GSPC members were arrested during that campaign (Council on Foreign Relations, 2009). The group disbanded later in 2004 after many of its leaders were arrested or killed, and other members joined GSPC/AQIM (Stanford University, n.d.).

Hezbollah

Two events marked the immediate beginning of the Hezbollah movement, the Iranian Revolution and Israel's invasion of Lebanon. The Israeli invasion served as the "last straw event." The 1979 Iranian Revolution re-sparked the Islamic revolution in the area. The Revolution created a space for resurgence in the Shiite momentum in 1982 (Karagiannis, 2009). An integral part of Hezbollah's ideology is the concept of guardianship of the Islamic jurist. This was first introduced in 1970 by Ayatollah Khomeini, leader of the Iranian Revolution (Karagiannis, 2009).

Israel and the Israeli Defense Force (IDF) began its invasion of Lebanon in 1982 with Operation Peace for Galilee (Matthews, 2008). In September of 1982, Phalangists, commanded by Israel, killed an estimated 3,000 Palestinian and Lebanese people located in a Palestinian refugee; most of the victims were children, the elderly, and Shiite Muslims. A Lebanese resistance operation responded on the same day against Israelis in the city of Beirut (Harb, 2011).

Hezbollah, also called Hizbollah, was formed in the early 1980s by Shiite Muslims. Aggrieved citizens created Hezbollah, the "Party of God," as a direct response to the Israeli invasion and occupation of Southern Lebanon (Karagiannis, 2009).

Hezbollah, dubbed the "Habitat for Hezbollah," delivers a variety of community services that range from running hospitals to a television station. The group possesses two characteristics: devoted membership and a push for political and social change (Karagiannis, 2009). The duality of the organization allows it to supply military and political support as well as community activism.

Hezbollah's success is attributed to five factors (Harik, 2005). Firstly, Hezbollah's ability to advance the foreign policy agenda of Syria, Iran, and Lebanon, garnering their support. Secondly, it remains flexible enough to incorporate different groups and identities into its ideologies (sympathizers of Lebanon, Islam, Arabs, the deeply religious, etc.). Thirdly, factor of Hezbollah's success, in certain parts of Lebanese society, is its adaptation to the political needs of Lebanese society; it uses modern technology and political techniques to gain sympathizers. Fourthly, it has adopted television outlets that allow it to spread its message of resistance against Israel in Lebanon, Muslim, and Arab countries where its acts would not be considered terrorist, as similar ideologies against Israel are common. Lastly, Hezbollah's relationship with Syria has warded off several outside interventions (Harik, 2005). Hezbollah's current involvement in the Syrian Civil War, its impact on Lebanese society, and the possibility of outside intervention remains to be unseen.

Hezbollah served as a "presence" in Lebanese society for many years but was not officially created under the Hezbollah creed until 1982. Its origins are rooted in a splinter faction of the Amal movement, the Islamic Amal. The Islamic Amal, the Lebanese branch of Hizb al-Dawa al-Islamiya, was a radical Shiite group (Karagiannis, 2009). Hezbollah received support from Tehran, as Tehran hoped to spread the Islamic Revolution to Lebanon, and Damascus. Tehran helped the organization to gain weaponry, trained individuals, and provided inspiration (Bynum, 2003).

Hezbollah emerged in 1982 during Israel's invasion of Lebanon. It gained legitimacy through winning military tactics, providing community development, and reconstruction support (Cammett, 2006). In 1983 the group claimed responsibility for the death of nearly 300 U.S. and French troops in Beirut and for targeting Western military. The group denied responsibility for the accusations. A once ignored Lebanese population, the Shiite community, appeared at the forefront of political and economic matters in the country. The U.S. withdrew its troops in 1984, Israel followed by withdrawing most of its troops in 1985 (BBC News, 2018). The death of Khomeini in 1989 began a new phase in Hezbollah as a political party. The organization reached out to other Lebanese communities and presented itself as a non-government party (Haddad, 2006). With Syrian support, Hezbollah was able to rise in political and military power.

The Lebanese Civil War symbolically ended in 1989 with the signing of the Taif Agreement. The agreement did not stop Hezbollah from keeping a militia in Southern Lebanon, and the group continued into the 1990s. The Civil War formally ended in 1990, and the National Assembly ordered all militias, except Hezbollah, to disband in 1991 (BBC News, 2018). The South Lebanon Army (SLA) refused to comply.

The activities of Hezbollah during the 1990s were more characteristics of guerilla warfare than terrorism (Bynum, 2003). The organization continued attempting to expel the Israeli military from Lebanon. A 1999 ambush of an Israeli convoy was filmed and aired throughout Lebanon and Israel, via Hezbollah's station. Hezbollah used the media to lower Israeli public support for war by constantly producing human casualties and showcasing attacks on its media outlet. Al-Manar, a television station largely associated with Hezbollah, became a tactic to weaken Israeli morale for war (Matthews, 2008).

In the mid-1990s, the IDF used Hezbollah's strategy of attacking Lebanese civilians, as Hezbollah had successfully done, to force the Lebanese government to disband Hezbollah. The tactic created backlash; it attracted scorn from the international community and validated Hezbollah's mission in the viewpoint of some in the Lebanese public (Matthews, 2008). The IDF and Israeli troops withdrew from Southern Lebanon in 2000 after the collapse of the SLA (Matthews, 2008). Hezbollah viewed this as a victory and continued to support the destruction of Israel (Karagiannis, 2009). Hezbollah also cooperated with Hamas in order to achieve their mutual goal. In 2001, a funding cell was discovered by the FBI in North Carolina (Bynum, 2003). The dynamics of the Syrian-Hezbollah relationship shifted during this time.

In the 2002 State of the Union Address, former President George Bush labeled the organization as part of a "Terrorist Underworld" that threatened U.S. National Security (Karagiannis, 2009). The United States declared Hezbollah a terrorist organization, but other countries were not as quick to follow its lead. The Russian government did not recognize the organization as a terrorist organization, despite a newly relisted Russian manifesto of terrorist organizations (Karagiannis, 2009). Syria, Iran, and other Middle Eastern countries viewed Hezbollah as a legitimate resistance movement. Lebanon attempted to use legal precedents to justify Hezbollah's use of force in Southern Lebanon (Harik, 2005).

The 2004 U.N. Security Council resolution required the withdrawal of all foreign troops from Lebanon; Syria ignored the request (BBC News, 2018). In the same year, Rafik Hariri left his post as prime minister and was assassinated in Beirut in 2005. Some suspected Syrian involvement in the assassination; others attributed it to Israel trying to destabilize the country (Fitzgerald & Annon, 2005). However, anti-Syrian sentiments sparked several demonstrations, both violent and nonviolent, that became dubbed the "Cedar Revolution."

Hezbollah strategically placed sites in several parts of Lebanon for access to inner Israel in case of an invasion (Matthews, 2008). Between 2000 and 2006, Hezbollah placed missile launcher sites in several villages. A 34-day war emerged between Israel and Hezbollah in 2006; a war Hezbollah strategically planned for almost half a decade (Matthews, 2008). Israel launched attacks on Lebanon. Hezbollah, not the Lebanese government, responded by launching streams of rockets into Northern Israel.

The U.N. established a ceasefire in August. By the summation of the 34-day war, Hezbollah launched more than 3,700 rockets into Israel; 42 civilians were killed, and 4,262 others were wounded. In addition to those killed or wounded, 2,773 Israeli citizens were treated from "shock and anxiety" (Matthews, 2008). Post Israeli and Lebanon War, Hezbollah emerged as the reconstruction agent to rebuild Lebanon (Cammett, 2006). Hezbollah provided medical support, hospitals, and displacement services for Lebanese citizens harmed by the war; services that the Lebanese government was not able to provide on such a large scale.

In 2009, the Hague released the four generals suspected of assassinating former Prime Minister Hariri. Hezbollah's leader, Hassan Nasrallah, boycotted the tribunal. The Hague cited insufficient evidence to charge the pro-Syrian Lebanese guards. Nasrallah claimed that the tribunal was "in league with Israel" (BBC News, 2018). Hezbollah continued its activities in Lebanese society and politics, with both a military faction and a political arm of the organization.

Islamic State of Iraq and Syria

The history of the Islamic State is closely linked with the evolution of Al-Qaeda. The Islamic State, or the Islamic State of Iraq and Syria (ISIS), the Islamic State in Iraq and the Levant (ISIL), or Daesh, is a Salafist Jihadist terror organization founded in 2013 (Weiss & Hassan, 2015). By June 2014, the Sunni Islamist group reemerged as The Islamic State, marking the beginning of its global caliphate. Previously, the Islamic State was named Tanzim Qa'idat al-Jihad fi Bilad al-Rafidayn (or the Al-Qaeda Group in the Land of the Two Rivers/Al-Qaeda in Iraq [AQI]) (United Nations Security Council, n.d.). Dubbed as both a terrorist organization and as a mafia, for its involvement in the illicit markets of oil and arms trafficking, ISIS has also exhibited aspects of a military organization. The origins of the Islamic State start with a Jordanian group, al-Tawhid, in 1993 (Gerges, 2016). It morphed into AQI in 2004 and then the Islamic State that became known for beheadings and radicalization too extreme for Al-Qaeda.

The group's founder is Abu Musab al-Zarqawi, born Ahmad Fadhil Nazzal al-Khalaykah (Weiss & Hassan, 2015). Zarqawi created his alternative name after a neighborhood in Jordan, Zarqa, due to the biblical and historical significance of the town. A place that was once the location of a struggle between God and Jacob in the Bible, and the location of the oldest Palestinian refugee camp in Jordan, Zarqa is a sight of religious and political significance.

al-Zarqawi's path to the formation of ISIS is one that includes a parallel, but socially different, trajectory than that of Osama bin Laden. al-Zarqawi was semi-literate in Arabic and dropped out of school. Once his father died, he became involved in criminal activities.

In hopes of thwarting a life of crime for her son, Um Sayel, his mother, enrolled him in Al-Husayn Ben Ali Mosque religious classes (Weiss & Hassan, 2015). There he learned about Salafism and a more stringent interpretation of Islam.

Parallel to al-Zarqawi's path, the dynamics of the soon-to-be Al-Qaeda group began to shift. Ayman al-Zawahiri, the Egyptian surgeon who was once a part of Jamaat al-Jihad, or the Jihad group, created an ideological rift between his friend Osama bin Laden and his mentor Abdullah Azzam (Weiss & Hassan, 2015). In 1986 al-Zawahiri began forming a more extreme ideology that included *takfirism* or excommunication that preceded death. Abdullah Azzam, the leader of MAK and the architect of Al-Qaeda, was fundamentally opposed to Muslims killing Muslims. Bin Laden was receptive to the ideology. The rift between Azzam and bin Laden culminated in November 1989 when Azzam and his two sons were assassinated in a roadside bomb. The suspects for the assassination range from bin Laden to the United States (Rogell, n.d.). Osama bin Laden continued the quest for global jihad from Saudi Arabia. Al-Zawahiri operated from Egypt with the EIJ in the hopes of creating an Egyptian caliphate. Simultaneously, in December of 1989, Huthaifa Azzam, son of Abdullah Azzam, picked up a group of Jordanian Arab-Afghans from the airport to fight in the dwindling Arab-Afghan War. Abu Musab al-Zarqawi was among the group of fighters.

In 1989, al-Zarqawi traveled to Afghanistan to fight as a mujahideen and remained in the region until 1993. During that time, he created a network of allies among those that remained in Afghanistan vying for control of the country post-Soviet Invasion (Weiss & Hassan, 2015). He connected with Khalid Sheikh Mohammed (mastermind of the 9/11 attacks), Mohammed Shobana (publisher of a Jihadist magazine), and Salah al-Hami (a journalist). As the power struggle continued in Afghanistan, al-Zarqawi decided to side with Gulbuddin Hekmatyar in his attempt to control the country. This was a losing choice as Hekmatyar was overthrown by the Taliban and Hekmatyrar fled to Iran (Weiss & Hassan, 2015).

With Hekmatyar gone, al-Zarqawi went to train at Al-Qaeda's Sada al-Malahim camp, among some other camps as well. Sada al-Malahim had three phases of training (Weiss & Hassan, 2015). The first lasted for 15 days and included psychological and moral exhaustion. This was done to help weed out candidates. The second phase lasted for roughly 45 days and included military preparation. During this time, they received arms training, ranging from some small arms to heavier artillery. The final phase included learning guerilla war tactics. With the politics of Afghanistan settled and the Soviets gone from the region, al-Zarqawi returned to Jordan in 1993 (Gerges, 2016).

Soon after returning to Jordan, al-Zarqawi, with his mentor Abu Mohammed al-Maqdisi, created an underground group named Al-Tawhid. The group promoted the *Dawa* pillar of Islam, promoting or inviting people to Islam. The group would later become Bayat al-Imam, with al-Zarqawi focusing on the "near" enemy of Arab governments. By 1994, he and his mentor, were arrested for establishing an illegal jihadist organization (Gerges, 2016). A 15-year sentence resulted in al-Zarqawi being sent to al-Suwaqah/Swaqa prison. Like many prisoners in the Arab world report, torture and solitary confinement were common occurrence. Al-Zarqawi received eight and half months of solitary confinement at one time and reportedly lost all of his toenails due to infections from the torture he received there (Gerges, 2016).

Those who knew him before and after his incarceration noted a notable change in his mentality and personality. Although he was always an aggressive person, he became more extreme in his beliefs and his mission. During his time at al-Suwaqah, he was able to make a name for himself, isolating himself from his mentor and emerging as a vicious and determined prison leader (Gerges, 2016).

In May of 1999, King Abdallah II of Jordan granted amnesty to thousands of prisoners (Gerges, 2016). After five years in prison, al-Zarqawi was released. Almost immediately, he returned to Afghanistan more emboldened, hardened, and determined than before. Initially, Al-Qaeda Central's leaders avoided working directly with him but allowed him to use a training camp in Herat. Both bin Laden and Zawahiri approved the setup. Al-Zarqawi was reluctant to pledge allegiance with Al-Qaeda and was open to using their camps as a base for training his new recruits. Al-Qaeda carried out one of the deadliest terrorist attacks in modern history, the September 11, 2001 attacks in New York City.

In October 2001, the United States bombed Herat and subsequently invaded Afghanistan, causing both Al-Qaeda and affiliates to relocate to Kandahar and then Tora Bora (Gerges, 2016). al-Zarqawi and his recruits found themselves fighting alongside the Taliban and Al-Qaeda in the December 2001 Battle of Tora Bora. On foot, he and his affiliates went to Iran following the Tora Bora battle. Around this time, al-Zarqawi pledged *biya* to bin Laden and used "seed money" from him to further upstart his organization. He was also involved in the 2002 assassination of a USAID official in Jordan and with a toxins network throughout Europe and the Middle East (Defense Intelligence Agency, n.d.). Also receiving help from Hekmatyar, the leader banished from Afghanistan by the Taliban in the 1990s, he was involved in many illicit activities.

An Iranian government crackdown, precipitated by the U.S. government, resulted in nearly 80% of Zarqawi's men being arrested and deported (Gerges, 2016). With what men he had left, he and his fighters crossed into Iraq in 2003 (Defense Intelligence Agency, n.d.). In Iraq, al-Zarqawi gained new recruits, and the attention and support of bin Laden. He was still fundamentally opposed to the central stance of Al-Qaeda Central. He was a point person for al-Qaeda (AQ) while in Iraq, especially after the U.S. invasion of Afghanistan dispersed many in the AQ leadership Iraq (Gerges, 2016).

al-Zarqawi began working with the Sunni Jihadist group Ansar al-Islam in Iraqi Kurdistan. However, another subsequent invasion, this time the 2003 invasion of Iraq, led to the rebranding of Ansar al-Islam to Ansar al-Sunna. The shift allowed them to bring al-Zarqawi and his men into the "Sunni Triangle" (Gerges, 2016). This network provided him with additional resources and connections. In 2003, al-Zarqawi became the founder of al-Tawid wa al-Jihad. In 2004, the group became AQI, with al-Zarqawi officially pledging allegiance to Al-Qaeda in October of the same year (Defense Intelligence Agency, n.d.). The allegiance gained him access to transnational operations and to veterans of the Iraq jihad. al-Zarqawi went from 30 men to an estimated 5,000 full-time fighters quickly (Gerges, 2016). Homegrown Iraqi radicals, fueled by the U.S. involvement in the region at the time, were fast recruits. In 2006, the group renamed itself as the Islamic State in Iraq (ISIQ) and by 2014, the Islamic State (IS). Although he was killed in June 2006, al-Zarqawi was able to execute more high-profile operations in Iraq that Osama bin Laden was able to do globally (Defense Intelligence Agency, n.d.). Abu al-Masri assumed leadership of the group until his death in 2010

Leadership for the group includes its Amir and founder, Abu Musab al-Zarqawi, from the early 2000s until his death via U.S. drone strike in 2006 (National Counterterrorism Center, n.d.). Abu Bakr al-Baghdadi (AKA Ibrahim Awaad Ibrahim Ali al-Badri) assumed control of the group in 2010. Under his leadership, the "caliphate" was created, and he proclaimed himself the "caliph" in 2014. Baghdadi was killed by U.S. forces in Syria in October of 2019.

Immediately succeeding al-Baghdadi was Hajji 'Abdallah (AKA Amir Muhammad Said Abdal-Rahman al-Mawla) in October of 2019. 'Abdullah self-detonated an explosive, killing himself, during a U.S. military raid aimed at capturing him in February of 2022 (Vergun, 2022). The current leader of ISIS/IS is Abu al-Hassan al-Qurayshi (National Counterterrorism Center, n.d.).

Attacks by the group are vast, as the evolution to the Islamic State began with al-Zarqawi in the early 2000s. Jama'at al-Tawhid Wa'al-Jihad (JTJ) was responsible for the August 2003 bombing of the United Nations headquarters in Baghdad (United Nations Security Council, n.d.). The attack killed 23 people. In 2006, Abu Bakr Naji released the *Management of Savagery*, which calls for the unbridled use of terror to wield an Islamic caliphate. The author makes the claim that public torture and killings are needed to frighten one's enemy and to keep civilians in check (White, 2020). ISIS uses Naji's "management" style to rationalize its excessive use of violence and force. In 2009, the Iraqi Prime Minister began targeting Sunni leaders, this triggered support for ISI in Sunni tribal areas. They conducted a suicide attack in Baghdad that killed hundreds of people (Wilson Center, 2019).

In 2011, the Islamic State in Iraq (ISI) went to Syria to establish an Al-Qaeda affiliate, al-Nusra Front. In January 2012, the newly formed Salafist group announced its goal to overthrow the Assad regime and take control of Syria (National Counterterrorism Center, n.d.). In 2013 Baghdadi announced that the Islamic State in Iraq would merge with al-Nusra Front to create the Islamic State in Iraq and Al Sham (ISIS). Despite this, a rift was growing between the two groups as a merger would have threatened the autonomy of al-Nusra. In April 2013, the leader of al-Nusra, Abu Muhammad al-Jawlani, publicly pledged allegiance with Al-Qaeda/Ayman al-Zawahiri (National Counterterrorism Center, n.d.). Baghdadi's decision to attempt to merge the groups was a move that Al-Qaeda did not support, and eventually severed ties with ISIS the following year. In August of that year, ISIS attacked rebel groups like Liwa al-Tawhid, Ahrar al-Sham, and al-Nusra Front (Wilson Center, 2019).

In January of 2014, ISIS took control of Raqqa and declared the city the capital of its "caliphate." The following month, Al-Qaeda officially cut all ties with the group. In a surprisingly effective offensive, ISIS took control of Mosul in June, killing over 600 inmates at a Badoush prison (Wilson Center, 2019). This began the group's claiming territory in Iraq, including Mosul, Raqqa, Sinjar, and Mosul Dam by August of that year.

The video of the beheading of American journalist James Foley in August 2014 not only garnered media attention but also showcased the brutality of the group. This began a series of publicized beheadings and executions by ISIS that included James Foley (U.S.), Steven Sotloff (U.S.), David Haines (British), Herve Gourdal (French), and many others (Wilson Center, 2019). The U.S. executed its first airstrike in Syria against ISIS in September 2014. Later, the U.S. named the campaign against ISIS as "Operation Inherent Resolve."

In 2015, the group transitioned into the height of its operations, during which it controlled large areas in Iraq and Syria. ISIS started the year with an attack on a French newspaper, Charlie Hebdo, killing 11 people. In February, in its operational background, the group abducted over 200 Assyrian Christians in Syria. The following month, affiliates of the group bombed two mosques in Yemen, killing 137 people. From May to June 2015, ISIS gained territory in Iraq, Syria, and Libya. Attacks by ISIS and its affiliates occurred from Yemen to Kuwait. ISIS launched attacks within and beyond its controlled territories (Congressional Research Service, 2024). ISIS's Yemeni affiliates also engaged in several attacks.

In October, the first American died in combat during a hostage rescue mission in northern Iraq. That same month, an ISIS affiliate in Egypt, the Islamic State Sinai, bombed a Russian passenger plane, killing 224 people (Wilson Center, 2019). The lethality and frequency of attacks by the group and its affiliates, continued at an alarming pace with multiple attacks occurring each month. On November 13, 2015, ISIS carried out six coordinated attacks in Paris, leaving 130 civilians dead (BBC News, 2015). The Paris attacks prompted France to increase its airstrikes in Syria.

January 2016 began with attacks in Istanbul (suicide bomber) and Indonesia (firearms and bombs), respectively (Fuller, 2016). The Iraqi forces were able to capture the town of Hit from the group but ISIS was able to recapture a Syrian town, Rai, from the Free Syrian Army on the same day (Wilson Center, 2019). Although ISIS was able to reclaim some towns, the group began losing territory as various rebel groups and governments ramped up their attacks against the group.

On August 30 of that year, ISIS acknowledged that Abu Muhhammad al Adnani was killed by a U.S. airstrike in Syria. In October, the U.S. continued its counterterrorism policy by conducting more than 30 airstrikes against the group throughout that month, impacting the fast trajectory of the group. Later that month, a U.N. report indicated that the group used thousands of men, women, and children as human shields in Mosul (Kennedy, 2016). The tactic of the group aimed to slow down Iraqi forces from advancing on their stronghold, an indicator of distress by the group. Another sign of distress was a November press release by Abu Bakr al-Baghdadi addressing affiliates, followers, and sympathizers. Baghdadi urged more of them to join the fight, citing them as essential for the group's survival. The message was echoed again in December when Abi al-Hassan al Muhajer, the new spokesperson for the group, called for more attacks by sympathizers and for current fighters to stand their ground on the battlefields (Wilson Center, 2019).

At the close of 2016, a U.S. military report indicated that more than 50,000 ISIS fighters were killed since the U.S. involvement two years prior. Additionally, Iraqi security forces began the second phase of their campaign to regain Mosul from ISIS. By January 2017, the Iraqi government recaptured an estimated 70% of Mosul (Wilson Center, 2019). Around that time, a U.S. airstrike killed at least 80 ISIS fighters in Sirte. In February, the Turkish government detained over 400 people suspected of being a part of the Islamic State and killed 45 ISIS fighters, while the U.S. backed Iraqi forces in a ground offensive in Mosul (Wilson Center, 2019). By the end of February, ISIS fighters were being killed at a rate they couldn't sustain. As countries like Iraq, France, Turkey, and the United States increased their pressure, and ground strikes on ISIS, civilians who went to join the Islamic State also began to request a return to their home countries.

In March 2016, both ISIS's commander of Mosul and its leader of the Egyptian branch were killed in battle. A close associate of Abu Bakr al-Baghdadi, Abdurakhmon Uzbeki, was killed in Syria in April (Wilson Center, 2019). In the same month, two leaders of Abu Sayyaf, the Philippines branch, were killed by Philippine soldiers. In continued offenses with governments, rebel groups, and other organizations, the Islamic State killed a senior Taliban official, complicating the group's status in the region.

During the month of June in 2017, the U.S. joined the Philippine government in the battle against Abu Sayyaf. At the time, ISIS controlled 20% of Marawi City. During the same month, Baghdadi officially claimed a "caliphate," or an Islamic State, and destroyed two mosques in Mosul to commemorate the occasion (Wilson Center, 2019). By the end of the same month, Iraqi troops captured important locations in Mosul, the Syrian Democratic Force (SDF) closes supply routes to Raqqa, ISIS fighters withdrew from their last stronghold in Aleppo, and with the help of the U.S., the SDF broke Raqqa's Old City.

The decline of the Islamic State was solidified when the Iraqi Prime Minister declared victory over ISIS in the city of Mosul in July. Days later, the head of the Islamic State in Afghanistan was killed in a U.S. airstrike in the Kunar province, followed by Egyptian security forces killing a prominent figure in the ISIS-Sinai Peninsula branch (Reuters, 2017). The same month brought the dismantling of an Islamic State cell by Algerian forces. It is at this point that Hezbollah, another designated Foreign Terrorist Organization (FTO), declared that it will join the fight against the Islamic State and shortly thereafter began using drones to attack ISIS fighters at the Lebanon-Syria border.

In August of 2017, the University of Maryland published a report citing the Islamic State as the deadliest militant group of 2016, despite both territory loss and the death of many of its fighters. As previously noted, ISIS, although short-lived, was able to carry out more attacks than its Al-Qaeda predecessor.

The final stage of the Islamic State as a "caliphate" was in October when the group lost its last stronghold (Hawija) in northern Iraq and the loss of its last territories in central Syria. Additionally, Abu Sayyaf, an ISIS affiliate in the Philippines, lost its hold on the city of Marawi. After a four-month campaign, U.S. President Donald Trump declared the recapture of ISIS's former capital of Raqqa in October (Wilson Center, 2019). The loss of Raqqa was a significant and symbolic loss for the group. The Syrian Defense Forces declared victory over the Islamic State in November, followed by the same declaration from the Iraqi government in December (BBC News, 2019). The year ended with ISIS having fewer than 1,000 fighters left in Iraq and Syria.

With a large depletion of land in the "caliphate," the West Point Counterterrorism Center reports that the group had reverted to insurgent tactics and was using caves in northern Iraq in 2018. Baghdadi was killed during a Special Forces raid in 2019, with Ibrahim al Hashemi al Qurayshi taking on the role of leader/emir (Wilson Center, 2019). The group has relied on affiliate groups since 2019 to carry out attacks.

Financially, ISIS and its cells/affiliates, rely on various activities to raise revenue. Typically, ISIS, based in Syria and Iraq, relies on kidnapping, looting (including the selling of artifacts and antiquities), extortion of local businesses, and collecting "taxes" from drug trafficking as revenue (Department of Treasury, 2022). The Department of Treasury estimated that in 2020, the group had about $20–25 million in cash reserves dispersed throughout the region. The group has also engaged in cyber terror to finance its campaigns. Its largest expenditure is the salaries of its fighters and payments made to families of deceased or imprisoned members.

The Islamic State's attacks were generally concentrated in Iraq and Syria. However, they have affiliates in the Middle East and North Africa (MENA) and sub-Saharan Africa that allow them to have an extended reach (Congressional Research Service, 2024). Currently, the group uses its affiliates in Africa, the Middle East, and Asia to exert its presence globally. ISIS affiliates include Islamic State in Libya, Islamic State Khorasan Province (ISKP),

Islamic State in West African Province (ISWAP), Islamic State in the Sahel Province, Islamic State in the Democratic Republic of Congo, Islamic State in Mozambique, Islamic State in Somalia, and other affiliates in South Asia like Abu Sayaff (Congressional Research Service, 2024). The Islamic State in Libya began in 2014, but by 2016 it was considered "significantly degraded." It remains limited to Southern Libya and engages in illicit crimes like human trafficking and goods smuggling.

The Islamic State Khorasan Province (ISKP) is an Afghanistan-based affiliate established in 2015. Created by Pakistani, Afghan, and Central Asian militants, ISKP has amped up its attacks in Afghanistan after the 2021 country takeover by the Taliban (Congressional Research Service, 2024). Intelligence suggests that the group is still intent to attack the U.S. and other Western countries. In early 2024, the group conducted attacks in Russia, Iran, and Pakistan. In April 2024, both Italy and Turkey, on separate occasions, arrested ISKP member (Sayeh, 2024).

Without its territory, or caliphate, IS further expanded and depended, on its affiliates. This is particularly true of Africa. The 2024 Annual Threat Assessment (ATA) noted a shift of the "Sunni global jihad to Africa" (Congressional Research Service, 2024). The Islamic State in sub-Saharan and West Africa flourished. West Africa is a particular focus for terrorist groups. Corruption, weak and unstable governments, local grievances, and tribal/communal conflicts all aid for the infiltration of external groups. One such affiliate is the Islamic State—West African Province (ISWAP). Abubakar Shekau, of Boko Haram, claimed that the hostage-taking and kidnapping tactics coincide with the religious texts of the Quran and are acceptable tactics for the group (Hussein, 2015). This proclamation coincided with ISIS's leader Abubaker al-Baghdadi's similar claim for his group. Shortly after Shekau's proclamation, Boko Haram raised the ISIS flag in allegiance. An internal clash over the dispute led to the splintering of Boko Haram. ISWAP formed in 2015 after a group of members broke away from Boko Haram to pledge allegiance to the Islamic State (See ISWAP in the chapter on African terrorism).

Another African affiliate is the Islamic State in Sahel Province. Also formed in 2015, at the height of IS operations, the Islamic State in the Sahel Province is an offshoot of al-Mourabitoun (see al-Mourabitoun in the chapter on African terrorism). As a note, al-Mourabitoun was an offshoot of Al-Qaeda in the Maghreb. In 2022, the group gained the elevated status of a "province." It operates primarily in Mali, Niger, and Burkina Faso. The group is thought to have security ties with Russia (Congressional Research Service, 2024). Tactics of the group include civilian massacres that cross ethnic lines, making the group popular among a subset of the population.

In 2019, the Allied Democratic Forces (ADF) reemerged as the Islamic State in the Democratic Republic of Congo. Operating primarily in the Democratic Republic of Congo and Uganda, this group is a long-running organization. While the group's numbers have diminished, as of 2024, the group still maintains between 1,000–1,500 fighters (Congressional Research Service, 2024).

Also known as Ansar al-Sunna, the Islamic State in Mozambique (IS-M) began in 2017. Locally, the group is known as al-Shabaab, having no affiliation with the larger, and more widely known group by the same name (National Counterterrorism Center, n.d.). In 2019 the group aligned itself with the Islamic State. The Islamic State in Mozambique has displaced over 1.3 million people and is responsible for the deaths of an estimated 6,500 people. Counterterrorism policies beginning in 2024 have led to a decline in the group's numbers. However, various troops withdrawing from the region have led to a surge in numbers again (Congressional Research Service, 2024).

The final African Islamic State affiliate is the Islamic State—Somalia. An al-Shabaab split in 2015 led to the formation of Islamic State—Somalia. Al-Shabaab is one of Al-Qaeda's largest affiliates. Like ISWAP, IS-Somalia is a group that formed after members left their organization to start an IS branch. The group is based in the Puntland region of Somalia with an estimated 100–200 fighters (Congressional Research Service, 2024).

Five factors aided in the group's fast trajectory to a globally recognized terrorist organization (Defense Intelligence Agency, n.d.). First, the group benefited from large-scale support on the ground from Iraqi locals and other extremist groups. Second, the group used Al-Qaeda's model of a centralized but decentralized group. Third, its propaganda/ideology of creating an Islamic State was one that utilized Al-Qaeda's Saudi Salafism, jihadism, and politics (Gerges, 2016). The group's ability to intervene with a political framework with Salafi Jihadism created a solution to the political and structural vacuum caused by the U.S. invasions in the region. Fourth, MAK, the predecessor of Al-Qaeda, laid the foundation for addressing logistical pipeline shortcomings during the Afghan-Soviet war (Farrall, 2017). Al-Qaeda further thought about how to improve supply chains in the region. The Islamic State, via its relationship with Al-Qaeda, gained access to this network and improved on the logistical pipelines to replenish the loss of resources needed for operations (Defense Intelligence Agency, n.d.). Lastly, the group was able to quickly replace key personnel and assume new responsibilities.

While al-Zarqawi was able to draw many influences from Al-Qaeda, there are key differences between him and his predecessor. In January of 2004, he sent a letter to bin Laden pointing out the opportunity to use jihad as a means for battle. The letter proposed inciting war with Shia, among other targets, would provide prolonged instability and the opportunity to continue fighting. This would in turn incite more extremists from Sunni Iraqis and Sunni globally (Defense Intelligence Agency, n.d.).

Although the Islamic State and even some of its affiliates have ties with al-Qaeda, the two organizations are very different in their focus, tactics, and ideology. Al-Qaeda focuses on attacking the "far enemy," such as the United States and other Western countries. The Islamic State prefers focusing on the "near enemy," an approach that makes its targets more regional in scope. An example of this is its focus on Iran and Syria (Byman, 2015). IS targets other Muslims indiscriminately, a practice that is less favored by Al-Qaeda. The fundamental clash between the two groups, and what ultimately led Al-Qaeda to cut ties with Al-Qaeda in the Maghreb/ISIS/IS, was their ideological differences over the use of violence against other Muslims. Additionally, the brutality and lethality of IS are notably different. IS uses beheadings to garner popularity and media attention.

Al-Qaeda uses attacks to excite and mobilize the Muslim world. It favors large-scale attacks. Al-Qaeda plots against strategic and symbolic targets, like attacking the World Trade Center. It uses the long-term strategy of attacks to prompt countries to leave/retreat from Muslim lands. IS's strategy is to control land. This coincides with its goal of creating a caliphate, which it needs land in order to rule (Byman, 2015). It also seeks to conquer, so it uses many soldiers, lots of weapons, and brute force. Unlike Al-Qaeda, IS uses sensational tactics like rape, beheadings, etc., all in an attempt to terrorize the population into submission. It also attempts to "purify" the population, so it utilizes mass executions. Other tactics and targets of the group include kidnappings, targeted attacks, the use of

IEDs, ambushes, military assaults, and suicide attacks (National Counterterrorism Center, n.d.). The United Nations confirmed that the group used mustard gas in the town of Umm Hawsh against civilians in 2016 (Wilson Center, 2019). Another known tactic of the group is its reliance on media (videos, newspapers, social media, etc.) to spread its propaganda.

The two groups also differ on what their role should be in the Syrian conflict. Al-Qaeda's Zawahiri encouraged Iraqi jihadists and helped in the conflict (Byman, 2015). He initiated the start of al-Nusra Front as a means to help in the conflict. IS's Baghdadi only sent a few fighters to the conflict. He felt conflicted over the Syrian Al-Qaeda branch, al-Nusra, having so much control in the group but incorporated them into his organization at the behest of Zawahiri. Baghdadi would later separate from them in order to maintain his control.

While an early 2024 U.N. report deems the group as "effectively suppressed," they are still considered a threat. General Kurilla testified in March 2024 that if the region was left unchecked, from a U.S. withdrawal, that ISIS would be able to run independently within two years of such a departure from the region (Congressional Research Service, 2024). The SDF is holding around 9,000 IS fighters in its detention facilities. It also detained and then took into custody some 44,000 people linked to IS in hopes of thwarting radicalization among the civilian population (Congressional Research Service, 2024). The group may have lost the majority of its territory, but it remains active via its affiliates. Additionally, IS still has many members loyal to the organization. Some remain in prison and others are free. It is considered an active organization.

Aden Islamic Army

Aden Islamic Army, Jaysh Adan-Abiyan al-Islami, or Islamic Army of Aden (IAA), became a recognized terrorist organization in October of 2001. However, the Yemen-based Salafi Jihadist group formed in the mid-1990s shortly after Yemen unified into an independent country (United Nations Security Council, 2010). Not much is known about the initial, formative years of the organization. However, the group was formed by a mixture of veterans from the Soviet-Afghanistan War, a loose network of Islamist and guerilla fighters (United Nations Security Council, 2010). Initial leadership for the group was Abu Al-Hassan, also known as Zayn al-Abidin. He and many of the initial members of the group received training in Saudi Arabia in order to fight as part of the *mujahideen* in the Soviet-Afghan War. The Yemeni government sent between 5,000–7,000 volunteers/*mujahideen* to Saudi Arabia in 1984, many of which adopted the Salafi sect of Sunni Islam while training there (Encyclopedia, n.d.).

The Yemen government denied the existence of the group until May of 1998, when IAA issued a series of statements about the political state of Yemen and publicly supported Al-Qaeda after its attacks on the U.S. embassies in Kenya and Tanzania (Encyclopedia, n.d.). The group called for Yemeni people to kill Americans, destroy Americans property, and to overthrow the Yemeni government (McHugh, 2014).

Tactics of the group include suicide bombings, bomb attacks, kidnappings, and firearms (The Mackenzie Institute, 2016). The primary goal of the group focused on the secularism of Yemen and the ability for the country to establish a Sunni, Islamist government. Al-Hassan followed a literal interpretation of the Koran that stated, "12,000 warriors would emerge from Aden-Abyan to restore Islam." This belief placed geographical and religious importance on Yemen (Encyclopedia, n.d.).

Zayn al-Abidin, al-Hassan, was executed in 1999 for participation in the December 1998 kidnapping of 16 foreign tourists (The Mackenzie Institute, 2016). The attempted rescue by the Yemeni security forces left four hostages dead. Islamic Army of Aden used many hostages as human shields after negotiations proved fruitless and the Yemeni security forces raided the IAA safe house (Encyclopedia, n.d.). In addition to Zayn al-Abidin, two other members were sentenced to death and another to 20 years in prison.

In January of 2000, IAA first attempted to bomb a U.S. vessel, specifically the USS The Sullivans (The Mackenzie Institute, 2016). The group wasn't successful in its attempts until October of the same year, when two suicide bombers from the group crashed a watercraft loaded with explosives into the USS Cole. The al-Qaeda-supported explosion of the USS Cole in the Port of Aden killed 17 U.S. soldiers and wounded others (The Mackenzie Institute, 2016). Note that another group, Al-Qaeda in Yemen (AQY), is also thought to be responsible for the attack. However, both groups are Al-Qaeda affiliated and both may have claimed responsibility for the attack. Other attacks by the group include the 2002 attack on the French refueling vessel, the Limburg, the 2003 attacks on a military medical convoy, and failed attempts to bomb foreign embassies in Sana'a (Encyclopedia, n.d.). The United States dispatched Special Forces to the region to help aid Yemen in its counterterrorism campaign (Sergie, 2015). This led to the 2002 death of the group's leader Abu Ali al-Harithi by drone strike.

Over time, the group's linkage to al-Qaeda became more salient as it became apparent that IAA received funding and support from Al-Qaeda. In 2003, Abu-Hamzah al-Masri, the spiritual leader of IAA, announced that the group had joined Al-Qaeda (Encyclopedia, n.d.). The group's activities fizzled after the capture of Khalid al-Nabi. Some reports indicated that he was released and became less vocal, while other sources indicated that he was killed by Yemeni security forces in 2003 during his capture (The Mackenzie Institute, 2016). Either way, the group continued to decline until the release of several Al-Qaeda members from Yemeni jails. The new membership propelled the group into a new direction. In 2009, it is believed that the group merged and rebranded with others to become part of AQAP (Pearson, 2024).

Al-Qaeda in the Arabian Peninsula

Al-Qaeda in the Arabian Peninsula is a Sunni terrorist group that formed in January of 2009 (Stanford University, n.d.). This Yemen and Saudi Arabia-based group has been called "one of the most dangerous al-Qaeda affiliates" (Sergie, 2015). The group's popularity in the region is attributed to its core ideologies rooted in Al-Qaeda's concern of the "far enemy" and Western threat but it also uses a local narrative. Al-Qaeda in the Arabian Peninsula relays concerns about issues pertaining to Palestinians and concerns about Gaza, but also about inadequate services and the unequal distribution of resources in the region (Batal al-Shishani, 2012). This global but local message has proven to be an effective recruitment tool for the group. However, the group's ideology of violent jihad often conflicts with the local Yemeni method of finding solutions to conflict (Harris, 2010). The group controlled the majority of the Sunni areas in the Abyan area after the onset of the Yemeni civil war (Sergie, 2015).

The collapse, reformation, and morphing of several organizations led to the formation of AQAP. The group is a mixture of both Yemen and Saudi-based al-Qaeda-affiliated groups. Those groups include Islamic Jihad in Yemen (1990–94), IAA/Army of Aden-Abyan (AAIA) (1994–98), Al-Qaeda in Yemen/AQY (1998–2003), and a Saudi-based branch of Al-Qaeda (Sergie, 2015).

The Islamic Jihad in Yemen (IJY) was a loosely organized group that quickly dissolved. Many IJY members joined the newly founded IAA but IAA lost its momentum after its leader was killed by the Yemeni government in 2009.

Steep decline in the AQY's membership by 2003 led to a fizzling out of the group. This was precipitated by the death of the Al-Qaeda leader in Yemen, Abu Ali al-Harithi, in 2002 and the arrest of his replacement, Muhammad Hamdi al-Ahdal, in 2003 (Harris, 2010).

However, twenty-three convicted terrorists, many with ties to Al-Qaeda, escaped a high-security facility in Sana'a in February of 2006. This created a resurgence of interest in restoring Al-Qaeda's presence in the region as many of the convicted escapees vowed to restore Al-Qaeda's to the region (Sergie, 2015). Majority of the escapees banded together to form what is now known as AQAP. The group is able to consolidate under Osama bin Laden's former secretary, Nasir Abdel Karim al-Wuhayshi (aka Abu Basir), and begin more lethal and organized attacks (Harris, 2010). Another al-Qaeda-linked group based in Yemen also became more active, the Jund al-Yaman Brigades (Knights, 2008).

Simultaneously in the Kingdom of Saudi Arabia, a local al-Qaeda-affiliated group, not yet AQAP, launched three deadly attacks in Riyadh in May of 2003 that killed 35 people. In June of 2008, the Ministry of Interior announced more than 700 terrorism-related arrests (Knights, 2008). The crackdown in Saudi Arabia forced a local Al-Qaeda franchise to move across its borders and join forces with jihadists in Yemen. The various branches that merged formed AQAP (Council on Foreign Relations, 2009).

The goal of AQAP is to expel Western influences in Muslim countries and to establish a government based on Sharia law, and fundamentalist Islamic ideology (Council on Foreign Relations, 2009). This goal would require the group to change the current regime in Yemen and to attack Western affiliated civilians and property. As a result, AQAP has targeted the embassies of the United States, Italy, and Britain. The group has attempted to assassinate members of the royal Saudi family, attack civilians, attempted to bomb planes or cargo-carrying vessels headed to Western cities, etc (Council on Foreign Relations, 2009).

Targets for the group frequently include the oil and gas sectors (Knights, 2008). However, the group has been known to target civilians. The group has received scrutiny from bin Laden for targeting local Muslims and Yemeni security forces (Stenersen, 2017). He also criticized them for trying to declare an Islamic State in Yemen, as he felt it was counterproductive and too premature for the region. The group did so in 2011, but it should be noted that AQAP does not consider itself to be part of the IS (Stanford University, n.d.).

Osama bin Laden's former secretary, Nasir Abdel Karim al-Wuhayshi (aka Abu Basir), founded AQAP in 2009 and was its leader until his death in 2015 due to a drone attack (Stanford University, n.d.). The same month that the group officially formed as Al-Qaeda in the Arabian Peninsula, Said al-Shahri (killed in 2012) and Mohammed al-Aufi assumed leadership roles in the group. The two were Saudi returnees from Guantanamo Bay who made their way to Yemen (Boucek, n.d.). Additional leaders in the group included Anwar al-Awlaki (killed by drone strike in 2011), Nayif Mohammed Saeed al-Qhatani (killed by Saudi forces in 2010), and Qasim al-Raymi/al-Rimi (killed in 2020 by U.S. forces). The current leader of AQAP is Khalid Batarfi (Stanford University, n.d.).

Attacks by the group include the March 2009 suicide bombings that targeted Korean tourists in Southeast Yemen. In June of the same year, the group abducted nine foreigners, with at least three executed by AQAP (Stanford University, n.d.). In August of 2009, the group unsuccessfully attempted to assassinate Saudi's Prince Mohammed bin Nayef. Twice affiliates attempted to bomb cargo planes heading to Chicago but Saudi intelligence helped thwart the October 2010 attacks. In 2011, AQAP created Ansar al-Shariah Yemen (ASY) in southern Yemen. ASY was an offshoot organization attempting to rebrand the group and win over more Yemeni locals.

Former Yemen President Ali Abdullah was ousted by popular protests in February 2012. This was followed by a May 2012 attack by the group that left more than 90 Yemeni soldiers and a AQAP suicide bomber dead. Abdullah's successor, President Abd Rabbu Mansour Hadi, had to tackle both AQAP and Houthi rebels during his tenure (Sergie, 2015). The group continued to expand but met resistance for some of its tactics. The group received some pushback and ultimately apologized for its December 2013 attacks on the defense ministry and a military hospital. The attack left some 50 people dead, including unarmed health workers. AQAP affiliates/linked operatives in Umar Farouk Abdulmutallab, also known as the Christmas/Underwear Bomber, attempted to bomb a Detroit-bound plane (Council on Foreign Relations, 2009). The Nigerian students attempted the attack but AQAP claimed responsibility (Harris, 2010).

The group claimed responsibility for the January 2015 attack on Charlie Hebdo magazine, a police woman, and a Jewish supermarket in Paris that left 17 people dead (BBC News, 2020). Fourteen people were found guilty in connection with the attacks. Two French-born Algerian Muslim brothers, Saïd Kouachi, and Chérif Kouachi, were specifically responsible for the Hebdo attack (Salaun et al., 2020). While the group claimed responsibility for the attacks, some sources question whether the group directed the attacks or if they were merely the inspiration for the attacks (Council on Foreign Relations, 2009).

As a recruitment tool, AQAP has a bimonthly magazine, *Sada al-Malahim* ("The Echo of Battles"), that spreads its message and propaganda to a primarily Yemeni targeted population (Council on Foreign Relations, 2009).The magazine is known to support jihadist actions and ideology. Used as a recruitment tool, *Sada al-Malahim* outlines the grievances that many Yemenis face in everyday life. The publication also provides an analysis of who is to blame for those grievances, mobilizing the population and recruiting civilians for collective action (Harris, 2010). *Sada al-Malahim* intentionally targets Yemeni civilians, as this population is a large base of AQAP. Analysts have found that AQAP's membership has a breakdown of roughly 56% Yemenis, 37% Saudis, and 7% foreign (Batal al-Shishani, 2012). Although the group does not affiliate with IS, the civil war in Yemen and its ideology having close proximity to IS allows the group to maintain a space in Yemen. The group utilizes tribal alliances and political relationships, expressing grievances specific to Yemeni locals, and a local approach to maintain relevance in the region.

The Islamic Army in Iraq

The Islamic Army in Iraq (IAI) formed in 2003 in response to the United States' invasion of Iraq. The IAI is a nationalist, Sunni Islamist militant organization with the aim of expelling foreign troops from Iraq. IAI primarily operates in Iraq. Leadership for the group includes Sheikh Ahmed al-Dabash (2003-Present), a founding leader of the group, and Ishmael Jubouri (2004-Unknown) (Stanford University, n.d.).

The Islamic Army in Iraq has a long-standing alliance with the Mujahideen Army. The group both cooperated and clashed with AQI and has had a rocky relationship with the IS. Both IAI and IS share the common goal of overthrowing the Shiite-dominant Iraqi government and removing foreign troops from the region (Stanford University, n.d.).

From 2003–2011 the group primarily targeted U.S. coalition troops. They also attacked Shiite militias and Iraqi government troops. Between 2006–2007, they reportedly targeted AQI operatives. Since 2013, the majority of its attacks have been directed against the Iraqi army and police forces. In 2014, the group's leader suggested that IAI sever ties with IS (Stanford University, n.d.). Not much is known about the group's tactics. IAI has been connected to attacks that used improvised explosive devices and rocket-propelled grenades, so these are possible tactics. The group also claims responsibility for shooting down helicopters and Western hostage situations (some released, others executed) (Stanford University, n.d.).

The group dissolved in 2011 following the U.S. withdrawal from Iraq, but its members shortly after created a political activism group called the Sunni Popular Movement (Stanford University, n.d.). The IAI reactivated in December 2013 to fight the Maliki government, and its last known activity was in 2014. As of now, they are believed to be inactive.

Kurdistan Workers Party

The Kurdistan Workers Party (PKK) is a nationalist/separatist group founded by Abdullah Ocalan in 1978 (Stanford University, n.d.). The group is also known by the alias Partiya Karkeren Kurdistan (PKK) and has received the distinction by many as one of the oldest armed groups in the Middle East (Haner, Cullen, & Benson, 2019). The group is Marxist-Leninist with aspects of feminism, as it was co-founded by a woman, Sakine Cansiz (Haner, Cullen, & Benson, 2019). Based out of Turkish and Iraqi Kurdistan, the group also goes by the name of its armed faction, The People Defense Force (HPG) (Stanford University, n.d.). The aim of the organization is to create a semi-autonomous nation for Kurdish people. This would require the group to gain control of Kurdish areas that span from Turkey and Iraq to Syria (United Kingdom Government, 2023).

The eventual formation of the PKK was largely impacted by the pan-Islamist thought of Sultan Abdulhamid II. Between 1876 and 1909, the Sultan attempted to merge Muslims around the world under one umbrella, and consequently under the Ottoman Empire (Karaca, 2010). This attempt at unification allowed both Turkish and Kurdish people to unify under one religion. It also had a lasting impact of tying the Kurdish identity to that of faith/religion (Karaca, 2010).

With the imminent collapse of the Ottoman Empire looming after World War I, the Treaty of Sevres was signed in 1920. The treaty was significant for the Kurdish people in that it offered them the opportunity to create their own independent state. The leaders of the Kurds declined the opportunity as a sign of solidarity with the Turks (Karaca, 2010). Under the Islamic Ottoman Empire, Turks and Kurds were under one banner. The newly formed Turkey was secular, a democratic republic, and not beholden to the familiar ties of religion or unity under the Islamic faith. This inadvertently put the Kurdish people and the

Turkish government at odds, especially as sheiks lost both their feudal and religious power (Karaca, 2010). It should be noted that the eventual rift created between the PKK and the Turkish government also reflects the rift that grew between the PKK and Turkish society as a whole. This makes the group an ethno-nationalist separatist group.

The transition to a more democratic political structure in the 1950s created channels for disenchanted groups, Kurds and Turks alike, to petition their complaints to the government. Marxist and socialist ideologies were the prominent themes of the time. However, the military coup and newly formed government between 1971–1973 strengthened the Kurdish nationalist and socialist movement (Karaca, 2010). Many Kurds attempted to resolve their complaints through legitimate political channels, while others moved towards the Maoist/Marxist ideology of the PKK.

The group was founded in 1974 and in 1984, Oclan fully embraced Maoism and the use of violent tactics. The PKK increased its violent tactics in 1986, and by the early 1990s, the group increased its regions of operations (Karaca, 2010). The group has historically maintained its headquarters in Iraq. However, the group has training camps in Belgium, France, and other Middle Eastern countries (Stanford University, n.d.).

In 1993, Ocalan inactivated the group's first unilateral ceasefire, in a hope of achieving the groups objectives via legal/legitimate means (Karaca, 2010). In 1994 the PKK began bombing Turkish tourism spots. In the same year, the PKK formed a short-lived alliance with the Revolutionary People's Liberation Party. This affiliation fizzled out by March of 1998. Other PKK affiliations include the Patriotic Union of Kurdistan (PUK), with which they joined forces against the Kurdish Democratic Party (KDP) during the Kurdish Civil War between 1994 and 1998 (Karaca, 2010). However, the PKK worked with both the PUK and KDP in 2013 while attempting to thwart the Islamic State (IS/ISIS) (Stanford University, n.d.). Subsequently, the PKK had clashes with other Kurdish groups, like the Turkish Hizbullah, as the PKK has attempted to monopolize the space for Kurdish nationalism (Karaca, 2010).

At the group's fifth conference in 1995, the PKK decided to increase its strategy of using suicide bombings. Shortly thereafter, in 1996, the Turkish government increased its counterterrorism campaign and alienated the group to mountainous/rural areas. In 1999, the group's leader Abdullah Ocalan was captured in Kenya, an event that changed the immediate trajectory of the group. From 1999 to 2004 the group's operations were generally defensive in scope and they engaged more in acts of civil disobedience (Karaca, 2010). During this timeframe, the United States designated the group as a terrorist organization, ending any affiliations with the PKK. Also during this time, in 2002, the group renamed itself as the Kurdistan Democratic and Freedom Congress. This was a short-lived change, as the group went back to the name PKK in 2005 with a revamped mission to incorporate a pan-Kurdish ideology that included all Kurdish movements into its scope (Karaca, 2010).

From 2005–2008 the PKK expanded its activities to include urban terrorism, while maintaining its rural basis of operations and continued use of civil disobedience as a way to express their grievances (Karaca, 2010). The U.S. entered an intergovernmental counterterrorism pact with Turkey and Iraq. As a part of this pact, the U.S. provided PKK intelligence to Turkey. In 2009, the Turkish government began legislative reform against the group.

In 2013, the PKK signed a ceasefire agreement with the Turkish government. The agreement was nullified after the PKK was accused of killing two Turkish police that the PKK claimed were affiliated with IS (Stanford University, n.d.). By 2015, the violence between both the PKK and the Turkish government escalated. The Turkish government subsequently joined the war against IS but used the majority of its firepower against PKK camps in Iraqi Kurdistan (Stanford University, n.d.). In 2019, the Turkish government expanded its counterterrorism operations against the PKK into Northern Syria and Northern Iraq. Post Covid-19, most of the conflict between the government and the PKK occurred outside of Turkey's border (United Kingdom Government, 2023). A brief ceasefire occurred between the two when a deadly earthquake killed more than 60,000 Turkish people in February of 2023. It is estimated that close to 7,000 people have died due to acts of terrorism or in clashes between forces since the 2015 ceasefire failed (International Crisis Group, 2024).

The group receives support from a variety of places, ranging from state-sponsored to human trafficking. In regards to state-sponsored funding, several countries have intervened on the PKK's behalf: Greece supported the group mainly in the 1990s; Syria, until recently, was one of the most notable supporters of the group due to complex historical ties; Russia has been a supporter of the group due to its affiliation with Syria and its own history with the Turks (United Kingdom Government, 2023). Other notable state sponsors of funding include Iraq, where many of the PKK bases are located, and Iran. Iran was a supporter of the group during the First Gulf War but decided to cut ties with the group in 2004. The U.S. occupation of Iraq made the Iranian government wary of overextended and engaging with a group the U.S. placed on its FTO list (United Kingdom Government, 2023).

Armenia supported the PKK in the 1990s, and the United States has a heavily debated and contested linkage to the PKK. It is argued that in the 1980s, the U.S. supported the PKK in order to have a weakened Turkish government in the region. However, the U.S. stance on the group shifted throughout the various administrations and as the tactics of the PKK evolved (Karaca, 2010).

Other sources of funding for the group include engaging in human trafficking, drug trafficking, money laundering, and fabricating fake passports and other documents pertaining to migration. The group is also known to engage in processing raw drug materials to make illicit drugs like heroin, hashish, and morphine (Karaca, 2010). As the smuggling of drugs is a dangerous and risky business, the group began to manufacture its own using raw drugs.

The group utilizes a variety of tactics that include suicide bombings, kidnappings, IEDs, and car bombs (United Kingdom Government, 2023). The PKK tactics are a mixture of both guerrilla warfare and traditional terrorist tactics. The group attacks Turkish government personnel both within the country and in other strategic locations like Iraq and Syria. Within Turkey, the group has been known to conduct attacks in their stronghold locations as well as Ankara and Istanbul, utilizing urban terrorism (United Kingdom Government, 2023).

The PKK has a uniqueness to it in that it actively recruits women. The group promotes the messages of gender equality, justice, and egalitarianism, options that resonate with many young Kurds who do not align with traditional/tribal lines in Kurdish society (Haner, Cullen, & Benson, 2019). Its founding leader, Ocalan, wrote about the issue of gender equality and how women are essential to the separatist movement. In his book, *Liberating Life: Women's Revolution*, Ocalan encouraged women to rise up and fight against Turkey and the internal, tribal aspects of inequality within Kurdish society (Haner, Cullen, & Benson, 2019).

Men and women are trained in the same manner, both receiving lessons on political and military training. The groups are not segregated but are mixed, allowing women to receive combat training equivalent to men (Haner, Cullen, & Benson, 2019). This is an appealing recruitment tool for women.

Those with PKK membership or affiliation encounter new counterterrorism policies implemented by the Turkish government after the failed coup of 2016 (United Kingdom Government, 2023). Such policies allow measures typically reserved for when the country is in a state of emergency. For example, the counterterrorism arrest policies are scrutinized for curbing freedom of speech but cite the new laws as ensuring national security. Those suspected of affiliation or sympathizing with the PKK, such as lawyers or journalists, are also prosecuted under the newer counterterrorism policies. Charges include organized crime/terrorist crimes (United Kingdom Government, 2019). Human rights groups have warned that fair and impartial trials are irregular for PKK members, affiliates and suspected affiliates (United Kingdom Government, 2023). It is also noted by several sources that prison overcrowding is on the rise in Turkey, with less than legal conditions for some detained. Those with Kurdish ethnicity are treated worse than other prisoners, mainly identified by their language (DIS—Danish Immigration Service, 2021). The PKK remains active with the explicit goal of uniting the various Kurdish movements to create a state for ethnic Kurds in the region.

Harakat al-Muqawamah al-Islamiyaah

The Islamic Resistance Movement (Harakat al-Muqawamah al-Islamiyaah or HAMAS) began in 1987 as a spinoff from the Palestinian Muslim Brotherhood in Gaza during the First Intifada (December 1987–September 1993) (National Counterterrorism Center, 2014). Hamas is a Palestinian nationalist group. It includes elements of Islamic fundamentalism (Congressional Research Service, 2023). In 1997 the United States designated Hamas as a FTO (Maizland, Robinson, & Hoffman, 2024).

Base of operations for the group is the Gaza Strip, but it also operates in the West Bank and Lebanon. The group has controlled the Gaza Strip since it won against Fatah, a rival political party, in 2006/07 (Maizland, Robinson, & Hoffman, 2024). Some of the group's leaders and personnel live or work in Turkey and in neighboring Arab countries (Congressional Research Service, 2023).

Sheik Ahmed Yassin founded the group after becoming an activist in the local Muslim Brotherhood branch (Maizland, Robinson, & Hoffman, 2024). Yassin was a cleric that had both preached and provided aid in the West Bank and Gaza Strip. He witnessed inequalities and harsh treatment of civilians there. His time in the area also overlapped with Israel's 1967 Six Day War, where Israel utilized a heavily militaristic approach to the conflict and many Palestinian casualties (Maizland, Robinson, & Hoffman, 2024).

The origins of Hamas are largely intertwined with the evolution of the Palestinian Liberation Organization (PLO). The first Arab Summit was held in January of 1964. The summit led to the creation of the Palestinian National Council (PNC), an organization comprised mostly of Palestinian civilians. The PNC met in June of 1964 to discuss the fate of Palestinians and to create a body/organization that would govern them (Mapping Palestinian Politics, n.d.). The Palestinian Liberation Organization emerged at the conclusion of the PNC meeting as the new governing body for Palestinians. The PLO outlined its goals, which included the destruction of Israel, and was led by Ahmad Shuqairi (History Channel, 2018).

Slowly, the PLO was infiltrated by members of a group named Fatah, led by Yasser Arafat (History Channel, 2018). Over time, members of Fatah dominated the PLO and in 1979, Arafat became the PLO's chairman. He remained in that position until his death in 2004 (History Channel, 2018). In the 1960, the PLO was based in Jordan and launched attacks on Israel from there. However, the Black September confrontation in 1970/71 forced the group to move its home base to Lebanon (Mapping Palestinian Politics, n.d.).

In 1974, Arafat called for a cease of attacks outside of Israel. In October of 1974, the Arab League recognized the PLO as the "...sole legitimate representative of the Palestinian people" (History Channel, 2018). In 1982, Israel forced the PLO out of Lebanon and into Tunisia, where its headquarters remained until it relocated back to Gaza in 1994.

A precipitating event turned the tides of the Palestinian movement. On December 8, 1987, a driver of an Israeli military tractor-trailer crashed into two vans, killing four Palestinian workers and wounding seven others (Tamimi, 2010). The crash took place near Jabaliya refugee camp, as the workers were heading back home for the night. This crash is dubbed the "Accident that Sparked an Intifada," as it sparked outrage and triggered a shift in Palestinian society (Omer, 2011).

Immediately after the accident, unrest broke out with protests near the Jabaliya refugee camp and along the coastal area up to the West Bank (Omer, 2011). Israel Defense Forces (IDF) and the Israeli government responded to the protests with a heavy hand and brute force. Israel Defense Forces soldiers were photographed using live ammunition against Palestinians throwing rocks and stones (Omer, 2011). The imagery was broadcasted worldwide, inviting international attention of the conflict.

On December 9, 1987, just one day after the accident, seven senior leaders of al-Ikhwan al-Muslimoon (The Muslim Brotherhood, or the Ikhwan), held an emergency meeting to propel the Palestinian Resistance Movement into a cohesive body (Tamimi, 2010). Earlier that day, the Islamic University, under the behest of Sheikh Yassin and others, staged a strike to shut down the university, and protesters rallied at al-Shifa hospital.

The seven leaders of the Ikhwan were Abd al-Fattah Dukan, Dr Abd al-Aziz al-Rantisi, Muhammed Sham'ah, Ibrahim al-Yazuri, Salah Shihadah, "Isa al-Nashar," and Sheik Ahmad Yassin. At their December 9 meeting, the leaders decided to turn the Ikhwan organization into Harakat al-Muqawamah (HAMAS/Hamas) (Tamimi, 2010). Ten years in the making, Sheik Yasin had laid the foundation for the organization well before they knew it would be needed. As a note, the driver of the tractor-trailer was later acquitted of manslaughter for the four Palestinian deaths in an Israeli court in 1994 (Los Angeles Times, 1992).

Hamas positioned itself as the more religious and aggressive alternative to the secular Fatah movement, which was the political arm of the PLO. The group's tactics at the time included attacking Israeli citizens and military personnel, which was different from their PLO counterpart (Congressional Research Service, 2023).

In 1988, the group created a charter that outlined the group's aims to eliminate Israel as a nation state (Congressional Research Service, 2023). The charter also outlined the plan to create an Islamic State that would encompass present-day Israel, the Gaza Strip, and the West Bank. The proposed Islamic State would return all of the aforementioned land returned to Palestinians; a move that would revert the geopolitical landscape back to what it was before the inception of Israel (Congressional Research Service, 2023).

By April of 1993, the group incorporated the use of suicide bombings (Maizland, Robinson, & Hoffman, 2024). In September of the same year, the PLO, specifically Yasser Arafat, and Israel's then Prime Minister Yitzhak Rabin signed the Oslo Accords. The PLO entered into a political process with Israel to create the Palestinian Authority (PA), with the PA having limited rule of the West Bank and Gaza (Congressional Research Service, 2023). Hamas was fundamentally against this pact and was opposed to both parties involved in the creation of it (Maizland, Robinson, & Hoffman, 2024). Receiving support from both Iran and private Arab donors, Hamas positioned itself as the "rejectionist" group.

The Second Intifada (2000–2005) was a time of violent unrest with groups like Hamas, the PLO, the Palestinian Islamic Jihad (PIJ), and Fatah's Tanzim militia a part of the Palestinian Resistance Movement (Maizland, Robinson, & Hoffman, 2024). Immediately post-Second Intifada, Israel gives any governing responsibility to the PA but it maintains control over land, sea, and air access (Congressional Research Service, 2023). It is argued that Hamas became the de facto leadership in the area once Israel troops left the territories in 2005 (Maizland, Robinson, & Hoffman, 2024). However, in 2006, Hamas won the majority of the votes, taking over the new PA cabinet and ousting the PLO/Fatah from leadership. The group was able to garner votes by providing social services (like building schools, etc.) and remaining the "rejectionist" party. Fatah had increasingly came to be viewed as a corrupt party that was at the behest of Israel's wishes, not Palestinians' needs (Maizland, Robinson, & Hoffman, 2024).

The Middle East "Quartet" (the United States, Israel, the U.N. Secretary General, and the European Union) urged Hamas to recognize Israel, stop violent actions, and accept the previously agreed-upon Israeli-Palestinian policies. Hamas refused to acknowledge Israel as a legitimate state (Congressional Research Service, 2023). Although Hamas won the elections, the Quartet only interacted with and shared funding with PA President Mahmoud Abbas, a member of the Fatah party (Congressional Research Service, 2023).

Tensions and divisions, continued to grow until the West Bank and Gaza split in 2007. Hamas took control of the Gaza Strip, and Abbas seized control of the West Bank. Israel and Egypt imposed strict security-related restrictions on people coming in and out of the Gaza Strip (Congressional Research Service, 2023). Hamas then allowed groups like the Palestinian Islamic Jihad (PIJ) to launch attacks on Israel from Gaza (Congressional Research Service, 2023). From 2008 to 2021, Hamas and Israel engaged in major rounds of conflicts, notably 2008–2009, 2012, 2014, and 2021 (Congressional Research Service, 2023). Prior to October 2023, 2021 was one of the deadliest years of fighting between Hamas and the Israeli government. During an eleven-day conflict, Hamas and the PIJ launched some 4,000 rockets from Gaza. Ten Israeli citizens were killed, and more than 300 were wounded. The United States and Egypt were able to secure a ceasefire.

On October 7, 2023, Hamas launched "Operation al-Aqsa Storm" on Southern Israel on the Jewish Sabbath, an important Jewish holiday (Maizland, Robinson, & Hoffman, 2024). Hamas launched over 5,000 rockets and missiles into southern and central Israel (Vazirian, 2023). Hamas targeted Tel Aviv, Sderot, and Ashkelon. Operation al-Aqsa Storm was of a massive scale and shrouded in secrecy. Not only did the attack show the vulnerabilities of the Israeli government, but it also showed the strategy and planning capabilities of Hamas. The attack included rockets, missiles, and militants that were able to breach the heavily guarded Gaza border (Maizland, Robinson, & Hoffman, 2024).

Hamas militants live-streamed images of brutal attacks, sexual violence against hostages, and what the U.N. would later confirm as war crimes (Maizland, Robinson, & Hoffman, 2024). With the support of Iran, Hamas was able to leverage its anti-West, anti-Israel coalition, known as the Axis of Resistance, to plan and execute the large-scale attack that utilized air, sea, and land. Yahya Sinwar, the group's leader since 2017, is thought to be responsible for the October 7 Massacre that occurred against Israeli citizens (Congressional Research Service, 2023). The goals of the attack included disabling and destroying Israeli defenses and military bases with rocket attacks. Additionally, the group aimed to trade captured Israeli civilians and soldiers for imprisoned Hamas fighters (Vazirian, 2023).

Israel's Prime Minister, Benjamin Netanyahu, responded to the attack with a declaration of war and an immediate ground attack with the intention to destroy Hamas. Prime Minister Netanyahu's ground attack included a heavy bombardment and leveling of the Gaza Strip (Vazirian, 2023). As of June 2024, 1,200 Israelis and 37,084 Palestinians have been killed in the conflict, making it one of the deadliest in the Hamas-Israeli Conflict history (Al-Mughrabi, 2024). A lasting impact of the Hamas attack and counter-attacks by Israel is the large-scale humanitarian crisis. Neighborhoods have been destroyed, two-third of the population of Gaza is displaced/unhoused, and widespread malnutrition afflicts displaced Palestinians (Al-Mughrabi, 2024). One one three (31%) children under the age of two in Northern Gaza suffer from acute malnutrition (Canon, 2024).

The October 7 attacks drew attention to several points. First, it drew attention to conditions in Gaza that many Palestinians, analysts, and military strategists cited as part of Hamas's retaliatory attack. In 2022, 1.84 million Palestinians, around ⅓ of the population, did not have enough food to eat. In 2023, Gaza had electricity for 13 out of the 24 hours of the day (Sen, 2023). Water in Gaza is known to be contaminated with both sewage/waste and seawater. The most widely known complaint is the lack of free movement for Palestinians, going through frequent and sometimes invasive security checks.

Second, the attacks drew attention to vulnerabilities within the Israeli government. "Iranian Supreme Leader Ayatollah Ali Khamenei and Hassan Nasrallah, the leader of Hezbollah, have referred to Israel as 'weaker than a spider's web'" (Vazirian, 2023). This vulnerability gives a new perspective to Arab states that have had tenuous relationships with Israel in the past. Thirdly, the attack has flared concerns about relationships between Arab and Middle Eastern countries with those that ally with Israel (Vazirian, 2023). U.S. President Biden noted that one of the possible goals of the group was to sour improved relations between Israel and Saudi Arabia (Congressional Research Service, 2023). The staggering death toll of civilians has even garnered attention and raised criticism from the United Nations, which has suggested that both sides are guilty of war crimes (Maizland, Robinson, & Hoffman, 2024). It has also bolstered support for Hamas both regionally and internationally.

Leadership within Hamas is complicated and has various levels. Its formal leadership consists of a 15-member politburo that makes the major decisions for the organization. However, the politburo is elected by a Shura Council (Congressional Research Service, 2023). The current chair of the politburo/political chief, and former Palestinian Authority Prime Minister, is Ismail Haniyeh. Haniyeh has been based in Doha, Qatar, since 2017 due to restricted movements in and out of Gaza (Maizland, Robinson, & Hoffman, 2024). Yahya Sinwar has been Hamas leader in Gaza since 2017. Sinwar was part of the

2011 prisoner swap that exchanged more than 1,000 Palestinian prisoners for 1 captured Israeli soldier. Sinwar is thought to be the mastermind behind the October 2023 attacks (Congressional Research Service, 2023). Other senior Hamas leaders are thought to operate out of Turkey (Maizland, Robinson, & Hoffman, 2024). As of August 6, 2024, Hamas announced that Yahya Sinwar, the architect of the October 7 attacks, will become the political head of Hamas. This is a move that elevates Sinwar from the leader of Hamas in Gaza to the leader of the entire organization (New York Times, 2024).

Other members of leadership include Muhammed Deif and Marwan Issa, leading Hamas's military wing, also known as Izz al Din al Qassam Brigades (Congressional Research Service, 2023). Khaled Meshaal, former political chief, became leader of the diaspora office in a 2021 internal election. During that same election, Salameh Katawi became leader of the imprisoned members' affairs, and Saleh al-Arouri became leader of the West Bank branch. Al-Arouri died in an Israeli drone attack in January of 2024 (Maizland, Robinson, & Hoffman, 2024).

Graphic courtesy of the Council on Foreign Relations (Maizland, Robinson, & Hoffman, 2024).

Funding for Hamas has typically come from private donors throughout the Persian Gulf and Palestinians in various diasporas around the world. Iran is a large benefactor for Hamas, providing weapons, training, and funding. The State Department estimates that Iran provides up to $100 million a year to "Palestinian militants"; PIJ, Hamas, and other Palestinian

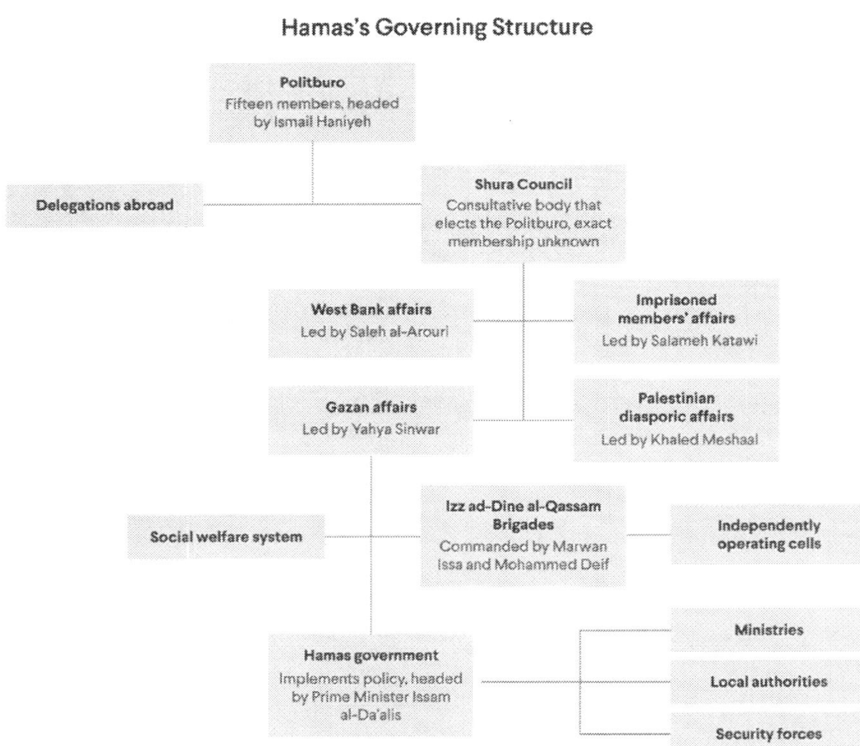

FIGURE 7.1

groups designated as terrorist (Congressional Research Service, 2023). Turkey has also served as a supporter of Hamas since the 2002 election of President Recep Tayyip Erdogan. While Turkey supports Hamas politically, it is unclear if, or how much, the country supports Hamas financially (Maizland, Robinson, & Hoffman, 2024). Additional supporters and financiers of Hamas include Algeria, Sudan, Qatar, and the United Arab Emirates.

When Egypt and Israel closed their borders to Gaza in 2006, it forced the group to look for additional ways to fund itself. Years after the blockade began, Hamas began collecting taxes and revenue from goods moving through its network of tunnels at the border (Maizland, Robinson, & Hoffman, 2024). The *Economist* estimates the group is able to collect more than $1 billion in revenue annually, with $360 million coming from taxed goods (Congressional Research Service, 2023). Other estimates suggest around $12 million per month in revenue from taxed goods (Maizland, Robinson, & Hoffman, 2024). Hamas receives another $750 million annually from foreign sources.

Initially, Hamas utilized guerrilla tactics, but in 1993 it implemented suicide attacks. The group's military and strategic capabilities have increased over time. Weaponry for the group includes small arms, drones, rockets, missiles, and man-portable air defense systems (Congressional Research Service, 2023). Although the group uses rockets and mortars, the range for them is as far as Southern Israel. Hamas also uses its intricate tunnel system within Gaza to transport weapons and personnel. The group gained the capability to make its own weaponry after training with Iran's Islamic Revolutionary Guard Corps (IRGC) in 2017, shortly after the IRGC supported Hamas via Hizbullah from 2012–2016 (Levitt, 2023).

Hamas's popularity among Palestinians is hard to determine. While Hamas champions itself as the protector of and fighting for, Palestinian rights, many polls/surveys prior to October 7 found that many Palestinians did not trust the Hamas led government (Congressional Research Service, 2023). Additionally, Palestinians were more in favor of Fatah and fewer violent escalations with Israel. On the other hand, an estimated 20% of Palestinians support Hamas and its policies. It is thought that the 2021 election was cancelled by PA President Mahmoud Abbas to prevent a Hamas victory. However, Israel's aggressive ground operations post-October 7 and high death toll for Palestinian civilians have led to a rise in support for Hama (Congressional Research Service, 2023). Researchers found an overall 4% increase in Hamas support, and quadrupled support in the West Bank in a December 2023 survey. It was noted in the findings that although support for Hamas has increased due to Israel's military response, the findings are not indicative of Palestinian support for the actions of Hamas on October 7. As of June 2024, a United States and United Nations-brokered ceasefire between Israel and Hamas was unresolved with continued strikes on both sides.

Conclusion

Whether groups subscribe to a global jihad or take a more local approach, the Middle East and North Africa remain an attractive destinations for many terrorist organizations. Established training grounds like Afghanistan and Pakistan continue to see an influx of fighters coming to train within their borders.

From the Al-Qaeda franchise to the IS affiliates, Islamic extremism has rooted itself in the Middle East and North Africa (MENA). The era of the "Islamic Resurgence" began in the 1960s. It revived the Islamic movements and was fueled by the works/writings of modern jihad writers like Mohammed Ibn Abdul Wahhab, Mawlana Mawdudi (Maududi), Sayyid Qutb and Muhammad al-Farag (Harik, 2005). A growing sense of secular invasion, government corruption and misrule and poverty grew.

Pivotal political events, like the Soviet-Afghan War, created a space for select mujahedeen to morph into global jihadists. The Islamic fundamentalism of Osama bin Laden trickled into the framework of Al-Qaeda and permeated its way into Al-Qaeda and Islamic State affiliates. This puritanical version of Islam has made its way to sub-Saharan Africa and further west to Southeast Asia.

Countries like Saudi Arabia and Pakistan, established with the intent of being Islamic nation, continuously support groups that aim to establish an Islamic State. Support for organizations are as tangible as money and places to train, or it may be as abstract as promoting Wahhabism via propaganda or groups that spread the ideology.

With the United States closely intertwined with countries like Israel, it has made U.S. counterterrorism policies complicated and aligned with its Israel ally. Groups like Hezbollah and Hamas exist with the primary purpose of destroying Israel and creating a state for ethnic Palestinians. The United States has found itself at odds with countries like Iran over this allyship but working with Afghan forces to thwart attacks from Al-Qaeda, the Taliban, and others. The current U.S. approach is both defensive and offensive, using drone attacks to address immediate threats and preemptive by supplying troops and resources to bolster weak borders and civil wars. However, post-October 7, 2023, Israel's Prime Minister Netanyahu and his policy choices against Hamas have created a tenuous relationship between the two nations. Groups like Hezbollah, and countries like Iran have signaled a possible entrance into the Hamas-Israel conflict, creating tension among MENA countries. Countries like Egypt, Syria, and Iraq, plus various militant groups, wait on the sidelines. The long-standing alliances of Western countries and the prominent Wahhabism of the region leave a looming question mark on the trajectory of Islamic extremism in the region.

References

Alam, J. (2024, August 1). Bangladesh bans Jamaat-e-Islami party following violent protests that left more than 200 dead. *Associated Press*. https://apnews.com/article/bangladesh-hasina-jamaat-party-banned-violence-campus-28d00e1af317e0325e8b09f010728ccd

Al-Mughrabi, N. (2024, June 9). Israel keeps pounding central Gaza as Palestinian death toll in hostage rescue raid rises to 274. *Reuters*. https://www.reuters.com/world/middle-east/israel-pounds-central-gaza-palestinian-death-toll-hostage-rescue-raid-rises-274-2024-06-09/

Amnesty International. (2021, June 14). Egypt: Death sentences upheld for 12 defendants after shameful mass trial. *Amnesty International*. https://www.amnesty.org/en/latest/press-release/2021/06/egypt-death-sentences-upheld-for-12-defendants-after-shameful-mass-trial/

Arrabyee, N. (2016, February). *Rising extremism in Yemen*. Carnegie Endowment for International Peace. https://carnegieendowment.org/sada/62832

Associated Press. (2021, July 2). A timeline of more than 40 years of war in Afghanistan. *AP News*. https://apnews.com/article/joe-biden-islamic-state-group-afghanistan-europe-middle-east-70451c485d46908ef5c6a83a1de9f0f6

Azani, E. (2009). *Hezbollah: The story of the party of god: From revolution to institutionalization*. Palgrave Macmillan.

Badawi, N. (2014). *Religion, war, and ethics: A sourcebook of textual traditions*. Cambridge University Press.

Batal al-Shishani, M. (2012). *Al-Qaeda: Geopolitical, strategic outlook and social composition*. The Emirates Centre for Strategic Studies and Research-Abu Dhabi.

BBC News. (2015, December 9). Paris attacks: What happened on the night. *BBC*. https://www.bbc.com/news/world-europe-34818994

BBC News. (2018, April 25). Lebanon profile - timeline. *BBC*. https://www.bbc.com/news/world-middle-east-14649284

BBC News. (2019, March 23). Islamic State group defeated as final territory lost, US-backed forces say. *BBC*. https://www.bbc.com/news/world-middle-east-47678157

BBC News. (2020, December 16). Charlie Hebdo: Fourteen guilty in 2015 Paris terror attacks trial. *BBC*. https://www.bbc.com/news/world-europe-55336094

Boucek, C. (n.d.). *Examining Saudi Arabia's 85 most wanted list – combating terrorism center at west point*. Combating Terrorism Center. https://ctc.westpoint.edu/examining-saudi-arabias-85-most-wanted-list/

Burke, J. (2009, October 27). Think again: Al Qaeda. Foreign Policy. https://foreignpolicy.com/2009/10/27/think-again-al-qaeda-4/

Byman, D. (2015, April 29). Comparing Al Qaeda and ISIS: Different goals, different targets | Brookings. *Brookings Institution*. https://www.brookings.edu/articles/comparing-al-qaeda-and-isis-different-goals-different-targets/

Bynum, D. (2003). Should Hezbollah be next? *Foreign Affairs*, 54–66.

Cammett, M. (2006, August 17). *Habitat for Hezbollah*. Foreign Policy. https://foreignpolicy.com/2006/08/17/habitat-for-hezbollah/

Canon, D. (2024, March 15). Acute malnutrition has doubled in one month in the north of Gaza strip: UNICEF. *PMNCH*. https://pmnch.who.int/news-and-events/news/item/15-03-2024-acute-malnutrition-has-doubled-in-one-month-in-the-north-of-gaza-strip-unicef

Central Intelligence Agency. (n.d.). *Terrorist organizations*. The World Factbook. https://www.cia.gov/the-world-factbook/references/terrorist-organizations/

Congressional Research Service. (2023, December 14). *Hamas: Background, current status, and U.S. Policy*. CRS Reports. https://crsreports.congress.gov/product/pdf/IF/IF12549

Congressional Research Service. (2024, May 6). *Al Qaeda: Background, current status, and U.S. Policy*. CRS Reports. https://crsreports.congress.gov/product/pdf/IF/IF11854

Congressional Research Service. (2024, May 6). *The Islamic state: Background, current status, and U.S. Policy*. CRS Reports. https://crsreports.congress.gov/product/pdf/IF/IF10328

Council on Foreign Relations. (2009, May 27). *Armed Islamic group (Algeria, Islamists)*. Council on Foreign Relations. https://www.cfr.org/backgrounder/armed-islamic-group-algeria-islamists

Counter Extremism Project. (n.d.). *Al-Qaeda*. Counter Extremism Project. https://www.counterextremism.com/threat/al-qaeda

Defense Intelligence Agency. (n.d.). *Abu Musab al-Zarqawi and Al-Qaida in Iraq* [Declassified Brief]. https://www.dia.mil/FOIA/FOIA-Electronic-Reading-Room/FileId/161443/

Department of Treasury. (2022). *2022 National terrorist financing risk assessment* (pp. 1–28). https://home.treasury.gov/system/files/136/2022-National-Terrorist-Financing-Risk-Assessment.pdf

DIS – Danish Immigration Service. (2021, March). *Turkey prison conditions*. https://www.ecoi.net/en/file/local/2048256/Turkey+Prison+conditions+FINAL.pdf

Encyclopedia. (n.d.). *Islamic army of aden*. Encyclopedia.com. https://www.encyclopedia.com/politics/legal-and-political-magazines/islamic-army-aden

Farrall, L. (2017). Revisiting al-Qaida's foundation and early history. *Perspectives on Terrorism*, *11*(6), 17–37.

Fitzgerald, P., & Annon, K. (2005). *Lebanon/assassination - mission of inquiry report - SecGen letter to SecCo President*. United Nations. https://www.un.org/unispal/document/auto-insert-183309/

Fuller, T. (2016, January 13). Jakarta attack raises fears of ISIS' spread in Southeast Asia (Published 2016). *The New York Times*. https://www.nytimes.com/2016/01/15/world/asia/jakarta-explosion.html

Gerges, F. A. (2016). *ISIS: A history*. Princeton University Press.

Haddad, S. (2006). The origins of popular support for Lebanon's Hezbollah. *Studies in Conflict & Terrorism*, *29*(1), 21–34.

Haner, M., Cullen, F. T., & Benson, M. L. (2019). Women and the PKK: Ideology, gender, and terrorism. *International Criminal Justice Review*, 1–23. https://doi.org/10.1177/1057567719826632
Harb, Z. (2011). *Channels of resistance in Lebanon: Liberation propaganda, Hezbollah and the media*. IB Tauris.
Harik, J. P. (2005). *Hezbollah: The changing face of terrorism*. IB Tauris & Co Ltd.
Harris, A. (2010). Exploiting grievances: Al-Qaeda in the Arabian Peninsula. *Carnegie Endowment for International Peace*. http://www.jstor.org/stable/resrep12735
History Channel. (2018, May 7). *Middle eastern history: PLO*. PLO. https://www.history.com/topics/middle-east/plo
Hussein, W. (2015, March). The Islamic State in Africa. *Al- Monitor: The Pulse of the Middle East*. http://www.al-monitor.com
International Crisis Group. (2024, March 3). *Türkiye's PKK conflict: A visual explainer*. Crisis Group. https://www.crisisgroup.org/content/turkiyes-pkk-conflict-visual-explainer
Jofee', G. (2010). *Radicalism, extremism and government in North Africa: International terrorism post 9/11: Comparative dynamics and responses*. Routledge.
Karaca, A. (2010). *Disrupting terrorist networks an analysis of the PKK terrorist organization*. Diss. Naval Postgraduate School.
Karagiannis, E. (2009). Hizballah as a social movement organization: A framing approach. *Mediterranean Politics*, *14*(3), 365–383.
Kennedy, M. (2016, October 28). U.N.: ISIS is using tens of thousands of civilians as human shields in Mosul. *NPR*. https://www.npr.org/sections/thetwo-way/2016/10/28/499767161/u-n-isis-is-using-tens-of-thousands-of-civilians-as-human-shields-in-mosul
Knights, M. (2008, September). *The current state of Al-Qa`ida in Saudi Arabia – combating terrorism center at west point*. Combating Terrorism Center. https://ctc.westpoint.edu/the-current-state-of-al-qaida-in-saudi-arabia-2/
Laub, Z. (2019, August 15). *Egypt's muslim brotherhood*. Council on Foreign Relations. https://www.cfr.org/backgrounder/egypts-muslim-brotherhood
Levitt, M. (2023, November). The hamas-iran relationship – the jerusalem strategic tribune. *The Jerusalem Strategic Tribune*. https://jstribune.com/levitt-the-hamas-iran-relationship/
Los Angeles Times. (1992, March 7). Israeli acquitted in traffic mishap that sparked arab riots. *Los Angeles Times*. https://www.latimes.com/archives/la-xpm-1992-03-07-mn-3555-story.html
Lumen Learning. (n.d.). *The United States and the Mujahideen | History of Western Civilization II*. Lumen Learning. https://courses.lumenlearning.com/suny-hccc-worldhistory2/chapter/the-united-states-and-the-mujahideen/
The Mackenzie Institute. (2016, January 7). *Islamic Army of Aden (IAA)*. The Mackenzie Institute. Retrieved February 7, 2024, from https://mackenzieinstitute.com/2016/01/islamic-army-of-aden-iaa/
Maizland, L., Robinson, K., & Hoffman, B. (2024, April 18). *What is hamas?* Council on Foreign Relations. https://www.cfr.org/backgrounder/what-hamas
Mapping Palestinian Politics. (n.d.). *Palestine Liberation Organisation (PLO) | ECFR*. European Council on Foreign Relations. https://ecfr.eu/special/mapping_palestinian_politics/plo/
Masters, J., & Laub, Z. (2015). *Al-Qaeda in the Islamic Maghreb*. Council on Foreign Relations. https://www.cfr.org/backgrounder/al-qaeda-islamic-maghreb
Matthews, M. M. (2008). *We were caught unprepared: The 2006 Hezbollah-Israeli war*. U.S. Army Combined Arms Center, Combat Studies Institute Press:.
McHugh, R. (2014, September 7). *Aden-Abyan islamic army*. Encyclopedia Britannica. https://www.britannica.com/topic/Aden-Abyan-Islamic-Army
Migaux, P. (2007). Al Qaeda. In *The history of terrorism: From antiquity to Al Qaeda* (p. 330). University of California Press.
National Counterterrorism Center. (n.d.). *Al nusra front*. Counterterrorism Guide. https://www.dni.gov/nctc/groups/al_nusrah_front.html
National Counterterrorism Center. (n.d.). *Al-Qa'ida in the Lands of the Islamic Maghreb (AQIM)*. Counter Terrorism Guide. https://www.dni.gov/nctc/groups/aqim.html
National Counterterrorism Center. (n.d.). *Counter terrorism guide: Islamic state mozambique*. National Counterterrorism Center. https://www.dni.gov/nctc/ftos/isis_mozambique_fto.html
National Counterterrorism Center. (n.d.). *Islamic state of iraq and Ash-Sham (ISIS)*. National Counterterrorism Center | FTOs. https://www.dni.gov/nctc/ftos/isis_fto.html

National Counterterrorism Center. (2014, January). *Hamas*. National Counterterrorism Center | HAMAS. https://www.dni.gov/nctc/groups/hamas.html

New York Times. (2024, August 6). Hamas names an architect of Oct. 7 attacks as new political leader. *The New York Times*. https://www.nytimes.com/live/2024/08/06/world/israel-iran-hezbollah-gaza?smid=nytcore-ios-share&referringSource=articleShare

Omer, M. (2011, December 4). The accident that sparked an Intifada. *The Jerusalem Post*. https://www.jpost.com/features/in-thespotlight/the-accident-that-sparked-an-intifada

Pearson, E. (2024, February 11). Al-Qaeda | history, meaning, terrorist attacks, & facts. *Britannica*. https://www.britannica.com/topic/al-Qaeda

Pew Research Center. (2010, September 15). Muslim brotherhood and Jama'at-i Islami. *Pew Research Center*. https://www.pewresearch.org/religion/2010/09/15/muslim-networks-and-movements-in-western-europe-muslim-brotherhood-and-jamaat-i-islami/

Reuters. (2017, July 18). Egyptian security forces kill prominent Islamic State militant in North Sinai. *Reuters*. https://www.reuters.com/article/world/egyptian-security-forces-kill-prominent-islamic-state-militant-in-north-sinai-idUSKBN1A326A/

Richardson, L. (2021, August 3). A fuller picture of Osama bin Laden's Life (Published 2021). *The New York Times*. https://www.nytimes.com/2021/08/03/books/review/the-rise-and-fall-of-osama-bin-laden-peter-bergen.html

Rogell, D. E. (n.d.). *Abdullah Azzam*. The Investigative Project on Terrorism. https://www.investigativeproject.org/profile/103/abdullah-azzam

Ronald Reagan Presidential Library. (n.d.). *Photo Op. President reagan meeting with freedom fighters from Afghanistan (Mujahideen) Oval Office*. Ronald Reagan Presidential Library. https://www.reaganlibrary.gov/archives/video/photo-op-president-reagan-meeting-freedom-fighters-afghanistan-mujahideen-oval

Salaun, T., Pineau, E., Lough, R., & MacSwan, A. (2020, August 28). Five years on, France to try suspects in Charlie Hebdo killings. *Reuters*. https://www.reuters.com/article/idUSKBN25O2J2/

Sayeh, J. (2024, June 10). *ISKP's transnational reemergence*. FDD. https://www.fdd.org/analysis/op_eds/2024/06/10/iskps-transnational-reemergence/

Sen, S. (2023, October 8). There is nothing surprising about Hamas's operation | Gaza. *Al Jazeera*. https://www.aljazeera.com/opinions/2023/10/8/there-is-nothing-surprising-about-hamass-operation

Sergie, M. (2015, June 19). *Al-Qaeda in the Arabian Peninsula (AQAP)*. Council on Foreign Relations. https://www.cfr.org/backgrounder/al-qaeda-arabian-peninsula-aqap

Shehata, S. (2015, August 27). Egypt: The new founders. *Wilson Center*. https://www.wilsoncenter.org/article/egypt-the-new-founders

Stanford University. (n.d.). *MMP: Al Qaeda in the Arabian Peninsula*. Center for International Security and Cooperation. https://cisac.fsi.stanford.edu/mappingmilitants/profiles/al-qaeda-arabian-peninsula

Stanford University. (n.d.). *MMP: Al Qaeda in the Islamic Maghreb*. Center for International Security and Cooperation. https://cisac.fsi.stanford.edu/mappingmilitants/profiles/aqim

Stanford University. (n.d.). *MMP: Islamic Army in Iraq*. Center for International Security and Cooperation. https://cisac.fsi.stanford.edu/mappingmilitants/profiles/islamic-army-iraq#highlight_text_12777

Stanford University. (n.d.). *MMP: Kurdistan workers party*. Center for International Security and Cooperation. https://mappingmilitants.org/mmp-group/kurdistan-workers-party

Stenersen, A. (2017). Thirty years after its foundation – where is al-Qaida going? *Perspectives on Terrorism*, *11*(6), 5–16. http://www.jstor.org/stable/26295953

Tamimi, A. (2010). *Hamas: A history from within*. Interlink Publishing Group Incorporated.

Thurston, A. (2017). Algeria's GIA: The first major armed group to fully subordinate jihadism to salafism. *Islamic Law and Society*, *24*(4), 412–436. JSTOR. https://www.jstor.org/stable/26571284

Toutounji, Y. (2017). *The Double-edged Sword: Globalization and international islamic terrorism*. American University in Cairo, Master's Thesis. AUC Knowledge Fountain. https://www.google.com/url?sa=t&source=web&rct=j&opi=89978449&url=https://fount.aucegypt.edu/cgi/viewcontent.cgi%3Farticle%3D1696%26context%3Detds

United Kingdom Government. (2019, June 17). *Report of a home office fact-finding mission Turkey: Kurds, the HDP and the PKK*. https://www.ecoi.net/en/document/2020297.html

United Kingdom Government. (2023, October 26). *Country policy and information note: Kurdistan Workers' party (PKK).* GOV.UK. https://www.gov.uk/government/publications/turkey-country-policy-and-information-notes/country-policy-and-information-note-kurdistan-workers-party-pkk-turkey-october-2023-accessible

United Nations Security Council. (n.d.). *AL-QAIDA IN IRAQ.* United Nations. https://main.un.org/securitycouncil/en/sanctions/1267/aq_sanctions_list/summaries/entity/al-qaida-in-iraq

United Nations Security Council. (2010, September). *Islamic of Aden | United nations security council.* The United Nations. https://www.un.org/securitycouncil/sanctions/1267/aq_sanctions_list/summaries/entity/islamic-army-of-aden

United Nations Security Council. (2018, June 27). *Armed Islamic group.* The United Nations. https://www.un.org/securitycouncil/sanctions/1267/aq_sanctions_list/summaries/entity/armed-islamic-group

Vazirian, A. H. (2023, November 7). The 'Al-Aqsa storm' surprises israel and upsets plans for a new security order. *Stimson Center.* https://www.stimson.org/2023/the-al-aqsa-storm-surprises-israel-and-upsets-plans-for-a-new-security-order/

Vergun, D. (2022, February 3). Leader of ISIS dead following U.S. Raid in Syria. *Department of Defense.* https://www.defense.gov/News/News-Stories/Article/Article/2922796/leader-of-isis-dead-following-us-raid-in-syria/

Weiss, M., & Hassan, H. (2015). *ISIS: Inside the army of terror.* Regan Arts.

White, J. (2020). *Terrorism and homeland security* (9th ed.). Wadsworth.

Wilson Center. (2019, October 28). Timeline: The rise, spread, and fall of the Islamic State. *Wilson Center.* https://www.wilsoncenter.org/article/timeline-the-rise-spread-and-fall-the-islamic-state

8

TERROR GROUPS IN SOUTHEAST ASIA

Ashlie Perry Banerjee

Historical Background of Southeast Asia

Southeast Asia is not exempt from experiencing attacks by extremist groups. Factors like colonialism, grievances with the government, lack of accountability by regimes, weak governments, and corruption all leave room for extremism. Like the previously discussed Middle East and North Africa (MENA) and sub-Saharan Africa, a growing sense of secular invasion, government corruption, and misrule has laid the foundation for violent clashes between civilians and governments. However, a small subset of the civilian population expands the group's tactics to include terrorism to achieve their desired goal.

For example, the Pattani United Liberation Organization (PULO) was established in 1968 to fight for the creation of an independent Islamic State. Formed in India, the group set out to meet its objective through armed struggle. With active attacks from 1977 to 2016, the group has sought to separate from the Thailand government, which it viewed as colonizers, and to create a separate Pattani Darussalam State ("Pattani United Liberation Organization (PULO)," n.d.) Founded by disenfranchised Malay Muslims, PULO continues to be one of the most influential separatist movements in Southern Thailand with the intention to form an Islamic State (White, 2020).

Similarly, the Barisan Revolusi Nasional Coordinate (BRN) formed in 1963 with the objective of creating an independent Islamic State separate from the Thai government. Accusation of brute force and human rights abuses on both sides have led to prolonged conflict. Human Rights Watch estimates that more than 7,000 lives, mostly civilians, have been lost in the area (Phasuk, 2022).

The Thai government's response to Malay Muslims' grievances has opened the door for an 18-year conflict where the BRN justifies the use of violence based on its interpretation of Islam.

While extremism is not new to Southeast Asia, the end of the colonialism era saw a rise in the number of groups active in the region, from Sikh to Islamic movements. Darul Islam (DI) formed in the late 1940s as a rebellion, looking to establish an Islamic State

DOI: 10.4324/9781003375265-12

in Indonesia. From 1948 until 1962, the political group attempted to establish its goal (Gunaratna, 2015).

The group inspired many others, like Komando Jihad of Indonesia. Komando Jihad, an offshoot of Darul Islam, led the region's first major attack when the group hijacked a plane in 1981 (Bakhshi & Rousselle, 2024).

The group called for the release of prisoners, the removal of Israelis from Indonesia and for money. The motive of the act is thought to be a similar plane hijacking that took place earlier that year in Pakistan, a common form of attack at the time. From 1968–1982, the CIA reports that more than 108 hijackings took place in the region.

Religion, like many other countries discussed in previous chapters, plays a role in the formation of many groups. Coupled with colonialism, religion is a surface factor for tensions. Things like lack of resources, disenfranchisement, being on the periphery of the political process, etc., are more internal and harder to pinpoint sources of conflict. Muslim rulers, up until the decline of the Mughal Empire, ruled over their majority Hindu subjects in Southeast Asia. Differing from their Middle Eastern counterparts, Muslim leaders did not attempt to enforce full Sharia law (Haqqani, 2005).

Instead, Muslims, from laymen to ulema (scholars), enjoyed the prestige that came along with the religious affiliation. However, colonialism changed the tide of power in many Southeast Asian countries. When the British formally declared India as part of the British Empire in 1857, Muslim rule, and said privileges, ended. The decline in political power triggered a rise in Islamic identity and eventually the need for an Islamic State. Divided communities and attacks perpetrated by both Hindus and Muslims have exacerbated conditions in both the subcontinent of India and throughout Southeast Asia. Recruitment into various extremist groups feeds off the fear and politics of their respective communities.

Sikh Extremism in India

The British colonial era and the impact of colonization are linked to the formation of the Sikh identity into a separate "race" or "nation." The Sikh and government relationships, the subsequent Khalsa nation movement included, preceded the 1980s and dated back to the colonial era. The British colonial elites referred to them as *quams,* a specific "race" or "nationality" of people, a separate identity within the region (Shani, 2000). The British believed that the Sikhs were a separate race, isolating the Keshdhari Sikhs as a distinct community within society.

Prior to the colonial era, the Sikh identity lacked a single definition and a homogenous community. The 1870s Singh Sabha movement started, it was a turning point in modern Sikh identity (Shani, 2000). Between 1915 and 1925, British colonials detained thousands of Sikhs for participating in nonviolent demonstrations, or morchas. In 1925, the Sikh Gurdwara Act, an institutionalized opposition to British rule was passed. This act solidified a uniform Sikh identity. The Act predated the formation of the Shiromani Gurdwara Prabandhak Committee (SGPC) and the Akali Dal, the political arm of the faction (Shani, 2000.)

From independence until 1962, leaders in the Akali fasted and self-immolated, for the creation of a Punjabi-speaking state. The Chief Khalsa Diwan (CKD) and the Akali Dal leadership requested a separate Sikh state in 1942. The Sikh Akali Dal (SAD) requested the creation of a Sikh state in 1946 (Shani, 2000).

The 1966 trifurcation of the Punjab region resulted in the splitting of the region into three states: Haryana, Himachal Pradesh, and Punjab. The trifurcation divided the region based upon communal identities. The Indian government created the Punjab region based on it having a Sikh majority, with Haryana and Himachal Pradesh having a Hindu majority.

During the 1960s and 1970s, the Sikhs were in the majority, but they were not able to obtain a political popular vote. The Akali Dal, the main Sikh party, was unable to exert political dominance over the Congress Party, the Hindu minority party, causing growing tension in the Sikh majority state. The Akali Dal created the Anandpur Sahib Resolution. The Anandpur Sahib Resolution asked the Indian government for a state independent of Punjab. The Indian government rejected the idea of Khalistan, the independent state that Sikhs requested. Growing frustration with the political system, a sense of injustice and the growing belief that Sikhs needed an independent state created a structural space for Sikh extremist organizations to form. The proposed Khalistan state, the Sikh state, included the three states that were part of the 1966 trifurcation: Haryana, Himachal Pradesh, and Punjab.

The tension between GurSikhs and Nirankari groups culminated in 1978 in Amritsar, leading to a massacre. The Nirankaris killed 13 GurSikhs, a religious Sikh sect, during the event. A group belonging to each sect was in Amritsar on the Vaisakhi day at the same time (Indla, 2020). GurSikh reported an ambush by the Nirankari without the help of police. Nirankari reported an attack by Sikhs. Irrespective of the event's origins, the Indian police did not de-escalate the clash. Murder charges were brought against the Nirankari leader, Singh, but he was acquitted by the Indian government. The GurSikh population, again, felt the political system did not work for them.

It is noted that this is not about "Sikhs" but the militants and those who violently pursued the goal of a "Khalistan" homeland. The Khalistan movement is both a resistance and a fundamentalist movement, largely influenced by religion, Sikhism (Mahmood, 1996). From the Christian Crusades to the Islamic extremists on a jihad mission, religion is a cultural influence on violence.

The 1978 Massacre was the beginning of a recruitment phase for the Sikh extremists. Bhindranwale heavily recruited civilians from rural areas and cities as well, using the rhetoric of the creation of a Sikh country and the creation of their own independent government (Indla, 2020).

Clashes between Sikhs and Hindus became common with an escalation of violence in the Punjab region. Bhindranwale was different from his modern-day successors of Sikh extremists, in that he urged using arms to protect themselves. He urged Sikhs to acquire firearms to defend themselves (Shani, 2000).

Bhindranwale's focus was on the perceived inequality of Sikhs in the Punjab region.

Bhindranwale's legacy on the Sikh extremist movement was the urge to disable the state's legitimacy of "morally sanctioned killing." Akali leaders had not called for violent means of obtaining their goal, and fasting was the preferred tactic used. Bhindranwale called for violence and mingled it with the Khalsa's militant tradition; it was justification enough for armed resistance (Shani, 2000). By 1983, Bhindranwale amassed a large number of weapons and followers. Bhindranwale used the Golden Temple in Amritsar as an operation base for the organization's terrorist activity. Babbar Khalsa International, a terrorist organization, was formed and operated out of the temple. One of its two founders was a widow of the 1978 Massacre (South Asia Terrorism Portal, n.d.). Indira Gandhi, the prime minister of India since the 1970s and during the 1978 Massacre, opted for a strong military response to the movement.

Hess and Martin hypothesized that a repressive event by a government can also lead to backlash, transforming the event into a social movement (Hess & Martin, 2006).

Two factors need to be present for a repressive event to create backfire: a group who views the event as unfair and violent repression of an event that is considered legitimate in nature. A common backfire includes police using violence or unnecessary force on non-violence protests. The Khalistan movement, a social movement that became intertwined with terrorism, exhibited periods of violent and nonviolent discontent with the government

Islamic Extremism

Before addressing the type of extremist groups that are present in Southeast Asia, the influences on Islamic extremism in the region should be addressed. Many of the terrorist groups in this chapter are rooted in the concept of the "global jihad." As mentioned in the previous chapter, many of these groups claim that their interpretation of jihad is linked to Islam's more classical roots. Generally, there are four recognized Sunni jurisprudence or schools of thought: Maliki (jurist Malik Ibn Anas jurist), Hafani (jurist Muhammed al-Sahybani), Shafi'i (jurist al-Shafi'i), and Hanbali (jurist Ibn Qudama) schools (Toutounji, 2017). Another, the Zahiri school (jurist Ibn Hazm), is frequently characterized as a fifth jurisprudence, but it should be noted that it is generally outlined as four schools of Sunni thought.

The classical jurists shaped the foundations of Islam and have been cited by many extremist groups as the explanation for the use of force, especially against non-Muslims. The "global jihad" that we think of today is more defensive than offensive (Toutounji, 2017). Many classical jurists understood jihad as offensive and generally held a spiritual connotation that aimed at internal struggles and desires. However, they did agree that the accidental killing of women and children was a consequence of war. They also made the stipulation that a non-Muslim needed to be invited to the faith before engaging in violence or fighting (Badawi, 2014). When we examine the interpretations of jihad by modern terrorist groups, jihad is rooted in the context of warfare. The stipulations for fighting are generally ignored, and the concept of jihad is intertwined with the sociopolitical views of the group, a practice that did not begin until modern authors of Islamic jihad. Instead, global jihad is largely influenced by a group of modern writers: Taqi al-Din Ibn Tamiyya, Mohammed Ibn Abdul Wahhab, Mawlana Mawdudi (Maududi), Sayyid Qutb, and Muhammad al-Farag.

The rise of Islamic fundamentalism predates Osama bin Laden and begins with Taqi al-Din ibn Taymiyya. Taymiyya was a philosopher who studied the Christian/Western crusades against Muslims and the Mongol attacks on Arab lands. He called for the destruction of invaders and heretics. He urged that jihad (struggle or effort) to be the sixth pillar of Islam (White, 2020). Taymiyya's philosophy had a direct effect on Mohammed ibn Abdul Wahhab, who led the 18th-century purification movement. Wahhab's movement took root in the then "Arabia," which advocated for a puritanical sect of Islam that removed certain practices introduced after the Prophet Mohammed's (PBUH) death (White, 2020). Wahhab's teachings appealed to those who favored a militant application of Islam. Such followers argued that they were attempting to restore Islam to the state it was before

Mohammed's death. This form of Islam, this Wahhabism, spread to India and other parts of Asia (White, 2020).

Additionally, modern writers like Mawlana Mawdudi/Maududi (1903–1979), Sayid Qub (1906–1966), and Muhammad Abd al-Salam Faraj (1952–1982) impacted the concept of global jihad. Mawdudi challenged the classical writers by taking away the need to invite people to Islam. He didn't believe that non-believers (*kuffars*) would want to change their faith (Toutounji, 2017). Additionally, he sought to apply Islamic law to modern-day political problems. Mawdudi viewed British and French colonialism as one of the main hindrances to Muslim rule in the Middle East and South Asia (Toutounji, 2017).

In 1941, Maududi founded Jamaat e-Islami in British India, while the country was still under British rule. He was opposed to nationalism, as it was mainly associated with Hindu secular identity, not one around an Indian Islamic State. He also sought to change society by using Islamic values.

The creation of Jamaat e-Islami as a political party and social organization had the same goals as the Muslim Brotherhood in Egypt. Both hoped to create a non-secular nation rooted in Islam. Maududi interpreted jihad as a way to bring about the Islamic State, by using war/violence to liberate Muslims. In his first major writing, *On the Islamic Law of War and Peace*, and other works, Mawdudi challenged the classical jurist by asserting that the purpose of jihad was to protect Muslims from both "injustice (fasad) abd violence (fitnah)" through the use of war/violence in the pursuit of a universal Islamic State (Toutounji, 2017). Along the lines of rejecting secular nationalism, Mawdudi later campaigned against the creation of Bangladesh as an independent state in 1971 (Alam, 2024).

Similarly, the Egyptian Muslim Brotherhood had a mission of creating an Islamic State. The Brotherhood began in 1928 by Hassan al-Banna. Originally, he started the Brotherhood as a social welfare and religious club that promoted Islamic values. However, during the time of the Brotherhood's inception, Egyptians were living under the British occupation of Egypt (1882–1952) (Laub, 2019). Many were experiencing severe economic hardship, and colonialism was stifling the progress of many Egyptians. The Muslim Brotherhood promoted the importance of civil society in Egypt and campaigned for an Islamic party that would expand beyond Egypt's border (Harik, 2005).

In 1954 an attempted assassination of Gamal Nasser, led to Nasser viewing the group as a political threat and calling for the arrest of hundreds of its members (Pew Research Center, 2010). Around this time, a young Egyptian scholar and teacher had joined the Muslim Brotherhood upon his return from the United States. Sayyid Qutb, the young teacher, was appalled by the Western culture he saw there and was drawn to the ideology of a single Islamic State with Islamic culture. Qutb was arrested by the Nasser government during one of its crackdowns. His most famous body of work was *Milestones*, published in 1965, and it outlined the ideology of jihadist revolution. Qutb called for the destruction of all enemies and expanded on the concept of *Jahiliyyah*. His views were in direct opposition to the government, he deemed as "secular and nationalistic" and he was arrested again in 1966 (White, 2020). He was hanged shortly thereafter, and his death would become a form of martyrdom. Qutb gave a "call to action," where Muslims could use jihad against non-Muslim authorities, transcending national borders. He is dubbed the "father" of modern-day jihadism (Toutounji, 2017).

The last modern writer to greatly impact the concept of global jihad, especially in Southeast Asia, is Muhammad al-Farag (or Muhammad Abd al-Salam Faraj). Faraj

(1952–1982) was also an Egyptian whose father was a member of the Muslim Brotherhood (Pearson, n.d.). In the late 1970s, Faraj helped form the Egyptian Islamic Jihad, or Tanzim al-Sihad, after merging several smaller groups (Toutounji, 2017). Less of a scholar and more of a writer for the layperson, Faraj wrote the Neglected Duty (1981), outlining his ideology and thoughts on jihad. He advocated for the use of violence by Muslims, in pursuit of the Islamic State. He rejected finding peaceful ways to achieve the goal and advocated for the use of violent jihad. He and his comrades were committed to the use of violence when they planned and executed the assassination of Egyptian President Anwar Sadat in 1981. Six months later, Faraj was executed in April 1982 (Pearson, n.d.). The idea of armed jihad became a platform of the group. The Egyptian Islamic Jihad (EIJ) split with some members forming the Islamic Group with Omar Abdul Rahman as their leader. In the 1980s, then leaders Sayyid Imam al-Sharif and Ayman al-Zawahiri traveled to Afghanistan and became acquainted with Osama bin Laden. Al-Zawahiri would later become a leader in Al-Qaeda.

The Al-Qaeda Era of Extremism

The Al-Qaeda era of influence includes the 1990s–2000s. Some extremists from the Philippines, Malaysia, and Indonesia had made their way to Afghanistan to fight as mujahideen in the Soviet-Afghan war. During that time, they either made contact with Al-Qaeda or the Taliban. Some adopted the ideologies of the groups, received financing/support from al-Qaeda, or were inspired by the groups and their leaders (Bakhshi & Rousselle, 2024). Al-Qaeda helped with the creation of Jemaah Islamiyah, an Indonesian group that would go on to be one of the deadliest Southeast Asia groups in the 2000s. Al-Qaeda, along with Moro National Liberation Front (MNLF), helped to start the Philippines-based Abu Sayyaf Group (ASG). Jemaah Islamiyah is closely linked to Kumpulan Mujahidin Malaysia (KMM), creating a network of groups in the Southeast Asia region. Mujahidin Indonesia Timor started as an Al-Qaeda affiliate but later pledged allegiance to ISIS (Temby, 2020).

The Influence of ISIS' and Dissidents

The 2010s ushered in a new wave of inspiration. In the Middle East, the Islamic State began its turbulent and violent trajectory on the international stage, inspiring some. Other groups formed from dissidence within their group. In the early and mid-2010s, many groups began to form in Indonesia and the Philippines as more extreme members splintered from larger organizations. For example, internal conflict between Moro Islamic Liberation Front (MILF) members led to some breaking away to form Bangsamoro Islamic Freedom Fighters (BIFF). Other disagreements within MILF led to the creation of Maute group, Ansar Khilafah Philippines (AKP), and a few others.

Jemaah Islamiyah is a large terrorist network and movement, with many members. It too saw dissidence from within that led to spin-off groups, as many as 18 new groups forming in Indonesia from its large network (Bakhshi & Rousselle, 2024). Examples of such groups include Jamaah Anshuarut Daulah (JAD), a pro-Islamic State group. Another such group was Jamaah Ansharut Tauhid (JAT). The group was founded by Abu Bakar Ba'asyir, a former Jemaah Islamiyah leader (Temby, 2020).

The influence of ISIS on Southeast Asia includes the formation of Katibah Nusantara. Formed by all Southeast Asian fighters, this affiliate of ISIS was formed in the Middle East (Bakhshi & Rousselle, 2024). They trained other Southeast Asian recruits, fought against the Kurdish, and handled requested operational tasks for ISIS. Meanwhile, terrorist groups, and/or leaders, in the Southeast Asia region claimed allegiance to ISIS in their respective countries. Groups like Abu Sayyaf, which received an official nod from ISIS as an affiliate, the East Indonesia Mujahideen, BIFF, the Maute group, and others. In 2018, ISIS officially recognized Wilayat Sharq Asiyya (East Asia Province). This recognition formed the Islamic State East Asia Province, a loosely held together "umbrella" organization of organizations that pledged allegiance to ISIS.

Pakistan

The jihadist group operated in India and present-day Pakistan and Afghanistan in the 19th century. The group originally fought regional Sikh rulers, a group that will be discussed in more detail, but shifted to the British Empire. The movement's leader, Sayyid Ahmed of Bareili, was influenced by the writings of Muhammad ibn Abdul Wahhab, the founder of Wahhabism (Haqqani, 2005). The formation of Pakistan as an independent nation in 1947 was the result of many years of struggle. The country was formed with the intent to have a Muslim-majority country, as India simultaneously became a mostly Hindu independent nation. The move at the time was championed as a path for Muslims to have a collective future. In 1949, the Constituent Assembly stated that Pakistan was created so that South Asian Muslims could live in harmony with the teachings of Islam. There were proposals that went as far as to suggest changing the national script of Bengali from Sanskrit to an Arabic-Persian based script (Haqqani, 2005). The Muslim League declared Pakistan as the beginning of Islamistan or a pan-Islamic State. Pakistan's role in Islamic extremism has been an undeniable effort to support and sponsor various terrorist groups that promote the aim of an Islamic State. Over time, Pakistan's political commitment to an Islamic State has morphed into supporting various jihadist groups, especially during and post the 1971 Bangladesh war for independence.

Networks

Jemaah Islamiyah

Jemaah Islamiyah (The Islamic Community), or al-Jemaah al-Islamiyah, is an Islamist militant group on a campaign to establish a pan-Islamic State in Malaysia, Singapore, Indonesia, southern Philippines, and Singapore (The World Factbook, n.d.). Founder Abdullah Sungkar (1937–1999) was rooted in the DI movement. An "ideological hybrid," the group embraces ideology from DI and Wahhabism. Sungkar drew inspiration from Hassan al-Banna, founder of the Muslim Brotherhood, and Sayyid Qutb, the "father" of modern-day jihadism (Golburt, n.d.). Sungkar did not believe in nationalism and he asserted that Islam does not teach the concept. So, to him, a nation state is un-Islamic and did not exist. Due to this rationale, he rejected national flags or any type of nationalist symbol. He favored a universal, transnational, pan-Islamic State.

Darul Islam was founded with the intent to reject the national government and create an Islamic State in Indonesia. Darul Islam evolved over several phases from the 1950s to the creation of Jemaah Islamiyah or Jamaat Islamiyya (Gunaratna, 2015). The initial phase of the group includes when the group self-identified as DI. Darul Islam was a movement campaigning for an Islamic State in Indonesia. From 1948 to 1962, separatists were run by Sekarmadji Kartosuwiryo, who viewed the government as too secular (Yunanto & Damayanti, 2017). Kartosuwiryo was sentenced to death in 1962, and the group entered a second phase that included maintaining a low profile and consolidating smaller movements into a larger group. Recruitment for the group included the Egyptian-developed *Usroh* method; around five recruits would receive specific Islamic teachings but then be given militarized training. During this time, some DI activists were also going by the name of Komando Jihad. Members of Komando Jihad shared the Kartosuwiryo ideology.

In 1971, the Pondok Ngruki schooling network, co-founded by Abdullah Sungkar and Abu Bakr Ba'asyir, opened in Central Java (Golburt, n.d.). The two were never a part of the original DI but fully embraced the ideology. In 1976, the Indonesian government deemed that they were "inducted" into DI due to their affiliation and network connections. In an attempt to weaken the Komando Jihad uprising, in 1977 the government detained over 185 activists. Sungkar and Ba'asyir were part of the roundup of activists. In 1978, they were sentenced to nine years in prison, but their sentence was reduced on appeal and they were released shortly thereafter.

Komando Jihad remained active and was responsible for the 1981 Garuda airplane hijacking that led to President Suharto giving in to some of their demands (New York Times, 1981). However four of the five hijackers and two military personnel were killed. Dubbed the Woyla tragedy, the 55 passengers were released by the group.

In 1985, the court ordered Sungkar and Ba'asyir back to prison. The men decided to flee to Malaysia to live in exile and establish a *dakwa* movement there (Yunanto & Damayanti, 2017). While in Malaysia, they networked with businessmen in an effort to continue to fundraise for their movement for an Islamic Indonesia. They traveled to Saudi Arabia in search of additional funds and made connections with mujahideen fighters there (Gunaratna, 2015). While still based in Malaysia, they sent their fighters to train in Pakistan and fight in the Soviet-Afghan war in early 1985. The group continued to send DI activists to train at camps led by Abdul Rasul Sayyaf, a veteran of the Soviet-Afghan war and well-connected within the bin Laden/Al-Qaeda network, and fight in Afghanistan until 1995. Some DI members also went to the Philippines to support MILF fighters. The connection with the Al-Qaeda network introduced them to global jihad and the leaders formed the "ideological hybrid" that Jemaah Islamiyah is known for. The group embraces ideology from both DI (a pan-Islamic State in Southeast Asia) and Wahhabism (the use of violent force in jihad).

Sungkar and Ba'asyir proposed the idea of jihad as a way to overthrow local governments. Many members of DI were not comfortable with the proposal. In 1993, Sungkar, Ba'asyir, and followers left DI to form their own organization. Sungkar and Ba'asyir founded Jemaah Islamiyah in 1995 in Malaysia with the vision of creating an Islamic State, named Daulah Islamiyah Nusantara, officially breaking away from DI (Golburt, n.d.). That same year, Sungkar based Jemaah Islamiyah (JI) in Afghanistan after Saudi funding came to a slow halt. They plotted to bomb eleven U.S. commercial airliners in Asia but were not successful. In 1996, the Philippine Moro Liberation Front (MILF) established a JI cell at Camp Abu Bakr in Afghanistan.

Jemaah Islamiyah relocated to Indonesia in 1998 after the collapse of the Suharto regime. Sungkar died in 1999 and was succeeded by Ba'asyir as emir. JI began conducting attacks in 1999. In December of 2000, the group was linked to two major events: a wave of church bombings in Indonesia that killed 18 people and a series of bombings in Manila that killed 22 people (Council on Foreign Relations, n.d.). However, it was their 2002 attack that drew international attention.

Known as the Bali Bombing, the October 2002 bombing of a nightclub on the predominantly Hindu island of Bali targeted foreigners, including U.S., British, Australian, and Israeli diplomats. Amrozi bin Nurhasyim was convicted on August 8, 2003, for purchasing the vehicle that was the main explosive. A total of 33 JI members were arrested and convicted for their involvement in the attack (Council on Foreign Relations, n.d.).

Its leader at the time, Riduan Isamuddin, also known as Hambali, was a close associate of the 9/11 architect, Khalid Sheikh Mohammed. Through this connection, Isamuddin was able to secure funding from Al-Qaeda to support JI's attack in Bali in October 2022. The Bali Bombings were Southeast Asia's highest profile terror attack at the time. More than 200 people were killed, with just as many wounded (Bakhshi & Rousselle, 2024). Captured JI operatives pointed to both the U.S. invasion of Afghanistan and Israel's attack on Palestinians in Jenin that year as motivating factors for the attack.

The group launched several attacks from 2003–2009. A faction of JI led an attack on a Marriott hotel in August 2003. In 2004, JI attacked the Australian embassy with a car bomb in Jakarta, killing 3 and wounding over 100 others. They attacked an Australian embassy again in Bali with a suicide bombing in 2005, killing 20 and injuring 129 more (Council on Foreign Relations, n.d.). The group again attacked a Marriott hotel, in addition to a Ritz Carlton, in July 2009.

Tactics of the group include targeting Christians and Westerners. They particularly target tourist sites and typically use small arms and IEDs. The group aims to harm civilians and frequently attack locations like hotels and nightclubs (The World Factbook, n.d.).

The structure of JI is complex, with various tiers of leadership. At the top of the hierarchy is the Amir (emr). The Amir selects and oversees who is appointed to the various councils: religious, fatwa, disciplinary, and governing councils. The various councils have specific tasks and individuals that preside over the councils. Past leaders for the group, in chronological order, include Abdullah Sungkar (deceased), cofounder of JI; Abu Bakar Ba'asyir, "spiritual leader" and cofounder of JI who created a faction group; Azhari Husin (deceased), bomb maker for the group; Mohammed Noordin Top (deceased), also became a leader of a faction group; Abu Jibril (aka Mohamad Iqbal Abdurrahman), second in command and primary recruiter until arrested; Hambali (aka Riduan Isamuddin, deceased), operational leader; Sanusi (deceased), senior leader; and Zarkasih, currently detained.

Membership for the group is composed mostly of young men, foot soldiers, who were inspired by their religious teachers (Golburt, n.d.). During the earlier times of DI, the young men were recruited through social ties. During later iterations of the group, they were recruited through the Pondok Ngruki network. Children of leaders and siblings/relatives of members (often brought in through marriage) are another way the group brings in members. Recruitment for the group includes money/stipends. Religious ideology allows for a variety of members, both well-educated and those who are not wealthy. Recruitment happens in multiple countries with senior members trying to recruit from conflict areas. "Terrorism scholar Zachary Abuza believes that Ba'asyir ordered the Bali bombings to hurt the Indonesian economy, which in turn would attract people to religion and JI preaching" (Golburt, n.d.)

There is disagreement on how strong these ties are to Al-Qaeda. It is known that the group embraces Al-Qaeda's global focus but beyond that, it is not clear the level of affiliation between the groups. Financing for JI comes from various charities, many of which have ties to Al-Qaeda.

It is believed that Hambali (aka Riduan Isamuddin) was the leader with the greatest connection/affiliation with Al-Qaeda (Council on Foreign Relations, n.d.). Hambali arranged for Yazid Sufat to be the leader of the anthrax attacks that occurred shortly after Al-Qaeda's 9/11 attacks (Golburt, n.d.).

JI is also linked to JAT, which was founded by Ba'aysir after disagreements within the group about leadership. Links to other Islamic extremist groups, including JAT, Front Pembela Islam, Majelis Mujahidin Indonesia, KOMPAK, Lashkar Jundullah, and Majelis Dakwah Umat Indonesia, MILF.

Countries like Singapore and Malaysia have banned the group and arrested suspected members. Indonesia has had a mixed history of dealing with the group, ranging from denying JI's existence to purporting that targeting terrorists could increase public support. However, after the 2002 Bali Bombings, the government became more stringent in cracking down on the organization (Council on Foreign Relations, n.d.). The group was significantly weakened by the late 2000s due to counterterrorism policies, but it remains active.

Al-Qaeda in Southeast Asia

There have been ties found between groups such as ISIS and al-Qaeda and extremist groups in Southeast Asia. One such network of groups is Al-Qaeda in Southeast Asia. Al-Qaeda in Southeast Asia refers to the regional operations and networks of the global terrorist organization Al-Qaeda. The presence of Al-Qaeda in Southeast Asia emerged in the 1990s as the group sought to expand its influence beyond its base in the Middle East and South Asia (Naval History and Heritage Command, n.d.). Al-Qaeda's presence in Southeast Asia was facilitated by existing Islamist extremist networks and militant groups in the region. Al-Qaeda (AQ) is a transnational terrorist organization founded by Osama bin Laden in the late 1980s. Al-Qaeda is known for its involvement in numerous terrorist attacks, including the September 11, 2001, attacks in the United States (Naval History and Heritage Command, n.d.).

Al-Qaeda in Southeast Asia (AQSA) primarily operates in Southeast Asia. As this is a loosely linked network of groups, each group has individual ideologies. However, AQSA supports a Salafi-jihadist ideology and aims to establish global Islamic rule based on its interpretation of Sunni Islam.

Al-Qaeda's leadership has undergone changes over the years due to U.S.-led counterterrorism efforts and internal power struggles. Osama bin Laden served as the group's founder and leader until his death in 2011 (International Crisis Group, 2002). Other prominent leaders have included Ayman al-Zawahiri, Abu Musab al-Zarqawi, and various regional commanders responsible for overseeing operations in Southeast Asia. This network of groups has their own individual leaders but subscribes to the overall mission and leadership of Al-Qaeda.

Al-Qaeda helped facilitate the creation of extremist groups in the area, such as Jema'at Islamiyah and ASG, which are also a part of the network. However, some groups within

AQSA also have ties to ISIS. Al-Qaeda has often aided in funding other groups in the region and provided training to members of terrorist organizations.

Al-Qaeda in Southeast Asia's membership includes individuals from diverse backgrounds, including local militants, foreign fighters, and sympathizers (International Crisis Group, 2002). Many members are radicalized individuals drawn to the group's jihadist ideology and anti-Western rhetoric. Recruitment efforts often target vulnerable populations, including young men disillusioned with government policies, economic hardship, and perceived injustices against Muslims.

Al-Qaeda in Southeast Asia recruits members primarily from local Islamist extremist networks, militant groups, and disenfranchised youth sympathetic to its jihadist ideology. Recruitment efforts often target individuals with grievances against the government, perceived injustices against Muslims, or a desire to participate in the global jihad against Western powers.

Al-Qaeda in Southeast Asia has been involved in various terrorist activities, including bombings, assassinations, and attacks on Western interests, government installations, and civilian targets (International Crisis Group, 2002). The group has also provided ideological and logistical support to local Islamist extremist groups and insurgent organizations in the region. Al-Qaeda in Southeast Asia's activities have included the planning and execution of terrorist attacks, recruitment and training of operatives, fundraising, and propaganda dissemination.

Al-Qaeda in the Indian Subcontinent

Ayman al-Zawahiri announced the formation of Al-Qaeda in the Indian subcontinent (AQIS) in September 2014. Founded by al-Zawahiri and Asim Umar, AQIS in 2014 as Al-Qaeda's fifth official chapter. Al-Qaeda in the Indian subcontinent is a Salafist Islamic group that operates in Afghanistan, Pakistan, India, Burma, Bangladesh, and the Kashmir region (Counter Extremism Project, n.d.).

The group uses "defensive" jihad to establish a Caliphate in the Indian subcontinent. As an affiliate, it supports the overarching goals of Al-Qaeda of a global jihad. Al-Qaeda in the Indian subcontinent ideology utilizes the *Ghazwa-e-Hind*, "final battle in India" prophecy found in the Hadith. Both Al-Qaeda and AQIS believe in a prophecy that an apocalyptic war with the Indian state will result in the demise of a Hindu nation and begin that of an Islamic State. Pakistan will come under this Sharia law and is not viewed as an enemy, as it was built on Islamic principles.

It's believed that al-Zawahiri created AQIS to draw attention to, and recruit for, Al-Qaeda's brand. It appears that AQC is planning a comeback for Al-Qaeda in a post "ISIS dominated" era, where grievances are still high in the MENA and Southeast Asia regions. Al-Qaeda in the Indian subcontinent took two years to create and its founder aimed to consolidate several factions of jihadist groups on the Indian subcontinent (Hoffman, 2019). The decision to do so was a strategic one, with al-Zawahiri looking to preserve Al-Qaeda safe havens in Afghanistan and Pakistan with an Al-Qaeda-based group on the ground on the Indian subcontinent (Counter Extremism Project, n.d.).

While groups like ISIS and its affiliates, take the approach of sensationalizing to garner media attention, groups like Al-Qaeda and AQIS take the infiltration route. AQIS operates and promotes its ideology in a manner that garners very little attention.

The relative success of AQIS is attributed to two tactics: a "glo-cal" jihad and a "Code of Conduct" (Hoffman, 2019). AQIS stability, unlike ISIS, over the last decade is attributed to its ability to propagate Al-Qaeda's global jihad message while keeping local politics and grievances in mind. In other words, AQIS uses a local narrative found in that respective community but gives it a global aspiration. This deliberate strategy continues to center locals at the heart of the "jihad" and encourages recruitment from the region as the narrative focuses on their grievances. Another key component of success for the group is a published "Code of Conduct" that rejects the practices of coercion and fear that groups like ISIS practiced. AQIS engages with local leaders and community members to establish rapport and communication. Importantly, the group touts that its code of conduct doesn't allow for members to attack noncombatant Christians, Hindus, Buddihists, etc (Hoffman, 2019). In contrast to ISIS, the group claims that religious places of worship would not be attacked. Their Code of Conduct reiterates that their primary targets are military-related (Counter Extremism Project, n.d.). This important move garners the support of less radical community members and jihadist groups, setting the tone that not every person is viewed as an "enemy." This strategy, put forward by Al-Qaeda Central (AQC), hopes to recruit members into leadership at both the AQIS and Al-Qaeda ranks.

A small-scale group, AQIS has engaged in limited attacks. In February 2013, the group claimed responsibility for the murder of Bangladeshi activist Rajib Haider (Counter Extremism Project, n.d.). AQIS claimed responsibility for the foiled September 2014, Pakistan navy frigate attack in Karachi. The attack highlighted the group's capability of launching attacks as a fairly new organization. Also in September, the group murdered an Islamic scholar, Mohammad Shakil Auj, in Pakistan. They also murdered sociology professor Shafiul Islam, in Bangladesh in 2014 and blogger Avijit Roy in 2015, also in Bangladesh.

Counterterrorism policies from 2014–2015 led to the loss of key AQIS members. However, the group's close proximity to AQC has allowed it to remain relatively stable (Hoffman, 2019). In April 2016, the group claimed responsibility for an attack on two editors, LGBTQIA+ activists Xulhaz Mannan and Mahbub Tonoy, of a human rights magazine in Bangladesh. The two were hacked to death. A month later, Bangladeshi police arrested Shariful Islam Shihab in connection with the attacks. In November of that same year, Pakistan's Counterterrorism department arrested a high-ranking member of AQIS, Muhammad Uzair, in a series of raids. Abdul Raheem, an Al-Qaeda commander and possible commander for AQIS, was killed in a drone attack in Pakistan in early 2017. In December 2017, Mar bin Khatab, a top AQIS leader, was killed in a joint U.S./Afghan mission (Counter Extremism Project, n.d.). The group's last claim of responsibility for an attack was in 2017. In March 2019, more than 30 AQIS members were killed by Afghan forces.

In a joint effort between the U.S. and the Afghan military, a raid in Musa Qala, Afghanistan, resulted in the death of AQIS leader Asim Umar, in September of 2019. Six other AQIS members were also killed in the raid. To date, the group continues to experience the arrest or death of several of its members. Currently, some of its members are known to collaborate with the Taliban, as the group remains low profile but active.

The group has claimed responsibility for the deaths of several secular activists, ranging from Bangladesh to Pakistan. Tactics of the group include targeting members of the military, security personnel, foreigners, foreign aid workers, students, professors, members of political parties, etc. They typically use small arms, IEDs, and machetes.

Tensions and conflicts between Hindus and Muslims in India are used by AQIS to bolster support and recruitment from the Muslim population. The group utilizes propaganda on social media, and in Urdu, to enrage local Muslims (Hoffman, 2019). Prior to the formation of AQIS, Al-Qaeda recruited members from the Kashmir region. However, AQIS now uses *Ghazwa-e-Hind* as online propaganda to recruit members in the subcontinent. Recruitment within India is still a difficult task for Al-Qaeda, as many Indian Muslims are more reluctant to join the call than Muslims in the Kashmir or Pakistan regions. In 2016, AQIS began translating its propaganda material into Tamil and Malayalam in hopes of recruiting South Indians.

Not much is known about how AQIS trains its soldiers. A possible AQIS training camp in Kandahar, Afghanistan, was destroyed by U.S. and Afghan forces in 2015. Another possible camp is in Waziristan, Pakistan (Counter Extremism Project, n.d.). In 2016, the group released video footage of the site to entice possible new recruits. Intelligence suggests that AQIS provides two weeks of indoctrinating, religious courses. The recruit is then exposed to military training.

While overall funding for the group is not publicly known, it is highly suspected that AQC provides support to the group. Other known sources of funding for the group includes kidnapping for ransom, money from other terrorist groups (i.e., Lakshar e Tobia), state sponsorship, trading in counterfeit currency, and a diverse portfolio of charitable and individual donations. An estimated one-third of the group's budget comes from civilian donations, so it has been challenging for governments to hamper the funding sources (Britannica, 2024). As previously noted, the group remains active. In January 2024, AQIS released a new edition of Nawa-i-Ghazwa-e-Hind calling for Muslims to answer the call and fight against Hindu, American, and Israel interests, a "glo-cal" jihad.

Bangladesh, Pakistan, and the Kashmir Region

Organized jihadi movements that operate militarily post-Soviet-Afghan war are generally put into three categories: the Jamaat-e-Islami groups, the Deobandi movements, and the Wahhabi groups. Jamaat-e-Islami is not a terror group but an ideology that groups subscribe to, like Wahhabism. Jamaat-e-Islami is a Pakistan-based Islamist political movement. It is also prominent, and has branches, in the United Kingdom (Pew Research Center, 2010).

Jama'at-e-Islami is a political party with many similarities to that of the Muslim Brotherhood. Both have an organizational aspect and an ideological component. The ideology at the root of Jamaat-e-Islami comes from an Islamic scholar and founder of the group, Maulana Abul Ala Maududi.

When Maududi founded Jamaat-e-Islami in British India in 1947, British rule was negatively impacting the lives of everyday citizens. He could see the impact of colonialism on the country. When it was time for the creation of an independent Indian nation, Maududi was opposed to nationalism. He associated it with a Hindu secular identity, not one around an Indian Islamic State. He sought to change society by using Islamic values but creating that change via violent jihad. Maududi challenged the classical jurist by asserting that the purpose of jihad was to protect Muslims from both "injustice (fasad) abd violence (fitnah)" through the use of war/violence in the pursuit of a universal Islamic State (Toutounji, 2017).

Beginning with its inception in 1941 until the early 1990s, Jamaat-e-Islami received support from Saudi Arabia, especially as Saudi Arabia is more likely to support Salafist/ Sunni organizations. In 1992, the group failed to support Saudi Arabia in the Gulf War as Saudi Arabia felt it was needed. Funding for the group slowly stopped for Jamaat-e-Islami and picked up for Wahhabist groups, like some mentioned in this chapter. Jamaat-e-Islami and Saudi Arabia were able to repair the relationship, but the period without funding elevated some groups in the region and diminished Jamaat-e-Islami's status in the international scene.

Jamaat-e-Islami's principles are rooted in Maududi's ideology. The group's call for revolutionary change was not as appealing a recruitment tool as the group had hoped for; however, the social service structure, like the Brotherhood, and the call for jihad through war/violence is one that had greater appeal.

Harakat ul-Mujahidin

Harkat-ul-Mujahideen (HuM) is a Salafist, jihadist terrorist organization based in Pakistan, specifically in Muzaffarabad, Rawalpindi, and several other towns (United Nations Security Council, 2011). HuM was formed in 1985 by Maulana Fazlur Rahman Khalil as a splinter group of Harakat ul-Jihad e Islami (HuJI). Formed during the Soviet-Afghan war, HuM and HuJI were initially anti-Soviet militants that received support from both the United States and Pakistan. However, after the Soviet withdrawal from Afghanistan in 1989, the goal of the group became the annexation of Jammu and Kashmir through violent jihad (Stanford University, 2017).

The operated training camps in eastern Afghanistan until U.S. drone strikes in 2001. Splintering occurred in the group in 2000 when a large number of members left to establish Jaish-e-Mohammad (The World Factbook, n.d.). In an attempt to rebrand the group, HuM changed its name to Jamiat ul-Ansar in 2003. Pakistan officially banned the group that same year.

The group is responsible for several attacks, many of which are directed towards Indian troops, government officials, Western targets, and even civilians. Between 2005 and 2013, the group's strategy was to target civilians. In 2002, the group targeted a bus carrying foreign workers via a suicide bombing. Around 20 people were wounded and 15 people were killed.

Tactics of the group includes bombs, suicide bombs, hijackings, kidnappings, assassination, the use of small arms, grenades, and IEDs. The only source of funding currently is donations from wealthy supporters in Pakistan. Although the group is based in Pakistan, it primarily operates in Afghanistan and in the Indian state of Jammu and Kashmir (The World Factbook, n.d.). The group has affiliations with Al-Qaeda and/or the Taliban (United Nations Security Council, 2011). It also has affiliations with Lashkar-e-Taiba, Jaish-e-Muhammad, and Lashkar-e-Jhangvi. The group has not claimed responsibility for an attack since 2018. The group is estimated to have a small number of active members.

Philippines

Abu Sayyaf Group

Abu Sayyaf Group is a Sunni extremist group. The group was formed in 1991 after splintering from the MILF. It was founded by Abdurajak Abubakar Janjalani with the goal of establishing an independent Islamic State in the southern Philippines (Stanford University, n.d.-a). Abu Sayyaf Group is a small but violent, Salafist separatist group. It is considered the most violent of the Islamic insurgent groups in the Philippines (National Counterterrorism Center, 2014).

ASG operates in the Philippines and has a presence in Malaysia. They're primarily present in Western Mindanao and the Sulu Archipelago of the Philippines. Specifically, the group operates mainly in the Basilan, Sulu, and Tawi-Tawi Provinces in the Sulu Archipelago (National Counterterrorism Center, 2014). The death of leader Janjalani in a 1998 shootout resulted in a large fragmentation of the group, splintering ASG into two groups. Janjalani's brother, Khadaffy, led one, and Galib Andang led another group. Fragmentation within the group led to a period where ASG pursued kidnapping tactics more and relied on terrorist tactics less (Stanford University, n.d.-a).

Tactics of the group includes a history of high-profile bombings, kidnappings for ransoms, assassinations, robbery, beheadings, murder, and extortion (Naval History and Heritage Command, n.d.). Attacks focused on military and civilian defense forces, as well as anyone considered to be working against the group's interests or against interpretations of Islamic law. Most attacks focus on receiving money for the group. In the early 2000s, the group conducted many high-profile bombings. Currently, it focuses on kidnapping for ransom. Increase in profit-driven activities and a decrease in political attacks. The last recorded attack by ASG was in January 2022. Due to its small size, some consider the group a criminal group rather than a terrorist organization. However, it is considered to be the most radical of Philippine Islamic separatist groups.

Attacks by the group have been numerous. In April of 2000, the group kidnapped 21 people, 10 of them being Westerners, from a Malaysian resort. That same year, they kidnapped three U.S. citizens and 17 Filipinos, later murdering several of the hostages (National Counterterrorism Center, 2014). The 9/11 attack by Al-Qaeda was felt throughout the jihadist world, as the United States engaged in an active "War against Terrorism." The U.S. and the Armed Forces of the Philippines actively targeted jihadist groups in Southeast Asia, ASG included. The U.S. deployed over 1,650 troops to the Philippines in 2002. ASG suffered losses in leadership during this time. However, the group reconsolidated its split factions and carried out its deadliest attack in 2004.

In February of 2004, ASG bombed a ferry in Manila Bay, one of the largest-scale attacks for the group, killing 16 people. In February of 2005, engaging in simultaneous bombings, they killed eight people and injured over 150 others. This attack was carried out by the Janjalani faction of ASG. In 2007, ASG and MILF collaborated in an attack on Philippine forces, killing 14. The group continued with bombings, like the 2007 motorcycle bombing, and kidnappings, like the 2009 International Red Cross workers kidnapping, for several years. In February 2010, Albader Parad was killed by Philippine marines. Parad was one of ASG's most violent sub-group/faction commanders (National Counterterrorism Center, 2014). The group continued to suffer loss of leadership, with "Dr Abu" in 2012 and Khair

Mundos in 2014. Also in 2014, the group claimed to have made peace with the Philippine government. The group carried out a series of attacks from 2017–2019 but Bangsamoro, the autonomous Muslim territory for the Moro people that they claimed to fight for, was created in 2018.

The leadership of ASG is fragmented. The current leader is Radullan Sahiron. However, past leaders include Abdurajak Abubakar Janjalani (Deceased) was the group's founder and leader from 1991 to 1998; Khadaffy Janjalani (Deceased) assumed the role of leadership after Abdurajak Abubakar Janjalani's death from 1998 to 2006; Radullan Sahiron (Unknown to Present) is known as Commander Putol; Alhamser Limbong (Deceased) was in leadership from an unknown time until 2002; Galib Andang (Deceased) led one faction after Abdurajak Janjalani's death from 1998 to 2003; Abu Sulaiman (Deceased) led until 2007; Abdul Basir Latip (Unknown to 2009) was arrested; Albader Parad (Deceased) led until 2010; Gumbahali Jumdail (Deceased) led until 2012; Isnilon Totoni Hapilon (Deceased) was killed near the end of the Marawi Crisis; Yasser Igasan (2007 to the present) is a current leader of the ASG, and Hatib Hajan Sawadjaan (unknown to present) is a sub-leader of a faction (Stanford University, n.d.-a).

ASG has affiliations with Al-Qa'ida and Jemaah Islamiyah (Naval History and Heritage Command, n.d.). Ramzi Yousef, a member of Al-Qaeda and participant in the 1993 WTC bombing, traveled to the Philippines in 1991 and 1992 and trained ASG members in 1994 (Stanford University, n.d.-a). Khalid Shaikh Mohammed, another Al-Qaeda member, worked with Yousef and ASG members on the Bojinka plot, where 12 planes were to be shot down over the Pacific Ocean.

Some subgroups of ASG aligned with the Islamic State and Islamic State East Asia (ISEA). In 2014, a faction of the group, under the leadership of Isnilon Hapilon, an ASG leader, pledged allegiance to ISIS (Stanford University, n.d.-a). They formed ISIS's Philippines branch and were highlighted in a 2016 ISIS propaganda video highlighting the Philippines branch of "battalions."

It is estimated that there are fewer than 400 members, with the membership ranging from teenagers to older adults. Many members come from impoverished backgrounds with limited formal education. However, there are some educated individuals and university graduates in the group. Due to its small size, some consider the group a criminal group rather than a terrorist organization. However, it is considered to be the most radical of Philippine Islamic separatist groups. Recruitment tactics of the group include exploiting grievances related to poverty, marginalization, and perceived injustice against Muslims by the Philippine government. They target vulnerable populations in an effort to recruit. Targets of attacks include Christians, military personnel, and foreigners, as well as larger individual targets such as politicians and business people. The group remains active.

Indonesia

Moro National Liberation Front

Moro National Liberation Front is an Islamic separatist movement that began in 1972 (Stanford University, 2019). The goal of the group is to create an independent, democratic Islamic State for the Filipino Muslim minority, known as the Moro people, who live primarily in the Philippines' Mindanao region.

Soon after the group began its insurgency in 1972, launching attacks on various targets in Marawi City (Stanford University, 2019). Soon after, President Ferdinand Marcos imposed martial law (Britannica, 2024). The military branch of the group, the Bangsa Moro Army, had more than 30,000 members at the group's height in the 1970s. In 1974, MNLF fighters entered Jolo and attempted to declare Mindanao's independence. They held the city captive for days before the military was able to retake the city.

In a pivotal moment for MNLF, in 1975 the Marcos administration acknowledged and affirmed, the economic grievances that MNLF/Moros had against Christian landowners. However, Marcos stopped short of granting autonomy for the Moros islands. With mediations assisted by Libya, MNLF and the Philippine government signed the Tripoli Agreement on December 23, 1976. However, the agreement did not go as planned, and MNLF ended the peace talks demanding full independence (Stanford University, 2019).

The group decided to boycott the Mindanao elections. This gave legislative control to the National Society Movement. The decision to sit out the election created a rift within the organization, resulting in a series of factional splits. In 1977, Hashim Salamat and other members broke from the organization to form the New MNLF, later called the MILF, a primary rival group of MNLF. Another such split resulted in the Bangsa Moro Liberation Organization (Britannica, 2024). Also in 1977, a MNLF commander lured a Philippine military general under the false pretense of a ceasefire meeting, but MNLF forces ambushed the general and his men. A total of 34 Philippine soldiers were killed.

Although martial law was lifted in 1981, the group continued to use guerrilla warfare. In February 1981, MNLF attacked soldiers on the island of Pata, killing more than 120 troops. In 1986, a change in the presidential administration led to fresh ceasefire talks. And in 1987, MNLF dropped its demand for an independent state, aiming for an autonomous entity (Britannica, 2024). However, several MNLF members frustrated with the MNLF's strategy broke off to form the ASG (Stanford University, 2019). In 1989, through a series of peace accords, the Autonomous Region in Muslim Mindanao (ARMM) was formed. However, many Moros thought the system was weak and didn't provide the level of independence they were seeking as ARMM deferred many issues to the Philippine government (START, n.d.).

In November of 2001, a group of Misuari's followers attacked several military camps in Jolo in an attempt to undermine the ARMM elections that Misuari was very likely to lose. Over 100 people were killed in the attacks. In the three decades that the group has existed, fighting between the Moro guerrilla group and the Philippine government has resulted in over 100,000 deaths (Britannica, 2024). The group remains active.

Tactics of the group include guerrilla warfare, kidnapping, boat and airplane hijackings, and attacks on civilians. Typically, they engage in armed struggle and negotiations as a tactic. In more recent decades the group began to engage in conventional warfare. Targets of the group include the Philippine government and Christian groups; some attacks on civilians but are mostly focused on the government.

Leadership for the group has weakened over time/since its creation. Leadership for the group includes Nur Misuari (1972 to the present) is the founding chairman and leads one faction; Dimas Pundato (1982 to 1985) established the faction Moro National Liberation Front-Reformist Group; Muslimin Sema (2001 to the present) led an anti-Misuari faction called the Executive Council of 15 (EC-15); Hatimil Hassan (2001 to the present) is a leading figure within the Executive Council of 15 (EC-15); Abul Khayr Alonto (2014 to the present) assumed leadership after Misuari was ousted in 2014; Habib Mujahab Hashim (unknown to present) currently leads the MNLF's Islamic Command Council (MNLF-ICC); Hadja Bainon Karon (unknown to the present) currently leads the MNLF's Islamic Command Council (MNLF-ICC); and Alvarez Isnaji (unknown to unknown) established the Isnaji Group (Stanford University, 2019).

The group receives support from the Malaysian government. They also receive support, money, and training from Libya. It is suspected that they have received support from the OIC (Organization of the Islamic Conference). Although less active then in the 1970s, the group remains an active terrorist organization.

Moro Islamic Liberation Front

The MILF formed in 1977 when Hashim Salamat and others, decided to break away from the MNLF (National Consortium for the Study of Terrorism and Responses to Terrorism). Like MNLF, the MILF is an Islamic separatist movement with the intention to create an independent Islamic or autonomous region in the Philippines. Specifically, the MILF advocates for the Moro people, the Filipino Muslim minority who live in the Philippines' Mindanao region. The MILF is the largest and strongest militant organization in the Philippines. It currently controls territory in the southern Philippines.

Salamat formed the group after MNLF's first attempt, of many, at peace talks with the Philippine government. The peace talks resulted in the creation of ARMM in 1989. However, MILF felt that ARMM was not autonomous enough as MNLF continued to defer issues to the Philippine government. From the 1980s to the 1990s, MILF utilized being in a secluded geographical location and increased in military power and social influence. Undermining the ARMM system established by MNLF, MILF established its own Muslim communities that were governed by MILF's own governing and judicial system. This created a de facto "Islamic State" under the ARMM's jurisdiction. MILF became a stronger representative of the Moro people than the MNLF's ARMM system.

The first attack by the group was a September 1986 bombing where MILF members threw a grenade into a Catholic church during a wedding. Ten people were killed and 90 people wounded in the attack (Stanford University, 2019). The group engaged in numerous attacks from 1986 until the present. Some such attacks include the February 200 bombings of a bus that killed over 40 people and the bombing of a Catholic radio station that wounded 7.

In 2001, newly elected President Gloria Macapagal-Arroyo reversed the previous administration's war policy on MILF in hopes of quelling the violent attacks by the group. By 2003, a ceasefire agreement between MILF and the Philippine government was signed in good faith to start peace talks. However, all talks came to a halt when the Philippine Supreme Court denied the proposal of Bangsamoro in October 2008 (National Consortium for the Study of Terrorism and Responses to Terrorism, n.d.). Up until this point, violence between MILF and the Philippine military forces had continued, but the dismissal by the court triggered widespread fighting. An estimated 600,000 people were displaced and more than a dozen were killed when various "rogue" cells of the MILF attacked mainly Christian villages. In July of 2009, the MILF and the Philippine government resumed ceasefire talks to allow for new negotiations for an autonomous Moro nation. This time, named Memorandum of Understanding, the two sides sought to establish a Muslim Moro community. On January 25, 2014, the Framework Agreement on the Bangsamoro (FAB) was signed off by both MILF and the Philippine government (National Consortium for the Study of Terrorism and Responses to Terrorism, n.d.).

While there are prominent individual leaders, MILF uses a unique strategy of collective leadership (Stanford University, 2019). Known individual leaders for the group include Hashim Salamat (1984–2003) helped break away from MNLF in 1977 and formed what later would be MILF; Al Haj Murad Ebrahim (2003 to the present) led the Bangsamoro Islamic Armed Forces (BIAF) and other leadership roles in MILF; Mohagher Iqbal (Unknown to the present) is a major spokesperson for the group and was the Peace Panel Chairman; and Abdullah Macapaar (Unknown to the present) a rouge member known as Commander Bravo, who carries out deadly attacks (Stanford University, 2019).

The group receives support from state and non-state actors. MILF has received support from countries like Libya, Malaysia, and other Islamic States. However, the group is not without competitors. The group's main rival was MNLF after MILF split from the group in 1977 (Stanford University, 2019). The group has formally condemned the ASG, another splinter group of MNLF. All things withstanding, there is some evidence that suggests low-level cooperation between the groups. In 2003/2004, the group cut ties with JI, AQ, ASG, and other organizations.

The group has targeted local officials, Christian groups, business leaders (in order to receive money), and the Philippine military (University of Central Arkansas, n.d.). The group has not engaged in indiscriminate civilian attacks, as they focused on targeting non-Muslims. Tactics of the group include guerrilla attacks against the military, bombings, and kidnappings. In 2018, the New York Times estimated the group to have 30–40,000 armed soldiers. However, the group has an estimated 2–3 million base supporters in the Moro community (Stanford University, 2019). While the group is active, it is in the process of disarmament (Stanford University, 2019).

The Philippine Communist PartyThe Communist Party of the Philippines (CPP), or New People's Army (NPA), is also known as The Philippine Communist Party. The group formed in 1968, and its armed faction, NPA, formed shortly thereafter in 1969. As the two groups are very closely intertwined, they are often referred to as one entity, The Communist Party of the Philippines—New People's Army (CPP-NPA). The group is a Marxist-Leninist-Maoist revolutionary group seeking to overthrow the Philippine government and incite the working class to revolt (The World Factbook, n.d.). The group was founded by former student activist Jose Maria Sison. Sison was the longtime leader of the group until his death in December 2022. Sison was originally associated with Partido Komunista ng Pilipinas (PKP), a Russian-supported organization, until he broke away in the late 1960s (Buenaventura, 2023). While the peak of operations for the group was the 1970s and 1980s, the group is still active and is the oldest existing communist insurgency(Stanford University, 2018). As a Maoist group, they focused on the peasantry and creating revolutionary change in the lower classes.

The CPP-NPA targeted military and security forces, government officials, infrastructure, and government facilities (The World Factbook, n.d.). They also attack U.S. interests in the Philippine economy and U.S. employees (embassy personnel, soldiers, etc.). The group also targets off-duty soldiers and police officers. The Communist Party of the

Philippines—New People's Army also targeted businesses that did not pay the "taxes" due to them (Buenaventura, 2023). However, the group carried out executions and ambushed anyone that they perceived to be "state collaborators." Since its inception, the group is responsible for the death of more than 40,000 civilian and combatant deaths (The World Factbook, n.d.). The group justifies the attacks on civilians as "revolutionary justice." Tactics for the group include propaganda units, rural and urban guerilla tactics, ambushes, extortions, assassinations, and bombings.

The first attack of the group took place in Manila's Plaza in 1971, when the group threw four grenades onto a stage at a rally, killing nine people and wounding over 90 others (Stanford University, 2018). Other large-scale attacks include the 1989 assassination of U.S. Army Colonel James Rowe while he provided assistance to the Philippine government. In August of 2010, around 40 CPP-NPA members used two improvised explosive devices (IEDs) and gunfire to ambush a police vehicle, killing eight people (Stanford University, 2018). The following year, 30 group members kidnapped mayor of Linging, Henry Dano, and his two bodyguards. They released all captured in the attack after a public apology by Dano in October.

In October 2011, the group carried out a large-scale attack where more than 200 CPP-NPA members attacked three mining companies in Surigao del Norte. The group took four hostages and caused an estimated $ one billion in damages (Stanford University, 2018). In 2013 some 30 CPP-NPA members fired at a truck carrying policemen, killing 9 and wounding 12. Another attack by the group took place in 2015 when CPP-NPA launched two attacks in Agusan del Sur, killing one and wounding one person. Between 2016 and 2019, the Philippine government and CPP-NPA engaged in several attempts to establish a ceasefire or a peace agreement, to no avail. In 2019, CPP-NPA used bombs to kill six Philippine *troops*, one of its deadliest attacks to date (The World Factbook, n.d.).

The group has multiple leaders at one time, with Jose Maria Sison being the founder and primary leader until his death in 2022. Other leaders include Bernabé Buscayno (1969–1976), Rodolfo Salas (1976–1986), Romulo Kintanar (Unknown to Unknown), Benito Tiamzon (Unknown to Unknown), Wilma Tiamzon (Unknown to 2014), and Adelberto Silva (2014 to Unknown) (Stanford University, 2018).

In the past, the group secured support from China, but Chinese support is now limited. CPP-NPA sought support from like-minded organizations, but with the decline of communist groups, this has been more or less an unsuccessful endeavor. The group has alleged cooperation with MNLF and MILF, but not collaboration. In the past, they have cooperated with the Japanese Red Army (JRA), the Maoist factions of the Palestinian Liberation Organization (PLO), the Sandinistas, the Communist Party of El Salvador, and many other organizations (Stanford University, 2018).

In the early 1990s, the Second Great Rectification Movement led to a split within the CPP-NPA (Buenaventura, 2023). The divide created reaffirmists and rejectionists with Alex Boncayao Brigade (ABB) resulting as one of the splinter groups. Both CPP-NPA and ABB have engaged in hostile clashes, with ABB working with the Philippine government against the CPP-NPA. A 2018 estimate of membership for the group is around 3,700 and even though the group is not as active as it once was, it is still the longest-running communist insurgency (The World Factbook, n.d.).

India and Sri Lanka

Khalistan Terrorist Groups

Violent mobilization (increased and decreased mobilization) for the Khalistan movement was precipitated by three main events: the 1978 Massacre, the 1984 Temple Raid, and the 1988 Temple Raid. The 1978 Sikh Massacre served as the catalyst for the creation of several Punjab terrorist organizations. In the same year, the Anandpur Sahib Resolution that requested a separate state from the Indian government, resurfaced in importance. The Resolution was not fulfilled by the government. Frustration and a growing sense of injustice created structural conduciveness for a Sikh extremist movement (the Khalistan movement). The Hindu minority (the Congress Party) controlled politics in the Sikh majority state, which created additional political strain.

The Khalistan movement, a social movement that became intertwined with terrorism, exhibited periods of violent and nonviolent discontent with the government. A violent backlash against the Indian government occurred after the 1978 Massacre.

The Golden Temple, one of the holiest sites of the Sikh religion, was the primary location that the Indian government decided to raid in relation to growing Sikh dissidence. This, in turn, created a separate space within society where it was perceived that the government attacked Sikhs (as a religion and culture). The Indian government's raid on the Golden Temple, known as Operation Blue Star, was a poorly planned attack on a subsequent social movement linked to terrorism. The operation was heavily military-based, excessive force was used and they rejected media coverage of the event. Due to the lack of transparency over the event, the estimated number of deaths during the raid remains contested. The Indian government stated that 493 civilians/terrorists were killed, Reuters News reported upwards of 1,000 killed, an Amritsar crematorium worker reported over 3,000 bodies cremated, and eyewitness accounts marked the deaths around 8,000 (BBC News, 2018). Innocent bystanders/civilians who prayed in the temple and lived near the temple were killed. Military soldiers also took children and women captive, starved them for days even though it was apparent that they were not armed terrorists. Another mishap of the raid was that the terrorists were warned of the raid by the government, this allowed for additional time to bring more reinforcements into the temple (Crenshaw, n.d.). Coupled with the undisclosed deaths from the temple raid were the 5–8,000 people that were reported missing in the days following.

Eyewitness reports on the ground became undisputed truths of the perceived biased actions by the government due to the lack of media coverage. The operation received widespread backlash. The Indian government lost the support of many Sikhs who had remained neutral since the 1978 Massacre. Brute use of force, a destroyed sacred temple, the loss of innocent civilian lives, and lack of transparency delegitimized the Indian government and Gandhi's claim to restore peace in the Punjab region. Disenfranchised Sikhs joined the Khalistan movement, and subsequently, recruitment into terrorist organizations increased. Militants killed during the raid became martyrs and symbols of the Khalistan movement.

By 1984, Sikh terrorists gained members and became an opponent of the Indian government. The 1984 Golden Temple raid by the government included innocent bystanders. Terrorism activity drastically increased after the 1984 temple raid as civilians joined terrorist organizations as part of the government backlash. Incidents of terrorism in India went from an average of 14 in 1983 to a total of 95 in 1984(Perry, 2014). The Khalistan movement became legitimized as the government lost popular support.

Khalistan Terrorist Organizations in India

Prior to the Temple Raid of 1988, negotiations were made by Sikh extremists but were not kept. In 1985, the Punjab Accord was signed between Prime Minister Rajiv Gandhi and Sant Longowal, Akali Dal leader. Many Sikh extremists had not agreed with the Accord, and Longowal was assassinated shortly after the Accord (Butani, 1986).

Bhinderwale Tiger Force of Khalistan (BTHK) was responsible for incidents of terrorism from 1988 to 1992. Babbar Khalsa International (BKI) first terrorism incident occurred in 1988. Activity for the organization decreased the following year and continued to decrease until BKI was no longer attributed to committing physical acts of terrorism. Babbar Khalsa, an offshoot of BKI, was responsible for one physical act of terrorism beyond 1998, a terror attack that occurred in 2007 (Perry, 2014). Active for two years, Dishmish Regiment was responsible for 43 of the terrorism incidents related to the Khalistan movement. After 1984, the group's activity decreased to zero.

The Khalistan Liberation Front (KLF) formed in 1986 and began committing acts of terrorism during the same year. The peak of the group's activity was in 1986 (N = 7), followed by decreased activity. The Khalistan Commando Force (KCF) had a sum of 20 terrorism incidents between 1987 and 1995. The peak of its activity was in 1989. "Sikh Extremists," non-affiliated persons, accounted for the largest number of terrorism incidents in the GTD related to Sikh extremism, separatist movement, in India. The number of attacks between 1984 and 1995 was over 700. Three main peaks in activity were visible: 1984, 1988 and 1991, coinciding with governmental responses to the Sikh movement. There was a noticeable decline in activity beginning in 1990 before the group was no longer attributed to terrorism incidents by 1995 (Perry, 2014). Three governmental interventions are identified for India and the Khalistan movement: the 1984 Golden Temple raid (Operation Blue Star), Operation Black Thunder (Golden Temple Raid of 1989), and Operation Rakshak I (1991).

TABLE 8.1

Organization	*Operation dates*	*Origin location*	*Classification*	*Status*
All India Sikh Student (AISSF)	1888/1937	Punjab, India	Nationalist/Separatists	Active
Bhinderwale Tiger Force of Khalistan (BTHK)	1984–1995	Punjab, India	Nationalist/Separatists	Inactive
Dishmish Regiment	1984–1986	Punjab, India	Nationalist/Separatists	Inactive
Khalistan Liberation Front (KLF)	1986	Punjab, India	Nationalist/Separatists	Active
Khalistan Commando Force (KCF)	1986–2006	Punjab, India	Nationalist/Separatists	Inactive
Khalistan Zindabad Force (KZ)	Early 1990s	Jammu & Kashmir, India	Nationalist/Separatists	Active
Khalistan Tiger Force (KTF)	Early 1980s	Punjab, India	Nationalist/Separatists	Active

The 1984 Golden Temple raid served as a catalyst for several terrorist organizations, as many as 12. While Operation Black Thunder was a transparent attack that minimized the space for discontent and new ideologies to form. Several additional structural deficiencies were addressed in the 1988 Raid. For example, the Indian government also tightened the Pakistan border and reduced the flow of people and arms into the region (Crenshaw, n.d.).

The raid resulted in more transparency and it gained Sikh public opinion. The government allowed the media to show Sikh terrorists as gunned down extremists who killed Sikh and Hindu police. This delegitimized the extremists in the eyes of members of a social movement. The raid is noted as one of the main reasons for the collapse of the growing militancy in the region. Support for the government increased among the general population. Terrorist activity decreased around 1995 in the Punjab region.

Khalistan Tiger Force

The Khalistan Tiger Force (KTF) is a Sikh separatist militant organization formed by Jagtar Singh Tara. The group emerged in the 1980s in the context of the Khalistan movement. The group primarily operates in the Punjab region of India. The main objective of the group is creating an independent Sikh state, named Khalistan, in the Punjab region. The group has had many leaders over the years, as leadership roles change due to security concerns and government crackdowns. Some of the prominent leaders include Jagtar Singh Tara and Hardeep Singh Nijjar.

The Khalistan Tiger Force has received funding from ISI and jihadi groups such as Lashkar-e-Toiba (LeT). The Khalistan Tiger Force membership levels fluctuate overtime due to government crackdowns. Targets include the Indian government officials, security forces, and perceived collaborators. Recruitment for the group includes targeting members of the Sikh community, particularly those disillusioned with Indian government policies and see themselves as victims of religious discrimination. Their tactics include bombings, assassinations, armed attacks, propaganda, and fundraising activities. The group was officially designated as a terrorist organization by India in 2023 (UAPA, 2023).

Tamil Nadu Liberation Army

Tamil Nadu Liberation Army (TNLA) is a separatist, nationalist terror organization formed in the early 1980s. A large number of separatist groups were present in Tamil Nadu during the 1980s, including the TNLA. The group originated in the Naxal ranks, but differences of opinion between the Tamil Nadu unit and all India unit, Communist Party of India—Marxist-Leninist (CPI-ML), led to a formal split in the CPI-ML and the formation of TNLA (South Asia Terrorism Portal, n.d.). The group primarily operates in Tamil Nadu. The goal of the group is independence of Tamil Nadu from Indian rule. For leadership, it is believed to have splintered into factions after the death of leader Thamizharasan.

The TNLA is believed to have several front organizations that it operates under. Among them are the Tamizhina Viduthalai Kazhagam (Liberation Party), Vivasayigal Urpathiyalar Sangham (Farmers' Union), Tamil Desiya Pengal Viduthalai Iyakkam (Women's Liberation Movement), Urimai Koruvaar Orungamaippu (Federation of Rights Activists), Tamil Nadu Ilaignar Peravai (Youth Association), and the Tamizhaga Odukapattor Viduthalai Iyakkam (Movement for the Liberation of the Downtrodden) (South Asia Terrorism Portal, n.d.). Their tactics include bombings, murders, looting banks, attacking police stations, and abductions. They have been mostly unsuccessful in recruiting members and taking territory.

Leadership for the group has included Thamizharasan (deceased due to bomb blast); Lenin (deceased due to bomb blast); and Maran (incarcerated). The last major attack of the group was in 2005. Tamil Nadu Liberation Army has close ties with the LTTE (Liberation Tigers of Tamil Eelam). They are also associated with the forest brigand Veerappan.

> When Maran was looking to safeguard himself and his gang members from the police dragnet, one of his gang members, who had met Veerappan earlier, suggested the latter's name. Furthermore, TNLA always remained a Vanniya dominated organization, headed only by Vanniya leaders.
>
> *(SATP)*

Liberation Tigers of Tamil Eelam

Liberation Tigers of Tamil Eelam (LTTE) is a separatist, and nationalist group that fought for an independent Tamil homeland in Northern and Eastern Sri Lanka. Impacting some three million people, the Tamil movement was a large-scale and violent movement. The group was founded by Velupillai Prabhakaran in 1976 (Britannica, 2024). The origins of the group's struggles began with the formation of India as an independent nation post-World War II (White, 2020). Another push factor for the Tamils were the concerns that the ethnic Tamil minority raised in a majority Sinhalese Sri Lanka. Claiming that the Sri Lankan government was dominated by Tamils, the Sinhalese majority adopted a Sinhalese-only policy in government, making many Tamils feel increasingly marginalized. Both religious and ethnic differences combined to propel the group to advocate for a Tamil homeland.

Liberation Tigers of Tamil Eelam initially emerged as a social movement and as a revolutionary group. However, the group adopted guerrilla warfare and violent tactics. In 1983, the LTTE killed 13 Sri Lankan soldiers using guerrilla warfare (Britannica, 2024). The Sri Lankan government responded with retaliatory brute force. The Sinhalese majority responded with a series of anti-Tamil riots (White, 2020). This led to large-scale violence and casualties. Some Tamils fled and took refuge in India, while members of LTTE remained to use terrorist tactics.

After 1983, the group began to incorporate a variety of tactics, including guerilla warfare, uniformed and plainclothes fighting, bombings, suicide bombs, small arms, etc. By 1985, the LTTE gained control of territory in Northern Sri Lanka, mainly Jaffna and most of the Jaffna Peninsula (Britannica, 2024). The group widely used suicide bombings starting in 1987 and began proficient in the use of them. A special unit, known as the Black Tigers, consisted of suicide bombers (White, 2020). They were known for swallowing cyanide capsules if caught to avoid disclosing any LTTE secrets if tortured. In 1988 and 1992, the group sought to control more territory/land so they switched to guerrilla tactics in uniformed cells. When driven into the jungle, the group would practice "jungle" terrorism, utilizing the jungle to attack Sri Lankan soldiers. In 1990, the group expanded its operations by converting a fishing fleet into a navy/water unit. The group waged a bombing and assassination campaign between 1994 and 1995. (White, 2020).

Simultaneously, LTTE was fighting rival groups. By 1987, LTTE had eliminated most of its rival Tamil factions. However, in 1987 the group lost its Jaffna territory. In 1990, with renewed strength, LTTE launched a series of successful attacks. With increased manpower and momentum, the group was able to complete high-profile attacks. The attacks included the May 1991 assassination of former Prime Minister Rajiv Gandhi via suicide bomber in the Indian State of Tamil Nadu; the August 1992 land mine explosion in Jaffna that killed ten senior Sri Lankan military officials; and the May 1993 assassination of Sri Lankan President Ranasinghe Premadasa (Britannica, 2024). The Sri Lankan government signed a peace agreement with the group in January 1995, when LTTE had a lot of momentum, but attacks continued by the group. In January 1996, a suicide bombing in Colombo killed over 100 people. The group started to experience blowback from the population, and the Sri Lankan government launched a full assault against the group in 1996. In December 2000, LTTE declared a unilateral ceasefire. Only a few months later, in July 2001, they attacked the Colombo airport, destroying half of Sri Lanka's commercial airlines. Fighting between the LTTE and the government intensified until the bilateral signing of a ceasefire agreement in 2002.

Civilians experienced the brunt of the violence between the government and LTTE. Fighting between the two groups reached a critical point after the European Union added LTTE to its list of terrorist organizations in 2006 (Britannica, 2024). Heavy fighting resulted in the deaths of thousands of civilians, and many citizens became disillusioned with LTTE, no longer supporting the group's cause.

In January 2008, the Sri Lankan government negated the 2002 ceasefire and set out to eradicate the group. In May 2009, the Sri Lankan government captured the last LTTE stronghold and killed the group's leader. The death of Prabhakaran led to the declaration of victory by the Sri Lankan government and the disarmament of LTTE fighters. The conflict between LTTE and the Sri Lankan government resulted in the death of an estimated 70,000–80,000 people from the 1980s until 2009 (Britannica, 2024). The number of LTTE fighters over time ranged from a thousand to over sixteen thousand. Funding for the group included illicit activities like drug trafficking, robbing banks, and extortion. They also received donations from their diaspora abroad (Britannica, 2024).

Conclusion

There appears to be five trends of Southeast Asian groups: fluidity, influence, splintering, collaboration, and familial/social ties. Many of the groups examined maintain a high level of fluidity. Members flow from one group to another, especially as many groups have very similar ideologies or splintered from a larger group. This coincides with the characteristic of splintering. In the Southeast Asian context, different viewpoints at the higher levels of leadership lead to members splintering off and creating offshoot organizations. However, the groups still collaborate with one another. For example, although the Moro Islamic National Liberation Front (MILF) was not active for some time, several of its members were involved in the 2017 Marawi siege initiated by the Islamic State East Asian Provence (Bakhshi & Rousselle, 2024). Additionally, the groups are influenced by global events. A hijacking by an extremist group may inspire another group to do so, the Soviet-Afghan war propelled many groups into action, and even the global attention that ISIS received sparked inspiration in local groups. Lastly, familial and social ties present another characteristic that makes Southeast Asian groups challenging to combat. Membership is linked to clan affiliations or family dynamics. Individuals follow in the footsteps of previous community or family members.

It appears that Wahhabism is a brand of Islam to which many extremist groups in Southeast Asia subscribe. This has been a gradual shift from a more moderate practice to a more puritanical one. Founders of many of the groups discussed were either indirectly influenced by Saudi-funded madrassas and/or Wahhabi mosques, or they were directly influenced by engaging in various conflicts that influenced their opinions of jihad (i.e., Afghan-Soviet War, formation of Pakistan as a state, DI conflicts, etc).

In dealing with a large Muslim population, Southeast Asia attempted to address internal and external factors influencing terrorism. The Southeast Asian model took both economics and grievances into consideration (i.e., 16 Point Counter Terrorism Program and Human Security Act). Working with the United States proved to be a sensitive subject for many Muslims, as many felt that the "Global War on Terror" was a war against Muslims and Islam (Tan, 2010). Domestic tension greatly influenced the foreign policy actions of the region. Southeast Asia used its previous experience with Muslim rebellions and populations and created a more comprehensive approach to counterterrorism. Both the Malacca Strait Patrols and the "Eye in the Sky" initiatives are considered a success, in that reducing domestic tension and security had priority.

References

Alam, J. (2024, August 1). Bangladesh bans Jamaat-e-Islami party following violent protests that left more than 200 dead. *AP News*. https://apnews.com/article/bangladesh-hasina-jamaat-party-banned-violence-campus-28d00e1af317e0325e8b09f010728ccd

Badawi, N. (2014). *Religion, war, and ethics: A sourcebook of textual traditions*. Cambridge University Press.

Bakhshi, U., & Rousselle, A. (2024, February 28). *The history and evolution of the Islamic State in Southeast Asia*. Hudson Institute. https://www.hudson.org/terrorism/history-evolution-islamic-state-southeast-asia

BBC News. (2018, April 25). Lebanon profile - Timeline. *BBC*. https://www.bbc.com/news/world-middle-east-14649284

Britannica, The Editors of Encyclopedia. (2024, March 22). *Moro National Liberation Front (MNLF)*. Britannica. https://www.britannica.com/topic/Moro-National-Liberation-Front

Britannica, The Editors of Encyclopedia. (2024, July 1). *Tamil tigers*. Encyclopedia Britannica. https://www.britannica.com/topic/Tamil-Tigers

Buenaventura, T. (2023, July 13). *The communist insurgency in the philippines: A 'protracted people's war' continues*. ACLED. https://acleddata.com/2023/07/13/the-communist-insurgency-in-the-philippines-a-protracted-peoples-war-continues/

Butani, D. (1986). *The third sikh war? Towards or away from Khalistan?* Promilla.

Council on Foreign Relations. (n.d.). *Jemaah Islamiyah (a.k.a. Jemaah Islamiah)*. Council on Foreign Relations. https://www.cfr.org/backgrounder/jemaah-islamiyah-aka-jemaah-islamiah

Counter Extremism Project. (n.d.). *Al-Qaeda in the Indian Subcontinent (AQIS)*. Counter Extremism Project. https://www.counterextremism.com/threat/al-qaeda-indian-subcontinent-aqis/report

Crenshaw, M. (n.d.). *Case narrative: Operation blue star*. National Consortium for the Study of Terrorism and Responses to Terrorism.

Golburt, Y. (n.d.). *An in-depth look at the Jemaah Islamiyah network Yanina Golburt*. CIAO: Columbia International Affairs Online. https://ciaotest.cc.columbia.edu/olj/aln/aln_fall04/aln_fall04b.pdf

Gunaratna, R. (2015, May 19). *The ideology of Al-Jama'ah Al-Islamiya*. Hudson Institute. https://www.hudson.org/national-security-defense/the-ideology-of-al-jama-ah-al-islamiya

Haqqani, H. (2005, May 19). *The ideologies of South Asian Jihadi groups*. Hudson Institute. https://www.hudson.org/national-security-defense/the-ideologies-of-south-asian-jihadi-groups

Harik, J. P. (2005). *Hezbollah: The changing face of terrorism*. IB Tauris & Co Ltd.

Hess, D., & Martin, B. (2006). Repression, backfire, and the theory of transformative events. *Mobilization: An International Quarterly*, *11*(2), 249–267.

Hoffman, B. (2019, January 19). *Al-qaeda in the Indian subcontinent: The Nucleus of Jihad in South Asia*. The Soufan Center. https://thesoufancenter.org/wp-content/uploads/2019/01/Al-Qaeda-in-the-Indian-Subcontinent-AQIS.pdf

Indla, A. (2020, January). Bhindranwale: How one controversial religious figure threatened the unity of India. *History in the Making*, *13*(15). https://scholarworks.lib.csusb.edu/cgi/viewcontent.cgi?article=1145&context=history-in-the-making

International Crisis Group. (2002, August 8). *Al-Qaeda in Southeast Asia: The case of the "Ngruki network" in Indonesia*. International Crisis Group (ICG). https://www.refworld.org/reference/countryrep/icg/2002/en/32276

Laub, Z. (2019, August 15). *Egypt's Muslim brotherhood*. Council on Foreign Relations. https://www.cfr.org/backgrounder/egypts-muslim-brotherhood

Mahmood, C. K. (1996). *Fighting for faith and nation: Dialogues with sikh militants*. University of Pennsylvania Press.

National Consortium for the Study of Terrorism and Responses to Terrorism. (n.d.). *Moro Islamic liberation front (MILF)*. START- UMD. https://www.start.umd.edu/baad/database/moro-islamic-liberation-front-milf-2012.html

National Counterterrorism Center. (2014, January). *Counter terrorism guide: Abu Sayyaf group*. National Counterterrorism Center. https://www.dni.gov/nctc/groups/abu_sayyaf.html

Naval History and Heritage Command. (n.d.). *Terrorism in Southeast Asia*. Naval History and Heritage Command. https://www.history.navy.mil/research/library/online-reading-room/title-list-alphabetically/t/terrorism-in-southeast-asia.html#r-pi

New York Times Archive. (1981, March 29). Hijackers force Indonesian plane with 57 to Thailand. *New York Times*. https://www.nytimes.com/1981/03/29/world/hijackers-force-indonesian-plane-with-57-to-thailand.html

Pearson, E. (n.d.). *Egyptian Islamic Jihad | Origins, Terrorist Attacks & Al-Qaeda*. Britannica. https://www.britannica.com/topic/Egyptian-Islamic-Jihad#ref1279725

Perry, A. (2014). *The impact of governmental strategies on collective action after backlash*. Rutgers University- Newark Dissertation. https://doi.org/doi:10.7282/T31N7ZDK

Pew Research Center. (2010, September 15). *Muslim brotherhood and Jama'at-i Islami*. Pew Research Center. https://www.pewresearch.org/religion/2010/09/15/muslim-networks-and-movements-in-western-europe-muslim-brotherhood-and-jamaat-i-islami/

Phasuk, S. (2022, January 21). Prioritize rights, justice in Southern Thailand peace efforts. *Human Rights Watch*. https://www.hrw.org/news/2022/01/21/prioritize-rights-justice-southern-thailand-peace-efforts

Shani, G. (2000). The construction of a sikh national identity. *South Asia Research*, *20*(1), 1–17.

South Asia Terrorism Portal. (n.d.). Terrorism. https://www.satp.org/

South Asia Terrorism Portal. (n.d.). *Tamil Nadu Liberation Army (TNLA)*. https://www.satp.org/satporgtp/countries/india/terroristoutfits/tnla.htm

Stanford University. (n.d.a). *MMP: Abu Sayyaf group*. Center for International Security and Cooperation. https://cisac.fsi.stanford.edu/mappingmilitants/profiles/abu-sayyaf-group

Stanford University. (2017, August 8). MMP: Harakat-ul-Mujahedeen. http://stanford.edu/group/mappingmilitants/cgi-bin/groups/print_view/219

Stanford University. (2018, August 1). *Communist party of the philippines - New people's army* [Mapping Militant Organizations]. https://mappingmilitants.org/profiles/communist-party-of-the-philippines-new-peoples-army#_ftn5

Stanford University. (2019, January 1). *MMP: Moro Islamic liberation front*. Center for International Security and Cooperation. https://mappingmilitants.org/profiles/moro-islamic-liberation-front

Stanford University. (2019, May 1). *MMP: Moro national liberation front*. Moro National Liberation Front. https://mappingmilitants.org/profiles/moro-national-liberation-front

START. (n.d.). *Pattani United Liberation Organization (PULO)*. Global Terrorism Database. https://www.start.umd.edu/gtd/search/Results.aspx?expanded=yes&casualties_type=&casualties

_max=&success=yes&perpetrator=536&ob=GTDID&od=desc&page=1&count=20#results-table

Tan, A. (2010). *Counter- terrorism in Southeast Asia post 9/11. International terrorism post 9/11: Comparative dynamics and responses*. Routledge.

Temby, Q. (2020). Terrorism in Indonesia after "Islamic State". *ISEAS- Yusof Ishak Institute, Trends in Southeast Asia, 3*, 1–28.

Toutounji, Y. (2017). *The double-edged sword: Globalization and international Islamic terrorism* (Master's Thesis). AUC Knowledge Fountain. https://www.google.com/url?sa=t&source=web&rct=j&opi=89978449&url=https://fount.aucegypt.edu/cgi/viewcontent.cgi%3Farticle%3D1696%26context%3Detds

UAPA. (2023, February 17). *Press release details: Press information Bureau*. PIB. https://pib.gov.in/PressReleseDetail.aspx?PRID=1900222

United Nations Security Council. (2011, October 7). *HARAKAT UL-MUJAHIDIN / HUM*. United Nations. https://main.un.org/securitycouncil/en/sanctions/1267/aq_sanctions_list/summaries/entity/harakat-ul-mujahidin/hum

University of Central Arkansas. (n.d.). *Philippines/Moro Islamic liberation front (1977-present)*. University of Central Arkansas. https://uca.edu/politicalscience/home/research-projects/dadm-project/asiapacific-region/philippinesmoro-islamic-liberation-front-1978-present/

White, J. (2020). *Terrorism and homeland security* (9th ed.). Cengage Learning.

The World Factbook. (n.d.). *Terrorist organizations*. CIA. https://www.cia.gov/the-world-factbook/references/terrorist-organizations/

Yunanto, S., & Damayanti, A. (2017, January). The root causes and nexus of militant islamic movements in Indonesia: Case studies of Darul Islam and Jemaah Islamiyah. *Journal of Asia Pacific Studies*, *1*(1), 28–39.

PART IV

Terrorism and Technology

9

CYBERTERRORISM AND CYBERTERRORIST OPERATIONS

Robin Valeri and Binneh Minteh

Introduction

In Chapter 2, we discuss the fact that there is no one universally agreed-upon definition of terrorism. Therefore, as you may well imagine, defining cyberterrorism is equally problematic. The difficulty stems, in part, from the fact that there is disagreement as to what constitutes cyberspace. Add to this the fact that there is no one agreed-upon definition of terrorism, and the result is varying opinions as to what constitutes cyberterrorism.

Let us start by defining cyberspace. When many of us think of cyberspace, we think of the Surface Web as opposed to the Deep Web or the Dark Web. As we previously discussed (Valeri & Minteh, 2023) the Surface Web, which is indexed and searchable, refers to all websites accessible to anyone with an internet connection and is hosted by browsers such as Internet Explorer, Firefox, and Google Chrome. In contrast, the Deep Web is neither indexed nor searchable. It consists of all the data behind firewalls, such as the data stored in company databases. Examples of this include medical records, banking information, and the content of personal email accounts. Many hackers, including cyberterrorists, target this type of information to engage in ransomware attacks, making this information inaccessible until a payment is made in exchange for renewed access, or doxing attacks, stealing private information and then making it accessible to the public. The Dark Web is a subset of the Deep Web, both of which are inaccessible from the Surface Web. Accessing the Dark Web typically requires an encrypted browser. Furthermore, the Dark Web allows the user to be anonymous, thus creating the opportunity for both beneficial and malicious activity. Criminals, hackers, and cyberterrorists use the Dark Web for buying and selling of illegal or stolen information, including weapons, drugs, and child pornography. As you will see, many cyberterrorist operations focus on hacking into information in the Deep Web or hampering access to information on the Surface Web or Deep Web. You will also note that as governments have tried to ban terrorists from the Surface Web, the terrorists have responded by moving many of their activities to the Dark Web.

Given the description of the Surface Web, Dark Web, and Deep Web we know that cyberspace contains information. But, does cyberspace contain more than information? As

DOI: 10.4324/9781003375265-14

previously discussed (Valeri & Minteh, 2023) that depends on one's definition of cyberspace. Hoffman (2022), when defining cyberspace, focuses on accessible information, defining cyberspace as being made up of all the information accessible via the internet as well as all the information stored on mobile devices such as smartphones, internet-connected appliances, and wearable technology that are connected to the internet. In contrast, Kremling and Parker (2022) offer a much broader definition of cyberspace, describing cyberspace in terms of four layers. There is a physical layer which is made up of all of the equipment, the computers, wires, networks, routers, etc. Next, there is the logic layer, meaning the codes of 0s and 1s that create and define the internet and its services. Then there is the information layer in which companies and organizations create and disseminate information through websites, social media, and the like. Finally, there is the personal layer consisting of websites, blogs, etc., created by individuals as well as individuals' online behaviors such as shopping, accessing videos, pictures, books, etc. (Kremling & Parker, 2022). For this chapter, we use Kremling and Parker's definition of cyberspace and consider any terrorist actions that occur in any of these layers to constitute cyberterrorism.

Given this definition of cyberspace, what is cyberterrorism? As with cyberspace, cyberterrorism may be narrowly or broadly defined. Narrow definitions of cyberterrorism are offered by Denning or the FBI.

> According to Dennings, cyberterrorism entails
> unlawful attacks and threats of attacks against computers, networks and the information stored therein when done to intimidate or coerce a government or its people in furtherance of political or social objectives...Serious attacks against critical infrastructures could be acts of cyberterrorism, depending on their impact. Attacks that disrupt nonessential services or that are mainly a costly nuisance. would not.
>
> *(Dennings, 2000, as cited by Weimann, 2004)*

In Denning's definition, a cyberterrorist attack can disrupt the functioning of computers or computer networks or disrupts access to the information contained therein. These attacks can include attacks against critical infrastructure.

The FBI definition of cyberterrorism also focuses on attacks against critical infrastructure. The FBI (2002) describes cyberterrorism as

> the use of cyber tools to shut down critical national infrastructures (such as energy, transportation, or government operations) for the purpose of coercing or intimidating a government or civilian population.

But terrorists do more in cyberspace than either of these definitions suggest. The United Nations, in its discussion of how terrorists use the internet, identifies

> six sometimes overlapping categories: propaganda (including recruitment, radicalization and incitement to terrorism); financing; training; planning (including through secret communication and open-source information); execution; and cyberattacks.
>
> *(UNODC, 2012, p. 3)*

The first five uses of the internet by terrorists can be thought of as cyber-enabled acts of terrorism, meaning that these acts can be committed offline but are facilitated by the internet. The power of cyberspace to support cyber-enabled terrorism cannot be overestimated. This power derives first, from the fact that the majority of the world's population can and does access cyberspace, and second, from the fact that communicating and sharing information via cyberspace, whether it is news, opinion, music, or video, is easy to do. In brief, the power of cyberspace to facilitate cyber-enabled terrorism stems from the fact that global communication can occur instantaneously, inexpensively, and anonymously. As was discussed in Chapter 2, many governments or intergovernmental agencies consider cyber-enabled acts of terrorism to be crimes. In this chapter, cyber-enabled acts of terrorism will be considered cyberterrorism and a discussion of them will be included in this chapter.

The last use of the internet described by the U.N., specifically cyberattacks, can be thought of as cyber-dependent uses of the internet, meaning that cyberattacks require information and communication technology for them to occur. Cyber-dependent cyberattacks are consistent with the narrower definitions of cyberterrorism offered by Denning and the FBI In this chapter, cyber-dependent acts of terrorism will be considered cyberterrorism and a discussion of them will also be included in this chapter.

Before leaving this section on definitions, it is important to note that when it comes to malicious activities in cyberspace, terrorists are not the only perpetrators. Perpetrators of malicious activities also include criminals, governments, or their agents. According to the United Nations,

> Cybercrime is an act that violates the law, which is perpetrated using information and communication technology (ICT) to either target networks, systems, data, websites and/or technology or facilitate a crime.
>
> *(UNODC, 2019a)*

Given this definition of cybercrime, cyberterrorism would be a type of cybercrime. But, if these same activities are carried out by one state against another, are they crimes or warfare? It depends, as you may surmise, on your definition of cyberwarfare. Similar to cyberterrorism, there is no one agreed-upon definition of cyberwarfare. However, the United Nations, in its description of cyberwarfare, states that "Only governments, organs of the state, or state-directed or state-sponsored individuals or groups can engage in cyberwarfare" (UNODC, 2019b). So while all illegal activity committed in cyberspace by a government or its agents may not be cyberwarfare, at least according to the United Nations, only governments or their agents can commit cyberwarfare.

In the end, what differentiates cyberterrorism from cybercrime or cyberwarfare is the who, meaning the perpetrator, and/or the why, meaning the motivation, for the crime. It can take time to investigate and determine the who or why behind a cyberattack. Also, it is important to note that criminals, terrorists, and governments may work together to carry out a cyberattack and that these groups learn strategies and tactics from each other.

Given these definitions, caveats, and difficulties in identifying who is behind a cyberattack, in this chapter some of the cyberattacks discussed are committed by state actors or their agents, others by criminals, and still others by terrorists. Therefore, while some of the attacks discussed may not be considered cyberterrorism, they are discussed here because it is only a matter of time before terrorist groups develop and deploy the same capabilities used by criminals and/or governments.

A Brief History of Extremism in Cyberspace

While cyberterrorism may be a relatively new phenomenon, terrorists' and extremist groups' use of the internet is not new. Extremists have been using the internet since it was invented. Prior to the internet, extremist groups communicated their message to current and prospective members primarily through print, in the form of flyers, posters, pamphlets, and books. Especially compared to the billions of people that can be reached instantaneously in cyberspace, these offline efforts were significantly slower and more limited in scope. Also, prior to the internet, becoming a member of an extremist group required a face-to-face declaration of one's beliefs, being vetted by, and accepted by current members. However, cyberspace has dramatically changed the radicalization process. Becoming radicalized can happen completely online, without communicating directly with anyone else and without any fear of rejection. Furthermore, all of the information necessary for carrying out a terrorist action can be garnered from the web.

Extremist groups were one of the first groups to embrace the internet as a means of communication. In 1984, only one year after the birth of the internet, extremist groups were establishing online bulletin boards. Louis Beam, a leader of the Aryan Nations and Grand Dragon of the Texas state unit of the Knights of the Ku Klux Klan, and two other white supremacists established the Aryan Nations Liberty Net (Ianniello, 1985; Southern Poverty Law Center (SPLC), n.d.a). A second anti-Semitic online bulletin board, Info International Network or Liberty Bell Net also went online in 1984 (Berlet, 2001; Ianniello, 1985; Miller, 1985). This bulletin board was run by George Dietz, who, prior to emigrating to the United States, was a German native and member of the Hitler Youth until the end of World War II (Ianniello, 1985; Miller, 1985). And, at some point in either late 1984 or early 1985, the White Aryan Resistance (WAR) bulletin board run by Thomas Metzger, who was well-known for his use of cable television and radio to spread white supremacist ideology, went online (Berlet, 2001; deLéon, 2020). While these are only three examples, other racist and extremist groups were also creating their own online bulletin boards. These early online bulletin boards not only highlight the power of the internet to reach a larger audience but also the borderless nature of the internet. Because online bulletin boards were available to anyone with internet access, they facilitated the spread of white supremacist literature from the United States to countries where such material was banned (Berlet, 2001).

By the mid-1990s, with the advent of the World Wide Web, many bulletin boards, including those of extremists, had disappeared or moved to the internet. The Stormfront webpage, created in 1995 by Don Black, is considered by many to be the first major hate site on the internet (SPLC, n.d.b). In the following years, Stormfront turned out to be one of many websites promulgated by racists, extremists, or terrorists. And, just as extremists first embraced the internet followed by the World Wide Web, they have now not only embraced all areas of cyberspace, but they have weaponized it. Today, they can be found communicating via social media, gaming platforms, instant messaging, and the Dark Web. From the very start, extremists have recognized the potential and power of what we now refer to as cyberspace. This is reflected as early as 1995, in this quote from Don Black when he said

> All of this [Internet] has had a pretty profound effect on a movement whose resources are limited...With the phenomenal growth of the Internet, tens of millions of people have access to our message if they wish...The access is anonymous and there is unlimited ability to communicate with others of a like mind.
>
> *(Schneider, 1995, p. A12)*

Beckers et al. (2000) noted that "it is the internet that provides the most opportunities [to spread hate and extremism] today." Twelve years later, this sentiment was echoed in a Bipartisan Policy Center Report (2012) which stated

> the Internet has also come to play an important—and, in many ways, unique—role in radicalizing homegrown and domestic terrorists. Supporters of Al Qaeda, Sovereign Citizens, white supremacists and neo-Nazis, environmental and animal liberationists, and other violent extremist groups all have embraced the Internet with great enthusiasm and vigor. They are using it as a platform to spread their ideas, connect with each other, make new recruits, and incite illegal and violent actions.
>
> *(Bipartisan Policy Center, 2012)*

Consider the fact that these uses of the internet by violent extremists align with the goals of terrorism and are also the same ones considered by many intergovernmental agencies to be crimes of terrorism. As you may recall from Chapter 1, groups and individuals engage in terrorism to promote their cause, instill fear in the public, gain recruits, raise morale, garner resources, and achieve their social, political, or religious goals (Weinberg, 2008). As noted in the Bipartisan Policy Center Report, all of these can be achieved in cyberspace. Also, as you may recall from Chapter 2, the Council of Europe, in an effort to prevent terrorism, made it a criminal act to recruit someone to engage in a terrorist offense or join a terrorist organization, to train someone in the methods or techniques for carrying out terrorism, to publicly provoke or advocate for terrorist offenses, or to fund terrorism. These are all activities that not only can but are being accomplished in cyberspace. In this chapter, we will explore how terrorists have accomplished these goals in cyberspace by examining examples of such efforts and discussing why they are effective. Note that oftentimes an example will serve multiple purposes. But, before we do this, a quick word on why terrorist and extremist groups cannot easily be banned from the internet.

Banning Cyberhate and Cyber-Extremism: A Sisyphean Task

While you might think that terrorist groups, extremists, and racists have or should be banned from cyberspace, this is a Sisyphean task. Setting aside issues of free speech, which is an entirely different discussion, trying to rid cyberspace of hate and extremism is like playing a game of "whack-a-mole." It is true that many internet service providers have terms and conditions or community standards that ban hate speech, messages that encourage violence or promote terrorism, and the like but individuals and groups find ways around these. Evidence of their tenacity can be seen following attempts to ban them. For example, following the death of Heather Heyer during the Unite the Right rally that took place in Charlottesville, Virginia, August 11–12, 2017, GoDaddy followed by Google banned the neo-Nazi website the Daily Stormer from their domains (Mettler & Selk, 2017). Paypal along with other payment companies cut off payments to more than three dozen hate groups and other extremist organizations (Berr, 2017). However, the Daily Stormer did not give up. Instead, it moved to the Dark Web, announcements of which were posted on Twitter, and continued to raise money in cryptocurrency (Bambenek, 2022; Finkle, 2021; Hayden & Squire, 2021; Kinetz & Hinnant, 2021). Similarly, after the January 6, 2023, attack on the United States Capitol Building, Facebook, Twitter, and YouTube kicked off Donald Trump and other extremists involved in planning the insurrection (Bond, 2022). But, like the Daily Stormer, these groups did not abandon cyberspace, they simply relocated to the encrypted messaging app Telegram, video streaming services DLive and Rumble, and social media sites like Parler, Gab, and Gettr (Holt, 2022). Thus, terrorists and other extremists have been able to maintain a presence in cyberspace by using a variety of techniques. They outsmart artificial intelligence that searches for specific language by purposefully adding typographical errors, misspelling words, or using coded language (Anti Defamation League (ADL), n.d.; Gröndahl et al., 2018; Meaker, 2019). They begin a video with a reputable report that, after a few minutes, becomes a message from them. When one of their web or social media pages is shut down, they may (1) repost it with a more innocuous-sounding name; (2) move it to a different service provider that is either less punctilious in enforcing their own standards, has less scrupulous standards, or promotes itself as a free speech platform; or (3) move to the Dark Web or use encrypted messaging platforms or techniques (Johnson, et al., 2019; Valeri, 2023).

Current Events in the Real World and Their Cyberspace Counterparts

To start, let us take a quick look at what is happening in cyberterrorism now, late 2023 through much of 2024, at the time of writing this chapter. Please keep in mind, from Chapters 1 and 2, that one person's terrorist is another person's freedom fighter.

War in Gaza

Currently, there is a war in Gaza between Israel and Hamas. From the first day of the surprise attack by Hamas on Israel, cyberspace was flooded with information, images, and commentaries about the war from news organizations, civilians, militants, and terrorists. According to an October 13, 2023, bulletin from the Institute for Strategic Dialogue (ISD), 128 posts glorifying terrorist violence were found on X (formerly known as Twitter) in the 24-hour period from 11–12 October (Ayad & Squirrell, 2023). These posts, which were primarily linked to the Izz ad-Din al-Qassem Brigades militia group, had over 16 million views (Ayad & Squirrell, 2023). According to the ISD bulletin, content appeared to circulate in Telegram prior to appearing on X.

Loadenthal (2023), shortly after the start of the war in Gaza, began examining how Palestinian militants were using Telegram videos. He conducted a content analysis of 192 videos posted on Telegram by eight Palestinian factions during the first six weeks of the war in Gaza (October 7, 2023–November 18, 2023) between Israel and Palestine. Loadenthal, in his analysis of the videos, states, "Many of the videos released on October 7 had lower production values, suggesting they were hastily prepared to capitalize on the surprise nature of the offensive." This statement highlights a key component of the internet's power in terrorism, its immediacy. It did not take weeks or days for the videos to become available. They were recorded, posted, and accessible all on the same day, the first day of the attack. Loadenthal's analyses reveal that all but 11 of the 192 videos included in the content analysis, included images of one or more weapons (rockets, mortars, rifles, drones, explosives, etc.). Loadenthal notes that while some of the images are real, showing drones, rifles, etc., others are fictionalized portrayals, such as images of engine-powered paragliders flying into Jerusalem's Haram al-Sharif. Why show so many images of weapons? These images convey to the militants themselves as well as to their supporters the power and strength of the militants. These images give both groups a sense of pride, the knowledge that "we," the Palestinian militants, are a threat, and "we" can succeed. Loadenthal also states that during the initial six weeks of the war, video production became more standardized and sophisticated. For example, the rocket-mortar launching video produced by Al-Quds Brigades, the armed component of the Palestinian Islamic Jihad.

> put greater emphasis on the persuasive power of dramatic video, with nearly half (48 percent) of its forty-two videos utilizing scripted, high production value content, and 67 percent adopting dramatic music. These scripted videos utilize high-definition video, multiple cameras capturing multiple angles, purposeful lighting, set design, and costuming.
>
> *(Loadenthal, 2023, p. 10)*

Obviously, these videos demonstrate a sophisticated level of production. But, more important to this chapter, is the persuasive impact of these videos. Loadenthal describes the videos as

> These high production value video portions are typically set to dramatic, patriotic, instrumental music, and show uniformed fighters in highly sophisticated, clandestine command and control facilities. Masked and uniformed fighters are shown preparing rockets, traveling in tunnels, and planning attacks in complex operational centers.
>
> *(Loadenthal, 2023, p. 11)*

Imagine the pride and hope an Al-Quds Brigade member or supporter must feel when watching the video. The patriotic music would make them feel like they are part of a well-organized, highly trained group fighting in defense of a noble and just cause. The video would serve to keep Al-Quds Brigade members firmly committed to the cause while also drawing new fighters to the Al-Quds Brigade, and bolstering support among Palestinians for the war. These videos, whether sophisticated or simple, achieve several of the goals of terrorism. They cause fear in their enemy, boost the morale of the fighters and the people they are championing, garner recruits and perhaps resources, and help the groups achieve their goals.

Al-Qaeda and the Islamic State (IS) are also using the war in Gaza as an opportunity to call for lone wolf attacks against the United States, Israel, Western interests, and Jewish communities (Burke, 2023; Dilanian et al., 2023). On January 4, 2024, the IS's spokesman Abu Hudhayfa Al-Ansari released an audio recording "And kill them where you find them" supporting the Muslims in Gaza and calling for attacks against civilians and military in Israel and the West (Dimensions, 2024; MEMRI, 2024). The audio recording was followed, on January 11, 2024, by the release of two posters. The posters, one of which depicts New York City in flames, encourage Muslims to attack civilians on the streets and in their homes through the use of explosives, knife attacks, shootings, and running people over (MEMRI, 2024). The text in the poster depicting New York City reads

> Lions of Islam: Chase your prey whether Jews, Christians, or their allies, on the streets and roads of America, Europe, and the world. Break into their homes, kill them and steal their peace of mind by any means you can lay hands on. Understand that you are the arm of the Islamic State hitting in the unbelievers' homelands, and are avenging the Muslims in Palestine, Iraq, Syria, and other Muslim countries....A sincere person will not lack the means to draw blood from the hearts of the Jews, the Christians, and their allies, and thus ease the suffering in the hearts of the believers.
>
> *(MEMRI, 2024)*

This poster ennobles attackers by calling them "lions of Islam" and the "arm of the IS." The phrase "a sincere person" suggests that someone who is a true adherent of Islam would find a way to carry out an attack. Finally, making people afraid, "stealing their peace of mind" is one of the main goals of terrorism (Monahan & Valeri, 2018).

Other anti-Semitic groups, specifically neo-Nazi groups and accelerationists are using the war in Gaza to encourage anti-Semitism. These groups are also sharing pro-Hamas videos in an effort to inspire attacks against Jewish communities (Ayad & Squirrell, 2023).

War in the Ukraine

In addition to the war in Gaza, there is also an ongoing war between Ukraine and Russia, which began on February 24, 2022. The war is not limited to the physical world but also extends to cyberspace and includes, depending on one's perspective, a propaganda or disinformation war. Since before the physical war began, Russia as well as pro-Kremlin organizations, defined here as organizations not clearly tied to Russia's government, were operating in cyberspace to discredit Ukraine and undermine international support for Ukraine (Belton, 2024; Bergengruen, 2023; EU Disinfo, 2024).

On February 24, 2022, just an hour before Russian troops invaded Ukraine, Russian hackers targeted the American satellite company Viasat, resulting in significant communication loss to the Ukrainian military (Greig, 2023; O'Neill, 2022). In addition to impacting the Ukrainian military, the hack of Viasat also impacted 5,800 internet-connected wind farms in Germany. Whether interfering with these wind farms was intentional or not is unknown. But the effect was to heighten Europe's interest in the war.

The hack of Viasat was preceded by a Russian hack of Ukrainian government computers with the intention of impacting the Ukrainian government's ability to respond to the attack (O'Neill, 2022). Ukrainian government and banking websites experienced distributed denial of service (DDoS) attacks, making these sites inaccessible to the public (McLaughlin, 2022). Sites impacted included the Ukrainian Defense Ministry and Armed Services, as well as two major banks. On the same day, the Ukrainian Cyber Police reported that there was a wave of fake SMS messages stating that ATMs were not operating (McLaughlin, 2022).

On February 25, 2022, Ukrainian cybersecurity officials reported that hackers associated with the Belarusian military were using a phishing campaign to steal passwords and break into the private emails of Ukrainian soldiers (Satter, 2022; TechCrunch, 2022).

Once access was obtained, the hackers could then send phishing messages to soldiers' contacts (Satter, 2022; TechCrunch, 2022). The use of phishing campaigns is popular among cyber-criminals.

Obviously, these attacks were meant to hinder Ukraine's response to the invasion and perhaps to intimidate the Ukrainian government and military into believing they could not stand up to the power of Russia. If that was the intention, Russia's efforts failed.

In December 2023, Kyivstar, Ukraine's major mobile network, was hacked leaving an estimated 24 million mobile customers and a million home internet users without service (Parker, 2023; Stern et al., 2023). This cyberattack also disrupted the early warning air raid system in Sumy and shut down many cash machines of PrivatBank, Ukraine's largest bank. This attack effectively disrupted the communication abilities of more than half of Ukraine's population, interfered with people's ability to obtain money, and left some Ukrainians more vulnerable to air raid attacks. Consider the fear and panic that many Ukrainians, unable to communicate, access money, and/or feeling more vulnerable, must have felt. Causing terror is one of the goals of terrorism. Who were the perpetrators? Investigations suggest that Russian-controlled hackers were responsible for this cyberattack.

Cyberattacks related to the war in Ukraine are not all one-sided. Ukraine had created its own cyber army, having appealed to domestic hackers for aid, and on February 26, 2022, the Kremlin's website was offline due to DDoS attacks (Pearson, 2022; Reuters, 2022; Schectman & Bing, 2022). The cyberattacks between Russia and the Ukraine, whether they are properly defined as cyberwarfare or cyberterrorism are presented here to reveal the blurred lines between governments, terrorists, and criminals, their willingness to learn from each other, and to work with each other.

To get a better glimpse of cyber-enabled terrorism associated with the war in Ukraine, specifically the propaganda aspect, research by Newsguard provides us with some insights. The organization Newsguard has been tracking disinformation campaigns on both sides of the war. Newsguard has identified 471 websites spreading disinformation (Roache et al., 2024). The majority of the websites are in English (238 sites) but include websites in French (60), German (54), Italian (45), and other languages (74). Most of these websites, but not all, are spreading pro-Russia/anti-Ukraine myths (Roache et al., 2024) in the hopes of undermining support for Ukraine. According to Newsguard, "[w]hile most myths disavow Russia's alleged atrocities and other abuses in Ukraine or demonize Ukrainians, Newsguard has also debunked some pro-Ukrainian and anti-Russian myths..." (Roache et al., 2024). The pro-Russian/anti-Ukraine myths being spread include disinformation that Russia is not blocking grain shipments to the West, that the massacre of civilians in Bucha, Ukraine, was staged, that Nazism is rampant in Ukrainian politics and society, and that Russian-speaking residents in Donbas, Ukraine, are being massacred (Roache et al., 2024). While some of the websites Newsguard is monitoring are part of the official Russian state media others are not. Because the European Union and the United States have placed bans on Russian state media since the start of the war, Russia has needed to rely on pro-Kremlin websites that include "proxy websites, bots, false social media personas, [and] cyber-enabled disinformation operations" to get their messages out (Global Engineering Center (GEC), 2020). Russia's success at getting their messages out demonstrates the ineffectiveness of bans. While much of Russia's current disinformation campaign has focused on undermining support for Ukraine, Russia's long-term disinformation efforts against the United States and other democracies are to amplify civil discord, foment ethnic, racial, and religious strife, and to undermine faith in government institutions and in the election process itself (GEC, 2020).

Animal Liberation Front

Current cyber-enabled terrorism is not limited to these two wars. Let us look at cyber-enabled terrorism from a leftist group, the Animal Liberation Front. On February 23, 2024, the New York Times (Shanahan, 2024) reported that Flaco, a Eurasian Eagle Owl who had been liberated from the Central Park Zoo in February 2023, had died. The cause of death appears to be from Flaco striking a building on West 89th Street. The perpetrators of the break-in at the Central Park Zoo who freed Flaco have never been caught. While some have speculated that the perpetrators were affiliated with the Animal Liberation Front, Jerry Vlasak, the spokesperson for the North American Animal Liberation Press Office (NAALPO), said that no one had contacted their office claiming responsibility for freeing Flaco (Offenhartz, 2024). However, earlier in the year, on January 5, 2024, the North American Animal Liberation Front Press Office did release its 2023 report (NAALFPO, 2024) "Unoffensives Report: 2023 Year in Review (Unoffensive Animal)." According to the report, 99 animal liberation actions were reported by their office. Of those actions, 40 were against the meat industry and 41 against hunting. The report also stated that in 2023 there were 50 ECO actions, the majority of which were related to the Atlanta Forest and Mountain Valley Campaigns in the United States. This report, in addition to providing basic statistics for members and supporters of these groups as well as news organizations, is obviously a propaganda tool. It helps to spread their message, bolster the commitment of current members, as well as recruit new supporters.

Artifical Inteligence (AI)

A discussion of current cyber-enabled terrorism would not be complete without a look at the emerging role of artificial intelligence in cyber-enabled terrorism. According to the Algorithms and Terrorism Report (2021) by the United Nations Interregional Crime and Justice Research Institute (UNICRI) and the United Nations Office of Counterterrorism (UNCCT), the major concern posed by artificial intelligence, with regard to cyber-enabled terrorism, is that artificial intelligence will be used to manipulate media content that can then be used to manipulate individuals. One concern is that AI can and is being used to create deepfake audio and video content that will lead people to believe they are hearing, seeing, or communicating with someone they know. Unfortunately, it is becoming increasingly difficult for either humans or AI to identify these deepfakes. If these deepfakes are successful, they could be used on a large scale to manipulate public opinion or sow doubt in government institutions, or on a small scale, to manipulate individuals into disclosing sensitive personal or financial information. One example of deepfake audio being used occurred in the run-up to the 2024 New Hampshire primary. AI was used to create a deepfake audio robocall impersonating President Joe Biden. The call instructed democrats not to vote in the upcoming primary (Seitz-Wald, 2024). Prior to that, in 2022, a deepfake video of Ukraine President Zelensky was created in which Zelensky is shown telling Ukrainian soldiers to lay down their arms and surrender to Russia (Allyn, 2022). The video circulated on social media as well as on a Ukrainian news website, placed there by hackers, before it was taken down (Allyn, 2022). A second concern is that terrorists and other malicious actors will one day be able to deploy AI to automatically read news headlines, change them to create false narratives consistent with their goals, and then widely disseminate the modified content on social media and other platforms (UNOCRI & UNCCT, 2021). At some point, AI may be used to identify individuals who are easily manipulated and radicalized and create radicalization narratives specifically customized to them (UNOCRI & UNCCT, 2021). A major fallout from the increase in misinformation, disinformation, and deepfake content is the public's increasing distrust in the media. Given hackers' ability to place fake news on legitimate news sources, the public is even becoming distrustful of sources once considered credible.

The preceding examples demonstrate the power of cyberspace. It offers the opportunity for any individual or group to share their views, opinions, and disinformation with a global audience. And anyone who has access to cyberspace can access those views and opinions. This is true for any group, whether they are Islamic extremists, far-right extremists, or animal rights activists. Individuals are able to seek out and find information and propaganda that is consistent with their beliefs and, often times, they can connect with individuals who will not only confirm their beliefs but bolster their self-image and strengthen their commitment to the cause.

Cyberterrorists Use of Cyberspace

Propaganda and Recruitment

Cyberspace provides terrorists with the opportunity to disseminate propaganda that can facilitate self-radicalization and encourage terrorist actions. People are often drawn to terrorist organizations during times of stress or a life transition, such as being let go from a job, searching for employment, reeling from the break-up of a relationship, or seeking friends in a new city. An individual may be searching for a place where they can belong, feel loved, accepted, and validated; are seeking meaning in their life or for God; or striving to do something important such as fighting for a political, social, or religious cause. Unfortunately, terrorist groups, in their propaganda, promise to fill any and all of these voids, and they do so in cyberspace. As you may recall, the perpetrator of the June 2015 shootings at the Emanuel African Methodist Episcopal Church said that he drew inspiration for his attack from information he found online (Bernstein & Horwitz, 2015; Lewis et al., 2015; O'Connor, 2015; Potok, 2015). The perpetrator of the May 14, 2022, mass shooting at the Tops Friendly Market in Buffalo, NY also said he acquired his beliefs online.

In the 21st Century, groups such as Al-Qaeda, the IS, many right-wing extremist groups, and, as mentioned previously, the Animal Liberation Front, each have their own media outlets or affiliates operating in cyberspace. Currently, the *Wolves of Manhattan* and *Mujahideen in the West* are online magazines generated by Al-Qaeda supporters. For some years prior to that, Al-Qaeda's *Inspire Magazine* was notorious. The IS, which had previously generated the online magazines *Dabiq* followed by *Rumiyah*, recently began publishing *The Voice of Khurasan*. These online magazines are filled with stories validating their cause, ennobling terrorists, and glorifying terrorist attacks.

A deep dive into the publications of the IS and Al-Qaeda reveal that they consistently encourage readers to make hijrah, defined as moving to territories controlled by them, or to engage in jihad, which they define, almost exclusively, as killing disbelievers. The magazine articles rely on two strategies to convince people to engage in these behaviors. They suggest that making hijrah or engaging in jihad is something that Muslims should do, which psychologists refer to as an injunctive norm, or that these behaviors are something that many good Muslims actually do, which psychologists refer to as descriptive norms. Research in psychology shows that when people are making decisions about their behavior, they are influenced by these two social norms (Deutsch & Gerard, 1955; Cialdini, Reno & Kallgren, 1990: Cialdini & Trost, 1988; Schultz, Nolan, Cialdini, Goldstein, & Griskevicius; 2007; Shultz, Khazian, & Zaleski, 2008; Sherif, 1936;). It is much easier for an individual to make a decision regarding their behavior when the injunctive norm, what they should do, suggests the same behavior as the descriptive norm, what most people or similar others do. The decision becomes more difficult when the injunctive norm and descriptive norm are inconsistent (Burger & Sheldon, 2011). In the propaganda of Islamic extremists, the injunctive and descriptive norms are consistent, both norms suggest that hijrah and jihad are the correct behaviors to engage in.

Injunctive norms, what one should do, are set forth by trustworthy authorities. Both Al-Qaeda and the IS, in their publications, use verses from the Quran or quotes from notable Islamic religious figures and scholars to convince people that someone who is a good Muslim ought to make hijrah or ought to engage in jihad. Perhaps the most powerful example of an injunctive norm for hijrah and jihad is the following quote from the Prophet (Rumiyah, Issue 3, p. 20), "The Prophet said I command you with 'five things with which Allah commanded me: the Jama'ah, listening, obeying, hijrah, and jihad' (Reported by Ahmad and at-Tirmidhi from al-Harith al-Ash'ari)." In *Inspire Magazine*, Issue 1, Shaykh Abu Basir is quoted as saying, "Jihad is an obligation from Allah. Young Muslims are brought up into it since the day the Messenger of Allah carried the sword until the last of this nation will fight against the False Messiah" (*Inspire Magazine* Issue 1, p. 13). *Dabiq* Issue 3 also makes it clear that jihad is an obligation "the worst of sins in modern times is that of qu'ūd (abandonment of jihād), jihād now is fard 'ayn (an obligation upon each individual)" (*Dabiqu* Magazine, Issue 3, p. 32). *Dabiq* Issue 15 also states that the obligation of jihad, as waging war against disbelievers, is consistent with the teachings of the Quran. "This is a divinely-warranted war between the Muslim nation and the nations of disbelief...Indeed, waging jihad—spreading the rule of Allah by the sword—is an obligation found in the Quran..." (Issue 15, p. 78). According to the IS, the injunctive norms regarding hijrah and jihad are clear. These are behaviors that one should engage in.

In contrast to injunctive norms, descriptive norms are determined either by consensus, what most people do, or by similarity, what people like you do. The IS and Al-Qaeda, through their many stories, either of people making hijrah or engaging in jihad, suggest that most good Muslims want to engage in hijrah or jihad and that people just like you, men and women, people with families, even pregnant women, are engaging in these activities. For example, in Dabiq Issue 8 there are several stories of women making hijrah, including the stories of two pregnant women who made hijrah.

> I met a sister who was six months pregnant accompanied by her husband coming from Britain. I was surprised by this adventurist, so I said, "Why didn't you wait a bit until

you gave birth to the baby you are carrying and then perform hijrah!" She answered, "We could not handle waiting any longer. We melted yearning for the Islamic State!"

(Issue 8, p. 35)

Similarly, in *Inspire Magazine*, Issue 12, the story of an American, Samir Khan, who made hijrah is recounted. Khan recalls, "This is an honest reflection from a Muslim who discarded his American citizenship for the sake of sacrificing his life for the Cause of Allāh...For me, it was either Hijrah to the land of Jihād or Jihād in America..." (*Inspire Magazine*, Issue 12, p. 23–25).

Al-Qaeda's and the IS's publications also imply that engaging in jihad is a common practice through such statements as "And the numbers of Muslims taking up arms in the name of jihād under the banner of the IS are growing, and they're growing fast" (*Dabiq Magazine,* Issue 5, p. 38). They also present stories of everyday Muslims engaging in jihad. For example, they tell the story of Abū Qudāmah who so longed for jihad that he left London for Syria two months before the birth of his daughter (*Dabiq Magazine,* Issue 7, p. 46).

Because the injunctive norms regarding hijrah and jihad are consistent with the descriptive norms, there is no ambiguity regarding the correct behaviors, both norms suggest that one should engage in hijrah and jihad. Because Quranic verses and quotes from Muslim clerics and scholars are used to justify hijrah and jihad, adherents are able to believe that what they are doing is sanctioned by Allah and that engaging in hijrah and jihad gives their lives meaning. Coupled with the belief that many other good Muslims, people just like them, are engaging in hijrah and jihad, not only allows them to feel as part of a group but also that they are fighting for religious justice.

Obviously, the sales pitches of right-wing extremists are somewhat different from those of Islamic extremists, in that they are not citing the Quran or asking people to make hijrah, but they are asking people to engage in jihad, to take up arms and kill others, but without calling it jihad. Interestingly, Islamic extremists and many right-wing extremists share some common enemies, specifically Jews, feminists, and liberals. However, right-wing extremists view non-whites as their enemy, while Islamic extremists do not. Obviously, right-wing extremists tend to be pro-Christian and anti-Muslim while the converse is true for Islamic extremists.

Today's right-wing extremists tend to package their ideology in terms of saving their race. As discussed by Valeri and Kellogg (2023), right-wing extremists make white people the victims, portraying them as being gradually eradicated from what they perceive to be historically white countries. The proximate causes of this "white-genocide" are immigration, both legal and illegal, and a decrease in the birth rate of white children. The distal causes of these are some combination of liberal politics, feminist ideology, and immorality, which, separately or together, have sanctioned birth control, abortion, racially mixed marriages, the rise of the LGBTQ movement, slack border regulations, and criminal behavior. Given the broad base of those responsible for the plight of whites, attacks on almost any group, non-whites, non-Christians, feminists, immigrants, the LGBTQ community, liberals, democrats, and enablers of these groups can be justified. The icing on the cake is that right-wing extremists have successfully sold the idea to their adherents that most people, blinded by liberal and feminist propaganda, are unaware of what is really happening, specifically that the white race and white culture are being eradicated. They sell the idea that only a small percent of people are smart enough and brave enough to realize the truth and fight for the survival of the white race. To those who have embraced this ideology, they have made taking up arms in the cause of saving the white race into a courageous and moral act that requires determination and self-sacrifice. As with the Islamic extremists, people who take up the cause of the right-wing extremist movement are made to feel valued, that they are part of a group of like-minded individuals, and are fighting for a just cause: to protect their people, their values, and their way of life.

When it comes to propaganda for Islamic extremists, it is the online magazines and videos of terrorist groups or their affiliates that seem to not only capture the public's and media's attention but also play a key role in the radicalization of others. In contrast, for right-wing extremists, the manifestos, online postings, and live-streamed attack videos of these individuals seem to play a key role in captivating the attention of the public and media and in driving self-radicalization. For example, the mass shooter at the Tops Friendly Market in Buffalo, New York, in his own manifesto, mentions the manifesto and video of the Christchurch, New Zealand Mosque mass shooter, who mentions the manifesto and postings of the Emanuel African Methodist Episcopal Church mass shooter. Each of these terrorists, in their writings, clearly states that they were not part of an organized terrorist group but were radicalized online.

An added incentive for carrying out a terrorist attack is that both Islamic extremists and right-wing extremists portray those who act in their cause, especially those who die for the cause, as martyrs, saints, or knights. In Issue 12 of the *Voice of Khurasan*, a quote from Mohammed describes the rewards of jihad. Allah's Messenger said:

> Allah has guaranteed the one who performs jihād for His cause, having left his home for no reason other than to perform jihād for His cause and to affirm the truth of His words, that He would enter him into Jannah or return him back home with all the rewards he has attained or the ghanīmah he has acquired.
>
> *(Voice of Khurasan, Issue 12, p. 28)*

In Issue 8 of *Rumiyah*, Abu Sulayman ash-Shami, when he died in an attack, was lionized as a martyr "[H]e [Abu Sulayman ash-Shami] achieved that which he desired most, and the story of his jihad ended just as he had wanted at its beginning: with martyrdom for the cause of Allah" (*Rumiyah*, Issue 8, p. 45).

The Christchurch mass shooter, who is often referred to as a "Saint" in far-right circles, refers to the 2011 Norway terrorist as "Knight Justiciar" Breivik (Am & Weimann, 2020). Thus, in the narratives of both right-wing extremists and Islamic terrorists becoming a martyr, saint, or knight is presented as something that is both achievable and desirable.

Weapons

The online magazines, posters, etc. of Al-Qaeda and the IS also provide extensive information on how to plan and implement a terrorist attack. For example, a regular feature of Al-Qaeda's *Inspire Magazine* was a "How to" column entitled "Open Source Jihad" which billed itself as

> A resource manual for those who loathe the tyrant; includes bomb making techniques, security measures, guerrilla tactics, weapons training, and all other jihad related activities...It allows Muslims to train at home instead of risking a dangerous travel abroad.
>
> (Inspire Magazine, *Issue 14, p. 63)*

The column provided step-by-step instructions for making bombs, the explosive acetone peroxide, car bombs, remote-control detonators, and other devices. It also included tips on several topics, including training with a handgun, causing road accidents, conducting assassination operations, and creating explosive packages that can avoid metal detection and canine detection. While the information in "Open Source Jihad" was written so that anyone could follow the instructions, the techniques and operations, by and large, required time, equipment, and skill to design and implement. The drawback to this is that this process also provides the opportunity for the potential perpetrator to have second thoughts, to question what they are doing, and decide to abort the plan. It also provided time for "leakage" meaning that the potential perpetrator might, intentionally or unintentionally, give away their plans to someone, who might in turn notify law enforcement of an impending attack.

In contrast, the magazines of the IS tended to promote simpler forms of jihad, encouraging adherents to grab a knife or gun and go out in the street, and kill people or drive a vehicle into a crowd.

> Therefore, O lions of the Ummah, and those living in Australia in particular, follow the path of these righteous souls for there is no other path. The Khilafah has called for you to mobilize from your dens to alleviate the pain afflicting the hearts of the Muslims by striking the kuffar in their homelands...So here before you are the doors of jihad—unhinged, and in their lands! Light the ground beneath them aflame and scorch them with terror...Stab them, shoot them, poison them, and run them down with your vehicles. Kill them wherever you find them until the hollowness of their arrogance is filled with terror.
>
> *(Rumiyah, Issue 1, p. 17)*

The benefit of these simple tactics is that they require little to no thought or planning. Someone who is angry, feeling wronged, hostile, or seeking revenge can act impulsively, without the chance for second thoughts, self-doubt, or "leakage" of plans to another.

For current right-wing extremists, the preferred weapon seems to be guns. Except for the perpetrator of the 2011 Norway attacks, who used both a vehicle bomb and guns, the perpetrators of the attacks at the Mosques in Christchurch, New Zealand, the Tops Market in Buffalo, New York, the Walmart in El Paso, the Synagogue in Pittsburgh, Pennsylvania, and the Emanuel Methodist Episcopal Church in Charleston, South Carolina, all used guns. The perpetrator of the Tops Market shooting, in his discord chat log, essentially created an instructional manual for future terrorists, providing information on target selection, planning, weapons selection and testing, and surveillance. Both this attacker and the Christchurch attacker live streamed their attacks.

Current left-wing extremists, such as the Animal Liberation Front and Extinction Rebellion, unlike Islamic extremists and right-wing extremists, do not try to kill humans as part of their efforts to bring about change. Rather, their efforts to protect animals and the earth typically involve sabotage and vandalism. Although both the Animal Liberation Front (ALF) and the Earth Liberation Front (ELF) have used arson as a weapon. For example, the ELF used arson to damage a ski facility in Vail, Colorado, and at the U.S. Forest Industries Office in Medford, Oregon. These organizations have their own "how to" training manuals. Importantly, both ALF and ELF, as part of their guidelines, state that all necessary precautions need to be taken to prevent harm to any animals, both human and non-human. Extinction Rebellion's strategy is one of nonviolent, disruptive civil disobedience.

Financing

As was mentioned in the section "Banning Cyberhate and Cyber Extremism," in 2017, when internet service providers started banning extremist websites and payment companies started cutting off payments to them, the Daily Stormer turned to funding through cryptocurrency. Much has been written about the adoption of cryptocurrency by extremists (Bambenek, 2022; Economist, 2022; Gartenstein-Ross et al., 2022; Hayden & Squire, 2021; Valeri & Kellogg, 2023). The Southern Poverty Law Center, in December 2021, reported over 600 cryptocurrency addresses associated with white supremacists and other far-right extremists (Hayden & Squire). Valeri and Kellogg (2023) explain that part of the appeal of cryptocurrency to these groups and their supporters is its anonymity, allowing donors, buyers, and sellers using cryptocurrency to remain unknown to each other as well as to the government. As one might imagine, anonymity is appealing to those conducting illegal transactions on the Dark Web. Also, the fact that cryptocurrency operates independently from central banks has a special appeal to anti-government groups such as sovereign citizens as well as to many conspiracy theorists, including those who are anti-Semitic and believe that banking is controlled by Jews. A recent report by the United States Treasury (2024) discusses the IS's foray into cryptocurrency.

According to a recent United States Treasury Fact Sheet (US Treasury, 2024) the IS in Syria and Iraq currently has access to between 10 and 20 million dollars in funds. According to the report, while much of the IS's current revenues come from extortion, criminal activity, and local taxes, there is evidence that ISIS affiliates are using "virtual assets to raise and transfer funds across multiple jurisdictions." The United Nations, in their Algorithms and Terrorism Report, also speculated that the IS was using cryptocurrency to fund terrorist attacks, stating

> investigators in the 2019 Sri Lankan bombings that killed more than 250 people observed that the number of transactions in Bitcoin wallets used by ISIL to raise funds increased notably before the bombings, leading to the belief that these Bitcoins played a role in financing the attacks. Similar suspicions exist with respect to the Paris attacks in 2015 by ISIL, although evidence confirming these suspicions is lacking.
>
> *(UNICRI & UNCCT, 2021, p. 39)*

Governments are taking action to impede the use of virtual assets by terrorist groups. According to the U.S. Treasury report (2024) "...over a dozen countries have taken steps to regulate and supervise virtual asset service providers and have taken disruptive actions to deter ISIS and other terrorist groups from abusing the emerging financial technology sector." While many extremists believe that using cryptocurrency keeps buyers and sellers anonymous, governments, investigators, and hackers, if willing to invest the time and effort, can trace cryptocurrency transactions (Greenberg, 2022; WIRED, 2023). Of course, criminals and extremists are trying to keep that from happening.

A discussion of terrorist financing via the web would not be complete without an example of terrorists engaged in typical cyber-scams. One such example that combines terrorists, cyber-scams, and cryptocurrency comes from the IS. In 2020, amid the COVID-19 Pandemic, ISIS and some of its affiliates were selling fake N95 masks on a website FaceMaskCenter.com and through Facebook accounts (Choi, 2020; Greenberg, 2020).

> Among the jihadist fundraising efforts the DOJ has nixed, however, one stands out as particularly brazen. Court documents detail how an ISIS agent allegedly ran a scam website for Covid-19 personal protective equipment, or PPE, known as FaceMaskCenter.com.
>
> *(Greenberg, 2020)*

Complaints from the public brought the scam to the attention of the Department of Justice.

> In a series of civil and criminal complaints and forfeiture notices...the Justice Department has revealed that it seized hundreds of bitcoin and ethereum accounts, millions of dollars, and four websites from known Islamic extremist groups that were using those accounts and funds to support terrorist operations. Prosecutors say the forfeited crypto assets from the groups, which include ISIS, the al-Qassam Brigades, and al Qaeda, represent "the government's largest-ever seizure of cryptocurrency in the terrorism context." The cryptocurrency haul alone totals more than $1 million.
>
> *(Greenberg, 2020)*

This COVID-19 PPE scam provides another example of the overlap between terrorism and typical criminal behavior. Terrorists are willing to learn from and adopt the tactics of criminals to achieve their goals.

Cyberattacks

Infrastructure includes the basic power, communication, and energy structures that a city, region, or country relies upon to function effectively. Because many of these systems rely on information and communication technology to function, they are vulnerable to cyberattacks

In May 2021, Colonial Pipeline, one of the United States' largest fuel pipelines, was hit by a ransomware attack, a cyberattack in which hackers prevent an organization from being able to access their own files or data until a ransom is paid (Nakashima et al., 2021; Perlroth; 2021). Colonial Pipeline supplies approximately 45% of gas, diesel, and jet fuel to the U.S.'s East Coast. This attack caused Colonial Pipeline to shutdown its entire network as a precautionary measure, causing fluctuations in the financial markets and highlighted the vulnerability of this critical infrastructure. In this incident, initially an Eastern-European gang was suspected of carrying out the ransomware attack. However, the FBI was eventually able to trace the attack to the Russian-based criminal group Darkside (FBI, 2021).

Conclusion

As discussed in this chapter, cyberspace is a critical component of both cyber-enabled and cyber-dependent terrorism. There is no doubt that terrorists are operating in cyberspace. This chapter makes clear that when it comes to operating in cyberspace, their abilities should not be underestimated. They are successful at using all of the tools available in cyberspace, from cryptocurrency to artificial intelligence, and all of the available platforms, from the Dark Web to gaming platforms. They can and do create propaganda on multiple platforms and in multiple forms (text, audio, video) allowing them to reach vast audiences almost instantaneously. The effectiveness of their propaganda to recruit adherents, train people in terrorist tactics, and inspire attacks is evident from their ability to recruit adherents to their territories or to carry out attacks around the world. The resiliency of these groups is evident from their ability to maintain a presence in cyberspace even when faced with efforts to ban them and cutoff their financing. The tenacity of these groups is evident from their willingness to work with or for governments and cyber-criminals and to learn from and adopt their techniques. While we have provided evidence of cyber-enabled counterterrorism efforts to successfully thwart some of their capabilities, these efforts need to expand. Cyber-enabled counterterrorists need to continue to anticipate the strategies and tactics of the cyberterrorists and put countermeasures in place before the cyberterrorists strike.

Acknowledgment

The authors would like to acknowledge, with appreciation, the research of Tinna Kasemsuwannakaeth, B.S. in Cyber Security, St. Bonaventure University, 2024.

References

Allyn, B. (2022, March 16). Deepfake video of Zelensky could be 'tip of the iceberg' in info wars, experts warn. *NPR News*. https://www.npr.org/2022/03/16/1087062648/deepfake-video-zelenskyy-experts-war-manipulation-ukraine-russia

Am, A. B., & Weimann, G. (2020, October). Fabricated martyrs: The warrior-saint icons of far-right terrorism. *Perspectives on Terrorism*, *14*(5), 130–147. https://pt.icct.nl/article/fabricated-martyrs-warrior-saint-icons-far-right-terrorism

Anti-Defamation League. (n.d.). *Hate on display/Echo*. Anti-Defamation League. https://www.adl.org/resources/hate-symbol/echo

Ayad, M., & Squirrell, T. (2023, October 13). Illegal, violent terrorist content relating to Hamas-Israel conflict reaches millions on X. *Institute for Strategic Dialogue*. https://www.isdglobal.org/digital_dispatches/illegal-violent-terrorist-content-relating-to-hamas-israel-conflict-reaches-millions-on-x/

Bambenek, J. (2022). Bitcoin: The currency of white supremacists. In J. Bacigalupo, K. Borgeson, & R. M. Valeri (Eds.), *Cyberhate: The far right in the digital age* (pp. 65–86). Lexington Press.

Becker, P. J. Byers, B., & Jipson, A. J. (2000). The contentious American debate: The first amendment and internet-based hate speech. *International Review of Law Computers & Technology, 14*, 33–41. doi: 10.1080/13600860054872

Belton, C. (2024, February 16). Kremlin runs disinformation campaign to undermine Zelensky, documents show. *Washington Post*. https://www.washingtonpost.com/world/2024/02/16/russian-disinformation-zelensky-zaluzhny/

Bergengruen, V. (2023, February 22). Inside the Kremlin's year of propaganda. *Time*. https://time.com/6257372/russia-ukraine-war-disinformation/

Berlet, C. (2001, April 28). *When hate went online*. Paper presented at the Northeast Sociological Assocaition, Spring Conference. Fairfield, CT. https://simson.net/ref/leaderless/berlet_when_hate_went_online.pdf
Bernstein, L., & Horwitz, S. (2015, June 20). Charleston shooting suspect left racist manifesto on Web site, authorities say. *The Washington Post*. https://www.washingtonpost.com/national/health-science/authorities-investigate-whether-racist-manifesto-was-written-by-sc-gunman/2015/06/20/f0bd3052-1762-11e5-9ddc-e3353542100c_story.html?utm_term=.9f66955ee0ff
Berr, J. (2017, August 16). PayPal cuts off payments to right-wing extremists. *CBS News*. https://www.cbsnews.com/news/paypal-suspends-dozens-of-racist-groups-sites-altright-com/
Bipartisan Policy Center. (2012, December). *Countering online radicalization in America*. https://bipartisanpolicy.org/download/?file=/wp-content/uploads/2019/03/BPC-_Online-Radicalization-Report.pdf
Bond, S. (2022, January 6). Kicked off Facebook and Twitter, far-right groups lose online clout. *National Public Radio*. https://www.npr.org/2022/01/06/1070763913/kicked-off-facebook-and-twitter-far-right-groups-lose-online-clout
Burger, J. M., & Shelton, M. (2011). Changing everyday health behaviors through descriptive norm manipulations. *Social Influence, 6*, 69–77.
Burke, J. (2023, October, 22). Al-Qaida and IS call on followers to strike Israel, US, and Jewish targets. *The Guardian*. https://www.theguardian.com/world/2023/oct/22/al-qaida-and-is-call-on-followers-to-strike-israeli-us-and-jewish-targets
Choi, D. (2020, August 29). Fake N95 face masks were being sold on this ISIS-linked website — and it shows how terror groups are using COVID-19 as a propaganda tool. *Business Insider*. https://www.businessinsider.com/fake-face-mask-website-isis-2020-8
Cialdini, R. B., Reno, R. R., & Kallgren, C. A. (1990). A focus theory of normative conduct: Recycling the concept of norms to reduce littering in public places. *Journal of Personality and Social Psychology, 58*, 1015–1026.
Cialdini, R. B., & Trost, M. R. (1998). Social influence: Social norms, conformity, and compliance. In D. T. Gilbert, S. T. Fiske, & G. Lindzey (Eds.), *The handbook of social psychology* (pp. 151–192). McGraw-Hill.
deLéon, C. (2020, November 12). Thomas Metzger, notorious white supremacist, dies at 82. *New York Times*. https://www.nytimes.com/2020/11/12/us/tom-metzger-dead.html
Deutsch, M., & Gerard, H. B. (1955). A study of normative and informational social influences upon individual judgement. *Journal of Abnormal and Social Psychology, 51*, 629–636.
Dilanian, K. Ainsley, J., Winter, T., & Dienst, J. (2023, October18). Pro-Hamas extremists and neo-Nazis flood social media with calls for violence. *NBC News*. https://www.nbcnews.com/news/us-news/-hamas-extremists-neo-nazis-flood-social-media-calls-violence-rcna121043
Dimensions. (2024, January 17). Does Ansari's speech indicate more Islamic State attacks are likely in Europe? *Dimensions Center for Strategic Studies*. https://www.dimensionscenter.net/ar/Does-Ansaris-Speech-Indicate-More-Islamic-State-Attacks-are-Likely-in-Europe
Economist. (2022, February 5). The charm of cryptocurrencies for white supremacists. *The Economists*. https://www.economist.com/united-states/2022/02/05/the-charm-of-cryptocurrencies-for-white-supremacists
EU Disinfo Lab. (2024, February 2). Doppelganger operation. *EU Disinfo Lab*. https://www.disinfo.eu/doppelganger-operation/
FBI. (2021, June 7). *Department of justice seizes $2.3million in cryptocurrency paid to the ransomware extortionist darkside*. https://www.justice.gov/opa/pr/department-justice-seizes-23-million-cryptocurrency-paid-ransomware-extortionists-darkside
FBI. (2002, February 6). *Testimony of Dale L. Watson on the terrorist threat confronting the United States before the senate select committee on intelligence*. https://archives.fbi.gov/archives/news/testimony/the-terrorist-threat-confronting-the-united-states
Finkle, J. (2021, September 30). Neo-Nazi group moves to "Dark Web" after website goes down. *Reuters*. https://www.reuters.com/article/idUSKCN1AV1HY/
Gartenstein-Ross, D., Koduvayur, V., & Hodgson, S. (2022, August 4). Profit of hate: How domestic extremist are embracing cryptocurrency. *Foundation for the Defense of Democracy*. https://www.fdd.org/wp-content/uploads/2022/03/fdd-monograph-crypto-fascists.pdf
Global Engagement Center. (2020, August). GEC special report: Pillars of Russia's disinformation and propaganda ecosystem. *U.S. Department of State*. https://www.state.gov/wp-content/

uploads/2020/08/Pillars-of-Russia%E2%80%99s-Disinformation-and-Propaganda-Ecosystem_08-04-20.pdf

Greenberg, A. (2020, August 13). ISIS allegedly ran a Covid19 PPE scam site. *Wired*. https://www.wired.com/story/isis-allegedly-ran-a-covid-19-ppe-scam-site/

Greenberg, A. (2022). *Tracers in the dark: The global hunt for the crime lords of cryptocurrency*. Doubleday.

Greig, J. (2023, August 11). NSA, Viasat say 2022 hack was two incidents; Russian sanctions resulted from investigation. *The Record: Recorded Future News*. https://therecord.media/viasat-hack-was-two-incidents-and-resulted-in-sanctions

Gröndahl, T., Pajola, L. Junti, M., Conti, M., & Asokan, N. (2018, October). *All you need is "love": Evading hate speech detection*. Proceedings of the 11th ACM Workshop on Artificial Intelligence and Security (AISec). doi: 10.1145/3270101.3270103. https://arxiv.org/pdf/1808.09115.pdf

Hayden, M. E., & Squire, M. (2021, July 15). Neo-Nazi's bitcoin history suggests Russian darknet link. *Southern Poverty Law Center*. https://www.splcenter.org/hatewatch/2021/07/15/neo-nazis-bitcoin-history-suggests-russian-darknet-link

Hoffman, M. (2022). Welcome to cyberspace. In J. Bacigalupo, K. Borgeson, & R. M. Valeri (Eds), *Cyberhate: The far right in the digital age*. Lexington Books.

Holt, J. (2022, January). After the insurrection: How domestic extremists adapted and evolved after the January 6 Capitol attack. *Digital Forensic Research Lab*. Atlantic Council. https://www.atlanticcouncil.org/in-depth-research-reports/report/after-the-insurrection-how-domestic-extremists-adapted-and-evolved-after-the-january-6-us-capitol-attack/#platforms

Ianniello, L. (1985). *Computerized networks of hate: An ADL fact finding report*. Anti-Defamation League of B'nai B'rith.

Johnson, N. F., Leahy, R., Restrepo, N. J. Valesquez, N., Zheng, M., Manrique, P., Devkota, P., & Wuchty, S. (2019). Hidden resilience and adaptive dynamics of the global online hate ecology. *Nature*, *573*, 261–265. https://doi.org/10.1038/s41586-019-1494-7

Kinetz, E., & Hinnant, L. (2021, September 27). 'White dissedents' raise money in cryptocurrency. *PBS*. https://www.pbs.org/wgbh/frontline/article/far-right-extremists-raise-millions-cryptocurrency-bitcoin/

Kremling, J., & Parker, A. (2022). *Cyberspace, cybersecurity, and cybercrime*. Sage Publications.

Lewis, P., Holpuch, A., & Glenza, J. (2015, June 21). Dylann Roof: FBI probes manifesto and website linked to Charleston suspect. *The Guardian*. https://www.theguardian.com/us-news/2015/jun/20/dylann-roof-fbi-website-manifesto-charleston-shooting

Loadenthal, M. (2023, December 12). *How palestinian militants use Telegram videos in the mideast conflict*. Digital Forensic Research Lab (DFRLab) of the Atlantic Council (blog). https://dfrlab.org/2023/12/12/how-palestinian-militants-use-telegram-videos-in-the-mideastconflict/

Meaker, M. (2019, February 28). 'Hate is way more interesting than that:' Why algorithms can't stop toxic speech online. *Pacific Standard Magazine*. https://psmag.com/ideas/neo-nazi-hate-speech-foiling-algorithms

McLaughlin, J. (2022, February 15). Ukraine says government websites and banks were hit with denial of service attack. *National Public Radio*. https://www.npr.org/2022/02/15/1080876311/ukraine-hack-denial-of-service-attack-defense

MEMRI. (2024, January 11) Pro-ISIS posters incite attacks on New York City: 'Go get them, oh monotheists'. *Jihad and Terrorism Threat Monitor*. https://www.memri.org/jttm/pro-isis-posters-incite-attacks-new-york-city-go-get-them-oh-monotheist

Mettler, K., & Selk, A. (2017, August 14). GoDaddy – then Google - ban neo-Nazi site daily stormer for disparaging Charlottesville victim. *The Washington Post*. https://www.washingtonpost.com/news/morning-mix/wp/2017/08/14/godaddy-bans-neo-nazi-site-daily-stormer-for-disparaging-woman-killed-at-charlottesville-rally/

Miller, T. (1985, July 14). The electronic fringe. *The Washington Post*. https://www.washingtonpost.com/archive/lifestyle/magazine/1985/07/14/the-electronic-fringe/17955294-9c94-4b5d-99e4-9af799b45eae/

Monahan, T. & Valeri, R. M. (2018). Terrorism and fear: "Terrorists want a lot of people afraid – not a lot of people dead". In R. M. Valeri & K. Borgeson (Eds.), *Terrorism in America* (pp. 213–230). Routledge.

Nakashima, E., Torbati, Y., & Englund, W. (2021, May 8). Ransomware attack leads to shutdown of major U.S. pipeline system. *The Washington Post*. https://www.washingtonpost.com/business/2021/05/08/cyber-attack-colonial-pipeline/

North American Animal Liberation Press Office. (2024, January 5). *Unoffensives report: 2023 year in review (Unoffensive animal)*. https://animalliberationpressoffice.org/NAALPO/2024/01/05/unoffensive-reports-2023-year-in-review-unoffensive-animal/

O'Connor, B. (2015, June 20). Here is what appears to be Dylann Roof's racist manifesto. *Gawker*. http://gawker.com/here-is-what-appears-to-be-dylann-roofs-racist-manifest-1712767241

Offenhartz, J. (2024, February 1). Who freed Flaco the owl? One year later, celebrity owl's escape from Central Park Zoo remains a mystery. *Associated Press*. https://animalliberationpressoffice.org/NAALPO/2024/02/01/who-freed-flaco-one-year-later-celebrity-owls-escape-from-central-park-zoo-remains-a-mystery/

O.Neill, P. H. (2022, May 10). Russia hacked an American satellite company one hour before the Ukraine invasion. *MIT Technology Review*. https://www.technologyreview.com/2022/05/10/1051973/russia-hack-viasat-satellite-ukraine-invasion/

Parker, J. (2023, December 12). Ukraine mobile network Kyivstar hit by 'cyber-attack'. *BBC News, Kyiv*. https://www.bbc.com/news/world-europe-67691222

Pearson, J. (2022, February 26). Ukraine launches "IT army," takes aim at Russian cyberspace. *Reuters*. https://www.reuters.com/world/europe/ukraine-launches-it-army-takes-aim-russian-cyberspace-2022-02-26/

Perlroth, N. (2021, May 13). Colonial pipeline paid 75 bitcoin, or roughly 5 million, to hackers. *The New York Times*. https://www.nytimes.com/2021/05/13/technology/colonial-pipeline-ransom.html

Potok, M. (2015, October 27). Carnage in Charleston. Intelligence report, 2015 (Winter). *Southern Poverty Law Center*. https://www.splcenter.org/fighting-hate/intelligence-report/2015/carnage-charleston

Reuters. (2022, February 26). Official Kremlin website down amid war in Ukraine. *Reuters*. https://www.reuters.com/world/europe/official-kremlin-website-down-amid-war-ukraine-2022-02-26/

Roache, M., et al. (2024, March 8). Russia-Ukraine Disinformation Tracking Center: 471 websites spreading war disinformation and the top myths they publish. *Newsguard*. https://www.newsguardtech.com/special-reports/russian-disinformation-tracking-center/

Satter. R. (2022, February 25). Ukraine says its military are being targeted by Belarusian hackers. *Reuters*. https://www.reuters.com/world/europe/ukraine-says-its-military-is-being-targeted-by-belarusian-hackers-2022-02-25/

Schectman, J., & Bing, C. (2022, February 24). Exclusive Ukraine calls on hacker underground to defend against Russia. *Reuters*. https://www.reuters.com/world/exclusive-ukraine-calls-hacker-underground-defend-against-russia-2022-02-24/

Schneider, K. (1995, March 13). Hate groups use tools of the electronic trade. *New York Times*, A12.

Schultz, P. W., Khazian, A. M., & Zaleski, A. C. (2008). Using normative social influence to promote conservation among hotel guests. *Social Influence, 3*, 4–23.

Schultz, P. W., Nolan, J. M., Cialdini, R. B., Goldstein, N. J., & Griskevicius, V. (2007). The constructive, destructive and reconstructive power of social norms. *Psychological Science, 18*, 429–434.

Seitz-Wald, A. (2024, February 6). N.H. attorney general says he found source of fake Biden calls. *NBC News*. https://www.nbcnews.com/politics/2024-election/nh-attorney-general-says-found-source-fake-biden-robocalls-rcna137499

Shanahan, E. (2024, February 23). Flaco, escaped Central Park Zoo owl and defier of doubts, is dead. *The New York Times*. https://www.nytimes.com/2024/02/23/nyregion/flaco-owl-central-park-zoo-dead.html?campaign_id=60&emc=edit_na_20240223&instance_id=0&nl=breaking-news&ref=cta&regi_id=56375098&segment_id=159017&user_id=a94e7817afa3b6b591fe53032fb4f26c

Sherif, M. (1936). *The psychology of social norms*. New York: Harper & Row.

Southern Poverty Law Center. (n.d.a). *Louis beam*. https://www.splcenter.org/fighting-hate/extremist-files/individual/louis-beam

Southern Poverty Law Center. (n.d.b). *Stormfront*. https://www.splcenter.org/fighting-hate/extremist-files/group/stormfront

Stern, D. L., O'Grady, S., Ryan, M., & Hrabchuk, K., (2023, December 12). Cyberattack hits Kyiv as Zelensky pitches U.S. for lifeline in war. *The Washington Post*. https://www.washingtonpost.com/world/2023/12/12/zelensky-washington-cyberattack-kyiv-ukraine/

TechCrunch. (2022, February 25). Ukraine says Belarusian hackers are targeting its defense forces. *Techcrunch*. https://techcrunch.com/2022/02/25/belarus-hackers-ukraine/

United Nations Interregional Crime and Justice Research Institute and United Nations Counter-Terrorism Center. (2021). *Algorithms and terrorism: The malicious use of artificial intelligence for terrorism purposes*. United Nations. https://unicri.it/News/Algorithms-Terrorism-UNICRI-UNOCCT#:~:text=With%20a%20proven%20track%20record,driving%20cars%2C%20augmenting%20cyberattacks%20on

UNODC. (2012). *The use of the internet for terrorist purposes*. United Nations Office of Drug and Crime.

UNODC. (2019a). *Cybercrime module 1: Introduction to cybercrime*. United Nations Office of Drug and Crime. https://sherloc.unodc.org/cld/en/education/tertiary/cybercrime/module-1/key-issues/cybercrime-in-brief.html

UNODC. (2019b). *Cybercrime module 14 key issues: Cyberwarfare*. United Nations Office of Drug and Crime. https://www.unodc.org/e4j/en/cybercrime/module-14/key-issues/cyberwarfare.html

United States Treasury (2024, February 27). *Fact sheet: Countering ISIS financing*. United States Treasury. https://home.treasury.gov/system/files/136/Fact-Sheet-Countering-ISIS-Financing-2-27-24.pdf

Valeri, R. M. (2023). Turning the time of hate. In R. M. Valeri & K. Borgeson (Eds.), *Hate crimes: Victims, motivations and typologies* (2nd ed.). Carolina Academic Press.

Valeri, R. M., & Kellogg, B. (2023). Crossing the divide: From virtual hate to actual harm. In R. M. Valeri & K. Borgeson (Eds.), *Hate crimes: Victims, motivations and typologies* (2nd ed.). Carolina Academic Press.

Valeri, R. M., & Minteh, B. (2023). Cybercrime, cyberterrorism and information warfare: Threats to democracy, governance and national security. In Y. R. Kamalipour & J. Pavlik (Eds.), *Communicating global crisis: Media, war, climate, and politics*. Rowman & Littlefield.

Weimann, G. (2004, December). *Cyberterrorism: How real is the threat?* United States Institute of Peace, Special Report 119.

Weinberg, L. (2008). *Global terrorism*. Oneworld Publications.

WIRED. (2023, February 9). Cryptocurrency's myth of anonymity. *WIRED*. https://www.wired.com/story/gadget-lab-podcast-585/

PART V

Criminal Justice and Counterterrorism

10

EXTREMISM ON TRIAL

Domestic Counterterrorism in a Divided Age

James Bacigalupo

Introduction

While the likelihood of falling victim to terrorism remains exceedingly low, its unpredictable nature keeps a persistent demand for heightened security measures. Victimology is useful to understand why terrorism works as a tool of fear. Terrorists, motivated by political objectives, exploit fear to advance their ideological goals, victimizing not only their direct targets but the wider population. The principles of victimology can be controversial because they can be interpreted as "blaming the victim." However, it is undoubtedly true that individuals often possess agency in minimizing or exacerbating their vulnerability to crime with decision-making.

Victim precipitation implies that behavior prior to a crime can contribute to victimization. An example of this would be if an individual goes to a high-crime neighborhood after midnight to purchase illicit drugs and gets robbed. The decision to enter the crime-ridden area clearly increased the individual's likelihood of being victimized. Victim facilitation occurs when a victim unintentionally aids the perpetrator. An example would be leaving the car running with the keys inside while going into a store. Lastly, victim provocation can be described as an individual provoking another person, resulting in their victimization. Even if someone has never heard of these terms, they still abide by them. This is why an elderly woman, who would certainly be vulnerable to victimization, is much less likely to be victimized than a male in his 20s. Knowing that she is vulnerable, she may not go out at night, especially alone, parks her car in a place that is observed by others, and she doesn't provoke fights. These principles allow people to have some control over the likelihood of their victimization.

Terrorism operates outside of these conventional rules of victimization, maximizing the fear that it casts over a population. Bombings and mass shootings at places such as concerts, subways, festivals, even the Boston Marathon are intended to threaten any sense of security. Terrorists want people to fear participating in society. Shichor (2007) describes it as such:

DOI: 10.4324/9781003375265-16

> Victims of terrorist acts might feel more helpless than victims of street crimes because they have less control over their own fate. They hardly can identify anything that they have done wrong or could have done better to avoid victimization, thus they do not have clear guidelines for protecting themselves from further attacks.
>
> *(p. 275)*

The susceptibility to feeling unreasonably vulnerable in the wake of an attack should be considered when contemplating counterterrorism policies. An overreaction is often a goal of the attackers, which can result in laws that trade freedoms for a perception of security. Nevertheless, national security remains a fundamental responsibility of the federal government, encompassing the realm of counterterrorism. When it comes to domestic counterterrorism, military intervention is not an option, leaving the criminal justice system as the core framework to combat this threat. This chapter will delve into the legal aspects of domestic counterterrorism and assess how the current political climate impacts prospective measures.

The Adjudication of Terrorist Defendants

Brent L. Smith's (1994) groundbreaking book, *Terrorism in America: Pipe Bombs and Pipe Dreams*, marked the first empirical examination of the criminal justice answer to terrorism. Smith applied theoretical frameworks to the response, such as Emile Durkheim's consensus theory and Karl Marx's conflict theory, as well as Turk's (1982) concepts of "explicit politicality" and "exceptional vagueness" to describe prosecutorial strategies. Additionally, his analysis includes the politicization of trials by terrorist defendants, the laws used to prosecute these offenders, patterns of guilty pleas, conviction rates, extralegal characteristics in sentencing, and disparities in punishment between terrorist and ordinary offenders facing similar charges. Smith founded the American Terrorism Study (ATS), which includes data from terrorism-related federal court records spanning from 1980 to the present day. It is regarded as the most comprehensive legal database for federal terrorism in the United States (Jackson et al., 2023). His work laid the foundation for research that has since expanded to include cases involving terrorist defendants that have come since, both foreign and domestic, and their adjudication in the court of law.

Theoretical Explanations

Smith (1994) applied both consensus and conflict theory to the government's response to terrorism. These perspectives developed by Emile Durkheim and Karl Marx, respectively, provide two contrasting views of how society responds to the terrorist threat. Durkheim believed that people possessed insatiable desires and viewed social institutions as necessary to control the evil impulses of humans. Marx was optimistic about human nature, but according to him, a shortage of good and services forced humanity into conflict. While he was not an advocate of terrorism, many of his followers viewed the tactic as a way to bring about class consciousness. According to Smith, perspectives extracted from the conflict model tend to be suspicious of governmental actions, whereas the consensus framework has produced perspectives that assumes the government acts in the best interest of its constituents.

Smith and Damphousse (1996) tested these theories empirically with terrorist sentencing data from the ATS matched with traditional federal offender data. Consensus theory was operationalized as having a fairly strong relationship between sentencing outcomes and legal variables because theoretically, "legal codes reflect the evolution and influence of widely shared societal values upon which a consensus of moral solidarity is presumed" (p. 294). In contrast, conflict theory suggests that because legal codes reflect the interests of those holding power, legal variables should have a moderate relationship with sentence severity, but it predicts a stronger relationship with extralegal variables that pose a threat to existing power relationships. Smith and Damphousse also applied structural-contextual theory, developed by Hagan (1989), which posits that sentence outcomes are more predictable for certain crimes. Hagan posits that the various subsystems that make up the criminal justice system work independently for most crimes, resulting in a lack of consistency. For crimes that are given a high priority, such as terrorism, there is a tightening effect between police, prosecutors, and judges resulting in a decrease of discretion in each component (Hagan, 1989). Because of the collaborative nature of terrorism investigations and prosecutions, Hagan argues, there is less variation in sentencing, and terrorist sentences are more predictable.

Smith and Damphousse (1996) found support for each of these perspectives. Political motive was found to be the strongest correlate of sentence length in a sample that compared terrorist and non-terrorist offenders charged with the same crimes, which supports structural-contextual theory in that political motive represents a tightening of the system that would result in harsher punishment with less variation. Structural-contextual theory has continued to be used to explain variation in sentencing (or lack thereof) of terrorist defendants (Smith & Damphousse, 1998; Bradley-Engen, 2009). It was also used to explain why terrorists are less likely to plead guilty, as it was proposed that plea-bargaining may decrease in the proactive political environment that terrorism produces (Shields et al., 2006). It was partially supported in explaining the prosecutorial strategies and outcomes following major terrorist attacks, as Damphousse and Shields (2007) found prosecutors and investigators increase the number of terrorism-related indictments for relatively less serious offenses in the two-year period following a major terrorism event. Murray (2018) contends that structural-contextual theory may be helpful in explaining variation in conviction outcomes of domestic terrorists by their ideological affiliation. She found that eco-terrorists were treated much more leniently, and that it may be due to the more high-profile nature of terrorist cases motivated by other ideologies, which unify the criminal justice system.

Prosecutorial Strategies and Trends

Austin Turk (1982) claimed that the government would take one of two approaches in prosecuting terrorists: explicit politicality and exceptional vagueness. Smith (1994) applied these concepts in his analysis of terrorist prosecutions in the 1980s. Exceptional vagueness is when prosecutors portray terrorists as mere criminals, motivated by personal rather than political objectives. Conversely, explicit politicality refers to criminal charges that are political in nature, such as treason, sedition, and subversive activities. In Smith's analysis, he found that more than a third of the counts used to prosecute terrorists were for racketeering or RICO violations. The second category of crimes most commonly used by prosecutors were "presumed" or "inferred liability" statutes where the assumption of intent is assumed with possession of items such as weapons, drugs, or explosive material. Overall, the use of politically motivated statutes was rarely invoked in the 1980s. Cases falling under these statutes had the highest acquittal rates when compared to any other category of crime. Smith et al. (2005) eventually added a third category, "subtle innuendo," to the typology after observing prosecutors adopting a middle ground by occasionally hinting at terrorist associations.

In Smith's (1994) study of 1980s-era terrorist prosecutions, it was revealed that prosecutors opted to politicize the sentencing as opposed to the prosecution. Pre-sentence reports and pre-sentence memoranda tended to emphasize the political nature of the defendant's behavior, activities, and associations that were not themselves illegal but could be used as aggravating factors for harsher punishment. The increased punishment was confirmed through various studies that compared the sentences of terrorist defendants and non-terrorist defendants who were convicted of the same crime (Smith, 1994; Smith & Damphousse, 1996, 1998; Bradley-Engen et al., 2009). While this may seem like a potential injustice, courts allow the consideration of uncharged and unconvicted conduct at sentencing. This is an effective strategy because it only requires a preponderance of the evidence, as opposed to beyond a reasonable doubt, which is the standard of proof at trial (Smith, 1994).

There was a shift in politicizing these cases more in the 1990's compared to the 1980s, likely due to the increase of international terrorism (Smith et al., 2002, 2005). In response to high-profile attacks such as the 1993 World Trade Center bombing and the Oklahoma City bombing, Congress passed the Antiterrorism and Effective Death Penalty Act of 1996 (AEDPA). This legislation significantly enhanced the federal government's capacity to combat terrorism by imposing harsher penalties for terrorism-related offenses and authorizing the Secretary of State to create a list of foreign terrorist organizations, among other measures (Pearson, 1998). Associating with groups on this list would later serve as the basis for a majority of terrorism convictions. In the wake of 9/11, the use of political charges increased for terrorism cases, but almost exclusively for internationally linked terrorists. According to Jensen and Akers (2024), between the years of 2014 and 2019, approximately 72% of international terrorism cases resulted in terrorism charges, while only 4.5% of domestic terrorism cases used these laws.

Outcomes

One of the most consistent findings in this area of research is that terrorists plead guilty at approximately half the rate of conventional offenders (Smith, 1994; Smith & Damphousse, 1996, 1998). Moreover, their decision to plead guilty is influenced by whether the charges against them are political. Terrorists have a strategic incentive for this tactic; when they take their chances at trial, they win acquittals at a higher rate. This is especially true when the charges are politicized. According to Damphousse and Shields (2007), politicized charges often require a prosecutor to prove the defendant's motivation. Typically avoided in American law, motive adds to the difficulty that prosecutors must overcome to convict terrorist defendants. Despite some success in securing convictions for seditious conspiracy among international terrorists in the 1990s, prosecutors still favored the safer "presumed liability" charges (Smith et al., 2002). Smith and colleagues (2005) found that terrorist defendants whose cases were explicitly politicized, pled guilty in 40% of cases, while nearly three-fourths of terrorist defendants tried as conventional offenders pleaded guilty to one or more charges. Of those who went to trial, 30% of the defendants subjected to either "subtle innuendo" or "explicit politicality" from the prosecutor were either acquitted of all charges or all charges were dismissed (Smith et al., 2005).

The Defense

Another unique aspect of trials involving political extremists is the nature of their defense. In his analysis of terrorist defendants in the 1980s, Smith (1994) notes that it was the defendants that would attempt to politicize the trial. More often, it was left-wing terrorists who would proclaim affiliation with an organization and claim political prosecution. For right-wing defendants, it was the opposite. They frequently attempted to prevent prosecutors from using the name of the group that they associated with. In some instances, the prosecutors would invoke the ideology of a defendant if they thought it would benefit their prosecution. Smith described this tactic in the 1985 trial of the white supremacist terrorist group The Order:

> Although the white supremacist motives of the group were brought out frequently by the prosecution, these motives were not intrinsic elements of the racketeering charges brought against the defendants in this case. The fact that these defendants espoused a radical philosophy highly offensive to most persons was utilized by federal prosecutors as an extenuating circumstance that enhanced the probability of conviction and severe sentencing. Had it appeared to the prosecution that widespread public sympathy existed for the racist goals of the group, mention of these motives could have been minimized during the proceedings with little effect on the outcome of the trial.
>
> *(p. 162)*

Smith et al. (2005) identified six defenses used by terrorist defendants. The first is a "political persecution" defense, where the defendant claims he or she is being targeted for their political beliefs. The second is dissociation, where the defendant attempts to distance themselves from other members of the terrorist group. The third defense identified by Smith and colleagues is "civil disobedience," which is when the offender claims to be justified in their actions and is willing to accept the consequences. "Freedom fighter" is the defense where the defendant claims to be part of a legitimate effort to replace the existing government. The next defense, commonly used by individuals in the Sovereign Citizens movement, argues that the government lacks jurisdiction in the case. Finally, there is the purely legal defense, where the defendant uses a traditional defense related to legal matters such as the admissibility of evidence. Overall, the most successful strategy was found to be dissociation (Smith et al., 2005).

Extralegal Factors in Sentencing

Extralegal factors, such as personal characteristics, have been shown to influence sentencing in criminal trials (Spohn, 2009). This issue has been explored in the sentencing of terrorist offenders as well. In Smith's (1994) analysis of 1980s terrorist defendants, he found that females were sentenced approximately 25% less than males, but the small sample size of female terrorists prevented conclusive findings. Left-wing and right-wing terrorists were sentenced virtually the same, and no variation in sentencing was found between white and non-white terrorists. The biggest impact on sentencing was found to be the defendant's role in the terrorist group. The most severe sentences were imposed on the leaders, who averaged 27-year terms, while non-leaders received sentences shorter than 12 years. Smith notes that this disparity was in part due to the prosecutor's strategy of having members testify against the leaders for reduced sentences and witness protection. A more recent study by Yon and Milton (2021), using data from 1947 to 2017, also found that terrorist leadership roles were related to longer prison sentences.

Sentencing disparities between domestic and international terrorists became more of a factor with the passage of time. In his initial study, Smith (1994) found that international terrorists were punished less severely than their domestic counterparts. This trend reversed in the 1990's (Smith, 2002), and has continued to the present day with increased use of terrorism laws resulting in harsher treatment for individuals linked to international terrorism (Yon & Milton, 2021; Jensen & Akers, 2024). Sentences for international terrorists averaged 13.9 years, while domestic terrorists' sentences were less than half, with an average of 6.2 years (Jensen & Akers, 2024).

Jackson et al. (2021) examined how gender impacts the criminal justice response and found that women are treated more leniently, which is a consistent finding for criminal sentencing generally. With data from both federal and state cases, Corradi (2023) investigated the role of gender as well and found females received shorter sentences. Other key findings concerning extralegal variables revealed that having a history of mental health issues results in a longer prison term, while being affiliated with an environmental extremist group (ALF/ELF) was related to more lenient punishment—an observation also corroborated by Murray (2018).

Policy Implications

To address the increase in domestic political violence, the most common proposal has been to create domestic terrorism legislation to prosecute such offenses. While 18 U.S.C. §2331 (5) defines domestic terrorism, it does not function as an enforcement statute on its own (Johl, 2023). Advocates claim that these new laws would "fill this gap" (McCord, 2019, p. 3), and establish "moral equivalency" (p. 3) between domestic and international terrorism. The main legal argument is as follows: existing terrorism laws inadequately address the modus operandi of domestic extremists, particularly their use of firearms to target civilians. For example, 18 U.S.C. §2339A, which bans providing material support to terrorists, requires a predicate offense of over 50 crimes ranging from producing a virus to targeting federal employees. However, none of these 50 crimes include the use of targeting civilians with firearms, rendering the statute not applicable to many domestic cases. This section will use findings of studies on the adjudication of terrorism defendants and partisan impacts on terrorist punishment to illustrate why this is an unnecessary measure, and how it could potentially lead to unintended consequences.

Politicization and Partisan Dynamics

As the memory of the 9/11 terrorist attacks gradually recedes from the collective consciousness of Americans, and the influence of global jihadist groups like ISIS and al-Qaeda are perceived to be in decline, interest in the U.S. war on terror is diminishing as well. In recent years, political polarization has increased (Tyler & Iyengar, 2024), and homegrown extremists have replaced the international threat as the primary national security concern (Wray, 2023). The agencies and departments that have been tasked to fight the global war on terror now have their sights on domestic threats (Patel & Kurzman, 2023). A focus shift from international jihadist terrorism to domestic terrorism introduces additional obstacles. Domestic political extremism is intricately linked with mainstream political issues, involving beliefs, groups, and movements that often align themselves with positions within the current political divides. Unlike radical jihadists, who adhere to an ideology that is detached from the American left-right political spectrum, domestic extremists are often aligned with, or at least adjacent to, relatively popular political ideologies. This is especially true in the current extremist landscape, where political violence has become intertwined with mainstream political views and electoral politics. This makes domestic counterterrorism a contentious issue with allegations of real and perceived partisan bias.

Research has demonstrated that political partisans prefer to punish their political adversaries more harshly than radicals on their side of the aisle when they break the law (Silver & Shi, 2023; Edwards & Arnon, 2021). With the use of a survey experiment, Silver and Shi found that overall, respondents' political ideology predicted support for different government responses when violence or harm occurred at protests that were more ideologically aligned or more ideologically opposed, with strong liberals and conservatives both preferring to punish the other side's activists more severely than their own. In a sample of survey respondents in both the U.S. and Israel, Edwards and Arnon found that support for repressing nonthreatening political rivals was just as large as support for repressing a threatening in-group.

Partisanship has been suspected of being implemented in terrorism laws in some instances. For example, Oregon's new domestic terrorism law has been alleged to have been crafted to address right-wing extremist activity while ignoring far-left tactics by specifically addressing paramilitary activity (Selsky, 2023). It is not just conservatives suspicious over unequal treatment. Left-leaning journalist Natasha Lennard (2023) opposed the Oregon measure citing the expansion of the Georgia domestic terrorism law in 2017. The expansion of the law came in response to the racist mass shooting perpetrated by Dylan Roof in neighboring South Carolina; however, critics at the time raised concerns that the law would be used against left-wing activists. This concern materialized when more than 40 leftists were arrested on state terrorism charges for their activities opposing the planned Atlanta Public Safety Training Center, commonly referred to as "Cop City" (Mansoor, 2023). Conversely, a recent example of alleged politically motivated prosecution resulted in a successful motion to dismiss for the right-wing group Rise Above Movement, or RAM (Mejia, 2024). Judge Cormac J. Carney granted their motion and wrote, "Prosecuting only members of the far-right and ignoring members of the far-left leads to the troubling conclusion that the government believes it is permissible to physically assault and injure Trump supporters to silence speech" (Mejia, 2024).

A new domestic terrorism statute could exacerbate the current political divides. Emphasizing the criminality of domestic terrorists with nonpolitical laws takes the politics of the defendant out of the equation and reduces trials from political events to routine law and order processes. While politics are contentious, crime is more black and white; therefore, separating them makes for a less politically contentious legal proceeding. Research has demonstrated that defendants of terrorism often employ political defenses at trial and use the stage to promote their political cause (Smith, 1994; Smith et al., 2005). Unlike traditional offenders, terrorists' goals are ideological, and a high-profile criminal trial provides a platform where these defendants can disseminate their worldview and depict themselves as political prisoners or freedom fighters. A guilty plea would deny these defendants the spotlight. While terrorist defendants plead guilty at a much lower rate than traditional defendants overall, this is especially true when the charges are political. A domestic terrorism law may motivate these offenders to opt for a trial which would amplify their visibility and increase their exposure. Politicized jury trials have shown to result in a high number of acquittals (Smith et al., 2005; Damphousse & Shields, 2007). Focusing on conventional criminality could avoid these effects.

Gap or Overlap?

Describing the absence of a dedicated statute for domestic terrorism as a "gap" inaccurately portrays there to be a loophole exploited by extremists. In reality, domestic terrorism is already illegal and prosecuted through various legal avenues including federal charges that involve a political motive such as treason, sedition, and other subversive activities (U.S.C. 18 Ch.115), formal terrorism charges (U.S.C. 18 Ch. 113B), various civil rights and hate crime laws (U.S.C. 18 Ch. 13), as well as nonpolitical traditional federal criminal laws. Sentencing enhancements can also be applied at the sentencing phase, including the terrorism enhancement (§3A1.4) and hate crime enhancement (§3A1). This is aside from the numerous terrorism laws, hate crime laws, standard criminal laws, and sentencing enhancements that can be enforced at the state level. It is also true that even when nonpolitical crimes are used to prosecute terrorists, they still pay a penalty for their ideological motivation, as shown through studies analyzing sentence lengths between politically motivated and traditional defendants charged with the same crime (Smith, 1994; Smith & Damphousse, 1996, 1998; Bradley-Engen et al., 2009).

In advocating for new legislation, McCord (2019) refers to five right-wing terrorists or their attacks, arguing that if they had pledged allegiance to the leader of ISIS, then they would have been charged with multiple terrorism crimes. Instead, four out of five of them were convicted or pleaded guilty to federal hate crime charges resulting in either life imprisonment or the death penalty. Terrorism laws would only serve a symbolic purpose in these cases as they were already dealt deservingly harsh punishments in their absence. The fifth extremist mentioned by McCord, Christopher Hasson, is a better example for her case. The Coast Guard Lieutenant stockpiled weapons and intended to carry out a racially motivated mass shooting. He pleaded guilty to numerous (nonpolitical) crimes and was sentenced to over 13 years in federal prison followed by four years of supervised release (DOJ, 2020). While a case could be made that he should have been charged more severely, overall, the outcome of these five cases makes for a better argument against the necessity of new legislation than it does for it.

Sentencing Equity

Studies have revealed that individuals connected to international terrorist organizations are punished more harshly than domestic terrorists (Smith et al., 2002; Jensen & Akers, 2024). In a sample of terrorism cases initiated between 2014 and 2019, the biggest disparity between international and domestic terrorists regarding terrorism charges was for §2339B, which bans providing material support to a designated foreign terrorist organization (FTO) (Jensen & Akers, 2024). The data showed 57 of the 116 international terrorists were prosecuted for this crime, while none of the domestic terrorists were. This creates an ideological disparity between Islamic extremists and domestic terrorists who are committed to political or religious belief systems largely detached from international terrorist organizations. In prosecuting terrorist defendants, the state prefers to charge crimes that are most likely to result in a conviction (Smith, 1994; Smith et al., 2002; Damphousse & Shields, 2007). The material support charge is commonly used because the requisite elements of the offenses are easy to prove (Jensen & Akers, 2024). The other part of the law, §2339A, does not require an FTO, but does have limitations. Aaronson (2019) highlights the case of the Patriots Defense Force, a militia based in Utah, where a member, believing he was planting a real bomb as part of an FBI sting operation, only faced two years in prison, followed by three years of probation because of the government's decision to not pursue multiple terrorism charges that would have been applicable to the case. Aaronson contends that the disparity between domestic and internationally linked terrorism is primarily due to the discretion of the Department of Justice who has prioritized the use of these laws on al-Qaeda and ISIS-related extremists.

Terrorism scholars Hoffman and Ware (2024) argue that some right-wing groups should also be designated as FTOs, including The Base, a white supremacist paramilitary group currently being operated out of Russia. It is certainly true that this organization adheres to a hate-fueled ideology and has demonstrated a willingness to engage in violence, including a foiled plot to attack a pro-gun rally in hopes of igniting a racial civil war (Vakil, 2021). The legal distinction and subsequent punishments between individuals associated with global jihadist organizations such as ISIS and those affiliated with far-right groups like The Base may be justified based on their respective operational capabilities and scale of attacks. The attacks carried out by al-Qaeda and ISIS are of a much greater magnitude than those conducted by any contemporary right-wing group. Focusing on group-level attacks by the far-right ignores the reality of fatal violent extremism in the U.S., which is being perpetrated overwhelmingly by unaffiliated lone actors.

A Tailored Approach

Addressing the lone actor phenomenon should prioritize preventing attacks from occurring, rather than solely focusing on punishment after the fact. According to the Anti-Defamation League (ADL) (2023), extremist linked fatalities are predominantly being carried out with firearms. Therefore, preventing individuals who have expressed a willingness to engage in violent extremism from accessing these deadly weapons should be a primary objective. Red flag gun laws, or ERPOs have been used to disarm potential terrorists with success. For example, in 2019, the leader of the Washington chapter of Atomwaffen Division, a clandestine neo-Nazi paramilitary group responsible for a string of murders in the United States, was stripped of his arsenal. Kaleb James Cole, who played a key role in organizing "hate camp" trainings and creating propaganda, had five rifles, a shotgun, three semiautomatic handguns, and four lower receivers confiscated by the Seattle Police after the department obtained an ERPO against Cole (Winston, 2019).

What Are Extreme Risk Protection Orders?

Red flag gun laws or ERPOs refer to state-level legislation that permits specified individuals (i.e., law enforcement, family) to petition a civil court for an order to temporarily remove guns from dangerous situations. If the court finds that someone poses a serious risk of injuring themselves or others with a firearm, that individual is temporarily prohibited from purchasing and possessing guns. According to Everytown for Gun Safety (2024), which is a research organization that advocates for gun control and opposes gun violence, 21 states have now adopted these laws. The specifics of who is legally allowed to petition for an order varies. For example, California allows law enforcement, immediate family members, employers, coworkers, teachers, roommates, people with a child in common, and those who are in a dating relationship to petition for an order. While other states, such as Indiana, only allow law enforcement to do so.

The Rationale for Extreme Risk Protection Orders in Addressing Domestic Terrorism

As noted, fatal violent extremism is largely a gun violence issue. According to the ADL (2023), from 2013 to 2022, there have been 444 extremist killings in the U.S. Over 75% or 335 of these homicides were carried out with a firearm. Almost all of the mass casualty attacks during this period were carried out with firearms as well. While a bit more speculative, there is reason to believe that domestic extremists rely on purchasing their weapons legally in comparison to traditional homicide offenders. Many of these lone wolf attackers appear to be socially isolated with a limited social network, which makes acquiring a weapon illegally more challenging. Lastly, "leaking," or disclosing intentions or plans prior to an attack is common for terrorists. According to Dudenhoefer et al. (2021), up to 90% of terrorist offenders showed some type of leaking prior to the attacks. This presents an opportunity for someone to learn of a potential attack and then file a petition for an ERPO.

Just as most gun control measures face fierce resistance, these laws are not embraced by all. However, unlike other gun control laws, these are applied at the individual level. They impose no obstacles to individuals wishing to safely exercise their 2nd Amendment rights. They are only applicable to those who have demonstrated that they are a serious risk to themselves or others. Due process is not violated as judges hold hearings, usually within ten days, where the individual can challenge any evidence and make their case as to why the order should not be issued. The order only remains in effect for a specified amount of time, such as a year. States such as New York require high standards of proof, as well as clear and convincing evidence for a yearlong order (Whitehurst et al., 2022). For many states, these laws also include penalties for individuals who submit false applications.

Although red flag gun laws have only been enacted in 21 states, another concern is that they are being underutilized in the states where they do exist. Often, these laws are being passed without any guidance for police departments and without adequate policies to enforce them (Lipari, 2023). While these measures can be effective if implemented correctly, it appears that many members of the public are not aware that these protections are available. In many instances, mass shootings could have been prevented if these laws were utilized. A recent example is white supremacist Payton Gendron, who in 2022, opened fire in a Buffalo, New York, grocery store, killing ten. He was able to buy an AR-15 style rifle, even after he made a threat at school that resulted in a State Police response and a mental health evaluation at a hospital (Whitehurst et al., 2022). Because no petitions were made to remove his firearms, he was able to commit this heinous act.

Conclusion

As this chapter has demonstrated, terrorist defendants undergo a unique experience within the criminal justice system, encompassing their prosecution, defense, and punishment. Individuals with ties to domestic extremist movements and organizations face an increased level of scrutiny from law enforcement and face increased punishment for these affiliations if they commit a crime and are prosecuted for it—irrespective of the charged crime being political. Creating new legislation to charge domestic terrorists may fuel polarization and lead to actual or alleged partisan bias in an already politicized criminal justice system. Instead of isolating domestic terrorism with a dedicated law, it is advisable to address the deadly lone actor threat within the broader framework of mass shooter prevention, employing measures such as red flag gun laws. This approach directly interacts with the tactics used by the most deadly extremists while focusing on violent intentions rather than ideology.

References

Aaronson, T. (2019, March 23). Homegrown material support: The domestic terrorism law the justice department forgot. *The Intercept*. https://theintercept.com/2019/03/23/domestic terrorism-material-support-law/

Anti-Defamation League. (2023). Murder & extremism in the United States in 2022. *Anti-defamation league: Center on extremism*. https://www.adl.org/sites/default/files/pdfs/2023-02/Murder-and-Extremism-in-the-United-States-in-2022.pdf

Bradley-Engen, M. S., Damphousse, K. R., & Smith, B. L. (2009). Punishing terrorists: A re examination of U.S. federal sentencing in the postguidelines era. *International Criminal Justice Review*, *19*(4), 433–455.

Corradi, A. (2023). Disparities in extreme contexts: The impact of gender and mental health status on the criminal justice outcomes of extremists. *Journal of Criminal Justice*, *88*, 102104.

Damphousse, K. R., & Shields, C. (2007). The morning after: Assessing the effect of major terrorism events and prosecution strategies and outcomes. *Journal of Contemporary Criminal Justice*, *23*(2), 174–194.

DOJ. (2020, January 1). Christopher Hasson sentenced to more than 13 years in federal prison on federal charges of illegal possession of silencers, possession of firearms by an addict to and unlawful user of a controlled substance, and possession of a controlled substance. *Department of Justice*. https://www.justice.gov/usao-md/pr/christopher-hasson sentenced-more-13-years-federal-prison-federal-charges-illegal

Dudenhoefer, A. L., Niesse, C., Görgen, T., Tampe, L., Megler, M., Gröpler, C., & Bondü, R. (2021). Leaking in terrorist attacks: A review. *Aggression and Violent Behavior*, *58*, 101582.

Edwards, P., & Arnon, D. (2021). Violence on many sides: Framing effects on protest and support for repression. *British Journal of Political Science*, *51*(2), 488–506.

Everytown for Gun Safety. (2024, January 4). Which states have extreme risk laws? *Everytown for Gun Safety*. https://everytownresearch.org/rankings/law/extreme-risk-law/

Hagan, J. (1989). Why is there so little criminal justice theory? Neglected macro- and micro level links between organization and power. *Journal of Research in Crime and Delinquency*, *26*, 116–135.

Hoffman, B., & Ware, J. (2024). *God, guns, and sedition: Far-right terrorism in America*. Columbia University Press.

Jackson, S. M., Ratcliff, K., & Gruenewald, J. (2021). Gender and criminal justice responses to terrorism in the United States. *Crime & Delinquency*, *69*(5), 1044–1070.

Jensen, M. A., & Akers, E. (2024). Prosecuting terror in the homeland: An empirical assessment of sentencing disparities in United States federal terrorism cases. *Perspectives on Terrorism*, *18*(1), 8–36.

Johl, M. (2023). Activism or domestic terrorism? how the terrorism enhancement is used to punish acts of political protest. *Fordham Urban Law Journal, 50*(3), 465–504.
Lennard, N. (2023, April 24). Oregon domestic terrorism law targets the far right. Here's how it'll backfire. *The Intercept*. https://theintercept.com/2023/04/24/oregon-domestic terrorism-law/#:~:text=If%20passed%2C%20H.B.%202772%20would,prison%20and%2 a%20 %24250%2C000%20fine
Lipari, L. (2023, March 8). Utilizing red flag laws: Preparing your agency to execute extreme risk protection orders. *Police Chief Magazine*. https://www.policechiefmagazine.org/utilizing-red -flag-laws/
Mansoor, S. (2023, May 4). Georgia is using a domestic terrorism law expanded after Dylann Roof against 'cop city' protesters. *Time*. https://time.com/6276994/georgia-domestic terrorism-law-cop-city/
McCord, M. (2019, August). Filling the gap in our terrorism statutes. *The George Washington University Program on Extremism*, 1–15.
Mejia, B. (2024, February 21). Judge clears charges against alleged white supremacists, says there's a bias against the far right. *Los Angeles Times*. https://www.latimes.com/california/story/2024-02 -21/judge-again-dismisses-charges against-members-of-california-white-nationalist-group
Murray, K. (2018). A comparative analysis of conviction outcomes of American domestic terrorists. *International Journal of Comparative and Applied Criminal Justice*, *42*(1), 75–88.
Patel, F., & Kurzman, C. (2023, May 8). U.S. domestic terrorism prosecutions: The reality behind the government's inflated numbers. *Just Security*. https://www.justsecurity.org/86456/u-s-domestic -terrorism-prosecutions-the-reality-behind-the-governments-inflated-numbers/
Pearson, A. (1998). The anti-terrorism and effective death penalty act of 1996: A return to guilt by association. *William Mitchell Law Review*, *24*(4), 1185–1215.
Selsky, A. (2023, February 17). Oregon, a hotbed of extremism, seeks to curb paramilitaries. *The Associated Press*. https://apnews.com/article/politics-oregon-state-government-portland 39f77e0b5572fc9678687b1f0aaced6e
Shichor, D. (2007). Thinking about terrorism and its victims. *Victims & Offenders: An International Journal of Evidence-Based Research, Policy, and Practice*, *2*(3), 269–287.
Shields, C. A., Damphousse, K. R., & Smith, B. L. (2006), Their day in court: Assessing guilty plea rates among terrorists. *Journal of Contemporary Criminal Justice*, *22*(3), 261–276.
Silver, J. R., & Shi, L. (2023). Punishing protesters on the "other side": Partisan bias in public support for repressive and punitive responses to protest violence. *Socium*, *9*, 1–16.
Smith, B. L. (1994). *Terrorism in America: Pipe bombs and pipe dreams*. State University of New York Press.
Smith, B. L., & Damphousse, K. R. (1996). Punishing political offenders: The effect of political motive on federal sentencing decisions. *Criminology*, *34*(3), 289–322.
Smith, B. L., & Damphousse, K. R. (1998). Terrorism, politics, and punishment: A test of structural-contextual theory and the "liberation hypothesis." *Criminology*, *36*(1), 67–92.
Smith, B. L., Damphousse, K. R., Jackson, F., & Sellers, A. (2002). The prosecution and punishment of international terrorists in federal courts: 1980–1998. *Criminology*, *1*(3), 311–338.
Smith, B. L., Damphousse, K. R., Song, Y., & Ginther, C. (2005). Prosecuting politically motivated offenders: The impact of the "terrorist" label on criminal case outcomes. *International Journal of Contemporary Sociology*, *42*(2), 209–226.
Spohn, C. (2009). *How do judges decide? The search for fairness and justice in punishment* (2nd ed.). Sage Publications.
Turk, A. T. (1982). *Political criminality: The defiance and defense of authority*. Sage Publications.
Tyler, M., & Iyengar, S. (2024). Testing the robustness of the ANES feeling thermometer indicators of affective polarization. *American Political Science Review*, 18(3):1570–1576.
Vakil, C. (2021, November 5). FBI says white supremacists were recorded plotting terror attacks in Virginia. *The Hill*. https://thehill.com/policy/national-security/580220-fbi-recordings revea l-two-members-of-the-base-group-plotting-terror/
Whitehurst, L., Tarm, M., & Anderson, J. (2022, May 17). Buffalo shooter's previous threat raises red-flag questions. *The Associates Press*. https://apnews.com/article/red-flag-gun-laws buffalo-su permarket-shooting-fecdd8a10f1a1e0f99ac5c4d17db145a
Winston, A. (2019, October 19). Atomwaffen division's Washington state cell leader stripped of arsenal in U.S., banned from Canada. *The Daily Beast*. https://www.thedailybeast.com/kaleb

-james-cole-atomwaffen-divisions-washington-state-leader-stripped-of-arsenal-in-us-banned-from-canada

Wray, C. A. (2023, October 31). *Statement of Christopher A. Wray, director, federal bureau of investigation, before the committee on homeland security and governmental affairs.* United States Senate at a Hearing Entitled "Threats to the Homeland." https://www.hsgac.senate.gov/wp-content/uploads/Testimony-Wray-2023-10-31.pdf

Yon, R., & Milton, D. (2021). Examining the outcome of investigations and prosecutions of extremism in the United States. *Studies in Conflict & Terrorism*, 47, 622–644.

CONCLUSION

The Future of Terrorism

Binneh Minteh

In the end, it is important to look at the central theme of the book as provided in the introduction. The book attempted to analyze the changing nature of terrorism into new phases by defining terrorism through a global lens, outlining the history of terrorism in the United States, the causes of terrorism as provided by various theoretical lenses, including political, sociological, psychological, and some relevant criminology theories that explain the function of human behavior in both individual and group contexts.

In both theoretical and empirical terms, various forms of terrorism and terrorist groups were used to understand the concept of terrorism. Prominent among some of the groups used, include right wing and left-wing extremist groups in the United States, domestic Jihadist attackers in the U.S. and Europe, terror groups in Sub-Saharan Africa, terror groups in the Middle East, and terror groups in Southeast Asia.

Furthermore, the New Phase of Global Terrorism exhaustively captured the impact of technology on terrorist operations and activities. In that context, the concepts of cyberterrorism and cyberspace are extensively discussed. An important aspect of cyberterrorism is terrorist use of the vulnerabilities of cyberspace to recruit, spread propaganda, and communicate operational plans and activities in the complex web of cyberspace. An analysis of terrorist activities in cyberspace shows that technology will continue to be a vital resource for terrorist groups around the world.

In the context of counterterrorism, the United States made considerable progress in combatting domestic terrorism. Internationally, U.S. efforts have led to the growth of partnerships and cooperation across various parts of the world in combating terrorism. The growth of splinter terror groups in Sub-Saharan Africa and the Middle East raises questions around geopolitics and global power dynamics. More research will be needed to understand the role of geopolitics in the emboldening of terror groups around the world. Similarly, more research will be needed to understand the effectiveness of state and regional organizations' response in global counterterrorism efforts. Furthermore, in the wake of the August 2024 terrorist attacks by an Al-Qaida linked terrorist group, Jamaat Nusrat al-Islam that claimed the lives of over 150 citizens in Burkina Faso, West Africa, research is additionally needed in explaining the impact of geopolitical tensions on terrorism.

DOI: 10.4324/9781003375265-17

INDEX

Kolibri 360 GmbH
Ferdinand-Jühlke-Straße 7
99095 Erfurt, Deutschland
produktsicherheit@kolibri360.de